S·O·U·R·C·E·S

Notable Selections in Economics

About the Editors

BELAY SEYOUM is an associate professor of international business at Nova Southeastern University. He earned an L.L.B. from the University of Daresalaam, Tanzania, and master's and doctoral degrees in international business from McGill University in Canada. He is the author of *Technology Licensing in Eastern Africa* (Gower Press, 1990) and numerous journal articles on intellectual property rights, technology transfer, export subsidies, and foreign exchange rates. He is currently writing a book on exports and imports, which is due to be published by Haworth Press. Dr. Seyoum has taught a variety of courses in economics, international trade, export-import marketing, and research methods. In addition, he has consulted extensively for Canadian companies and the United Nations.

REBECCA ABRAHAM is an associate professor of business administration at Nova Southeastern University. She earned a bachelor's degree in chemistry from Madras University, India, and master's and doctoral degrees in business administration from United States International University in San Diego, California. She is the author of several journal articles on option pricing theory, interest rate theory, emotional dissonance, offshore manufacturing, and expatriate acculturation. Dr. Abraham has taught a variety of undergraduate and graduate courses in economics, finance, statistics, operations research, and business policy.

S·O·U·R·C·E·S

Notable Selections in Economics

EDITED BY

BELAY SEYOUM
Nova Southeastern University

REBECCA ABRAHAM
Nova Southeastern University

Dushkin/McGraw-Hill
A Division of The McGraw-Hill Companies

This book is dedicated to Susan Jacob, Mark Zikiye, and Memenasha Abay.

Manufactured in the United States of America

First Edition

123456789FGRFGR3210

Library of Congress Cataloging-in-Publication Data

Main entry under title:

Sources: notable selections in economics/edited by Belay Seyoum and Rebecca Abraham.—1st ed.

Includes bibliographical references and index.

1. Economics. I. Seyoum, Belay, *ed.* II. Abraham, Rebecca, *ed.* III. Title.

330.1′5

0-07-303590-4 ISSN: 1525-2612

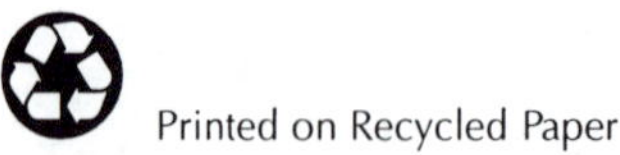

Preface

Over the past several decades, many undergraduate programs in business and economics have included a course entitled The History of Economic Thought, which surveys the work of leading economists of the past and present. In forging this link, students develop a conceptual framework of economic ideas that have aroused the interest of economists over time, including inequality, the role of factors of production in trade and growth, capital formation and theories of interest, human welfare, partial versus general equilibrium, and so on. A knowledge base of this form is invaluable in making students informed participants in the economic debates of our times, be they on social security, welfare, or foreign aid.

An examination of the course outline would likely reveal the use of multiple texts, texts that briefly summarize the work of the economists, with the exclusion of the period from about 1970 to the present. We felt that the needs of such a course would be best served by a single, comprehensive book of selections covering the entire period from the eighteenth century to the present. It seemed obvious that the book should be composed of selections, as only in such a book could the greatest thinkers of the past and present disseminate their views in their own words, which are clearly more powerful than any paraphrasing of their ideas. For example, according to Adam Smith, "Self-interest in a free society would lead to rapid growth" is not nearly as effective in delivering its message as "It is not from the benevolence of the butcher, the brewer, or the baker that we expect our dinner, but from their regard to their own self-interest" (Smith, 1776). However, to provide a context in terms of time and political events, we recommend that this book be used in conjunction with a book that describes the historical development of economics.

Sources: Notable Selections in Economics is a compilation of 41 selections. It represents the work of the leading economists of the past three centuries. While a typical course in the history of economic thought may include the work of 75 economists, to preserve parsimony we feel that it would be appropriate for students to read the original works of the leading economists in this book in conjunction with others that summarize the contributions of lesser economists.

While there is a core group of traditional economists of the Cambridge, Austrian, Chicago, and Stockholm schools of economics whose work is included in every text and every course on the subject, there is less agreement as to the relative value of the work of contemporary economists. We initially chose to include the work of every Nobel Prize winner, recognizing that it is the premier award of excellence in the field. However, a closer examination revealed that an appreciation of the work of certain laureates requires a knowledge of mathematics that is well beyond the capabilities of most undergraduate students. They have, therefore, been omitted. Also, several recent winners have focused on investments, portfolio theory, and option pricing theory, all of which are topics in finance and therefore not within the scope of this book.

Organization of the book. The selections are organized topically around the major schools of economic thought and the major subject areas in the discipline. Part 1 describes the Mercantilist, Physiocratic, and Classical Schools; Part 2, the Marxian, Neoclassical, Libertarian, and Chicago Schools; Part 3, the Keynesian and Institutionalist Schools; and Part 4, welfare, trade economics, and growth and development. The first three parts have been arranged in chronological order in accordance with the evolution of economic thought from the seventeenth to the mid-twentieth centuries. The last part focuses on the work of contemporary economists. We believe that most users of this book will preserve the ordering of selections in the first three parts, as they represent the prevailing opinions of their schools of thought. In contrast, the heterogeneity of ideas presented in the last part permits these selections to be rearranged and read in any order that meets the needs of an instructor or course. Each selection is preceded by a brief headnote that establishes the relevance of the selection, provides biographical information on the author, and notes the selection's key concept.

On the Internet. Each part in this book is preceded by an *On the Internet* page that contains a list of Web sites that may be accessed for additional information, including further readings on the schools of economic thought and the work of individual economists, autobiographies, and organizations that seek to promote the work.

A word to the instructor. An *Instructor's Manual With Test Questions* (multiple-choice and essay) is available through the publisher for instructors using *Sources* in the classroom.

Sources: Notable Selections in Economics is only one title in the Sources series. If you are interested in seeing the table of contents for any of the other titles, please visit the Sources Web site at `http://www.dushkin.com/sources/`.

Acknowledgements. We would like to thank David Dean, former list manager for the Sources series; Ted Knight, current list manager; and Rose Gleich, administrative assistant at Dushkin/McGraw-Hill for keeping us abreast of developments throughout the publication process. Among the staff at Nova Southeastern University, we are particularly grateful to Daniel Brodsky and Patricia Bender at the Einstein Library for their assistance in procuring most of the material for this book and to Helen Tragou and Natalie Lewis for research support.

We welcome comments and suggestions for future editions of the text and instructor's manual from students, faculty, and other users of this book.

Belay Seyoum
Nova Southeastern University

Rebecca Abraham
Nova Southeastern University

Contents

CHAPTER 12 Economics of Growth and Development 283

PART ONE

The Mercantilist, Physiocratic, and Classical Schools

On the Internet . . .

Sites appropriate to Part One

This Web site traces the evolution of physiocracy as the first scientific school of economics.

http://echonyc.com:70/0/Cul/HGS/fizcrats/

The McMaster University Archive for the History of Economic Thought contains information on David Hume, Adam Smith, Thomas Robert Malthus, David Ricardo, Jean-Baptiste Say, and John Stuart Mill. Useful information is also available on Karl Marx, Alfred Marshall, Irving Fisher, Carl Menger, William Stanley Jevons, Frank H. Knight, John Maynard Keynes, Thorstein Veblen, Vilfredo Pareto, Joseph A. Schumpeter, and John R. Commons.

http://socserv2.socsci.mcmaster.ca/~econ/ugcm/3113/index.html

This Web site describes the influence of the Classical School on other major schools of economic theory.

http://www.unipr.it/~deyoung/1preface.htm

This is the home page of the Adam Smith Institute, founded in 1977 and based in the United Kingdom. It is an independent economic policy institute comprised of both a domestic and an international division, which advises governments on market-based economic reforms.

http://www.adamsmith.org.uk

CHAPTER 1 The Mercantilist School

1.1 THOMAS MUN

England's Treasure by Forraign Trade

Thomas Mun (1571–1641) was born into an influential English family. He rose to prominence during the economic depression of 1620, which was held to have been caused by the shortage of money. Mun's books, *A Discourse of Trade from England unto the East-Indies* (1621) and *England's Treasure by Forraign Trade* (published posthumously in 1664), from which the following selection has been taken, along with his membership on a commission to make policy recommendations brought into the public debate all of the economic variables that confronted England at the time.

In the mercantilist tradition, Mun believed that the profit of the individual is distinct from the profit of the national economy so that the gain of one is achieved at the expense of the other. Likewise, a nation achieves profitable trade at the expense of its trading partners. However, his work is noted for its practical liberalism. In *A Discourse of Trade from England unto the East-Indies,* Mun responded to charges that the East India Company's export of silver was responsible for the depression. He held that the reexport of East Indian goods earned more silver than that used in their export. Mun's more significant work, *England's Treasure by Forraign Trade,* promotes export expansion through low export prices, low duties on imports, encouragement of reexports, efficient commercial procedures, and the efficient employment of human resources. His major insight is the need to adjust the balance of payments in the face of changing economic circumstances, typically rising foreign competition with Holland. Mun defends his position that the export of money increases national wealth.

Key Concept: the benefits of foreign trade

The Exportation of our Moneys in Trade of Merchandize is a means to encrease our Treasure.

This Position is so contrary to the common opinion, that it will require many and strong arguments to prove it before it can be accepted of the Multitude, who bitterly exclaim when they see any monies carried out of the Realm; affirming thereupon that wee have absolutely lost so much Treasure, and that this is an act directly against the long continued laws made and confirmed by the wisdom of this Kingdom in the High Court of Parliament, and that many places, nay Spain it self which is the Fountain of Mony, forbids the exportation thereof, some cases only excepted. To all which I might answer, that Venice, Florence, Genoa, the Low Countreys and divers other places permit it, their people applaud it, and find great benefit by it; but all this makes a noise and proves nothing, we must therefore come to those reasons which concern the business in question.

First, I will take that for granted which no man of judgment will deny, that we have no other means to get Treasure but by forraign trade, for Mines wee have none which do afford it, and how this mony is gotten in the managing of our said Trade I have already shewed, that it is done by making our commodities which are exported yearly to over ballance in value the forraign wares which we consume; so that it resteth only to shew how our moneys may be added to our commodities, and being jointly exported may so much the more encrease our Treasure.

We have already supposed our yearly consumption of forraign wares to be for the value of twenty hundred thousand pounds, and our exportations to exceed that two hundred thousand pounds, which sum wee have thereupon affirmed is brought to us in treasure to ballance accompt. But now if we add three thousand pounds mor in ready mony unto our former exportations in wares, what profit can we have (will some men say) although by this means we should bring in so much ready mony more than wee did before, seeing that wee have carried out the like value.

To this the answer is, that when wee have prepared our exportations of wares, and sent out as much of every thing as wee can spare or vent abroad: It is not therefore said that then we should add our mony thereunto to fetch in the more mony immediately, but rather first to enlarge our trade by enabling us to bring in more forraign wares, which being sent out again will in due time much encrease our Treasure.

For although in this manner wee do yearly multiply our importation to the maintenance of more Shipping and Mariners, improvement of His Majesties

Customs and other benefits: yet our consumption of those forraign wares is no more than it was before; so that all the said encrease of commodities brought in by the means of our ready mony sent out as is afore written, doth in the end become an exportation unto us of a far greater value than our said moneys were, which is proved by three several examples following.

1. For I suppose that 100000 £. being sent in our Shipping to the East Countreys, will buy there one hundred thousand quarters of wheat cleer aboard the Ships, which being after brought into England and housed, to export the same at the best time for vent thereof in Spain or Italy, it cannot yield less in those parts than two hundred thousand pounds to make the Merchant but a saver, yet by this reckning wee see the Kingdom hath doubled that Treasure.

2. Again this profit will be far greater when wee trade thus in remote Countreys, as for example, if wee send one hundred thousand pounds into the East-Indies to buy Pepper there, and bring it hither, and from hence send it for Italy or Turkey, it must yield seven hundred thousand pounds at least in those places, in regard of the excessive charge which the Merchant disburseth in those long voyages in Shipping, Wages, Victuals, Insurance, Interest, Customes, Imposts, and the like, all which notwithstanding the King and the Kingdom gets.

3. But where the voyages are short & the wares rich, which therefore will not employ much Shipping, the profit will be far less. As when another hundred thousand pounds shall be employed in Turkey in raw Silks, and brought hither to be after transported from hence into France, the Low Countreys, or Germany, the Merchant shall have good gain, although he sell it there but for one hundred and fifty thousand pounds: and thus take the voyages altogether in their Medium, the moneys exported will be returned unto us more than Trebled. But if any man will yet object, that these returns come to us in wares, and not really in mony as they were issued out.

The answer is (keeping our first ground) that if our consumption of forraign wares be no more yearly than is already supposed, and that our exportations be so mightly encreased by this manner of Trading with ready money as is before declared: It is not then possible but that all the over-ballance or difference should return either in mony or in such wares as we must export again, which, as is already plainly shewed will be still a greater means to encrease our Treasure.

For it is in the stock of the Kingdom as in the estates of private men, who having store of wares, doe not therefore say that they will not venture out or trade with their mony (for this were ridiculous) but do also turn that into wares, whereby they multiply their Mony, and so by a continual and orderly change of one into the other grow rich, and when they please turn all their estates into Treasure; for they that have Wares cannot want mony.

Neithr is it said that Mony is the Life of Trade, as if it could not subsist without the same; for we know that there was great trading by way of commutation or bartr when there was little mony stirring in the world. The Italians and some other Nations have such remedies against this want, that it can neither decay nor hinder their trade, for they transfer bills of debt, and have Banks both publick and private, wherein they do assign their credits from one to another daily for very great sums with ease and satisfaction by writings only, whilst in the mean time the Mass of Treasure which gave foundation to these credits is employed in Forraign Trade as a Merchandize, and by the said means they have little other use of mony in those countreys more than for their ordinary expences. It is not therefore the keeping of our mony in the Kingdom, but the necessity and use of our wares in forraign Countries, and our want of their commodities that causeth the vent and consumption on all sides, which makes a quick and ample Trade. If wee were once poor, and now having gained some store of mony by trade with resolution to keep it still in the Realm; shall this cause other Nations to spend more of our commodities than formerly they have done, whereby we might say that our trade is Quickned and Enlarged? no verily, it will produce no such good effect: but rather according to the alteration of times by their true causes we may expect the contrary; for all men do consent that plenty of mony in a Kingdom doth make the native commodities dearer, which as it is to the profit of some private men in their revenues, so is it directly agains the benefit of the Publique in the quantity of the trade; for as plenty of mony makes wares dearer, so dear wares decline their use and consumption, as hath been already plainly shewed . . . upon that particular of our cloth; And although this is a very hard lesson for some great landed men to learn, yet I am sure it is a true lesson for all the land to observe, lest when wee have gained some store of mony by trade, wee lose it again by not trading with our mony. I know a Prince in Italy (of famous memory) Ferdinando the first, great Duke of Tuscanie, who being very rich in Treasure, endevoured therewith to enlarge his trade by issuing out to his Merchants great sums of money for very small profit; I my self had forty thousand crowns of him gratis for a whole year, although he knew that I would presently send it away in Specie for the parts of Turkey to be employed in wares for his Countries, he being well assured that in this course of trade it would return again (according to the old saying) with a Duck in the mouth. This noble and industrious Prince by his care and diligence to countenance and favour Merchants in their affairs, did so encrease the practice thereof, that there is scarce a Nobleman or Gentleman in all his dominions that doth not Merchandize eithr by himself or in partnership with others, whereby within these thiry years the trade to his port of Leghorn is so much encreased, that of a poor little town (as I my self knew it) it is now become a fair and strong City, being one of the most famous places for trade in all Christendom. And yet it is worthy our observation, that the multitude of Ships and wares which come thither from England, the Low Countreys, and other places, have little or no means to make their returns from thence but only in ready mony, which they may and do carry away freely at all times, to the incredible advantage of the said great Duke of Tuscanie and his subjects, who are much enriched by the continual great concourse of Merchants from all the States of the neighbour Princes, bringing them plenty of mony daily to supply their wants of the said wares. And thus we see that the current of Merchandize which carries away their Treasure, becomes a flowing stream to fill them again in a greater measure with mony.

There is yet an objection or two as weak as all the rest: that is, if wee trade with our Mony wee shall issue out the less wares; as if a man should say, those Countreys which heretofore had occasion to consume our Cloth, Lead, Tin, Iron, Fish, and the like, shall now make use of our monies in the place of those necessaries, which were most absurd to affirm, or that the Merchant had not rather carry our wares by which there is ever some gains expected, than to export mony which is still but the same without any encrease.

But on the contrary there are many Countreys which may yield us very profitable trade for our mony, which otherwise afford us no trade at all, because they have no use of our wares, as namely the East-Indies for one in the first beginning thereof, although since by industry in our commerce with those Nations we have brought them into the use of much of our Lead, Cloth, Tin, and other things, which is a good addition to the former vent of our commodities.

Again, some men have alleged that those Countries which permit mony to be carried out, do it because they have few or no wares to trade withall: but wee have great store of commodities, and therefore their action ought not to be our example.

To this the answer is briefly, that if we have such a quantity of wares as doth fully provided us of all things needful from beyond the seas: why should we then doubt that our monys sent out in trade, must not necessarily come back again in treasure; together with the great gains which it may procure in such manner as is before set down? And on the other side, if those Nations which send out their monies do it because they have but few wares of their own, how come they then to have so much Treasure as we ever see in those places which suffer it freely to be exported at all times and by whomsoever? I answer, Even by trading with their Moneys; for by what other means can they get it, having no Mines of Gold or Silver?

Thus may we plainly see, that when this weighty business is duly considered in his end, as all our humane actions ought well to be weighed, it is found much contrary to that which most men esteem thereof, because they search no further than the beginning of the work, which mis-informs their judgments, and leads them into error: For if we only behold the actions of the husbandman in the seed-time when he casteth away much good corn into the ground, we will rathr accompt him a mad man than a husbandman: but when we consider his labours in the harvest which is the end of his endeavours, we find the worth and plentiful encrease of his actions.

A Treatise of Taxes and Contributions

William Petty (1623–1687) was born in Rumsey, Hampshire, England. In 1648 he became an instructor in the emerging science of anatomy at Brasenose College in Oxford. A wealthy man, Petty's employment as a surveyor in Ireland earned him estates in every province of that country. He was knighted in 1662.

Adhering to mercantilist tradition, Petty believed that the security of a nation depended on the ability to create wealth through the productive use of the efforts of its subjects. His *Treatise on Taxes and Contributions* (1662), from which the following selection has been taken, has been hailed for its depth and insight into the consequences of alternative methods of raising taxes. Petty has meticulously compiled a list of expenditures of government including defense, administration of justice, religion, education, and welfare. These expenditures can be increased by wars or unwillingness to pay taxes. He then addresses the sources of unwillingness to pay taxes and remedies for the situation. The main thrust of this work involves comparisons of various proposals to raise money from taxes. These proposals include reserving a portion of the land as royal domain, or a fixed portion from the rent of lands. Petty asserts that export duties are only advisable on commodities in which the country has a natural monopoly, while import duties should be heavily levied on luxuries and lightly on tools of trade and semi-manufactured goods. Tonnage duties and marine insurance underwriting are other profitable means of extraction of taxes. In the following selection, Petty evaluates alternative tax proposals in light of their acceptance by the public.

Key Concept: methods of taxation

Of the Several wayes of Taxe, and first, of setting a part, a proportion of the whole Territory for Publick uses, in the nature of Crown Lands; and secondly, byt way of Assessement, or Land-taxe.

But supposing, that the several causes of Publick Charge are lessened, as much as may be, and that the people be well satisfied, and contented to pay their just shares of what is needfull for their Government and Protection, as also for the Honour of their Prince and Countrey: It follows now to propose the several wayes, and expedients, how the same may be most easily, speedily, and insensibly collected. The which I shall do, by exposing the conveniences and inconveniences of some of the principal wayes of Levyings, used of later years within the several States of Europe: unto which others of smaller and more rare use may be referred.

2. Imagine then, a number of people, planted in a Territory, who had upon Computation concluded, that two Millions of pounds per annum, is necessary to the publick charges. Or rather, who going more wisely to work, had computed a twenty fifth part of the proceed of all their Lands and Labours, were to be the Excisium, or the part to be cut out, and laid aside for publick uses. Which proportions perhaps are fit enough to the affairs of England, but of that hereafter.

3. Now the question is, how the one or the other shall be raised. The first way we propose, is, to Excize the very Land it self in kinde; that is, to cut out of the whole twenty five Millions, which are said to be in England and Wales, as much Land in specie, as whereof the Rack-rent would be two Millions, viz. about four Millions of Acres, which is about a sixth part of the whole; making the said four Millions to be Crown Lands, and as the four Counties intended to be reserved in Ireland upon the forfeitures were. Or else to excize a sixth part of the rent of the whole, which is about the proportion, that the Adventurers and Souldiers in Ireland retribute to the King, as Quit Rents. Of which two wayes, the latter is manifestly the better, the King having more security, and more obliges; provided the troubl and charge of this universal Collection, exceed not that of the other advantage considerably.

4. This way in a new State would be good, being agreed upon, as it was in Ireland, before men had even the possession of any Land at all; wherefore whosoever buyes Land in Ireland hereafter, is no more concerned with the Quit Rents wherewith they are charged, then if the Acres were so much the fewer; or then men are, who buy Land, out of which they know Tythes are to be paid. And truly that Countrey is happy, in which by Original Accord, such a Rent is reserved, as whereby the Publick charge may be born, without contingent, sudden, superadditions, in which lies the very Ratio of the burthen of all Contributions and Exactions. For in such cases, as was said before, it is not onely the Landlord payes, but every man who eats but an Egg, or an Onion of the growth of his Lands; or who useth the help of any Artisan, which feedeth on the same.

5. But if the same wer propounded in England, viz. if an aliquot part of every Landlords Rent were excinded or retrenched, then those whose Rents were settled, and determined for long times to come, would chiefly bear the burthen of such an Imposition, and others have a benefit thereby. For suppose A, and B, have each of them a parcel of Land, of equal goodness and value; suppose also that A hath let his parcel for twenty one years at twenty pound per annum, but that B is free; now there comes out a Taxe of a fifth part; hereupon B will not let under 25£. that his remainder may be twenty, whereas A must be contented with sixteen neat; nevertheless the Tenants of A will sell the proceed of their bargain at the same rate, that the Tenants of B shall do. The effect of all this is; First, that the Kings fifth part of B his Farm shall be greater

then before. Secondly, that the Farmer to B shall gain more then before the Taxe. Thirdly, that the Tenant or Farmer of A shall gain as much as the King and Tenant to B both. Fourthly, the Tax doth ultimately light upon the Landlord A and the Consumptioners. From whence it follows, that a Land-taxe resolves into an irregular Excize upon consumptions, that those, bear it most, who least complain. And lastly, that some Landlords may gain, and onely such whose Rents are predetermined shall loose; and that doubly, viz. one way by the raising of their revenues, and the other by exhausting the prices of provisions upon them.

6. Another way is an Excisum out of the Rent of Houseing, which is much more uncertain then that of Land. For an House is of a double nature, viz. one, wherein it is a way and means of expence; the other, as 'tis an Instrument and Tool of gain: for a Shop in London of less capacity and less charge in building then a fair Dining-room in the same House unto which both do belong, shall nevertheless be of the greater value; so also shall a Dungeon, Sellar, then a pleasant Chamber; because the one is expence, the other profit. Now the way Land-taxe rates housing, as of the latter nature, but the Excize, as of the former.

7. We might sometimes adde hereunto, that housing is sometimes disproportionately taxed to discourage Building, especially upon new Foundations, thereby to prevent the growth of a City; suppose London, such excessive and overgrown Cities being dangerous to Monarchy, though the more secure when the supremacy is in Citizens of such places themselves, as in Venice.

8. But we say, that such checking of new Buildings signifies nothing to this purpose; forasmuch as Buildings do not encrease, until the People already have increased: but the remedy of the above mentioned dangers is to be sought in the causes of the encrease of People, the which if they can be nipt, the other work will necessarily be done.

But what then is the true effect of forbidding to build upon new foundations? I answer to keep and fasten the City to its old seat and ground-plot, the which encouragement for new Buildings will remove, as it comes to pas almost in all great Cities, though insensibly, and not under many years progression.

9. The reason whereof is, because men are unwilling to build new houses at the charge of pulling down their old, where both the old house it self, and the ground it stands upon do make a much dearer ground-plot for a new house, and yet far less free and convenient; wherefore men build upon new free foundations, and cobble up old houses, until they become fundamentally irreparable, at which time they become either the dwelling of the Rascality, or in process of time return to waste and Gardens again, examples whereof are many even about London.

10. Now if great Cities are naturally apt to remove their Seats, I ask which way? I say, in the case of London, it must be Westward, because the Windes blowing near ¾ of the year from the West, the dwellings of the West end are so much the more free from the fumes, steams, and stinks of the whole Easterly Pyle; which where Seacoal is burnt is a great matter. Now if it follow from hence, that the Pallaces of the greatest men will remove Westward, it will also naturally follow, that the dwellings of others who depend upon them will creep after them. This we see in London, where the Noblemens ancient houses are not become Halls for Companies, or turned into Tenements, and all the Palaces are gotten Westward; Insomuch, as I do not doubt but that five hundred years

hence, the King's Pallace will be near Chelsey, and the old building of Whitehall converted to uses more answerable to their quality. For to build a new Royal Pallace upon the same ground will be too great a confinement, in respect of Gardens and other magnificencies, and withall a disaccommodation in the time of the work; but it rather seems to me, that the next Palace will be buildt from the whole present contignation of houses at such a distance as the old Pallace of Westminster was from the City of London, when the Archers began to bend their bowes just without Ludgate, and when all the space between the Thames, Fleet-Street, and Holborn was as Finsbury-Fields are now.

11. Onely I think 'tis certain, that while ever there are people in England, the greatest cohabitation of them will be about the place which is now London, the Thames being the most commodious River of this Island, and the seat of London the most commodious part of the Thames; so much doth the means of facilitating Carriage greaten a City, which may put us in minde of employing our idle hands about mending the High-wayes, making Bridges, Cawseys, and Rivers navigable: Which considerations brings me back round into my way of Taxes, from whence I digrest.

12. But before we talk too much of Rents, we should endeavour to explain the mysterious nature of them, with reference as well to Money, the rent of which we call usury; as to that of Lands and Houses, afore-mentioned.

13. Suppose a man could with his own hands plant a certain scope of Land with Corn, that is, could Digg, or Plough, Harrow, Weed, Reap, Carry home, Tresh, and Winnow so much as the Husbandry of this Land requires; and had withal Seed wherewith to sowe the same. I say, that when this man hath subducted his seed out of the proceed of his Harvest, and also, what himself hath both eaten and given to others in exchange for Clothes, and other Natural necessaries; that the remainder of Corn is the natural and true Rent of the Land for that year; and the medium of seven years, or rather of so many years as makes up the Cycle, within which Dearths and Plenties make their revolution, doth givbe the ordinary Rent of Land in Corn.

14. But a further, though collateral question may be, how much English money this Corn or Rent is worth? I answer, so much as the money, which another single man can save, within the same time, over and above his expence, if he imployed himself wholly to produce and make it; viz. Let another man go travel into a Countrey where is Silver, there Dig it, Refine it, bring it to the same place where the other man planted his Corn; Coyne it, etc. the same person, all the while of his working for Silver, gathering also food for his necessary livelihood, and procuring himself covering, etc. I say, the Silver of the one, must be esteemed of equal value with the Corn of the other: the one being perhaps twenty Ounces and the other twenty Bushels. From whence it follows, that the price of a Bushel of this Corn to be an Ounce of Silver.

15. And forasmuch as possible there may be more Art and Hazzard in working about the Silver, then about the Corn, yet all comes to the same pass; for let a hundred men work ten years upon Corn, and the same number of men, the same time, upon Silver; I say, that the neat proceed of the Silver is the price of the whole neat proceed of the Corn, and like parts of the one, the price of like parts of the other. Although not so many of those who wrought in Silver, learned the Art of refining and coining, or out-lived the dangers and diseases of

working in the Mines. And this also is the way of pitching the true proportion, between the values of Gold and Silver, which many times is set but by popular errour, sometimes more, sometimes less, diffused in the world; which errour (by the way) is the cause of our having been pestred with too much Gold heretofore, and wanting it now.

16. This, I say, to be the foundation of equallizing and ballancing of values; yet in the superstructures and practices hereupon, I confess there is much variety, and intricacy; of which hereafter.

17. The world measures things by Gold and Silver, but principally the latter; for there may not be two measures, and consequently the better of many must be the onely of all; that is, by fine silver of a certain weight: but now if it be hard to measure the weight and fineness of silver, as by the different reports of the ablest Saymasters I have known it to be; and if silver granted to be of the same fineness and weight, rise and fall in its price, and be more worth at one place than another, not onely for being father from the Mines, but for other accidents, and may be more worth at present, then a moneth or other small time hence; and if it differ in its proportion unto the several things valued by it, in several ages upon the increase and diminution thereof, we shall endeavour to examine some other natural Standards and Measures, without derogating from the excellent use of these.

18. Our Silver and Gold we call by severall names, as in England by pounds, shillings, and pence, all which may be called and understood by either of the three. But that which I would say upon this matter is, that all things ought to be valued by two natural Denominations, which is Land and Labour; that is, we ought to say, a Ship or garment is worth such a measure of Land, with such another measure of Labour; forasmuch as both Ships and Garments were the creatures of Lands and mens Labours thereupon; This being true, we should be glad to finde out a natural Par between Land and Labour, so as we might express the value by either of them alone as well or better then by both, and reduce pence into pounds. Wherefore we would be glad to finde the natural values of the Fee simple of Land, though but no better then we have done that of the usus fructus above-mentioned, which we attempt as followeth.

19. Having found the Rent or value of the usus fructus per annum, the question is, how many years purchase (as we usually say) is the Fee simple naturally worth? If we say an infinite number, then an Acre of Land would be equal in value to a thousand Acres of the same Land; which is absurd, an infinity of unites being equal to an infinity of thousands. Wherefore we must pitch upon some limited number, and that I apprehend to be the number of years, which I conceive one man of fifty years old, another of twenty eight, and another of seven years old, all being alive together may be thought to live; that is to say, of a Grandfather, Father, and Childe; few men having reason to take care of more remote Posterity: for if a man be a great Grandfather, he himself is so much the nearer his end, so as there are but three in a continual line of descent usually co-existing together; and as some are Grandfathers at forty years, yet as many are not till above sixty, and sic de eteteris.

20. Wherefore I pitch the number of years purchase, that any Land is naturally worth, to be the ordinary extent of three such persons their lives. Now in England we esteem three lives equal to one and twenty years, and consequently

the value of Land, to be about the same number of years purchase. Possibly if they thought themselves mistaken in the one, (as the observator on the Bills of Mortality thinks they are) they would alter in the other, unless the consideration of the force of popular errour and dependance of things already concatenated, did hinder them.

21. This I esteem to be the number of years purchase where Titles are good, and where there is a moral certainty of enjoying the purchase. But in other Countreys Lands are worth nearer thirty years purchase, by reason of the better Titles, more people, and perhaps truer opinion of the value and duration of three lives.

22. And in some places, Lands are worth yet more years purchase by reason of some special honour, pleasures, priviledge or jurisdiction annexed unto them.

23. On the other hand, Lands are worth fewer years purchase (as in Ireland) for the following reasons, which I have here set down, as unto the like whereof the cause of the like cheapness in any other place may be imputed.

First, In Ireland, by reason of the frequent Rebellions, (in which if you are conquered, all is lost; or if you conquer, yet you are subject to swarms of thieves and robbers) and the envy which precedent missions of English have against the subsequent, perpetuity it self is but forty years long, as within which time some ugly disturbance hath hitherto happened almost ever since the first coming of the English thither.

24. 2. The Claims upon Claims which each hath to the others Estates, and the facility of making good any pretence whatsoever by the favour of some one or other of the many Governours and Ministers which within forty years shall be in power there; as also by the frequency of false testimonies, and abuse of solemn Oaths.

25. 3. The paucity of Inhabitants, there being not above the 1/5th part so many as the Territory would maintain, and of those but a small part do work at all, and yet a smaller work so much as in other Countreys.

26. 4. That a great part of the Estates, both real and personal in Ireland, are owned by Absentees, and such as draw over the profits raised out of Ireland refunding nothing; so as Ireland exporting more then it imports doth yet grow poorer to a paradox.

27. 5. The difficulty of executing justice, so many of those in power being themselves protected by Offices, and protecting others. Moreover, the number of criminous and indebted persons being great, they favour their like in Juries, Offices, and wheresoever they can: Besides, the Countrey is seldom enough to give due encouragement to profound Judges and Lawyers, which makes judgements very casual; ignorant men being more bold to be apt and arbitrary, then such as understand the dangers of it. But all this with a little care in due season might remedy, so as to bring Ireland in a few years to the same level of values with other places; but of this also elsewhere more at large, for in the next place we shall come to Usury.

CHAPTER 2 The Physiocratic School

2.1 FRANÇOIS QUESNAY

Extract from the Royal Economic Maxims of M. De Sully

François Quesnay (1694–1774) was born in Mere, France. A doctor by profession, he was appointed as consulting physician to Louis XV. Quesnay is recognized as the founder of the physiocratic school. In his two-volume book *La Physiocratie* (1768), he underscored his belief in a natural order of things. Although medieval philosophers had stated the existence of natural laws, Quesnay and other physiocrats presented a more detailed explanation of the natural social order. They believed that for such an order to operate freely, there must be a strong monarch presiding over a free enterprise system whose structure is determined by the contributions of groups toward the national output. Farmers, farm laborers, landowners, and the sovereign were elevated as the productive class, while the contributions of merchants and industrialists were trivialized. Farmers contributed to the national product through outlays for fences, machinery, and raw materials, including seeds, fertilizer, etc. Landowners contributed by virtue of their ownership of land. The sovereign's contribution assumed the form of building public works and administering laws. Since merchants did not use land, and land was the only factor of production that yielded a surplus, merchants failed to make an economic contribution.

The following selection is taken from Marguerite Kuczynski and Ronald L. Meek, eds. and trans., *Quesnay's Tableau Économique* (Macmillan Press and A. M. Kelley, 1972). Quesnay's original masterpiece was published in 1766. In this selection, he maintains that the flow of income in an economic system is analogous to the circulation of blood. He elaborates on this concept, presenting a zig-zag flow of money through different sectors of the economy, thereby setting a precedent for the input-output models of Piero Sraffa and Wassily Leontief and the general equilibrium theory of Léon Walras and John Hicks. Quesnay presents an ideal economy in the form of maxims and advocates the use of large farms to lower costs of production, the restriction of monopolies, and limits on government intervention.

Key Concept: land as the preeminent source of positive net income

In this distribution it is assumed:

1. That the whole... revenue enters into the annual circulation, and runs through it to the full extent of its course; and that it is never formed into monetary fortunes, or at least that those which are formed are counterbalanced by those which come back into circulation; for otherwise these monetary fortunes would check the flow of a part of this annual revenue of the nation, and hold back the money stock or finance of the kingdom, to the detriment of the return of the advances, the payment of the artisans' wages, the reproduction of the revenue, and the taxes.

2. That no part of the sum of the revenues passes into the hands of foreign countries without return in money and commodities.

3. That the nation does not suffer any loss in its mutual trade with foreign countries, even if this trade is very profitable to the merchants through the gains they make out of their fellow-citizens on the sale of the commodities they import; for then the increase in the fortunes of these merchants represents a deduction from the circulation of the revenue, which is detrimental to distribution and reproduction.

4. That people are not taken in by a seeming advantage in mutual trade with foreign countries, through judging it simply with reference to the balance of the sums of money involved and not examining the greater or lesser profit which results from the particular commodities which are sold and purchased; for the loss often falls on the nation which receives a surplus in money, and this loss operates to the detriment of the distribution and reproduction of the revenue. In the mutual trade of the raw produce which is purchased from abroad and the manufactured commodities which are sold abroad, the disadvantage usually lies on the side of the latter commodities, because much more profit is yielded by the sale of raw produce.

5. That the proprietors and those engaged in remunerative occupations are not led by any anxiety, unforeseen by the Government, to give themselves

over to sterile saving, which would deduct from circulation and distribution a portion of their revenues or gains.

6. That the administration of finance, whether in the collection of taxes or in the expenditure of the Government, does not bring about the formation of monetary fortunes, which steal a portion of the revenue away from circulation, distribution, and reproduction.

7. That taxes are not destructive or disproportionate to the mass of the nation's revenue; that their increase follows the increase of the revenue; and that they are laid directly on the net product of landed property, and not on produce, where they would increase the costs of collection, and operate to the detriment of trade. That they are also not taken from the advances of the farmers of landed property; for the advances of a kingdom's agriculture ought to be regarded as if they were fixed property which should be preserved with great care in order to ensure the production of the taxes and the revenue of the nation. Otherwise taxation degenerates into spoliation, and brings about a state of decline which very soon ruins the state.

8. That the advances of the farmers are sufficient to enable the expenses of cultivation to reproduce at least 100 per cent; for if the advances are not sufficient, the expenses of cultivation are proportionately higher and yield less net product.

9. That the children of farmers are settled in the countryside, so that there are always husbandmen there. For if they are harassed into abandoning the countryside and withdrawing to the towns, they take there their fathers' wealth which used to be employed in cultivation. It is not so much men as wealth which must be attracted to the countryside; for the more wealth is employed in the cultivation of corn, the fewer men it requires, the more it prospers, and the more net profit it yields. Such is the large-scale cultivation carried on by rich farmers, in comparison with the small-scale cultivation carried on by poor *métayers* who plough with the aid of oxen or cows.

10. That the desertion of inhabitants who take their wealth out of the kingdom is avoided.

11. That no barriers at all are raised to external trade in raw produce; *for as the market is, so is the reproduction.*

12. That the prices of produce and commodities in the kingdom are never made to fall; for then mutual foreign trade would become disadvantageous to the nation. AS THE MARKET VALUE IS, SO IS THE REVENUE. *Abundance plus valuelessness does not equal wealth. Scarcity plus dearness equals poverty. Abundance plus dearness equals opulence.*

13. That people do not believe that cheapness of produce is profitable to the lower classes; for a low price of produce causes a fall in their wages, reduces their well-being, makes less work or remunerative occupations available for them, and reduces the nation's revenue.

14. That the well-being of the lower orders is not reduced; for then they would not be able to contribute sufficiently to the consumption of the produce which can be consumed only within the country, and the reproduction and revenue of the nation would be reduced.

15. That the breeding of livestock is encouraged; for it is livestock which provides the land with the manure which procures abundant crops.

16. That no encouragement at all is given to luxury in the way of ornamentation; for this is maintained only to the detriment of luxury in the way of subsistence, which sustains the market for raw produce, its proper price, and the reproduction of the nation's revenue.

17. That the Government's economic policy is concerned only with encouraging productive expenditure and external trade in raw produce, and that it refrains from interfering with sterile expenditure.

18. That means to meet the extraordinary needs of the state are expected to be found only in the prosperity of the nation and not in the credit of financiers; for *monetary fortunes are a clandestine form of wealth which knows neither king nor country.*

19. That the state avoids contracting loans which create rentier incomes, which burden the state with devouring debts, and which bring about a trade or traffic in finance, through the medium of negotiable bills, the discount on which causes a greater and greater increase in sterile monetary fortunes, which separate finance from agriculture, and which deprive the latter of the wealth necessary for the improvement of landed property and the cultivation of the land.

20. That a nation which has a large territory to cultivate, and the means of carrying on a large trade in raw produce, does not extend too far the employment of money and men in manufacturing and trading in luxury goods, to the detriment of the work and expenditure involved in agriculture; for more than anything else the kingdom ought to be well furnished with wealthy cultivators.

21. That the land employed in the cultivation of corn is brought together, as far as possible, into large farms worked by rich husbandmen; for in large agricultural enterprises there is less expenditure required for the upkeep and repair of buildings, and proportionately much less cost and much more net product than in small ones, because the latter employ uselessly, and at the expense of the revenue of the land, a greater number of the families of farmers, the extent of whose activities and means hardly puts them in a position to carry on wealthy cultivation. This multiplicity of farmers is less favourable to population than is the increase of revenue, because the population whose position is most assured, and which is most readily available for the different occupations and different kinds of work which divide men into different classes, is that maintained by the net product. All economies profitably made use of in work which can be done with the aid of animals, machines, rivers, etc., bring benefit to the population and the state, because a greater net product procures men a greater reward for other services or other kinds of work.

22. That each person is free to cultivate in his fields such products as his interests, his means, and the nature of the land suggest to him, in order that he may extract from them the greatest possible product. Monopoly in the cultivation of landed property should never be encouraged, for it is detrimental to the general revenue of the nation. The prejudice which leads to the encouragement of an abundance of produce of primary necessity in preference to that of less necessary produce, to the detriment of the market value of one or the other, is inspired by short-sighted views that do not extend as far as the effects of mutual external trade, which makes provision for everything and determines the price of the produce which each nation can cultivate with the most profit. It is

revenue and taxes which are the wealth of primary necessity in a state, in order to defend subjects against scarcity and against the enemy, and to maintain the glory and power of the monarch and the prosperity of the nation.

23. That the Government troubles itself less with economising than with the operations necessary for the prosperity of the kingdom; for an expenditure that is too high may cease to be excessive by virtue of the increase of wealth. But abuses must not be confused with simple expenditure, for abuses could swallow up all the wealth of the nation and the sovereign.

24. That less attention is paid to increasing the population than to increasing the revenue; for the greater well-being which a high revenue brings about is preferable to the greater pressure of subsistence needs which a population in excess of the revenue entails; and when the people are in a state of well-being there are more resources to meet the needs of the state, and also more means to make agriculture prosper.

Without these conditions, agriculture producing 100 per cent, as we have assumed it to do in the *tableau* and as it does in England, would be fictitious; but the principles would be no less certain, nor any less the true principles of the science of economic administration. This science is not confused here with the trivial and specious science of financial operations whose subject-matter is only the money stock of the nation and the monetary movements resulting from traffic in money, in which credit, the lure of interest, etc., as in the case of gambling, bring about nothing but a sterile circulation which only in exceptional circumstances can be of any benefit. It is in a knowledge of the true sources of wealth, and of the means of increasing and perpetuating them, that the science of the economic administration of a kingdom consists.

Economic administration opens up the sources of wealth; wealth attracts men; men and wealth make agriculture prosper, expand trade, give new life to industry, and increase and perpetuate wealth. Economic administration forestalls a decline in the affluence and strength of the nation. Upon the means which it abundantly provides, the success of the other branches of the kingdom's government depends. Economic administration strengthens the power of the state, attracts the respect of other nations, and safeguards the glory of the monarch and the happiness of the people. lit includes in its scope all the essential principles of a perfect system of government, in which authority is always a benevolent protectress and a beloved guardian, which can never be diverted from its course, which will not spread its influence too far, and which cannot cause anxiety. It maintains everywhere the interests of the nation, good order, the rights of the public, and the power and dominion of the sovereign.

2.2 ANNE-ROBERT-JACQUES TURGOT

Reflections on the Formation and Distribution of Wealth

Anne-Robert-Jacques Turgot (1727–1781), the baron de l'Aulne, was born in Paris, France, into the aristocracy. As chief administrative officer of the district of Limoges from 1761–1774, he sought to liberalize the local economy by abolishing the *taille* tax, adjusting taxes to the ability to pay, establishing an employment agency, and putting pressure on landowners to retain workers during a hunger crisis. In 1774, the financially insolvent government of Louis XVI appointed Turgot as minister of finance. Turgot ushered in an era of economic liberalism by lifting restrictions on the internal grain trade, taxing the nobility for public works, and destroying the trade monopolies of the guilds. The wrath of the aristocracy led to his dismissal in 1776.

A physiocrat and liberal, Turgot believed that land is the source of wealth. Furthermore, rent is equivalent to net product, wages tend toward subsistence, and savings determine the rate of interest and a risk premium. His economic treatise *Reflections on the Formation and Distribution of Wealth* (1770), from which the following selection has been taken, is based on the principle that each individual is the only competent judge of the best use of his lands and labor. Turgot underscores the importance of interest as the standard by which the level of capital may be judged, examines the factors determining the rate of interest, and notes the impact of interest on the overall economy.

Key Concept: the foundation of interest

True foundation of interest of money.

A man ... may lend his money as lawfully as he may sell it; and the possessor of money may either do one or the other, not only because money is equivalent to a revenue, and a means to procure a revenue: not only because the lender loses, during the continuance of the loan, the revenue he might have procured by it; not only because he risks his capital; not only because the borrower can employ it in advantageous acquisitions, or in undertakings from whence he will draw a large profit; the proprietor of money may lawfully receive the interest of it, by a more general and decisive principle. Even if none of these circumstances should take place, he will not have the less right to require an interest for his loan, for this reason only, that his money is his own. Since it is his own, he has a right to keep it, nothing can imply a duty in him to lend it; if then he does lend, he may annex such a condition to the loan as he chuses, in this he does no injury to the borrower, since the latter agrees to the conditions, and has no sort of right over the sum lent. The profit which money can procure the borrower, is doubtless one of the most prevailing motives to determine him to borrow on interest; it is one of the means which facilitates his payment of the interest, but this is by no means that which gives a right to the lender to require it; it is sufficient for him that his money is his own, and this is a right inseparable from property. He who buys bread, does it for his support, but the right the baker has to exact a price is totally independent of the use of bread; the same right he would possess in the sale of a parcel of stones, a right founded on this principle only, that the bread is his own, and no one has any right to oblige him to give it up for nothing. . . .

The rate of interest ought to be fixed, as the price of every other merchandize, by the course of trade alone.

. . . [T]he price of money borrowed, is regulated like the price of all other merchandize, by the proportion of the money at market with the demand for it: thus, when there are many borrowers who are in want of money, the interest of money rises; when there are many possessors who are ready to lend, it falls. It is therefore an error to believe that the interest of money in trade ought to be fixed by the laws of prices. It has a current price fixed like that of all other merchandize. This price varies a little, according to the greater or less security which the lender has; but on equal security, he ought to raise and fall his price in proportion to the abundance of the demand, and the law no more ought to fix the interest of money than it ought to regulate the price of any other merchandizes which have a currency in trade.

Money has in commerce two different valuations. One expresses the quantity of money or silver we give to procure different sorts of commodities; the other expresses the relation a sum of money has, in the interest it will procure in the course of trade.

It seems by this explanation of the manner in which money is either sold or lent for an annual interest, that there are two ways of valuing money in commerce. In buying and selling a certain weight of silver represents a certain quantity of labour, or of merchandize of every species; for example, one ounce of silver is equal to a certain quantity of corn, or to the labour of a man for a certain number of days. In lending, and in the commerce of money, a capital is the equivalent of an equal rent, to a determinate portion of that capital; and reciprocally an annual rent represents a capital equal to the amount of that rent repeated a certain number of times, according as interest is at a higher or lower rate.

These two valuations are independent of each other, and are governed by quite different principles.

These two different methods of fixing a value, have much less connection, and depend much less on each other than we should be tempted to believe at first sight. Money may be very common in ordinary commerce, may hold a very low value, answer to a very small quantity of commodities, and the interest of money may at the same time be very high.

I will suppose there are one million ounces of silver in actual circulation in commerce, and that an ounce of silver is given in the market for a bushel of corn. I will suppose that there is brought into the country in some manner or other, another million of ounces of silver, and this augmentation is distributed to every one in the same proportion as the first million, so that he who had before two ounces, has now four. The silver considered as a quantity of metal, will certainly diminish in price, or which is the same thing, commodities will be purchased dearer, and it becomes necessary, in order to procure the same measure of corn which he had before with one ounce of silver, to give more silver, perhaps two ounces instead of one. But it does not by any means follow from thence, that the interest of money falls, if all this money is carried to market, and employed in the current expences of those who possess it, as it is supposed the first million of ounces of silver was; for the interest of money falls only when there is a greater quantity of money to be lent, in proportion to the wants of the borrowers, than there was before. Now the silver which is carried to market is not to be lent; it is money which is hoarded up, which forms the accumulated capital for lending; and the augmentation of the money in the market, or the diminution of its price in comparison with commodities in the ordinary course of trade, are very far from causing infallibly, or by a necessary consequence, a decrease of the interest of money; on the contrary, it may happen that the cause which augments the quantity of money in the market, and which consequently increases the price of other commodities by lowering the value of silver, is precisely the same cause which augments the hire of money, or the rate of interest.

In effect, I will suppose for a moment, that all the rich people in a country, instead of saving from their revenue, or from their annual profits, shall expend the whole; that, not satisfied with expending their whole revenue, they dissipate a part of their capital; that a man who has 100,000 livres in money, instead of employing them in a profitable manner, or lending them, consumes them by degrees in foolish expences; it is apparent that on one side there will be more silver employed in common circulation, to satisfy the wants and humours of each individual, and that consequently its value will be lowered; on the other hand there will certainly be less money to be lent; and as many people will in this situation of things ruin themselves, there will clearly be more borrowers. The interest of money will consequently augment, while the money itself will become more plenty in circulation, and the value of it will fall, precisely by the same cause.

We shall no longer be surprised at this apparent inconsistency, if we consider that the money brought into the market for the purchase of corn, is that which is daily circulated to procure the necessaries of life; but that which is offered to be lent on interest, is what is actually drawn out of that circulation to be laid by and accumulated into a capital.

In comparing the value of money with that of commodities, we consider silver as a metal, which is an object of commerce. In estimating the interest of money we attend to the use of it during a determinate time.

In the market a measure of corn is purchased with a certain weight of silver, or a quantity of silver is bought with a certain commodity, it is this quantity which is valued and compared with the value of other commodities. In a loan upon interest, the object of the valuation is the use of a certain quantity of property during a certain time. It is in this case no longer a mass of silver, compared with a quantity of corn, but it is a portion of effects compared with a certain portion of the same, which is become the customary price of that mass for a certain time. Let twenty thousand ounces of silver be an equivalent in the market for twenty thousand measures of corn, or only for ten thousand, the use of those twenty thousand ounces of silver for a year is not worth less on a loan than the twentieth part of the principal sum, or one thousand ounces of silver, if interest is at five per cent.

The price of interest depends immediately on the proportion of the demand of the borrowers, with the offer of the lenders, and this proportion depends principally on the quantity of personal property, accumulated by an excess of revenue and of the annual produce to form capitals, whether these capitals exist in money or in any other kind of effects having a value in commerce.

The price of silver in circulation has no influence but with respect to the quantity of this metal employed in common circulation; but the rate of interest is governed by the quantity of property accumulated and laid by to form a capital. It is indifferent whether this property is in metal or other effects, provided these effects, are easily convertible into money. It is far from being the case, that the mass of metal existing in a state, is as large as the amount of the property lent on interest in the course of a year; but all the capitals in furniture, merchandize, tools, and cattle, supply the place of silver and represent it. A paper signed by a man, who is known to be worth 100,000 livres, and who promises to pay 100 marks in a certain time is worth that sum; the whole property of the man who has signed this note is answerable for the payment of it, in whatever the nature of these effects consists, provided they are in value 100,000 livres. It is not therefore the quantity of silver existing as merchandize which causes the rate of interest to rise or fall, or which brings more money in the market to be lent; it is only the capitals existing in commerce, that is to say, the actual value of personal property of every kind accumulated, successively saved out of the revenues and profits to be employed by the possessors to procure them new revenues and new profits. It is these accumulated savings which are offered to the borrowers, and the more there are of them, the lower the interest of money will be, at least if the number of borrowers is not augmented in proportion.

The spirit of oeconomy continually augments the amount of capitals, luxury continually tends to destroy them.

The spirit of oeconomy in any nation tends incessantly to augment the amount of the capitals, to increase the number of lenders, and to diminish that of the borrowers. The habit of luxury has precisely a contrary effect, and by what has been already remarked on the use of capitals in all undertakings, whether of cultivation, manufacture, or commerce, we may judge if luxury enriches a nation, or impoverishes it.

The lowering of interest proves, that in Europe oeconomy has in general prevailed over luxury.

Since the interest of money has been constantly diminishing in Europe for several centuries, we must conclude, that the spirit of oeconomy has been more general than the spirit of luxury. It is only people of fortune who run into luxury, and among the rich, the sensible part of them confine their expences within their incomes, and pay great attention not to touch their capital. Those who wish to become rich are far more numerous in a nation than those which are already so. Now, in the present state of things, as all the land is occupied, there is but one way to become rich it is either to possess, or to procure in some way or other, a revenue or an annual profit above what is absolutely necessary for subsistence, and to lay up every year in reserve to form a capital, by means of which they may obtain an increase of revenue or annual profit, which will again produce another saving, and become capital. There are consequently a great number of men interested and employed in amusing capitals.

Recapituation of the five different methods of employing capitals.

I have reckoned five different methods of employing capitals, or of placing them so as to procure a profit.

1st. To buy an estate, which brings in a certain revenue.

2d. To employ money in undertakings of cultivation; in leasing lands whose produce should render back, besides the expences of farming, the interest on the advances, and a recompense for the labour of him who employs his property and attention in the cultivation.

3d. To place a capital in some undertaking of industry or manufactures.

4th. To employ it in commerce.

5th. To lend it to those who want it, for an annual interest.

The influence which the different methods of employing money have on each other.

It is evident that the annual returns, which capitals, placed in different employs, will produce, are proportionate to each other, and all have relation to the actual rate of the interest of money.

Money invested in land, necessarily produces the least.

The person who invests his money in land let to a solvent tenant, procures himself a revenue which gives him very little trouble in receiving, and which he may dispose of in the most agreeable manner, by indulging all his inclinations. There is a greater advantage in the purchase of this species of property, than of any other, since the possession of it is more guarded against accidents. We must therefore purchase a revenue in land at a higher price, and must content ourselves with a less revenue for an equal capital.

Money on interest ought to bring a little more income, than land purchased with an equal capital.

He who lends his money on interest, enjoys it still more peaceably and freely than the possessor of land, but the insolvency of his debtor may endanger the loss of his capital. He will not therefore content himself with an interest equal to the revenue of the land which he could buy with an equal capital. The interest of money lent, must consequently be larger than the revenue of an estate purchased with the same capital; for if the proprietor could find an estate to purchase of an equal income, he would prefer that.

Money employed in cultivation, manufactures, or commerce, ought to produce more than the interest of money on loan.

By a like reason, money employed in agriculture, in manufactures, or in commerce, ought to produce a more considerable profit than the revenue of the same capital employed in the purchase of lands, or the interest of money on loan: for these undertakings, besides the capital advanced, requiring much care and labour, and if they were not more lucrative, it would be much better to secure an equal revenue, which might be enjoyed without labour. It is necessary then, that, besides the interest of the capital, the undertaker should draw every year a profit to recompence him for his care, his labour, his talents, the risque he runs, and to replace the wear and tear of that portion of his capital which he is obliged to invest in effects capable of receiving injury, and exposed to all kinds of accidents.

Meantime the freedom of these various employments are limited by each other, and maintain, notwithstanding their inequality, a species of equilibrium.

The different uses of the capitals produce very unequal profits; but this inequality does not prevent them from having a reciprocal influence on each other, nor from establishing a species of equilibrium among themselves, like that between two liquors of unequal gravity, and which communicate with each other by means of a reversed syphon, the two branches of which they fill; there can be no height to which the one can rise or fall, but the liquor in the other branch will be affected in the same manner.

I will suppose, that on a sudden, a great number of proprietors of lands are desirous of setting them. It is evident that the price of lands will fall, and that with a less sum we may acquire a larger revenue; this cannot come to pass without the interest of money rising, for the possessors of money would chuse rather to buy lands, than to lend at a lower interest than the revenue of the lands they could purchase. If, then, the borrowers want to have money, they will be constrained to pay a greater rate. If the interest of the money increases, they will prefer lending it, to setting out in a hazardous manner on enterprizes of agriculture, industry, and commerce: and they will be aware of any enterprizes but those that produce, besides the retribution for their trouble, an emolument by far greater than the rate of the lender's produce. In a word, if the profits, springing from an use of money, augment or diminish, the capitals are converted by withdrawing them from other employings, or are withdrawn by converting them to other ends, which necessarily alters, in each of those employments, the proportion of profits on the capital to the annual product. Generally, money converted into property in land, does not bring in so much as money on interest; and money on interest brings less than money used in laborious enterprises: but the produce of money laid out in any way whatever, cannot augment or decree without implying a proportionate augmentation, or decrease in other employments of money.

The current interest of money is the standard by which the abundance or scarcity of capitals may be judged; it is the scale on which the extent of a nation's capacity for enterprizes in agriculture, manufactures, and commerce, may be reckoned.

Thus the current interest of money may be considered as a standard of the abundance or scarcity of capitals in a nation, and of the extent of enterprizes of every denomination, in which she may embark: it is manifest, that the lower the interest of money is, the more valuable is the land. A man that has an income of fifty thousand livres, if the land is sold but at the rate of twenty years purchase is an owner of only one million; he has two millions, if the land is sold at the rate of forty. If the interest is at five per cent, any land to be brought into cultivation would continue fallow, if, besides the recovery of the advances, and the retribution due to the care of the cultivator, its produce would not afford five per cent. No manufactory, no commerce can exist, that does not bring in five per cent. exclusively of the salary and equivalents for the risque and trouble of the undertaker. If there is a neighbouring nation in which the interest stands only at two per cent. not only it will engross all the branches of commerce, from which the nation where an interest at five per cent. is established, is excluded, but its manufacturers and merchants, enabled to satisfy themselves with a lower interest, will also sell their goods at a more moderate price, and will attract the almost exclusive commerce of all articles, which they are not prevented to sell by particular circumstances of excessive dearth, and expences of carriages, from the nation in which the interest bears five per cent.

Influence of the rate of interest of money on all lucrative enterprizes.

The price of the interest may be looked upon as a kind of level, under which all labour, culture, industry, or commerce, acts. It is like a sea expanded over a vast country, the tops of the mountains rise above the surface of the water, and form fertile and cultivated islands. If this sea happens to give way, in proportion as it descends, sloping ground, then plains and vallies appear, which cover themselves with productions of every kind. It wants no more than a foot elevation, or falling, to inundate or to restore culture to unmeasurable tracts of land. It is the abundance of capitals that animates enterprize; and a low interest of money is at the same time the effect and a proof of the abundance of capitals.

CHAPTER 3 The Classical School

3.1 DAVID HUME

Of Commerce and of the Jealousy of Trade

David Hume (1711–1776), a Scottish historian and philosopher, is well known for his philosophical masterpieces. After entering the University of Edinburgh at the age of 14 and briefly studying law, Hume travelled to France in 1734 and started to write *A Treatise of Human Nature*, which is now considered a classic of the empiricist philosophy in the tradition of John Locke and Isaac Newton. In 1752, Hume became a librarian at the Advocates' Library in Edinburgh where he produced a six-volume history of England.

Hume's major works include *An Enquiry Concerning Human Understanding* (1742), *An Enquiry Concerning the Principles of Morals* (1748), and *Dialogues Concerning Natural Religion* (1779). In his *An Enquiry Concerning Human Understanding*, Hume stated that all ideas are derived from and represent impressions and that we have no rational basis for our feeling that the same cause must always have the same effect because it is neither a logical truth nor an empirically justified claim. An economic liberal, he rejected the mercantilist policy of maintaining a trade surplus in conjunction with imports of gold and silver by arguing that such imports pay for surpluses in exports, raising inflation and reducing exports until both exports and imports move back into balance. The following selection is taken from Eugene F. Miller, ed., *Essays: Moral, Political, and Literary*, rev. ed. (Liberty Classics, 1985). The book is based on the original 1777 editions. In it Hume views trade and industry as a stock of labor, which provides both necessities and public service. He strongly supports foreign trade for providing markets for those products that cannot be completely consumed at home and for expanding the array of products for domestic consumers while denouncing politicians who feel threatened by the rising economic power of their neighbors.

Key Concept: stock of labor and trade

OF COMMERCE

... Every thing in the world is purchased by labour; and our passions are the only causes of labour. When a nation abounds in manufactures and mechanic arts, the proprietors of land, as well as the farmers, study agriculture as a science, and redouble their industry and attention. The superfluity, which arises from their labour, is not lost; but is exchanged with manufactures for those commodities, which men's luxury now makes them covet. By this means, land furnishes a great deal more of the necessaries of life, than what suffices for those who cultivate it. In times of peace and tranquillity, this superfluity goes to the maintenance of manufacturers, and the improvers of liberal arts. But it is easy for the public to convert many of these manufacturers into soldiers, and maintain them by that superfluity, which arises from the labour of the farmers. Accordingly we find, that this is the case in all civilized governments. When the sovereign raises an army, what is the consequence? He imposes a tax. This tax obliges all the people to retrench what is least necessary to their subsistence. Those, who labour in such commodities, must either enlist in the troops, or turn themselves to agriculture, and thereby oblige some labourers to enlist for want of business. And to consider the matter abstractedly, manufactures encrease the power of the state only as they store up so much labour, and that of a kind to which the public may lay claim, without depriving any one of the necessaries of life. The more labour, therefore, is employed beyond mere necessaries, the more powerful is any state; since the persons engaged in that labour may easily be converted to the public service. In a state without manufactures, there may be the same number of hands; but there is not the same quantity of labour, nor of the same kind. All the labour is there bestowed upon necessaries, which can admit of little or no abatement.

Thus the greatness of the sovereign and the happiness of the state are, in a great measure, united with regard to trade and manufactures. It is a violent method, and in most cases impracticable, to oblige the labourer to toil, in order to raise from the land more than what subsists himself and family. Furnish him with manufactures and commodities, and he will do it of himself. Afterwards you will find it easy to seize some part of his superfluous labour, and employ it in the public service, without giving him his wonted return. Being accustomed to industry, he will think this less grievous, than if, at once, you obliged him to an augmentation of labour without any reward. The case is the same with regard to the other members of the state. The greater is the stock of labour of all kinds, the greater quantity may be taken from the heap, without making any sensible alteration in it.

A public granary of corn, a storehouse of cloth, a magazine of arms; all these must be allowed real riches and strength in any state. Trade and industry are really nothing but a stock of labour, which, in times of peace and tranquillity, is employed for the ease and satisfaction of individuals; but in the exigencies of state, may, in part, be turned to public advantage. Could we convert a city into a kind of fortified camp, and infuse into each breast so martial a genius, and such a passion for public good, as to make every one willing to undergo the greatest hardships for the sake of the public; these affections might now, as in ancient times, prove alone a sufficient spur to industry, and support the community. It would then be advantageous, as in camps, to banish all arts and luxury; and, by restrictions on equipage and tables, make the provisions and forage last longer than if the army were loaded with a number of superfluous retainers. But as these principles are too disinterested and too difficult to support, it is requisite to govern men by other passions, and animate them with a spirit of avarice and industry, art and luxury. The camp is, in this case, loaded with a superfluous retinue; but the provisions flow in proportionably larger. The harmony of the whole is still supported; and the natural bent of the mind being more complied with, individuals, as well as the public, find their account in the observance of those maxims.

The same method of reasoning will let us see the advantage of *foreign* commerce, in augmenting the power of the state, as well as the riches and happiness of the subject. It encreases the stock of labour in the nation; and the sovereign may convert what share of it he finds necessary to the service of the public. Foreign trade, by its imports, furnishes materials for new manufactures; and by its exports, it produces labour in particular commodities, which could not be consumed at home. In short, a kingdom, that has a large import and export, must abound more with industry, and that employed upon delicacies and luxuries, than a kingdom which rests contented with its native commodities. It is, therefore, more powerful, as well as richer and happier. The individuals reap the benefit of these commodities, so far as they gratify the senses and appetites. And the public is also a gainer, while a greater stock of labour is, by this means, stored up against any public exigency; that is, a greater number of laborious men are maintained, who may be diverted to the public service, without robbing any one of the necessaries, or even the chief conveniencies of life.

If we consult history, we shall find, that, in most nations, foreign trade has preceded any refinement in home manufactures, and given birth to domestic luxury. The temptation is stronger to make use of foreign commodities, which are ready for use, and which are entirely new to us, than to make improvements on any domestic commodity, which always advance by slow degrees, and never affect us by their novelty.

The profit is also very great, in exporting what is superfluous at home, and what bears no price, to foreign nations, whose soil or climate is not favourable to that commodity. Thus men become acquainted with the *pleasures* of luxury and the *profits* of commerce; and their *delicacy* and *industry*, being once awakened, carry them on to farther improvements, in every branch of domestic as well as foreign trade. And this perhaps is the chief advantage which arises from a commerce with strangers. It rouses men from their indolence; and presenting the gayer and more opulent part of the nation with objects of luxury, which they never before dreamed of, raises in them a desire of a more splendid way of life than what their ancestors enjoyed. And at the same time, the few merchants, who possess the secret of this importation and exportation, make great profits; and becoming rivals in wealth to the ancient nobility, tempt other adventurers to become their rivals in commerce. Imitation soon diffuses all those arts; while domestic manufactures emulate the foreign in their improvements, and work up every home commodity to the utmost perfection of which it is susceptible. Their own steel and iron, in such laborious hands, become equal to the gold and rubies of the INDIES.

When the affairs of the society are once brought to this situation, a nation may lose most of its foreign trade, and yet continue a great and powerful people. If strangers will not take any particular commodity of ours, we must cease to labour in it. The same hands will turn themselves towards some refinement in other commodities, which may be wanted at home. And there must always be materials for them to work upon; till every person in the state, who possesses riches, enjoys as great plenty of home commodities, and those in as great perfection, as he desires; which can never possibly happen. CHINA is represented as one of the most flourishing empires in the world; though it has very little commerce beyond its own territories....

OF THE JEALOUSY OF TRADE

Having endeavoured to remove one species of ill-founded jealousy [the fear that a nation's supply of money will be depleted by trade], which is so prevalent among commercial nations, it may not be amiss to mention another [the fear that trading will cause a nation harm insofar as it contributes to the improvement and prosperity of its neighbors], which seems equally groundless. Nothing is more usual, among states which have made some advances in commerce, than to look on the progress of their neighbours with a suspicious eye, to consider all trading states as their rivals, and to suppose that it is impossible for any of them to flourish, but at their expence. In opposition to this narrow and malignant opinion, I will venture to assert, that the encrease of riches and commerce in any one nation, instead of hurting, commonly promotes the riches and commerce of all its neighbours; and that a state can scarcely carry its trade and industry very far, where all the surrounding states are buried in ignorance, sloth, and barbarism.

It is obvious, that the domestic industry of a people cannot be hurt by the greatest prosperity of their neighbours; and as this branch of commerce is undoubtedly the most important in any extensive kingdom, we are so far removed from all reason of jealousy. But I go farther, and observe, that where an open communication is preserved among nations, it is impossible but the domestic industry of every one must receive an encrease from the improvements of the others. Compare the situation of GREAT BRITAIN at present, with what it was two centuries ago. All the arts both of agriculture and manufactures were then extremely rude and imperfect. Every improvement, which we have since made, has arisen from our imitation of foreigners; and we ought so far to esteem it happy, that they had previously made advances in arts and ingenuity. But this intercourse is still upheld to our great advantage: Notwithstanding the advanced state of our manufactures, we daily adopt, in every art, the inventions and improvements of our neighbours. The commodity is first imported from abroad, to our great discontent, while we imagine that it drains us of our money: Afterwards, the art itself is gradually imported, to our visible advantage: Yet we continue still to repine, that our neighbours should possess any art, industry, and invention; forgetting that, had they not first instructed us, we should have been at present barbarians; and did they not still continue their instructions, the arts must fall into a state of languor, and lose that emulation and novelty, which contribute so much to their advancement.

The encrease of domestic industry lays the foundation of foreign commerce. Where a great number of commodities are raised and perfected for the home-market, there will always be found some which can be exported with advantage. But if our neighbours have no art or cultivation, they cannot take them; because they will have nothing to give in exchange. In this respect, states are in the same condition as individuals. A single man can scarcely be industrious, where all his fellow-citizens are idle. The riches of the several members of a community contribute to encrease my riches, whatever profession I may follow. They consume the produce of my industry, and afford me the produce of theirs in return.

Nor needs any state entertain apprehensions, that their neighbours will improve to such a degree in every art and manufacture, as to have no demand from them. Nature, by giving a diversity of geniuses, climates, and soils, to different nations, has secured their mutual intercourse and commerce, as long as they all remain industrious and civilized. Nay, the more the arts encrease in any state, the more will be its demands from its industrious neighbours. The inhabitants, having become opulent and skilful, desire to have every commodity in the utmost perfection; and as they have plenty of commodities to give in exchange, they make large importations from every foreign country. The industry of the nations, from whom they import, receives encouragement: Their own is also encreased, by the sale of the commodities which they give in exchange.

But what if a nation has any staple commodity, such as the woollen manufacture is in ENGLAND? Must not the interfering of our neighbours in that manufacture be a loss to us? I answer, that, when any commodity is denominated the staple of a kingdom, it is supposed that this kingdom has some peculiar and natural advantages for raising the commodity; and if, notwithstanding these advantages, they lose such a manufacture, they ought to blame their own idleness, or bad government, not the industry of their neighbours. It ought also to be considered, that, by the encrease of industry among the neighbouring nations, the consumption of every particular species of commodity is also encreased; and though foreign manufactures interfere with them in the market, the demand for their product may still continue, or even encrease. And should it diminish, ought the consequence to be esteemed so fatal? If the spirit of industry be preserved, it may easily be diverted from one branch to another; and the manufacturers of wool, for instance, be employed in linen, silk, iron, or any other commodities, for which there appears to be a demand. We need not apprehend, that all the objects of industry will be exhausted, or that our manufacturers, while they remain on an equal footing with those of our neighbours, will be in danger of wanting employment. The emulation among rival nations serves rather to keep industry alive in all of them: And any people is happier who possess a variety of manufactures, than if they enjoyed one single great manufacture, in which they are all employed. Their situation is less precarious; and they will feel less sensibly those revolutions and uncertainties, to which every particular branch of commerce will always be exposed.

The only commercial state, that ought to dread the improvements and industry of their neighbours, is such a one as the DUTCH, who enjoying no extent of land, nor possessing any number of native commodities, flourish only by their being the brokers, and factors, and carriers of others. Such a people may naturally apprehend, that, as soon as the neighbouring states come to know and pursue their interest, they will take into their own hands the management of their affairs, and deprive their brokers of that profit, which they formerly reaped from it. But though this consequence may naturally be dreaded, it is very long before it takes place; and by art and industry it may be warded off for many generations, if not wholly eluded. The advantage of superior stocks and correspondence is so great, that it is not easily overcome; and as all the transactions encrease by the encrease of industry in the neighbouring states, even a people whose commerce stands on this precarious basis, may at first reap a considerable profit from the flourishing condition of their neighbours. The DUTCH, having mortgaged all their revenues, make not such a figure in political transactions as formerly; but their commerce is surely equal to what it was in the middle of the last century, when they were reckoned among the great powers of EUROPE.

Were our narrow and malignant politics to meet with success, we should reduce all our neighbouring nations to the same state of sloth and ignorance that prevails in MOROCCO and the coast of BARBARY. But what would be the consequence? They could send us no commodities: They could take none from us: Our domestic commerce itself would languish for want of emulation, example, and instruction: And we ourselves should soon fall into the same abject condition, to which we had reduced them. I shall therefore venture to acknowledge, that, not only as a man, but as a BRITISH subject, I pray for the flourishing commerce of GERMANY, SPAIN, ITALY, and even FRANCE itself. I am at least certain, that GREAT BRITAIN, and all those nations, would flourish more, did their sovereigns and ministers adopt such enlarged and benevolent sentiments towards each other.

3.2 ADAM SMITH

The Wealth of Nations

Adam Smith (1723–1790) was born in Kirkaldy, Scotland. He entered the University of Glasgow at the age of 14 and later accepted a scholarship to Balliol College in Oxford, England. After a few years spent delivering public lectures on rhetoric and the law in Kirkaldy, Smith returned to the University of Glasgow to teach logic. He gained fame with his book *The Theory of Moral Sentiments* (1759), which explored the origin of moral approval and disapproval. In 1776, Smith published *An Inquiry into the Nature and Causes of the Wealth of Nations,* which is still considered the source of free market economics. His book has been translated into almost every European language and has guided many governments about markets and economics.

In the following selection, taken from *The Wealth of Nations,* Smith introduces the concept of a system of natural liberty in which each person pursues his or her own self-interest. In this system, each party in an exchange concentrates on giving up a product of less value in order to obtain another of higher value. Both parties benefit from such transactions. A free society that permits the exercise of self-interest would achieve the highest possible levels of growth and wealth formation, according to Smith, who rejected any form of government intervention in business, limiting government involvement in society to the legal system, national defense, and public works.

Key Concept: self-interest

OF THE PRINCIPLE WHICH GIVES OCCASION TO THE DIVISION OF LABOUR

This division of labour, from which so many advantages are derived, is not originally the effect of any human wisdom, which foresees and intends that general opulence to which it gives occasion. It is the necessary, though very slow and gradual, consequence of a certain propensity in human nature which has in view no such extensive utility; the propensity to truck, barter, and exchange one thing for another.

Whether this propensity be one of those original principles in human nature, of which no further account can be given; or whether, as seems more probable, it be the necessary consequence of the faculties of reason and speech, it belongs not to our present subject to enquire. It is common to all men, and to be found in no other race of animals, which seem to know neither this nor any other species of contracts. Two greyhounds, in running down the same hare, have sometimes the appearance of acting in some sort of concert. Each turns her towards his companion, or endeavours to intercept her when his companion turns her towards himself. This, however, is not the effect of any contract, but of the accidental concurrence of their passions in the same object at that particular time. Nobody ever saw a dog make a fair and deliberate exchange of one bone for another with another dog. Nobody ever saw one animal by its gestures and natural cries signify to another, this is mine, that yours; I am willing to give this for that. When an animal wants to obtain something either of a man or of another animal, it has no other means of persuasion but to gain the favour of those whose service it requires. A puppy fawns upon its dam, and a spaniel endeavours by a thousand attractions to engage the attention of its master who is at dinner, when it wants to be fed by him. Man sometimes uses the same arts with his brethren, and when he has no other means of engaging them to act according to his inclinations, endeavours by every servile and fawning attention to obtain their good will. He has not time, however, to do this upon every occasion. In civilized society he stands at all times in need of the co-operation and assistance of great multitudes, while his whole life is scarce sufficient to gain the friendship of a few persons. In almost every other race of animals each individual, when it is grown up to maturity, is entirely independent, and in its natural state has occasion for the assistance of no other living creature. But man has almost constant occasion for the help of his brethren, and it is in vain for him to expect it from their benevolence only. He will be more likely to prevail if he can interest their self-love in his favour, and shew them that it is for their own advantage to do for him what he requires of them. Whoever offers to another a bargain of any kind, proposes to do this. Give me that which I want, and you shall have this which you want, is the meaning of every such offer; and it is in this manner that we obtain from one another the far greater part of those good offices which we stand in need of. It is not from the benevolence of the butcher, the brewer, or the baker, that we expect our dinner, but from their regard to their own interest. We address ourselves, not to their humanity but to their self-love, and never talk to them of our own necessities but of their advantages. Nobody but a beggar chuses to depend chiefly upon the benevolence of his fellow-citizens. Even a beggar does not depend upon it entirely. The charity of well-disposed people, indeed, supplies him with the whole fund of his subsistence. But though this principle ultimately provides him with all the necessaries of life which he has occasion for, it neither does nor can provide him with them as he has occasion for them. The greater part of his occasional wants are supplied in the same manner as those of other people, by treaty, by barter, and by purchase. With the money which one man gives him he purchases food. The old cloaths which another bestows upon him he exchanges for other old cloaths which suit him better, or for lodging, or for food, or for money, with which he can buy either food, cloaths, or lodging, as he has occasion.

As it is by treaty, by barter, and by purchase, that we obtain from one another the greater part of those mutual good offices which we stand in need of, so it is this same trucking disposition which originally gives occasion to the division of labour. In a tribe of hunters or shepherds a particular person makes bows and arrows, for example, with more readiness and dexterity than any other. He frequently exchanges them for cattle or for venison with his companions; and he finds at last that he can in this manner get more cattle and venison, than if he himself went to the field to catch them. From a regard to his own interest, therefore, the making of bows and arrows grows to be his chief business, and he becomes a sort of armourer. Another excels in making the frames and covers of their little huts or moveable houses. He is accustomed to be of use in this way to his neighbours, who reward him in the same manner with cattle and with venison, till at last he finds it his interest to dedicate himself entirely to this employment, and to become a sort of house-carpenter. In the same manner a third becomes a smith or a brazier; a fourth a tanner or dresser of hides or skins, the principal part of the clothing of savages. And thus the certainty of being able to exchange all that surplus part of the produce of his own labour, which is over and above his own consumption, for such parts of the produce of other men's labour as he may have occasion for, encourages every man to apply himself to a particular occupation, and to cultivate and bring to perfection whatever talent or genius he may possess for that particular species of business.

The difference of natural talents in different men is, in reality, much less than we are aware of; and the very different genius which appears to distinguish men of different professions, when grown up to maturity, is not upon many occasions so much the cause, as the effect of the division of labour. The difference between the most dissimilar characters, between a philosopher and a common street porter, for example, seems to arise not so much from nature, as from habit, custom, and education. When they came into the world, and for the first six or eight years of their existence, they were, perhaps, very much alike, and neither their parents nor playfellows could perceive any remarkable difference. About that age, or soon after, they come to be employed in very different occupations. The difference of talents comes then to be taken notice of, and widens by degrees, till at last the vanity of the philosopher is willing to acknowledge scarce any resemblance. But without the disposition to truck, barter, and exchange, every man must have procured to himself every necessary and conveniency of life which he wanted. All must have had the same duties to perform, and the same work to do, and there could have been no such difference of employment as could alone give occasion to any great difference of talents.

As it is this disposition which forms that difference of talents, so remarkable among men of different professions, so it is this same disposition which renders that difference useful. Many tribes of animals acknowledged to be all of the same species, derive from nature a much more remarkable distinction of genius, than what, antecedent to custom and education, appears to take place among men. By nature a philosopher is not in genius and disposition half so different from a street porter, as a mastiff is from a greyhound, or a greyhound from a spaniel, or this last from a shepherd's dog. Those different tribes of animals, however, though all of the same species, are of scarce any use to one another. The strength of the mastiff is not in the least supported either by the swiftness of the greyhound, or by the sagacity of the spaniel, or by the docility of the shepherd's dog. The effects of those different geniuses and talents, for want of the power or disposition to barter and exchange, cannot be brought into a common stock, and do not in the least contribute to the better accommodation and conveniency of the species. Each animal is still obliged to support and defend itself, separately and independently, and derives no sort of advantage from that variety of talents with which nature has distinguished its fellows. Among men, on the contrary, the most dissimilar geniuses are of use to one another; the different produces of their respective talents, by the general disposition to truck, barter, and exchange, being brought, as it were, into a common stock, where every man may purchase whatever part of the produce of other men's talents he has occasion for.

THAT THE DIVISION OF LABOUR IS LIMITED BY THE EXTENT OF THE MARKET

As it is the power of exchanging that gives occasion to the division of labour, so the extent of this division must always be limited by the extent of that power, or, in other words, by the extent of the market. When the market is very small, no person can have any encouragement to dedicate himself entirely to one employment, for want of the power to exchange all that surplus part of the produce of his own labour, which is over and above his own consumption, for such parts of the produce of other men's labour as he has occasion for.

There are some sorts of industry, even of the lowest kind, which can be carried on no where but in a great town. A porter, for example, can find employment and subsistence in no other place. A village is by much too narrow a sphere for him; even an ordinary market town is scarce large enough to afford him constant occupation. In the lone houses and very small villages which are scattered about in so desert a country as the Highlands of Scotland, every farmer must be butcher, baker and brewer for his own family. In such situations we can scarce expect to find even a smith, a carpenter, or a mason, within less than twenty miles of another of the same trade. The scattered families that live at eight or ten miles distance from the nearest of them, must learn to perform themselves a great number of little pieces of work, for which, in more populous countries, they would call in the assistance of those workmen. Country workmen are almost every where obliged to apply themselves to all the different branches of industry that have so much affinity to one another as to be employed about the same sort of materials. A country carpenter deals in every sort of work that is made of wood: a country smith in every sort of work that is made of iron. The former is not only a carpenter, but a joiner, a cabinet maker, and even a carver in wood, as well as a wheelwright, a ploughwright, a cart and waggon maker. The employments of the latter are still more various. It is impossible there should be such a trade as even that of a nailer in the remote and inland parts of the Highlands of Scotland. Such a workman at the rate of a thousand nails a day, and three hundred working days in the year, will make three hundred thousand nails in the year. But in such a situation it would be impossible to dispose of one thousand, that is, of one day's work in the year.

As by means of water-carriage a more extensive market is opened to every sort of industry than what land-carriage alone can afford it, so it is upon the sea-coast, and along the banks of navigable rivers, that industry of every kind naturally begins to subdivide and improve itself, and it is frequently not till a long time after that those improvements extend themselves to the inland parts of the country. A broad-wheeled waggon, attended by two men, and drawn by eight horses, in about six weeks time carries and brings back between London and Edinburgh near four ton weight of goods. In about the same time a ship navigated by six or eight men, and sailing between the ports of London and Leith, frequently carries and brings back two hundred ton weight of goods. Six or eight men, therefore, by the help of water-carriage, can carry and bring back in the same time the same quantity of goods between London and Edinburgh, as fifty broad-wheeled waggons, attended by a hundred men, and drawn by four hundred horses. Upon two hundred tons of goods, therefore, carried by the cheapest land-carriage from London to Edinburgh, there must be charged the maintenance of a hundred men for three weeks, and both the maintenance, and, what is nearly equal to the maintenance, the wear and tear of four hundred horses as well as of fifty great waggons. Whereas, upon the same quantity of goods carried by water, there is to be charged only the maintenance of six or eight men, and the wear and tear of a ship of two hundred tons burthen, together with the value of the superior risk, or the difference of the insurance between land and water-carriage. Were there no other communication between those two places, therefore, but by land-carriage, as no goods could be transported from the one to the other, except such whose price was very considerable in proportion to their weight, they could carry on but a small part of that commerce which at present subsists between them, and consequently could give but a small part of that encouragement which they at present mutually afford to each other's industry. There could be little or no commerce of any kind between the distant parts of the world. What goods could bear the expence of land-carriage between London and Calcutta? Or if there were any so precious as to be able to support this expense, with what safety could they be transported through the territories of so many barbarous nations? Those two cities, however, at present carry on a very considerable commerce with each other, and by mutually affording a market, give a good deal of encouragement to each other's industry.

Since such, therefore, are the advantages of water-carriage, it is natural that the first improvements of art and industry should be made where this conveniency opens the whole world for a market to the produce of every sort of labour, and that they should always be much later in extending themselves into the inland parts of the country. The inland parts of the country can for a long time have no other market for the greater part of their goods, but the country which lies round about them, and separates them from the sea-coast, and the great navigable rivers. The extent of their market, therefore, must for a long time be in proportion to the riches and populousness of that country, and consequently their improvement must always be posterior to the improvement of that country. In our North American colonies the plantations have constantly followed either the sea-coast or the banks of the navigable rivers, and have scarce any where extended themselves to any considerable distance from both.

The nations that, according to the best authenticated history, appear to have been first civilized, were those that dwelt round the coast of the Mediterranean Sea. That sea, by far the greatest inlet that is known in the world, having no tides, nor consequently any waves except such as are caused by the wind only, was, by the smoothness of its surface, as well as by the multitude of its islands, and the proximity of its neighbouring shores, extremely favourable to the infant navigation of the world; when, from their ignorance of the compass, men were afraid to quit the view of the coast, and from the imperfection of the art of ship building, to abandon themselves to the boisterous waves of the ocean. To pass beyond the pillars of Hercules, that is, to sail out of the Streights of Gibraltar, was, in the antient world, long considered as a most wonderful and dangerous exploit of navigation. It was late before even the Phenicians and Carthaginians, the most skilful navigators and ship-builders of those old times, attempted it, and they were for a long time the only nations that did attempt it.

Of all the countries on the coast of the Mediterranean Sea, Egypt seems to have been the first in which either agriculture or manufactures were cultivated and improved to any considerable degree. Upper Egypt extends itself nowhere above a few miles from the Nile, and in Lower Egypt that great river breaks itself into many different canals, which, with the assistance of a little art, seem to have afforded a communication by water-carriage, not only between all the great towns, but between all the considerable villages, and even to many farm-houses in the country; nearly in the same manner as the Rhine and the Maese do in Holland at present. The extent and easiness of this inland navigation was probably one of the principal causes of the early improvement of Egypt.

The improvements in agriculture and manufactures seem likewise to have been of very great antiquity in the provinces of Bengal in the East Indies, and in some of the eastern provinces of China; though the great extent of this antiquity is not authenticated by any histories of whose authority we, in this part of the world, are well assured. In Bengal the Ganges and several other great rivers form a great number of navigable canals in the same manner as the Nile does in Egypt. In the Eastern provinces of China too, several great rivers form, by their different branches, a multitude of canals, and by communicating with one another afford an inland navigation much more extensive than that either of the Nile or the Ganges, or perhaps than both of them put together. It is remarkable that neither the ancient Egyptians, nor the Indians, nor the Chinese, encouraged foreign commerce, but seem all to have derived their great opulence from this inland navigation.

All the inland parts of Africa, and all that part of Asia which lies any considerable way north of the Euxine and Caspian seas, the ancient Scythia, the modern Tartary and Siberia, seem in all ages of the world to have been in the same barbarous and uncivilized state in which we find them at present. The Sea of Tartary is the frozen ocean which admits of no navigation, and though some of the greatest rivers in the world run through that country, they are at too great a distance from one another to carry commerce and communication through the greater part of it. There are in Africa none of those great inlets, such as the Baltic and Adriatic seas in Europe, the Mediterranean and Euxine seas in both Europe and Asia, and the gulphs of Arabia, Persia, India, Bengal, and Siam, in Asia, to carry maritime commerce into the interior parts of that great continent: and the great rivers of Africa are at too great a distance from one another to give occasion to any considerable inland navigation. The commerce besides which any nation can carry on by means of a river which does not break itself into any great number of branches or canals, and which runs into another territory before it reaches the sea, can never be very considerable; because it is always in the power of the nations who possess that other territory to obstruct the communication between the upper country and the sea. The navigation of the Danube is of very little use to the different states of Bavaria, Austria and Hungary, in comparison of what it would be if any of them possessed the whole of its course till it falls into the Black Sea.

Adam Smith

3.3 THOMAS ROBERT MALTHUS

An Essay on the Principle of Population

Thomas Robert Malthus (1766–1834) was born at the Rookery in England, the county seat of his father. In 1784 he entered Jesus College, Cambridge, where he read mathematics and philosophy while studying for the clergy. He briefly practiced as a clergyman at a church in Okewood and later returned to Jesus College as a fellow in 1793.

In 1798, Malthus published *An Essay on the Principle of Population,* which later became one of the major building blocks of classical economics. In the following excerpt from this book, he states that population tends to increase unless it is kept in check by "misery and vice" and that population should not increase without the means of subsistence. Malthus argues that the problems of the poor are essentially moral and have their origins in two fundamental dilemmas: Food is necessary for the existence of man, and the passion between the sexes is necessary and will continue. This leads to a difficult outcome whereby the power of the population becomes infinitely greater than the power of the earth to produce subsistence to man. Malthus advocates for the abolition of the "poor laws," which had been instituted to alleviate poverty. He contends that although such laws could slightly alleviate the intensity of individual misfortune, they spread general evil over society.

Key Concept: the impact of population on subsistence

The different ratios in which population and food increase—The necessary effects of these different ratios of increase—Oscillation produced by them in the condition of the lower classes of society—Reasons why this oscillation has not been so much observed as might be expected—Three propositions on which the general argument of the Essay depends. . . .

[P]opulation, when unchecked, increase[s] in a geometrical ratio, and subsistence for man in an arithmetical ratio.

Let us examine whether this position be just.

I think it will be allowed that no state has hitherto existed (at least that we have any account of) where the manners were so pure and simple, and the means of subsistence so abundant, that no check whatever has existed to early marriages, among the lower classes, from a fear of not providing well for their families, or among the higher classes, from a fear of lowering their condition in life. Consequently in no state that we have yet known has the power of population been left to exert itself with perfect freedom.

Whether the law of marriage be instituted or not, the dictate of nature and virtue seems to be an early attachment to one woman. Supposing a liberty of changing in the case of an unfortunate choice, this liberty would not affect population till it arose to a height greatly vicious; and we are now supposing the existence of a society where vice is scarcely known.

In a state therefore of great equality and virtue, where pure and simple manners prevailed, and where the means of subsistence were so abundant that no part of the society could have any fears about providing amply for a family, the power of population being left to exert itself unchecked, the increase of the human species would evidently be much greater than any increase that has been hitherto known.

In the United States of America, where the means of subsistence have been more ample, the manners of the people more pure, and consequently the checks to early marriages fewer than in any of the modern states of Europe, the population has been found to double itself in twenty-five years.

This ratio of increase, though short of the utmost power of population, yet as the result of actual experience, we will take as our rule, and say, that population, when unchecked, goes on doubling itself every twenty-five years or increases in a geometrical ratio.

Let us now take any spot of earth, this Island for instance, and see in what ratio the subsistence it affords can be supposed to increase. We will begin with it under its present state of cultivation.

If I allow that by the best possible policy, by breaking up more land and by great encouragements to agriculture, the produce of this Island may be doubled in the first twenty-five years, I think it will be allowing as much as any person can well demand.

In the next twenty-five years, it is impossible to suppose that the produce could be quadrupled. It would be contrary to all our knowledge of the qualities of land. The very utmost that we can conceive is that the increase in the second twenty-five years might equal the present produce. Let us then take this for our rule, though certainly far beyond the truth, and allow that by great exertion, the whole produce of the Island might be increased every twenty-five years, by a quantity of subsistence equal to what it at present produces. The most enthusiastic speculator cannot suppose a greater increase than this. In a few centuries it would make every acre of land in the Island like a garden.

Yet this ratio of increase is evidently arithmetical.

It may be fairly said, therefore, that the means of subsistence increase in an arithmetical ratio. Let us now bring the effects of these two ratios together.

The population of the Island is computed to be about seven millions, and we will suppose the present produce equal to the support of such a number. In the first twenty-five years the population would be fourteen millions, and the food being also doubled, the means of subsistence would be equal to this increase. In the next twenty-five years the population would be twenty-eight millions, and the means of subsistence only equal to the support of twenty-one millions. In the next period the population would be fifty-six millions, and the means of subsistence just sufficient for half that number. And at the conclusion of the first century the population would be one hundred and twelve millions and the means of subsistence only equal to the support of thirty-five millions, which would leave a population of seventy-seven millions totally unprovided for.

A great emigration necessarily implies unhappiness of some kind or other in the country that is deserted. For few persons will leave their families, connections, friends, and native land, to seek a settlement in untried foreign climes, without some strong subsisting causes of uneasiness where they are, or the hope of some great advantages in the place to which they are going.

But to make the argument more general and less interrupted by the partial views of emigration, let us take the whole earth, instead of one spot, and suppose that the restraints to population were universally removed. If the subsistence for man that the earth affords was to be increased every twenty-five years by a quantity equal to what the whole world at present produces, this would allow the power of production in the earth to be absolutely unlimited and its ratio of increase much greater than we can conceive that any possible exertions of mankind could make it.

Taking the population of the world at any number, a thousand millions, for instance, the human species would increase in the ratio of—1, 2, 4, 8, 16, 32, 64, 128, 256, 512, &c. and subsistence as—1, 2, 3, 4, 5, 6, 7, 8, 9, 10, &c. In two centuries and a quarter, the population would be to the means of subsistence as 512 to 10, in three centuries as 4096 to 13, and in two thousand years the difference would be almost incalculable, though the produce in that time would have increased to an immense extent.

No limits whatever are placed to the productions of the earth; they may increase for ever and be greater than any assignable quantity; yet still the power of population being a power of a superior order, the increase of the human species can only be kept commensurate to the increase of the means of subsistence by the constant operation of the strong law of necessity acting as a check upon the greater power.

The effects of this check remain now to be considered.

Among plants and animals the view of the subject is simple. They are all impelled by a powerful instinct to the increase of their species, and this instinct is interrupted by no reasoning or doubts about providing for their offspring. Wherever therefore there is liberty, the power of increase is exerted, and the super-abundant effects are repressed afterwards by want of room and nourishment, which is common to animals and plants, and among animals, by becoming the prey of others.

The effects of this check on man are more complicated. Impelled to the increase of his species by an equally powerful instinct, reason interrupts his career and asks him whether he may not bring beings into the world, for whom he cannot provide the means of subsistence. In a state of equality, this would be the simple question. In the present state of society, other considerations occur. Will he not lower his rank in life? Will he not subject himself to greater difficulties than he at present feels? Will he not be obliged to labour harder? and if he has a large family, will his utmost exertions enable him to support them? May he not see his offspring in rags and misery, and clamouring for bread that he cannot give them? And may he not be reduced to the grating necessity of forfeiting his independence and of being obliged to the sparing hand of charity for support?

These considerations are calculated to prevent, and certainly do prevent, a very great number in all civilized nations from pursuing the dictate of nature in an early attachment to one woman. And this restraint almost necessarily, though not absolutely so, produces vice. Yet in all societies, even those that are most vicious, the tendency to a virtuous attachment is so strong that there is a constant effort towards an increase of population. This constant effort as constantly tends to subject the lower classes of the society to distress and to prevent any great permanent amelioration of their condition.

The way in which these effects are produced seems to be this.

We will suppose the means of subsistence in any country just equal to the easy support of its inhabitants. The constant effort towards population, which is found to act even in the most vicious societies, increases the number of people before the means of subsistence are increased. The food therefore which before supported seven millions must now be divided among seven millions and a half or eight millions. The poor consequently must live much worse, and many of them be reduced to severe distress. The number of labourers also being above the proportion of the work in the market, the price of labour must tend toward a decrease, while the price of provisions would at the same time tend to rise. The labourer therefore must work harder to earn the same as he did before. During this season of distress, the discouragements to marriage and the difficulty of rearing a family are so great that population is at a stand. In the mean time the cheapness of labour, the plenty of labourers, and the necessity of an increased industry amongst them, encourage cultivators to employ more labour upon their land, to turn up fresh soil, and to manure and improve more completely what is already in tillage, till ultimately the means of subsistence become in the same proportion to the population as at the period from which we set out. The situation of the labourer being then again tolerably comfortable, the restraints to population are in some degree loosened, and the same retrograde and progressive movements with respect to happiness are repeated.

This sort of oscillation will not be remarked by superficial observers, and it may be difficult even for the most penetrating mind to calculate its periods. Yet that in all old states some such vibration does exist, though from various transverse causes, in a much less marked, and in a much more irregular manner than I have described it, no reflecting man who considers the subject deeply can well doubt.

Many reasons occur why this oscillation has been less obvious, and less decidedly confirmed by experience, than might naturally be expected.

One principal reason is that the histories of mankind that we possess are histories only of the higher classes. We have but few accounts that can be depended upon of the manners and customs of that part of mankind, where these retrograde and progressive movements chiefly take place. A satisfactory history of this kind, of one people, and of one period, would require the constant and minute attention of an observing mind during a long life. Some of the objects of enquiry would be, in what proportion to the number of adults was the number of marriages, to what extent vicious customs prevailed in consequence of the restraints upon matrimony, what was the comparative mortality among the children of the most distressed part of the community and those who lived rather more at their ease, what were the variations in the real price of labour, and what were the observable differences in the state of the lower classes of society with respect to ease and happiness, at different times during a certain period.

Such a history would tend greatly to elucidate the manner in which the constant check upon population acts and would probably prove the existence of the retrograde and progressive movements that have been mentioned, though the times of their vibration must necessarily be rendered irregular, from the operation of many interrupting causes, such as the introduction or failure of certain manufactures, a greater or less prevalent spirit of agricultural enterprize, years of plenty, or years of scarcity, wars and pestilence, poor laws, the invention of processes for shortening labour without the proportional extension of the market for the commodity, and, particularly, the difference between the nominal and real price of labour, a circumstance which has perhaps more than any other contributed to conceal this oscillation from common view.

It very rarely happens that the nominal price of labour universally falls, but we well know that it frequently remains the same, while the nominal price of provisions has been gradually increasing. This is, in effect, a real fall in the price of labour, and during this period the condition of the lower orders of the community must gradually grow worse and worse. But the farmers and capitalists are growing rich from the real cheapness of labour. Their increased capitals enable them to employ a greater number of men. Work therefore may be plentiful, and the price of labour would consequently rise. But the want of freedom in the market of labour, which occurs more or less in all communities, either from parish laws, or the more general cause of the facility of combination among the rich, and its difficulty among the poor, operates to prevent the price of labour from rising at the natural period, and keeps it down some time longer; perhaps, till a year of scarcity, when the clamour is too loud and the necessity too apparent to be resisted.

The true cause of the advance in the price of labour is thus concealed, and the rich affect to grant it as an act of compassion and favour to the poor, in consideration of a year of scarcity, and, when plenty returns, indulge themselves in the most unreasonable of all complaints, that the price does not again fall, when a little reflection would shew them that it must have risen long before but from an unjust conspiracy of their own.

But though the rich by unfair combinations contribute frequently to prolong a season of distress among the poor, yet no possible form of society could prevent the almost constant action of misery upon a great part of mankind, if in a state of inequality, and upon all, if all were equal.

The theory on which the truth of this position depends appears to me so extremely clear that I feel at a loss to conjecture what part of it can be denied.

That population cannot increase without the means of subsistence is a proposition so evident that it needs no illustration.

That population does invariably increase where there are the means of subsistence, the history of every people that have ever existed will abundantly prove.

And that the superior power of population cannot be checked without producing misery or vice, the ample portion of these too bitter ingredients in the cup of human life and the continuance of the physical causes that seem to have produced them bear too convincing a testimony. . . .

The second, or positive check to population examined, in England—The true cause why the immense sum collected in England for the poor does not better their condition—The powerful tendency of the poor laws to defeat their own purpose—Palliative of the distresses of the poor proposed—The absolute impossibility from the fixed laws of our nature, that the pressure of want can ever be completely removed from the lower classes of society—All the checks to population may be resolved into misery or vice.

The positive check to population, by which I mean the check that represses an increase which is already begun, is confined chiefly, though not perhaps solely, to the lowest orders of society. This check is not so obvious to common view as the other I have mentioned, and to prove distinctly the force and extent of its operation would require, perhaps, more data than we are in possession of. But I believe it has been very generally remarked by those who have attended to bills of mortality that of the number of children who die annually, much too great a proportion belongs to those who may be supposed unable to give their offspring proper food and attention, exposed as they are occasionally to severe distress and confined, perhaps, to unwholesome habitations and hard labour. This mortality among the children of the poor has been constantly taken notice of in all towns. It certainly does not prevail in an equal degree in the country, but the subject has not hitherto received sufficient attention to enable anyone to say that there are not more deaths in proportion among the children of the poor, even in the country, than among those of the middling and higher classes. Indeed, it seems difficult to suppose that a labourer's wife who has six children, and who is sometimes in absolute want of bread, should be able always to give them the food and attention necessary to support life. The sons and daughters of peasants will not be found such rosy cherubs in real life as they are described to be in romances. It cannot fail to be remarked by those who live much in the country that the sons of labourers are very apt to be stunted in their growth, and are a long while arriving at maturity. Boys that you would guess to be fourteen or fifteen, are upon inquiry, frequently found to be eighteen or nineteen. And the lads who drive plough, which must certainly be a healthy exercise, are very rarely seen with any appearance of calves to their legs; a circumstance which can only be attributed to a want either of proper or of sufficient nourishment.

To remedy the frequent distresses of the common people, the poor laws of England have been instituted; but it is to be feared that though they may have alleviated a little the intensity of individual misfortune, they have spread the general evil over a much larger surface. It is a subject often started in conversation and mentioned always as a matter of great surprise that notwithstanding the immense sum that is annually collected for the poor in England, there is still so much distress among them. Some think that the money must be embezzled, others that the churchwardens and overseers consume the greater part of it in dinners. All agree that somehow or other it must be very ill-managed. In short the fact that nearly three millions are collected annually for the poor and yet that their distresses are not removed is the subject of continual astonishment. But a man who sees a little below the surface of things would be very much more astonished if the fact were otherwise than it is observed to be, or even if a collection universally of eighteen shillings in the pound instead of four, were materially to alter it. I will state a case which I hope will elucidate my meaning.

Suppose, that by a subscription of the rich, the eighteen pence a day which men earn now was made up five shillings, it might be imagined, perhaps, that they would then be able to live comfortably and have a piece of meat every day for their dinners. But this would be a very false conclusion. The transfer of three shillings and sixpence a day to every labourer would not increase the quantity of meat in the country. There is not at present enough for all to have a decent share. What would then be the consequence? The competition among the buyers in the market of meat would rapidly raise the price from six pence or seven pence, to two or three shillings in the pound, and the commodity would not be divided among many more than it is at present. When an article is scarce, and cannot be distributed to all, he that can shew the most valid patent, that is, he that offers most money becomes the possessor. If we can suppose the competition among the buyers of meat to continue long enough for a greater number of cattle to be reared annually, this could only be done at the expense of the corn, which would be a very disadvantageous exchange, for it is well known that the country could not then support the same population, and when subsistence is scarce in proportion to the number of people, it is of little consequence whether the lowest members of the society possess eighteen pence or five shillings. They must at all events be reduced to live upon the hardest fare and in the smallest quantity.

It will be said, perhaps, that the increased number of purchasers in every article would give a spur to productive industry and that the whole produce of the island would be increased. This might in some degree be the case. But the spur that these fancied riches would give to population would more than counterbalance it, and the increased produce would be to be divided among a more than proportionably increased number of people. All this time I am supposing that the same quantity of work would be done as before. But this would not really take place. The receipt of five shillings a day, instead of eighteen pence, would make every man fancy himself comparatively rich and able to indulge himself in many hours or days of leisure. This would give a strong and immediate check to productive industry, and in a short time, not only the nation would be poorer, but the lower classes themselves would be much more distressed than when they received only eighteen pence a day.

A collection from the rich of eighteen shillings in the pound, even if distributed in the most judicious manner, would have a little the same effect as that resulting from the supposition I have just made, and no possible contributions of sacrifices of the rich, particularly in money, could for any time prevent the recurrence of distress among the lower members of society whoever they were. Great changes might, indeed, be made. The rich might become poor, and some of the poor rich, but a part of the society must necessarily feel a difficulty of living, and this difficulty will naturally fall on the least fortunate members.

It may at first appear strange, but I believe it is true, that I cannot by means of money raise a poor man and enable him to live much better than he did before, without proportionably depressing others in the same class. If I retrench the quantity of food consumed in my house, and give him what I have cut off, I then benefit him, without depressing any but myself and family, who, perhaps, may be well able to bear it. If I turn up a piece of uncultivated land, and give him the produce, I then benefit both him and all the members of the society, because what he before consumed is thrown into the common stock, and probably some of the new produce with it. But if I only give him money, supposing the produce of the country to remain the same, I give him a title to a larger share of that produce than formerly, which share he cannot receive without diminishing the shares of others. It is evident that this effect, in individual instances, must be so small as to be totally imperceptible; but still it must exist, as many other effects do, which like some of the insects that people the air, elude our grosser perceptions.

Supposing the quantity of food in any country to remain the same for many years together, it is evident that this food must be divided according to the value of each man's patent, or the sum of money that he can afford to spend in this commodity so universally in request. It is a demonstrative truth, therefore, that the patents of one set of men could not be increased in value without diminishing the value of the patents of some other set of men. If the rich were to subscribe and give five shillings a day to five hundred thousand men without retrenching their own tables, no doubt can exist that as these men would naturally live more at their ease and consume a greater quantity of provisions, there would be less food remaining to divide among the rest, and consequently each man's patent would be diminished in value or the same number of pieces of silver would purchase a smaller quantity of subsistence.

An increase of population without a proportional increase of food will evidently have the same effect in lowering the value of each man's patent. The food must necessarily be distributed in smaller quantities, and consequently a day's labour will purchase a smaller quantity of provisions. An increase in the price of provisions would arise either from an increase of population faster than the means of subsistence, or from a different distribution of the money of the society. The food of a country that has been long occupied, if it be increasing, increases slowly and regularly and cannot be made to answer any sudden demands, but variations in the distribution of the money of a society are not unfrequently occurring, and are undoubtedly among the causes that occasion the continual variations which we observe in the price of provisions.

The poor-laws of England tend to depress the general condition of the poor in these two ways. Their first obvious tendency is to increase population without increasing the food for its support. A poor man may marry with little or no prospect of being able to support a family in independence. They may be said therefore in some measure to create the poor which they maintain, and as the provisions of the country must, in consequence of the increased population, be distributed to every man in smaller proportions, it is evident that the labour of those who are not supported by parish assistance will purchase a smaller quantity of provisions than before and consequently more of them must be driven to ask for support.

Secondly, the quantity of provisions consumed in workhouses upon a part of the society that cannot in general be considered as the most valuable part diminishes the shares that would otherwise belong to more industrious and more worthy members, and thus in the same manner forces more to become dependent. If the poor in the workhouses were to live better than they now do, this new distribution of the money of the society would tend more conspicuously to depress the condition of those out of the workhouses by occasioning a rise in the price of provisions.

Fortunately for England, a spirit of independence still remains among the peasantry. The poor-laws are strongly calculated to eradicate this spirit. They have succeeded in part, but had they succeeded as completely as might have been expected, their pernicious tendency would not have been so long concealed.

Hard as it may appear in individual instances, dependent poverty ought to be held disgraceful. Such a stimulus seems to be absolutely necessary to promote the happiness of the great mass of mankind, and every general attempt to weaken this stimulus, however benevolent its apparent intention, will always defeat its own purpose. If men are induced to marry from a prospect of parish provision, with little or no chance of maintaining their families in independence, they are not only unjustly tempted to bring unhappiness and dependence upon themselves and children, but they are tempted, without knowing it, to injure all in the same class with themselves. A labourer who marries without being able to support a family may in some respects be considered as an enemy to all his fellow-labourers.

I feel no doubt whatever that the parish laws of England have contributed to raise the price of provisions and to lower the real price of labour. They have therefore contributed to impoverish that class of people whose only possession is their labour. It is also difficult to suppose that they have not powerfully contributed to generate that carelessness and want of frugality observable among the poor, so contrary to the disposition frequently to be remarked among petty tradesmen and small farmers. The labouring poor, to use a vulgar expression, seem always to live from hand to mouth. Their present wants employ their whole attention, and they seldom think of the future. Even when they have an opportunity of saving they seldom exercise it, but all that is beyond their present necessities goes, generally speaking, to the ale-house. The poor-laws of England may therefore be said to diminish both the power and the will to save among the common people, and thus to weaken one of the strongest incentives to sobriety and industry, and consequently to happiness.

It is a general complaint among master manufacturers that high wages ruin all their workmen, but it is difficult to conceive that these men would not save a part of their high wages for the future support of their families, instead of spending it in drunkenness and dissipation, if they did not rely on parish assistance for support in case of accidents. And that the poor employed in manufactures consider this assistance as a reason why they may spend all the wages they earn and enjoy themselves while they can appears to be evident from the number of families that, upon the failure of any great manufactory, immediately fall upon the parish, when perhaps the wages earned in this manufactory while it flourished were sufficiently above the price of common country labour to have allowed them to save enough for their support till they could find some other channel for their industry.

A man who might not be deterred from going to the ale-house from the consideration that on his death, or sickness, he should leave his wife and family upon the parish might yet hesitate in thus dissipating his earnings if he were assured that, in either of these cases, his family must starve or be left to the support of casual bounty. In China, where the real as well as nominal price of labour is very low, sons are yet obliged by law to support their aged and helpless parents. Whether such a law would be advisable in this country I will not pretend to determine. But it seems at any rate highly improper, by positive institutions, which render dependent poverty so general, to weaken that disgrace, which for the best and most humane reasons ought to attach to it.

The mass of happiness among the common people cannot but be diminished, when one of the strongest checks to idleness and dissipation is thus removed, and when men are thus allured to marry with little or no prospect of being able to maintain a family in independence. Every obstacle in the way of marriage must undoubtedly be considered as a species of unhappiness. But as from the laws of our nature some check to population must exist, it is better that it should be checked from a foresight of the difficulties attending a family and the fear of dependent poverty than that it should be encouraged, only to be repressed afterwards by want and sickness.

It should be remembered always that there is an essential difference between food and those wrought commodities, the raw materials of which are in great plenty. A demand for these last will not fail to create them in as great a quantity as they are wanted. The demand for food has by no means the same creative power. In a country where all the fertile spots have been seized, high offers are necessary to encourage the farmer to lay his dressing on land from which he cannot expect a profitable return for some years. And before the prospect of advantage is sufficiently great to encourage this sort of agricultural enterprize, and while the new produce is rising, great distresses may be suffered from the want of it. The demand for an increased quantity of subsistence is, with few exceptions, constant every where, yet we see how slowly it is answered in all those countries that have been long occupied.

The poor-laws of England were undoubtedly instituted for the most benevolent purpose, but there is great reason to think that they have not succeeded in their intention. They certainly mitigate some cases of very severe distress which might otherwise occur, yet the state of the poor who are supported by parishes, considered in all its circumstances, is very far from being free from misery. But one of the principal objections to them is that for this assistance which some of the poor receive, in itself almost a doubtful blessing, the whole class of the common people of England is subjected to a set of grating, inconvenient, and tyrannical laws, totally inconsistent with the genuine spirit of the constitution. The whole business of settlements, even in its present amended state, is utterly contradictory to all ideas of freedom. The parish persecution of men whose families are likely to become chargeable, and of poor women who are near lying-in, is a most disgraceful and disgusting tyranny. And the obstructions continually occasioned in the market of labour by these laws, have a constant tendency to add to the difficulties of those who are struggling to support themselves without assistance.

These evils attendant on the poor laws are in some degree irremediable. If assistance be to be distributed to a certain class of people, a power must be given somewhere of discriminating the proper objects and of managing the concerns of the institutions that are necessary, but any great interference with the affairs of other people, is a species of tyranny, and in the common course of things the exercise of this power may be expected to become grating to those who are driven to ask for support. The tyranny of Justices, Churchwardens, and Overseers, is a common complaint among the poor, but the fault does not lie so much in these persons, who probably before they were in power were not worse than other people, but in the nature of all such institutions.

The evil is perhaps gone too far to be remedied, but I feel little doubt in my own mind that if the poor-laws had never existed, though there might have been a few more instances of very severe distress, yet that the aggregate mass of happiness among the common people would have been much greater than it is at present.

Mr. Pitt's Poor-bill has the appearance of being framed with benevolent intentions, and the clamour raised against it was in many respects ill directed and unreasonable. But it must be confessed that it possesses in a high degree the great and radical defect of all systems of the kind, that of tending to increase population without increasing the means for its support, and thus to depress the condition of those that are not supported by parishes, and, consequently, to create more poor.

To remove the wants of the lower classes of society is indeed an arduous task. The truth is that the pressure of distress on this part of a community is an evil so deeply seated that no human ingenuity can reach it. Were I to propose a palliative, and palliatives are all that the nature of the case will admit, it should be, in the first place, the total abolition of all the present parish-laws. This would at any rate give liberty and freedom of action to the peasantry of England, which they can hardly be said to possess at present. They would then be able to settle without interruption, wherever there was a prospect of a greater plenty of work and a higher price for labour. The market of labour would then be free, and those obstacles removed, which as things are now, often for a considerable time prevent the price from rising according to the demand.

Secondly, Premiums might be given for turning up fresh land, and all possible encouragements held out to agriculture above manufactures, and to tillage above grazing. Every endeavour should be used to weaken and destroy all those institutions relating to corporations, apprenticeships, &c., which cause the labours of agriculture to be worse paid than the labours of trade and manufactures. For a country can never produce its proper quantity of food while these distinctions remain in favour of artizans. Such encouragements to agriculture would tend to furnish the market with an increasing quantity of healthy work, and at the same time, by augmenting the produce of the country, would raise the comparative price of labour and ameliorate the condition of the labourer. Being now in better circumstances, and seeing no prospect of parish assistance, he would be more able, as well as more inclined, to enter into associations for providing against the sickness of himself or family.

Lastly, for cases of extreme distress, county workhouses might be established, supported by rates upon the whole kingdom, and free for persons of all counties, and indeed of all nations. The fare should be hard, and those that were able obliged to work. It would be desirable that they should not be considered as comfortable asylums in all difficulties, but merely as places where severe distress might find some alleviation. A part of these houses might be separated, or others built for a most beneficial purpose, which has not been unfrequently taken notice of, that of providing a place where any person, whether native or foreigner, might do a day's work at all times and receive the market price for it. Many cases would undoubtedly be left for the exertion of individual benevolence.

A plan of this kind, the preliminary of which should be an abolition of all the present parish laws, seems to be the best calculated to increase the mass of happiness among the common people of England. To prevent the recurrence of misery, is, alas! beyond the power of man. In the vain endeavour to attain what in the nature of things is impossible, we now sacrifice not only possible but certain benefits. We tell the common people that if they will submit to a code of tyrannical regulations, they shall never be in want. They do submit to these regulations. They perform their part of the contract, but we do not, nay cannot, perform ours, and thus the poor sacrifice the valuable blessing of liberty and receive nothing that can be called an equivalent in return.

Notwithstanding then, the institution of the poor-laws in England, I think it will be allowed that considering the state of the lower classes altogether, both in the towns and in the country, the distresses which they suffer from the want of proper and sufficient food, from hard labour and unwholesome habitations, must operate as a constant check to incipient population.

To these two great checks to population, in all long occupied countries, which I have called the preventive and the positive checks, may be added vicious customs with respect to women, great cities, unwholesome manufactures, luxury, pestilence, and war.

All these checks may be fairly resolved into misery and vice. And that these are the true causes of the slow increase of population in all the states of modern Europe, will appear sufficiently evident from the comparatively rapid increase that has invariably taken place whenever these causes have been in any considerable degree removed.

Bounties on Exportation, and Prohibitions of Importation

David Ricardo (1772–1823) was born in London into a large and prosperous family. He worked as a stockbroker from the age of 14, amassing a fortune over his lifetime. Ricardo's education was limited to a two-year period of instruction at a Portuguese synagogue in Amsterdam, the Netherlands. Upon retirement from the stock exchange in 1819, he entered Parliament as a representative from the borough of Portarlington.

Ricardo's interest in political economy came as a result of reading Adam Smith's *The Wealth of Nations* (1776). His first publication was in the form of three letters to the local newspaper on the price of gold in 1809. During the next two years Ricardo wrote two pamphlets supporting the bullionist position in the debate on currency depreciation. Another pamphlet, published in 1816, advocated a return to the gold standard. In 1817 he published *The Principles of Political Economy and Taxation,* from which the following selection has been excerpted. In it he advocates for free trade based on the principle of comparative advantage. This selection underscores Ricardo's commitment to free trade in corn with its prediction of the dire consequences of tariffs and export subsidies. This position is more fully developed in his *Essay on the Influence of a Low Price of Corn on the Profits of Stock* (John Murray, 1815) and his contribution to the parliamentary debate on the future of the Corn Laws.

Key Concept: bounties of exportation and prohibitions of importation

A bounty on the exportation of corn tends to lower its price to the foreign consumer, but it has no permanent effect on its price in the home market.

Suppose that to afford the usual and general profits of stock, the price of corn should in England be £4 per quarter; it could not then be exported to foreign countries where it sold for £3 15*s*. per quarter. But if a bounty of 10*s*. per quarter were given on exportation, it could be sold in the foreign market at

£3 10*s.*, and consequently the same profit would be afforded to the corn grower whether he sold it at £3 10*s.* in the foreign or at £4 in the home market.

A bounty then, which should lower the price of British corn in the foreign country, below the cost of producing corn in that country, would naturally extend the demand for British and diminish the demand for their own corn. This extension of demand for British corn could not fail to raise its price for a time in the home market, and during that time to prevent also its falling so low in the foreign market as the bounty has a tendency to effect. But the causes which would thus operate on the market price of corn in England would produce no effect whatever on its natural price, or its real cost of production. To grow corn would neither require more labour nor more capital, and, consequently, if the profits of the farmer's stock were before only equal to the profits of the stock of other traders, they will, after the rise of price, be considerably above them. By raising the profits of the farmer's stock, the bounty will operate as an encouragement to agriculture, and capital will be withdrawn from manufactures to be employed on the land, till the enlarged demand for the foreign market has been supplied, when the price of corn will again fall in the home market to its natural and necessary price, and profits will be again at their ordinary and accustomed level. The increased supply of grain operating on the foreign market, will also lower its price in the country to which it is exported, and will thereby restrict the profits of the exporter to the lowest rate at which he can afford to trade.

The ultimate effect then of a bounty on the exportation of corn is not to raise or to lower the price in the home market, but to lower the price of corn to the foreign consumer—to the whole extent of the bounty, if the price of corn had not before been lower in the foreign than in the home market—and in a less degree if the price in the home had been above the price in the foreign market.

A writer in the fifth volume of the *Edinburgh Review,* on the subject of a bounty on the exportation of corn, has very clearly pointed out its effects on the foreign and home demand. He has also justly remarked that it would not fail to give encouragement to agriculture in the exporting country; but he appears to have imbibed the common error which has misled Dr. [Adam] Smith, and, I believe, most other writers on this subject. He supposes, because the price of corn ultimately regulates wages, that therefore it will regulate the price of all other commodities. He says that the bounty, "by raising the profits of farming, will operate as an encouragement to husbandry; by raising the price of corn to the consumers at home, it will diminish for the time their power of purchasing this necessary of life, and thus abridge their real wealth. It is evident, however, that this last effect must be temporary: the wages of the labouring consumers had been adjusted before by competition, and the same principle will adjust them again to the same rate, by raising the money price of labour, *and, through that, of other commodities, to the money price of corn.* The bounty upon exportation, therefore, will ultimately raise the money price of corn in the home market; not directly, however, but through the medium of an extended demand in the foreign market, and a consequent enhancement of the real price at home: *and this rise of the money price, when it has once been communicated to other commodities, will of course become fixed.*"

If, however, I have succeeded in showing that it is not the rise in the money wages of labour which raises the price of commodities, but that such rise always affects profits, it will follow that the prices of commodities would not rise in consequence of a bounty.

But a temporary rise in the price of corn, produced by an increased demand from abroad, would have no effect on the money price of labour. The rise of corn is occasioned by a competition for that supply which was before exclusively appropriated to the home market. By raising profits, additional capital is employed in agriculture, and the increased supply is obtained; but till it be obtained, the high price is absolutely necessary to proportion the consumption to the supply, which would be counteracted by a rise of wages. The rise of corn is the consequence of its scarcity, and is the means by which the demand of the home purchasers is diminished. If wages were increased, the competition would increase, and a further rise of the price of corn would become necessary. In this account of the effects of a bounty nothing has been supposed to occur to raise the natural price of corn, by which its market price is ultimately governed; for it has not been supposed that any additional labour would be required on the land to insure a given production, and this alone can raise its natural price. If the natural price of cloth were 20*s.* per yard, a great increase in the foreign demand might raise the price to 25*s.*, or more, but the profits which would then be made by the clothier would not fail to attract capital in that direction, and although the demand should be doubled, trebled, or quadrupled, the supply would ultimately be obtained, and cloth would fall to its natural price of 20*s.* So, in the supply of corn, although we should export 200,000, 300,000, or 800,000 quarters annually, it would ultimately be produced at its natural price, which never varies, unless a different quantity of labour becomes necessary to production.

Perhaps in no part of Adam Smith's justly celebrated work are his conclusions more liable to objection than in the chapter on bounties. In the first place, he speaks of corn as of a commodity of which the production cannot be increased in consequence of a bounty on exportation; he supposes invariably that it acts only on the quantity actually produced, and is no stimulus to farther production. "In years of plenty," he says, "by occasioning an extraordinary exportation, it necessarily keeps up the price of corn in the home market above what it would naturally fall to. In years of scarcity, though the bounty is frequently suspended, yet the great exportation which it occasions in years of plenty must frequently hinder, more or less, the plenty of one year from relieving the scarcity of another. Both in the years of plenty and in years of scarcity, therefore, the bounty necessarily tends to raise the money price of corn somewhat higher than it otherwise would be in the home market."

Adam Smith appears to have been fully aware that the correctness of his argument entirely depended on the fact whether the increase "of the money price of corn, by rendering that commodity more profitable to the farmer, would not necessarily encourage its production."

"I answer," he says, "that this might be the case if the effect of the bounty was to raise the real price of corn, or to enable the farmer, with an equal quantity of it, to maintain a greater number of labourers in the same manner, whether liberal, moderate, or scanty, as other labourers are commonly maintained in his neighbourhood."

If nothing were consumed by the labourer but corn, and if the portion which he received was the very lowest which his sustenance required, there might be some ground for supposing, that the quantity paid to the labourer could, under no circumstances, be reduced—but the money wages of labour sometimes do not rise at all, and never rise in proportion to the rise in the money price of corn, because corn, though an important part, is only a part of the consumption of the labourer. If half his wages were expended on corn, and the other half on soap, candles, fuel, tea, sugar, clothing, etc., commodities on which no rise is supposed to take place, it is evident that he would be quite as well paid with a bushel and a half of wheat when it was 16*s.* a bushel, as he was with two bushels when the price was 8*s.* per bushel; or with 24*s.* in money as he was before with 16*s.* His wages would rise only 50 per cent. though corn rose 100 per cent. and, consequently, there would be sufficient motive to divert more capital to the land if profits on other trades continued the same as before. But such a rise of wages would also induce manufacturers to withdraw their capitals from manufactures, to employ them on the land; for, whilst the farmer increased the price of his commodity 100 per cent. and his wages only 50 per cent., the manufacturer would be obliged also to raise wages 50 per cent., whilst he had no compensation whatever in the rise of his manufactured commodity for this increased charge of production; capital would consequently flow from manufactures to agriculture, till the supply would again lower the price of corn to 8*s.* per bushel and wages to 16*s.* per week; when the manufacturer would obtain the same profits as the farmer, and the tide of capital would cease to set in either direction. This is, in fact, the mode in which the cultivation of corn is always extended, and the increased wants of the market supplied. The funds for the maintenance of labour increase, and wages are raised. The comfortable situation of the labourer induces him to marry—population increases, and the demand for corn raises its price relatively to other things—more capital is profitably employed on agriculture, and continues to flow towards it, till the supply is equal to the demand, when the price again falls, and agricultural and manufacturing profits are again brought to a level.

But whether wages were stationary after the rise in the price of corn, or advanced moderately or enormously, is of no importance to this question, for wages are paid by the manufacturer as well as by the farmer, and, therefore, in this respect they must be equally affected by a rise in the price of corn. But they are unequally affected in their profits, inasmuch as the farmer sells his commodity at an advanced price, while the manufacturer sells his for the same price as before. It is, however, the inequality of profit, which is always the inducement to remove capital from one employment to another; and, therefore, more corn would be produced, and fewer commodities manufactured. Manufactures would not rise, because fewer would be manufactured, for a supply of them would be obtained in exchange for the exported corn.

A bounty, if it raises the price of corn, either raises it in comparison with the price of other commodities or it does not. If the affirmative be true, it is impossible to deny the greater profits of the farmer, and the temptation to the removal of capital till its price is again lowered by an abundant supply. If it does not raise it in comparison with other commodities, where is the injury to the home consumer, beyond the inconvenience of paying the tax? If the manufacturer pays a greater price for his corn, he is compensated by the greater price at which he sells his commodity, with which his corn is ultimately purchased.

The error of Adam Smith proceeds precisely from the same source as that of the writer in the *Edinburgh Review;* for they both think "that the money price of corn regulates that of all other home-made commodities." "It regulates," says Adam Smith, "the money price of labour, which must always be such as to enable the labourer to purchase a quantity of corn sufficient to maintain him and his family, either in the liberal, moderate, or scanty manner, in which the advancing, stationary, or declining circumstances of the society oblige his employers to maintain him. By regulating the money price of all the other parts of the rude produce of land, it regulates that of the materials of almost all manufactures. By regulating the money price of labour, it regulates that of manufacturing art and industry; and by regulating both, it regulates that of the complete manufacture. *The money price of labour, and of every thing that is the produce either of land and labour, must necessarily rise or fall in proportion to the money price of corn.*"

This opinion of Adam Smith I have before attempted to refute. In considering a rise in the price of commodities as a necessary consequence of a rise in the price of corn, he reasons as though there were no other fund from which the increased charge could be paid. He has wholly neglected the consideration of profits, the diminution of which forms that fund, without raising the price of commodities. If this opinion of Dr. Smith were well founded, profits could never really fall, whatever accumulation of capital there might be. If, when wages rose, the farmer could raise the price of his corn, and the clothier, the hatter, the shoemaker, and every other manufacturer could also raise the price of their goods in proportion to the advance, although estimated in money they might be all raised, they would continue to bear the same value relatively to each other. Each of these trades could command the same quantity as before of the goods of the others, which, since it is goods, and not money, which constitute wealth, is the only circumstance that could be of importance to them; and the whole rise in the price of raw produce and of goods would be injurious to no other persons but to those whose property consisted of gold and silver, or whose annual income was paid in a contributed quantity of those metals, whether in the form of bullion or of money. Suppose the use of money to be wholly laid aside, and all trade to be carried on by barter. Under such circumstances, could corn rise in exchangeable value with other things? If it could, then it is not true that the value of corn regulates the value of all other commodities; for to do that, it should not vary in relative value to them. If it could not, then it must be maintained that whether corn be obtained on rich or on poor land, with much labour or with little, with the aid of machinery or without, it would always exchange for an equal quantity of all other commodities.

I cannot, however, but remark that though Adam Smith's general doctrines correspond with this which I have just quoted, yet in one part of his work he appears to have given a correct account of the nature of value. "The proportion between the value of gold and silver, and that of goods of any other kind, DEPENDS IN ALL CASES," he says, "*upon the proportion between the quantity of labour which is necessary in order to bring a certain quantity of gold and silver to market, and that which is necessary to bring thither a certain quantity of any other sort of goods.*" Does he not here fully acknowledge, that if any increase takes place in the quantity of labour required to bring one sort of goods to market, whilst no such increase takes place in bringing another sort thither, the first sort will rise in relative value? If no more labour than before be required to bring either cloth or gold to market, they will not vary in relative value, but if more labour be required to bring corn and shoes to market, will not corn and shoes rise in value relatively to cloth and money made of gold?

Adam Smith again considers that the effect of the bounty is to cause a partial degradation in the value of money. "That degradation," says he, "in the value of silver which is the effect of the fertility of the mines, and which operates equally, or very nearly equally, through the greater part of the commercial world, is a matter of very little consequence to any particular country. The consequent rise of all money prices, though it does not make those who receive them really richer, does not make them really poorer. A service of plate becomes really cheaper, and everything else remains precisely of the same real value as before." This observation is most correct.

"But that degradation in the value of silver, which, being the effect either of the peculiar situation or of the political institutions of a particular country, takes place only in that country, is a matter of very great consequence, which, far from tending to make anybody really richer, tends to make everybody really poorer. The rise in the money price of all commodities, which is in this case peculiar to that country, tends to discourage more or less every sort of industry which is carried on within it, and to enable foreign nations, by furnishing almost all sorts of goods for a smaller quantity of silver than its own workmen can afford to do, to undersell them, not only in the foreign, but even in the home market."

I have elsewhere attempted to show that a partial degradation in the value of money, which shall affect both agricultural produce and manufactured commodities, cannot possibly be permanent. To say that money is partially degraded, in this sense, is to say that all commodities are at a high price; but while gold and silver are at liberty to make purchases in the cheapest market, they will be exported for the cheaper goods of other countries, and the reduction of their quantity will increase their value at home; commodities will regain their usual level, and those fitted for foreign markets will be exported, as before.

A bounty, therefore, cannot, I think, be objected to on this ground.

If, then, a bounty raises the price of corn in comparison with all other things, the farmer will be benefited, and more land will be cultivated; but if the bounty do not raise the value of corn relatively to other things then no other inconvenience will attend it than that of paying the bounty; one which I neither wish to conceal nor underrate.

Dr. Smith states that "by establishing high duties on the importation, and bounties on the exportation of corn, the country gentlemen seemed to have imitated the conduct of the manufacturers." By the same means, both had endeavoured to raise the value of their commodities. "They did not, perhaps, attend to the great and essential difference which nature has established between corn and almost every other sort of goods. When by either of the above means you enable our manufacturers to sell their goods for somewhat a better price than they otherwise could get for them, you raise not only the nominal, but the real price of those goods. You increase not only the nominal, but the real profit, the real wealth and revenue of those manufacturers—you really encourage those manufactures. But when, by the like institutions, you raise the nominal or money price of corn, you do not raise its real value, you do not increase the real wealth of our farmers or country gentlemen, you do not encourage the growth of corn. The nature of things has stamped upon corn a real value which cannot be altered by merely altering its money price. Through the world in general that value is equal to the quantity of labour which it can maintain."

I have already attempted to show that the market price of corn would, under an increased demand from the effects of a bounty, exceed its natural price, till the requisite additional supply was obtained, and that then it would again fall to its natural price. But the natural price of corn is not so fixed as the natural price of commodities; because, with any great additional demand for corn, land of a worse quality must be taken into cultivation, on which more labour will be required to produce a given quantity, and the natural price of corn will be raised. By a continued bounty, therefore, on the exportation of corn, there would be created a tendency to a permanent rise in the price of corn, and this... never fails to raise rent. Country gentlemen, then, have not only a temporary but a permanent interest in prohibitions of the importation of corn, and in bounties on its exportation; but manufacturers have no permanent interest in establishing high duties on the importation, and bounties on the exportation of commodities; their interest is wholly temporary.

A bounty on the exportation of manufactures will, undoubtedly, as Dr. Smith contends, raise for a time the market price of manufactures, but it will not raise their natural price. The labour of 200 men will produce double the quantity of these goods that 100 could produce before; and, consequently, when the requisite quantity of capital was employed in supplying the requisite quantity of manufactures, they would again fall to their natural price, and all advantage from a high market price would cease. It is, then, only during the interval after the rise in the market price of commodities, and till the additional supply is obtained, that the manufacturers will enjoy high profits; for as soon as prices had subsided, their profits would sink to the general level.

Instead of agreeing, therefore, with Adam Smith, that the country gentlemen had not so great an interest in prohibiting the importation of corn, as the manufacturer had in prohibiting the importation of manufactured goods, I contend, that they have a much superior interest; for their advantage is permanent, while that of the manufacturer is only temporary. Dr. Smith observes that nature has established a great and essential difference between corn and other goods, but the proper inference from that circumstance is directly the reverse of that which he draws from it; for it is on account of this difference that rent is created, and that country gentlemen have an interest in the rise of the natural price of corn. Instead of comparing the interest of the manufacturer with the interest of the country gentleman, Dr. Smith should have compared it with the interest of the farmer, which is very distinct from that of his landlord. Manufacturers have no interest in the rise of the natural price of their commodities, nor have farmers any interest in the rise of the natural price of corn, or other raw produce, though both these classes are benefited while the market price of their productions exceeds their natural price. On the contrary, landlords have a most decided interest in the rise of the natural price of corn; for the rise of rent is the inevitable consequence of the difficulty of producing raw produce, without which its natural price could not rise. Now, as bounties on exportation and prohibitions of the importation of corn increase the demand, and drive us to the cultivation of poorer lands, they necessarily occasion an increased difficulty of production.

The sole effect of high duties on the importation, either of manufactures or of corn, or of a bounty on their exportation, is to divert a portion of capital to an employment which it would not naturally seek. It causes a pernicious distribution of the general funds of the society—it bribes a manufacturer to commence or continue in a comparatively less profitable employment. It is the worst species of taxation, for it does not give to the foreign country all that it takes away from the home country, the balance of loss being made up by the less advantageous distribution of the general capital. Thus, if the price of corn is in England £4, and in France £3 15*s*., a bounty of 10*s*. will ultimately reduce it to £3 10*s*. in France, and maintain it at the same price of £4 in England. For every quarter exported, England pays a tax of 10*s*. For every quarter imported into France, France gains only 5*s*., so that the value of 5*s*. per quarter is absolutely lost to the world by such a distribution of its funds, as to cause diminished production, probably not of corn, but of some other object of necessity or enjoyment.

Mr. [James] Buchanan appears to have seen the fallacy of Dr. Smith's arguments respecting bounties, and on the last passage which I have quoted very judiciously remarks: "In asserting that nature has stamped a real value on corn, which cannot be altered by merely altering its money price, Dr. Smith confounds its value in use with its value in exchange. A bushel of wheat will not feed more people during scarcity than during plenty; but a bushel of wheat will exchange for a greater quantity of luxuries and conveniences when it is scarce than when it is abundant; and the landed proprietors, who have a surplus of food to dispose of, will therefore, in times of scarcity, be richer men; they will exchange their surplus for a greater value of other enjoyments than when corn is in greater plenty. It is vain to argue, therefore, that if the bounty occasions a forced exportation of corn, it will not also occasion a real rise of price." The whole of Mr. Buchanan's arguments on this part of the subject of bounties appear to me to be perfectly clear and satisfactory.

Mr. Buchanan, however, has not, I think, any more than Dr. Smith or the writer in the *Edinburgh Review*, correct opinions as to the influence of a rise in the price of labour on manufactured commodities. From his peculiar views, which I have elsewhere noticed, he thinks that the price of labour has no connection with the price of corn, and, therefore, that the real value of corn might and would rise without affecting the price of labour; but if labour were affected, he would maintain with Adam Smith and the writer in the *Edinburgh Review* that the price of manufactured commodities would also rise; and then I do not see how he would distinguish such a rise of corn from a fall in the value of money, or how he could come to any other conclusion than that of Dr. Smith. In a note to page 276, vol. i. of the *Wealth of Nations*, Mr. Buchanan observes, "but the price of corn does not regulate the money price of all the other parts of the rude produce of land. It regulates the price of neither metals, nor of various other useful substances, such as coals, wood, stones, etc.; *and as it does not regulate the price of labour, it does not regulate the price of manufactures;* so that the bounty, in so far as it raises the price of corn, is undoubtedly a real benefit to the farmer. It is not on this ground, therefore, that its policy must be argued. Its encouragement to agriculture, by raising the price of corn, must be admitted; and the question then comes to be, whether agriculture ought to be thus encouraged?" —It is then, according to Mr. Buchanan, a real benefit to the farmer, because it does not raise the price of labour; but if it did, it would raise the price of all things in proportion, and then it would afford no particular encouragement to agriculture.

It must, however, be conceded that the tendency of a bounty on the exportation of any commodity is to lower in a small degree of the value of money. Whatever facilitates exportation tends to accumulate money in a country; and, on the contrary, whatever impedes exportation tends to diminish it. The general effect of taxation, by raising the prices of the commodities taxed, tends to diminish exportation, and therefore, to check the influx of money; and, on the same principle, a bounty encourages the influx of money....

The injurious effects of the mercantile system have been fully exposed by Dr. Smith; the whole aim of that system was to raise the price of commodities in the home market by prohibiting foreign competition; but this system was no more injurious to the agricultural classes than to any other part of the community. By forcing capital into channels where it would not otherwise flow, it diminished the whole amount of commodities produced. The price, though permanently higher, was not sustained by scarcity, but by difficulty of production; and, therefore, through the sellers of such commodities sold them for a higher price, they did not sell them, after the requisite quantity of capital was employed in producing them, at higher profits.

The manufacturers themselves, as consumers, had to pay an additional price for such commodities, and therefore, it cannot be correctly said, that "the enhancement of price occasioned by both (corporation laws and high duties on the importations of foreign commodities) is everywhere fully paid by the landlords, farmers, and labourers of the country."

It is the more necessary to make this remark as in the present day the authority of Adam Smith is quoted by country gentlemen for imposing similar high duties on the importation of foreign corn. Because the cost of production, and, therefore, the prices of various manufactured commodities, are raised to the consumer by one error in legislation, the country has been called upon, on the plea of justice, quietly to submit to fresh exactions. Because we all pay an additional price for our linen, muslin, and cottons, it is thought just that we should pay also an additional price for our corn. Because, in the general distribution of the labour of the world, we have prevented the greatest amount of productions from being obtained by our portion of that labour in manufactured commodities, we should further punish ourselves by diminishing the productive powers of the general labour in the supply of raw produce. It would be much wiser to acknowledge the errors which a mistaken policy has induced us to adopt, and immediately to commence a gradual recurrence to the sound principles of a universally free trade.

"I have already had occasion to remark," observes M. [Jean-Baptiste] Say, "in speaking of what is improperly called the balance of trade, that if it suits a merchant better to export the precious metals to a foreign country than any other goods, it is also the interest of the state that he should export them, because the state only gains or loses through the channel of its citizens; and in what concerns foreign trade, that which best suits the individual best suits also the state; therefore, by opposing obstacles to the exportation which individuals would be inclined to make of the precious metals, nothing more is done than to force them to substitute some other commodity less profitable to themselves and to the state. It must, however, be remarked that I say only *in what concerns foreign trade;* because the profits which merchants make by their dealings with their countrymen, as well as those which merchants make by their dealings with their countrymen, as well as those which are made in the exclusive commerce with colonies, are not entirely gains for the state. In the trade between individuals of the same country there is no other gain but the value of a utility produced; *que la valeur d'une utilité produite,*" vol. i. p. 401. I cannot see the distinction here made between the profits of the home and foreign trade. The object of all trade is to increase productions. If, for the purchase of a pipe of wine, I had it in my power to export bullion which was bought with the value of the produce of 100 days' labour, but government, by prohibiting the exportation of bullion, should oblige me to purchase my wine with a commodity bought with the value of the produce of 105 days' labour, the produce of five days' labour is lost to me, and, through me, to the state. But if these transactions took place between individuals in different provinces of the same country, the same advantage would accrue both to the individual, and through him, to the country, if he were unfettered in his choice of the commodities with which he made his purchases, and the same disadvantage if he were obliged by government to purchase with the least beneficial commodity. If a manufacturer could work up with the same capital more iron where coals are plentiful than he could where coals are scarce, the country would be benefited by the difference. But if coals were nowhere plentiful, and he imported iron, and could get this additional quantity by the manufacture of a commodity with the same capital and labour, he would, in like manner, benefit his country by the additional quantity of iron. . . . I have [elsewhere] endeavoured to show that all trade, whether foreign or domestic, is beneficial, by increasing the quantity and not by increasing the value of productions. We shall have no greater value whether we carry on the most beneficial home and foreign trade, or, in consequence of being fettered by prohibitory laws, we are obliged to content ourselves with the least advantageous. The rate of profits and the value produced will be the same. The advantage always resolves itself into that which M. Say appears to confine to the home trade; in both cases there is no other gain but that of the value of a *utilité produite.*

On Production

Jean-Baptiste Say (1767–1832) attracted the greatest attention and received more distinguished marks of approbation than any other economist since the publication of Adam Smith's *The Wealth of Nations* (1776). Say's works have been translated into several languages and adopted as textbooks at many universities. He lived in Saint-Clair Quay, a gathering place for merchants and traders, and ran his own business as a factory owner. Later Say became the first professor of political science in France.

Say's *A Treatise on Political Economy, or the Production, Distribution, and Consumption of Wealth* (A. M. Kelly, 1971), from which the following selection has been taken, was first published in 1803. In this selection, he rejects the notion that a glut of goods in the economy results from deficiencies in demand. Say asserts that industries with temporary overproduction experience a fall in prices, which causes them to shift production to other industries that are experiencing shortages. In other words, production is equal to demand, and the interest rate is the means by which full employment is attained. In the wake of a decline in demand due to an increase in the propensity to save, the rate of interest would fall sufficiently to stimulate investment demand to the extent that the additional investment demand would compensate for the reduction in consumer demand.

Key Concept: demand or market for products

OF THE DEMAND OR MARKET FOR PRODUCTS

It is common to hear adventurers in the different channels of industry assert, that their difficulty lies not in the production, but in the disposal of commodities; that products would always be abundant, if there were but a ready demand, or market for them. When the demand for their commodities is slow, difficult, and productive of little advantage, they pronounce money to be scarce; the grand object of their desire is, a consumption brisk enough to quicken sales and keep up prices. But ask them what peculiar causes and circumstances facilitate the demand for their products, and you will soon perceive that most of them have extremely vague notions of these matters; that their observation of facts is imperfect, and their explanation still more so; that they treat doubtful points as matter of certainty, often pray for what is directly opposite to their interests, and importunately solicit from authority a protection of the most mischievous tendency.

To enable us to form clear and correct practical notions in regard to markets for the products of industry, we must carefully analyse the best established and most certain facts, and apply to them the inferences we have already deduced from a similar way of proceeding; and thus perhaps we may arrive at new and important truths, that may serve to enlighten the views of the agents of industry, and to give confidence to the measures of governments anxious to afford them encouragement.

A man who applies his labour to the investing of objects with value by the creation of utility of some sort, can not expect such a value to be appreciated and paid for, unless where other men have the means of purchasing it. Now, of what do these means consist? Of other values of other products, likewise the fruits of industry, capital, and land. Which leads us to a conclusion that may at first sight appear paradoxical, namely, that it is production which opens a demand for products.

Should a tradesman say, "I do not want other products for my woollens, I want money," there could be little difficulty in convincing him that his customers could not pay him in money, without having first procured it by the sale of some other commodities of their own. "Yonder farmer," he may be told, "will buy your woollens, if his crops be good, and will buy more or less according to their abundance or scantiness; he can buy none at all, if his crops fail altogether. Neither can you buy his wool nor his corn yourself, unless you contrive to get woollens or some other article to buy withal. You say, you only want money; I say, you want other commodities, and not money. For what, in point of fact, do you want the money? Is it not for the purchase of raw materials or stock for your trade, or victuals for your support? Wherefore, it is products that you want, and not money. The silver coin you will have received on the sale of your own products, and given in the purchase of those of other people, will the next moment execute the same office between other contracting parties, and so from one to another to infinity; just as a public vehicle successively transports objects one after another. If you can not find a ready sale for your commodity, will you say, it is merely for want of a vehicle to transport it? For, after all, money is but the agent of the transfer of values. Its whole utility has consisted in conveying to your hands the value of the commodities, which your customer has sold, for the purpose of buying again from you; and the very next purchase you make, it will again convey to a third person the value of the products you may have sold to others. So that you will have bought, and every body must buy, the objects of want or desire, each with the value of his respective products transformed into money for the moment only. Otherwise, how could it be possible that there should now be bought and sold in France five or six times as many commodities, as in the miserable reign of Charles VI? Is it not obvious, that five or six times as many commodities must have been produced, and that they must have served to purchase one or the other?"

Thus, to say that sales are dull, owing to the scarcity of money, is to mistake the means for the cause; an error that proceeds from the circumstance, that almost all produce is in the first instance exchanged for money, before it is ultimately converted into other produce: and the commodity, which recurs so repeatedly in use, appears to vulgar apprehensions the most important of commodities, and the end and object of all transactions, whereas it is only the medium. Sales cannot be said to be dull because money is scarce, but because other products are so. There is always money enough to conduct the circulation and mutual interchange of other values, when those values really exist. Should the increase of traffic require more money to facilitate it, the want is easily supplied, and is a strong indication of prosperity—a proof that a great abundance of values has been created, which it is wished to exchange for other values. In such cases, merchants know well enough how to find substitutes for the product serving as the medium of exchange or money: and money itself soon pours in, for this reason, that all produce naturally gravitates to that place where it is most in demand. It is a good sign when the business is too great for the money; just in the same way as it is a good sign when the goods are too plentiful for the warehouses.

When a superabundant article can find no vent, the scarcity of money has so little to do with the obstruction of its sale, that the sellers would gladly receive its value in goods for their own consumption at the current price of the day: they would not ask for money, or have any occasion for that product, since the only use they could make of it would be to convert it forthwith into articles of their own consumption.

This observation is applicable to all cases, where there is a supply of commodities or of services in the market. They will universally find the most extensive demand in those places, where the most of values are produced; because in no other places are the sole means of purchase created, that is, values. Money performs but a momentary function in this double exchange; and when the transaction is finally closed, it will always be found, that one kind of commodity has been exchanged for another.

It is worth while to remark, that a product is no sooner created, than it, from that instant, affords a market for other products to the full extent of its own value. When the producer has put the finishing hand to his product, he is most anxious to sell it immediately, lest its value should diminish in his hands. Nor is he less anxious to dispose of the money he may get for it; for the value of money is also perishable. But the only way of getting rid of money is in the purchase of some product or other. Thus, the mere circumstance of the creation of one product immediately opens a vent for other products.

For this reason, a good harvest is favourable, not only to the agriculturist, but likewise to the dealers in all commodities generally. The greater the crop, the larger are the purchases of the growers. A bad harvest, on the contrary, hurts the sale of commodities at large. And so it is also with the products of manufacture and commerce. The success of one branch of commerce supplies more ample means of purchase, and consequently opens a market for the products of all the other branches; on the other hand, the stagnation of one channel of manufacture, or of commerce, is felt in all the rest.

But it may be asked, if this be so, how does it happen, that there is at times so great a glut of commodities in the market, and so much difficulty in finding a vent for them? Why cannot one of these superabundant commodities be exchanged for another? I answer that the glut of a particular commodity arises from its having outrun the total demand for it in one or two ways; either because it has been produced in excessive abundance, or because the production of other commodities has fallen short.

It is because the production of some commodities has declined, that other commodities are superabundant. To use a more hackneyed phrase, people have bought less, because they have made less profit: and they have made less profit for one or two causes; either they have found difficulties in the employment of their productive means, or these means have themselves been deficient.

It is observable, moreover, that precisely at the same time that one commodity makes a loss, another commodity is making excessive profit. And, since such profits must operate as a powerful stimulus to the cultivation of that particular kind of products, there must needs be some violent means, or some extraordinary cause, a political or natural convulsion, or the avarice or ignorance of authority, to perpetuate this scarcity on the one hand, and consequent glut on the other. No sooner is the cause of this political disease removed, than the means of production feel a natural impulse towards the vacant channels, the replenishment of which restores activity to all the others. One kind of production would seldom outstrip every other, and its products be disproportionately cheapened, were production left entirely free.

Should a producer imagine, that many other classes, yielding no material products, are his customers and consumers equally with the classes that raise themselves a product of their own; as, for example, public functionaries, physicians, lawyers, churchmen, &c., and thence infer, that there is a class of demand other than that of the actual producers, he would but expose the shallowness and superficiality of his ideas. A priest goes to a shop to buy a gown or a surplice; he takes the value, that is to make the purchase, in the form of money. Whence had he that money? From some tax-gatherer who has taken it from a tax-payer. But whence did this latter derive it? From the value he has himself produced. This value, first produced by the tax-payer, and afterwards turned into money, and given to the priest for his salary, has enabled him to make the purchase. The priest stands in the place of the producer, who might himself have laid the value of his product on his own account, in the purchase, perhaps, not of a gown or surplice, but of some other more serviceable product. The consumption of the particular product, the gown or surplice, has but supplanted that of some other product. It is quite impossible that the purchase of one product can be affected, otherwise than by the value of another.

From this important truth may be deduced the following important conclusions:—

1. That, in every community the more numerous are the producers, and the more various their productions, the more prompt, numerous, and extensive are the markets for those productions; and, by a natural consequence, the more profitable are they to the producers; for price rises with the demand. But this advantage is to be derived from real production alone, and not from a forced circulation of products; for a value once created is not augmented in its passage from one hand to another, nor by being seized and expended by the government, instead of by an individual. The man, that lives upon the productions of other people, originates no demand for those productions; he merely puts him-

self in the place of the producer, to the great injury of production, as we shall presently see.

2. That each individual is interested in the general prosperity of all, and that the success of one branch of industry promotes that of all the others. In fact, whatever profession or line of business a man may devote himself to, he is the better paid and the more readily finds employment, in proportion as he sees others thriving equally around him. A man of talent, that scarcely vegetates in a retrograde state of society, would find a thousand ways of turning his faculties to account in a thriving community that could afford to employ and reward his ability. A merchant established in a rich and populous town, sells to a much larger amount than one who sets up in a poor district, with a population sunk in indolence and apathy. What could an active manufacturer, or an intelligent merchant, do in a small deserted and semi-barbarous town in a remote corner of Poland or Westphalia? Though in no fear of a competitor, he could sell but little, because little was produced; whilst at Paris, Amsterdam, or London, in spite of the competition of a hundred dealers in his own line, he might do business on the largest scale. The reason is obvious: he is surrounded with people who produce largely in an infinity of ways, and who make purchases, each with his respective products, that is to say, with the money arising from the sale of what he may have produced.

This is the true source of the gains made by the towns' people out of the country people, and again by the latter out of the former; both of them have wherewith to buy more largely, the more amply they themselves produce. A city, standing in the centre of a rich surrounding country, feels no want of rich and numerous customers and, on the other hand, the vicinity of an opulent city gives additional value to the produce of the country. The division of nations into agricultural, manufacturing, and commercial, is idle enough. For the success of a people in agriculture is a stimulus to its manufacturing and commercial prosperity; and the flourishing condition of its manufacture and commerce reflects a benefit upon its agriculture also.

The position of a nation, in respect of its neighbours, is analogous to the relation of one of its provinces to the others, or of the country to the town; it has an interest in their prosperity, being sure to profit by their opulence. The government of the United States, therefore, acted most wisely, in their attempt, about the year 1802, to civilize their savage neighbours, the Creek Indians. The design was to introduce habits of industry amongst them, and make them producers capable of carrying on a barter trade with the States of the Union; for there is nothing to be got by dealing with a people that have nothing to pay. It is useful and honourable to mankind, that one nation among so many should conduct itself uniformly upon liberal principles. The brilliant results of this enlightened policy will demonstrate, that the systems and theories really destructive and fallacious, are the exclusive and jealous maxims acted upon by the old European governments, and by them most impudently styled *practical truths,* for no other reason, as it would seem, than because they have the misfortune to put them in practice. The United States will have the honour of proving experimentally, that true policy goes hand-in-hand with moderation and humanity.

3. From this fruitful principle, we may draw this further conclusion, that it is no injury to the internal or national industry and production to buy and

import commodities from abroad; for nothing can be bought from strangers, except with native products, which find a vent in this external traffic. Should it be objected, that this foreign produce may have been bought with specie, I answer, specie is not always a native product, but must have been bought itself with the products of native industry; so that, whether the foreign articles be paid for in specie or in home products, the vent for national industry is the same in both cases.

4. The same principle leads to the conclusion, that the encouragement of mere consumption is no benefit to commerce; for the difficulty lies in supplying the means, not in stimulating the desire of consumption; and we have seen that production alone, furnishes those means. Thus, it is the aim of good government to stimulate production, of bad government to encourage consumption.

For the same reason that the creation of a new product is the opening of a new market for other products, the consumption or destruction of a product is the stoppage of a vent for them. This is no evil where the end of the product has been answered by its destruction, which end is the satisfying of some human want, or the creation of some new product designed for such a satisfaction. Indeed, if the nation be in a thriving condition, the gross national re-production exceeds the gross consumption. The consumed products have fulfilled their office, as it is natural and fitting they should: the consumption, however, has opened no new market, but just the reverse.

Having once arrived at the clear conviction, that the general demand for products is brisk in proportion to the activity of production, we need not trouble ourselves much to inquire towards what channel of industry production may be most advantageously directed. The products created give rise to various degrees of demand, according to the wants, the manners, the comparative capital, industry, and natural resources of each country; the article most in request, owing to the competition of buyers, yields the best interest of money to the capitalist, the largest profits to the adventurer, and the best wages to the labourer; and the agency of their respective services is naturally attracted by these advantages towards those particular channels.

In a community, city, province, or nation, that produces abundantly, and adds every moment to the sum of its products, almost all the branches of commerce, manufacture, and generally of industry, yield handsome profits, because the demand is great, and because there is always a large quantity of products in the market, ready to bid for new productive services. And, *vice versâ*, wherever, by reason of the blunders of the nation or its government, production is stationary, or does not keep pace with consumption, the demand gradually declines, the value of the product is less than the charges of its production; no productive exertion is properly rewarded; profits and wages decrease; the employment of capital becomes less advantageous and more hazardous; it is consumed piecemeal, not through extravagance, but through necessity, and because the sources of profit are dried up. The labouring classes experience a want of work; families before in tolerable circumstances, are more cramped and confined; and those before in difficulties are left altogether destitute. Depopulation, misery, and returning barbarism, occupy the place of abundance and happiness.

Such are the concomitants of declining production, which are only to be remedied by frugality, intelligence, activity, and freedom.

OF THE BENEFITS RESULTING FROM THE QUICK CIRCULATION OF MONEY AND COMMODITIES

It is common to hear people descant upon the benefits of an active circulation; that is to say, of numerous and rapid sales. It is material to appreciate them correctly.

The values engaged in actual production cannot be realized and employed in production again, until arrived at the last stage of completion, and sold to the consumer. The sooner a product is finished and sold, the sooner also can the portion of capital vested in it be applied to the business of fresh production. The capital being engaged a shorter time, there is less interest payable to the capitalist; there is a saving in the charges of production; it is, therefore, an advantage, that the successive operations performed in the course of production should be rapidly executed.

By way of illustrating the effects of this activity of circulation, let us trace them in the instance of a piece of printed calico.

A Lisbon trader imports the cotton from Brazil. It is his interest that his factors in America be expeditious in making purchases and remitting cargoes, and likewise, that he meet no delay in selling his cotton to a French merchant; because he thereby gets his returns the sooner, and can sooner recommence a new and equally lucrative operation. So far, it is Portugal that benefits by the increased activity of circulation; the subsequent advantage is on the side of France. If the French merchant keep the Brazil cotton but a short time in his warehouse, before he sells it to the cotton-spinner, if the spinner after spinning sell it immediately to the weaver, if the weaver dispose of it forthwith to the calico printer, and he in his turn sell it without much delay to the retail dealer, from whom it quickly passes to the consumer, this rapid circulation will have occupied for a shorter period the capital embarked by these respective producers; less interest of capital will have been incurred; consequently the prime cost of the article will be lower, and the capital will have been the sooner disengaged and applicable to fresh operations.

All these different purchases and sales, with many others that, for brevity's sake, I have not noticed, were indispensable before the Brazil cotton could be worn in the shape of printed calicoes. They are so many productive fashions given to this product; and the more rapidly they may have been given, the more benefit will have been derived from the production. But, if the same commodity be merely sold several times over in a year in the same place, without undergoing any fresh modification, this circulation would be a loss instead of a gain, and would increase instead of reducing the prime cost to the consumer. A capital must be employed in buying and re-selling, and interest paid for its use, to say nothing of the probable wear and tear of the commodity.

Thus, jobbing in merchandise necessarily causes a loss, either to the jobber, if the price be not raised by the transaction, or to the consumer, if it be raised.

The activity of circulation is at the utmost pitch to which it can be carried with advantage, when the product passes into the hands of a new productive agent the instant it is fit to receive a new modification, and is ultimately handed over to the consumer, the instant it has received the last finish. All kind of activity and bustle not tending to this end, far from giving additional activity to circulation, is an impediment to the course of production—an obstacle to circulation by all means to be avoided.

With respect to the rapidity of production arising from the more skilful direction of industry, it is an increase of rapidity not in circulation, but in productive energy. The advantage is analogous; it abridges the amount of capital employed.

I have made no distinction between the circulation of goods and of money, because there really is none. While a sum of money lies idle in a merchant's coffers, it is an inactive portion of his capital, precisely of the same nature as that part of his capital which is lying in his warehouse in the shape of goods ready for sale.

The best stimulus of useful circulation is, the natural wish of all classes, especially the producers themselves, to incur the least possible amount of interest upon the capital embarked in their respective undertakings. Circulation is much more apt to be interrupted by the obstacles thrown in its way, than by the want of proper encouragement. Its greatest obstructions are, wars, embargoes, oppressive duties, the dangers and difficulties of transportation. It flags in times of alarm and uncertainty, when social order is threatened, and all undertakings are hazardous. It flags, too, under the general dread of arbitrary exactions, when every one tries to conceal the extent of his ability. Finally, it flags in times of jobbing and speculation, when the sudden fluctuations caused by gambling in produce, make people look for a profit from every variation of mere relative price: goods are then held back in expectation of a rise, and money in the prospect of a fall; and, in the interim, both these capitals remain inactive and useless to production. Under such circumstances, there is no circulation, but of such products as cannot be kept without danger of deterioration; as fruits, vegetables, grain, and all articles that spoil in the keeping. With regard to them, it is thought wiser to incur the loss of present sale, whatever it be, than to risk considerable or total loss. If the national money be deteriorated, it becomes an object to get rid of it in any way, and exchange it for commodities. This was one of the causes of the prodigious circulation that took place during the progressive depreciation of the French *assignats.* Everybody was anxious to find some employment for a paper currency, whose value was hourly depreciating; it was only taken to be re-invested immediately, and one might have supposed it burnt the fingers it passed through. On that occasion, men plunged into business, of which they were utterly ignorant: manufactures were established, houses repaired and furnished, no expense was spared even in pleasure; until at length all the value each individual possessed in *assignats* was finally consumed, invested or lost altogether.

3.6 JOHN STUART MILL

Of Direct Taxes

John Stuart Mill (1806–1873) was born in London, England. He was systematically educated by his father, James Mill, to follow in his footsteps as a champion of utilitarian philosophy. By the age of three, Mill's father had taught him Greek. By the age of eight, Mill had read Plato, Xenophon, and Diogenes in Greek and had begun learning Latin. When he was 20 years old, he became a leader of young philosophical radicals and was quite active in their intellectual pursuits. Mill worked at the East India Company for 35 years and later became a member of Parliament from 1865 to 1868.

Mill followed his father, David Ricardo, and Jeremy Bentham in expounding utilitarian philosophy. They believed in a democratic government with equal voting rights and an economic system of free competition and laissez-faire policies. They predicted that once political reform was achieved, voters, rather than laissez-faire policies, would become the architects of economic change. Mill concurred with Thomas Robert Malthus on the evils of overpopulation, attributing it to the inability of masses of laborers to see the impact of additional family members on wages. Nevertheless progress could be achieved over time, as it had been in England by capitalists, who as employers of the masses had accumulated substantial reserves of capital. Mill published his *System of Logic* (1843) and *Principles of Political Economy* (1848), from which the following selection has been taken, works that established his dominant position in Victorian intellectual life. His other major works include *Considerations on Representative Government* (1860), *On Liberty* (1859), *Utilitarianism* (originally published in *Fraser's* magazine in 1861), *Examination of Sir William Hamilton's Philosophy and of the Principal Philosophical Questions Discussed in His Writings,* and *Auguste Comte and Positivism* (1866). In the area of political economy, Mill's studies were often concerned with such issues as the Irish land question, slavery and the American Civil War, income and property taxation, tenure reform, and trade unionism. In the following excerpt of his writings on the general principles of taxation, he denounces taxes on profits for reducing England's capital.

Key Concept: direct taxes

1. TAXES ARE EITHER DIRECT OR INDIRECT A direct tax is one which is demanded from the very persons who, it is intended or desired, should pay it. Indirect taxes are those which are demanded from one person in the expectation

and intention that he shall indemnify himself at the expense of another: such as the excise or customs. The producer or importer of a commodity is called upon to pay a tax on it, not with the intention to levy a peculiar contribution upon him, but to tax through him the consumers of the commodity, from whom it is supposed that he will recover the amount by means of an advance in price.

Direct taxes are either on income, or on expenditure. Most taxes on expenditure are indirect, but some are direct, being imposed not on the producer or seller of an article, but immediately on the consumer. A house-tax, for example, is a direct tax on expenditure, if levied, as it usually is, on the occupier of the house. If levied on the builder or owner, it would be an indirect tax. A window-tax is a direct tax on expenditure; so are the taxes on horses and carriages, and the rest of what are called the assessed taxes.

The sources of income are rent, profits, and wages. This includes every sort of income, except gift or plunder. Taxes may be laid on any one of the three kinds of income, or a uniform tax on all of them. We will consider these in their order.

2. A TAX ON RENT FALLS WHOLLY ON THE LANDLORD There are no means by which he can shift the burthen upon any one else. It does not affect the value or price of agricultural produce, for this is determined by the cost of production in the most unfavourable circumstances, and in those circumstances... no rent is paid. A tax on rent, therefore, has no effect, other than its obvious one. It merely takes so much from the landlord, and transfers it to the state.

This, however, is, in strict exactness, only true of the rent which is the result either of natural causes, or of improvements made by tenants. When the landlord makes improvements which increase the productive power of his land, he is remunerated for them by an extra payment from the tenant; and this payment, which to the landlord is properly a profit on capital, is blended and confounded with rent; which indeed it really is, to the tenant, and in respect of the economical laws which determine its amount. A tax on rent, if extending to this portion of it, would discourage landlords from making improvements: but it does not follow that it would raise the price of agricultural produce. The same improvements might be made with the tenant's capital, or even with the landlord's if lent by him to the tenant; provided he is willing to give the tenant so long a lease as will enable him to indemnify himself before it expires. But whatever hinders improvements from being made in the manner in which people prefer to make them, will often prevent them from being made at all: and on this account a tax on rent would be inexpedient, unless some means could be devised of excluding from its operation that portion of the nominal rent which may be regarded as landlord's profit. This argument, however, is not needed for the condemnation of such a tax. A peculiar tax on the income of any class, not balanced by taxes on other classes, is a violation of justice, and amounts to a partial confiscation. I have already shown grounds for excepting from this censure a tax which, sparing existing rents, should content itself with appropriating a portion of any future increase arising from the mere action of natural causes. But even this could not be justly done, without offering as an alternative the market price of the land. In the case of a tax on rent which is not peculiar, but accompanied by an equivalent tax on other incomes, the objection grounded on its reaching the profit arising from improvements is less applicable: since, profits being taxed as well as rent, the profit which assumes the form of rent is liable to its share in common with other profits; but since profits altogether ought... to be taxed somewhat lower than rent properly so called, the objection is only diminished, not removed.

3. A TAX ON PROFITS, LIKE A TAX ON RENT, MUST, AT LEAST IN ITS IMMEDIATE OPERATION, FALL WHOLLY ON THE PAYER All profits being alike affected, no relief can be obtained by a change of employment. If a tax were laid on the profits of any one branch of productive employment, the tax would be virtually an increase of the cost of production, and the value and price of the article would rise accordingly; by which the tax would be thrown upon the consumers of the commodity, and would not affect profits. But a general and equal tax on all profits would not affect general prices, and would fall, at least in the first instance, on capitalists alone.

There is, however, an ulterior effect, which, in a rich and prosperous country, requires to be taken into account. When the capital accumulated is so great and the rate of annual accumulation so rapid, that the country is only kept from attaining the stationary state by the emigration of capital, or by continual improvements in production; any circumstance which virtually lowers the rate of profit cannot be without a decided influence on these phenomena. It may operate in different ways. The curtailment of profit, and the consequent increased difficulty in making a fortune or obtaining a subsistence by the employment of capital, may act as a stimulus to inventions, and to the use of them when made. If improvements in production are much accelerated, and if these improvements cheapen, directly or indirectly, any of the things habitually consumed by the labourer, profits may rise, and rise sufficiently to make up for all that is taken from them by the tax. In that case the tax will have been realized without loss to any one, the produce of the country being increased by an equal, or what would in that case be a far greater, amount. The tax, however, must even in this case be considered as paid from profits, because the receivers of profits are those who would be benefited if it were taken off.

But though the artificial abstraction of a portion of profits would have a real tendency to accelerate improvements in production, no considerable improvements might actually result, or only of such a kind as not to raise general profits at all, or not to raise them so much as the tax had diminished them. If so, the rate of profit would be brought closer to that practical minimum to which it is constantly approaching: and this diminished return to capital would either give a decided check to further accumulation, or would cause a greater proportion than before of the annual increase to be sent abroad, or wasted in unprofitable speculations. At its first imposition the tax falls wholly on profits: but the amount of increase of capital, which the tax prevents, would, if it had been allowed to continue, have tended to reduce profits to the same level; and at every period of ten or twenty years there will be found less difference between profits as they are, and profits as they would in that case have been: until at last there is no difference, and the tax is thrown either upon the labourer or upon the landlord. The real effect of a tax on profits is to make the country possess, at any given period, a smaller capital and a smaller aggregate production, and to make the stationary state be attained earlier, and with a smaller sum of national wealth. It is possible that a tax on profits might even diminish the existing capital of the country. If the rate of profit is already at the practical minimum, that is, at the point at which all that portion of the annual increment which would tend to reduce profits is carried off either by exportation or by speculation; then if a tax is imposed which reduces profits still lower, the same causes which previously carried off the increase would probably carry off a portion of the existing capital. A tax on profits is thus, in a state of capital and accumulation like that in England, extremely detrimental to the national wealth. And this effect is not confined to the case of a peculiar, and therefore intrinsically unjust, tax on profits. The mere fact that profits have to bear their share of a heavy general taxation, tends, in the same manner as a peculiar tax, to drive capital abroad, to stimulate imprudent speculations by diminishing safe gains, to discourage further accumulation, and to accelerate the attainment of the stationary state. This is thought to have been the principal cause of the decline of Holland, or rather of her having ceased to make progress.

Even in countries which do not accumulate so fast as to be always within a short interval of the stationary state, it seems impossible that, if capital is accumulating at all, its accumulation should not be in some degree retarded by the abstraction of a portion of its profit; and unless the effect in stimulating improvements be a full counter-balance, it is inevitable that a part of the burthen will be thrown off the capitalist, upon the labourer or the landlord. One or other of these is always the loser by a diminished rate of accumulation. If population continues to increase as before, the labourer suffers: if not, cultivation is checked in its advance, and the landlords lose the accession of rent which would have accrued to them. The only countries in which a tax on profits seems likely to be permanently a burthen on capitalists exclusively, are those in which capital is stationary, because there is no new accumulation. In such countries the tax might not prevent the old capital from being kept up through habit, or from unwillingness to submit to impoverishment, and so the capitalist might continue to bear the whole of the tax. It is seen from these considerations that the effects of a tax on profits are much more complex, more various, and in some points more uncertain, than writers on this subject have commonly supposed.

4. WE NOW TURN TO TAXES ON WAGES The incidence of these is very different, according as the wages taxed are those of ordinary unskilled labour, or are the remuneration of such skilled or privileged employments, whether manual or intellectual, as are taken out of the sphere of competition by a natural or conferred monopoly.

[I]n the present low state of popular education, all the higher grades of mental or educated labour are at a monopoly price; exceeding the wages of common workmen in a degree very far beyond that which is due to the expense, trouble, and loss of time required in qualifying for the employment. Any tax levied on these gains, which still leaves them above (or not below) their just proportion, falls on those who pay it; they have no means of relieving themselves at the expense of any other class. The same thing is true of ordinary wages, in cases like that of the United States, or of a new colony, where, capital increasing as rapidly as population can increase, wages are kept up by the increase of capital, and not by the adherence of the labourers to a fixed standard of comforts. In such a case some deterioration of their condition, whether by a tax or otherwise, might possibly take place without checking the increase of population. The tax would in that case fall on the labourers themselves, and would reduce them prematurely to that lower state to which, on the same supposition with regard to their habits, they would in any case have been reduced ultimately, by the inevitable diminution in the rate of increase of capital, through the occupation of all the fertile land.

Some will object that, even in this case, a tax on wages cannot be detrimental to the labourers, since the money raised by it, being expended in the country, comes back to the labourers again through the demand for labour.... [But] funds expended unproductively have no tendency to raise or keep up wages, unless when expended in the direct purchase of labour. If the government took a tax of a shilling a week from every labourer, and laid it all out in hiring labourers for military service, public works, or the like, it would, no doubt, indemnify the labourers as a class for all that the tax took from them. That would really be "spending the money among the people." But if it expended the whole in buying goods, or in adding to the salaries of employe's who bought goods with it, this would not increase the demand for labour, or tend to raise wages. Without, however, reverting to general principles, we may rely on an obvious *reductio ad absurdum*. If to take money from the labourers and spend it in commodities is giving it back to the labourers, then, to take money from other classes, and spend it in the same manner, must be giving it to the labourers; consequently, the more a government takes in taxes, the greater will be the demand for labour, and the more opulent the condition of the labourers. A proposition the absurdity of which no one can fail to see.

In the condition of most communities, wages are regulated by the habitual standard of living to which the labourers adhere, and on less than which they will not multiply. Where there exists such a standard, a tax on wages will indeed for a time be borne by the labourers themselves; but unless this temporary depression has the effect of lowering the standard itself, the increase of population will receive a check, which will raise wages, and restore the labourers to their previous condition. On whom, in this case, will the tax fall? According to Adam Smith, on the community generally, in their character of consumers; since the rise of wages, he thought, would raise general prices. We have seen, however, that general prices depend on other causes, and are never raised by any circumstance which affects all kinds of productive employment in the same manner and degree. A rise of wages occasioned by a tax, must, like any other increase of the cost of labour, be defrayed from profits. To attempt to tax day-labourers, in an old country, is merely to impose an extra tax upon all employers of common labour; unless the tax has the much worse effect of permanently lowering the standard of comfortable subsistence in the minds of the poorest class.

We find in the preceding considerations an additional argument for the opinion already expressed, that direct taxation should stop short of the class of incomes which do not exceed what is necessary for healthful existence. These very small incomes are mostly derived from manual labour; and, as we now see, any tax imposed on these, either permanently degrades the habits of the labouring class, or falls on profits, and burthens capitalists with an indirect tax, in addition to their share of the direct taxes; which is doubly objectionable, both as a violation of the fundamental rule of equality, and for the reasons which, as already shown, render a peculiar tax on profits detrimental to the public wealth, and consequently to the means which society possesses of paying any taxes whatever.

5. WE NOW PASS, FROM TAXES ON THE SEPARATE KINDS OF INCOME, TO A TAX ATTEMPTED TO BE ASSESSED FAIRLY UPON ALL KINDS; IN OTHER WORDS, AN INCOME TAX The discussion of the conditions necessary for making this tax consistent with justice, has been anticipated.... We shall suppose, therefore, that these conditions are complied with. They are, first, that incomes below a certain amount should be altogether untaxed. This minimum should not be higher than the amount which suffices for the necessaries of the existing population. The exemption from the present income [1857] tax, of all incomes under 100*l.* a year, and the lower percentage formerly levied on those between 100*l.* and 150*l.*, are only defensible on the ground that almost all the indirect taxes press more heavily on incomes between 50*l.* and 150*l.* than on any others whatever. The second condition is, that incomes above the limit should be taxed only in proportion to the surplus by which they exceed the limit. Thirdly, that all sums saved from income and invested, should be exempt from the tax: or if this be found impracticable, that life incomes, and incomes from business and professions, should be less heavily taxed than inheritable incomes, in a degree as nearly as possible equivalent to the increased need of economy arising from their terminable character: allowance being also made, in the case of variable incomes, for their precariousness.

An income-tax, fairly assessed on these principles, would be, in point of justice, the least exceptionable of all taxes. The objection to it, in the present low state of public morality, is the impossibility of ascertaining the real incomes of the contributors. The supposed hardship of compelling people to disclose the amount of their incomes, ought not, in my opinion, to count for much. One of the social evils of this country is the practice, amounting to a custom, of maintaining, or attempting to maintain, the appearance to the world of a larger income than is possessed; and it would be far better for the interest of those who yield to this weakness, if the extent of their means were universally and exactly known, and the temptation removed to expending more than they can afford, stinting real wants in order to make a false show externally. At the same time, the reason of the case, even on this point, is not so exclusively on one side of the argument as is sometimes supposed. So long as the vulgar of any country are in the debased state of mind which this national habit presupposes—so long as their respect (if such a word can be applied to it) is proportioned to what they suppose to be each person's pecuniary means—it may be doubted whether anything which would remove all uncertainty as to that point, would not considerably increase the presumption and arrogance of the vulgar rich, and their insolence towards those above them in mind and character, but below them in fortune.

Notwithstanding, too, what is called the inquisitorial nature of the tax, no amount of inquisitorial power which would be tolerated by a people the most disposed to submit to it, could enable the revenue officers to assess the tax from actual knowledge of the circumstances of contributors. Rents, salaries, annuities, and all fixed incomes, can be exactly ascertained. But the variable gains of professions, and still more the profits of business, which the person interested cannot always himself exactly ascertain, can still less be estimated with any approach to fairness by a tax-collector. The main reliance must be placed, and always has been placed, on the returns made by the person himself. No production of accounts is of much avail, except against the more flagrant cases of falsehood; and even against these the check is very imperfect, for if fraud is intended, false accounts can generally be framed which it will baffle any means of inquiry possessed by the revenue officers to detect: the easy resource of omitting entries on the credit side being often sufficient without the aid of fictitious debts or disbursements. The tax, therefore, on whatever principles of equality it may be imposed, is in practice unequal in one of the worst ways, falling heaviest on the most conscientious. The unscrupulous succeed in evading a great proportion of what they should pay; even persons of integrity in their ordinary transactions are tempted to palter with their consciences, at least to the extent of deciding in their own favour all points on which the smallest doubt or discussion could arise: while the strictly veracious may be made to pay more than the state intended, by the powers of arbitrary assessment necessarily intrusted to the Commissioners, as the last defence against the tax-payer's power of concealment.

It is to be feared, therefore, that the fairness which belongs to the principle of an income tax, cannot be made to attach to it in practice: and that this tax, while apparently the most just of all modes of raising a revenue, is in effect more unjust than many others which are *primâ facie* more objectionable. This consideration would lead us to concur in the opinion which, until of late, has usually prevailed—that direct taxes on income should be reserved as an extraordinary resource for great national emergencies, in which the necessity of a large additional revenue overrules all objections.

The difficulties of a fair income tax have elicited a proposition for a direct tax of so much per cent, not on income, but on expenditure; the aggregate amount of each person's expenditure being ascertained, as the amount of income now is, from statements furnished by the contributors themselves. The author of this suggestion, Mr. [John] Revans, in a clever pamphlet on the subject, contends that the returns which persons would furnish of their expenditure would be more trustworthy than those which they now make of their income, inasmuch as expenditure is in its own nature more public than income, and false representations of it more easily detected. He cannot, I think, have sufficiently considered, how few of the items in the annual expenditure of most families can be judged of with any approximation to correctness from the external signs. The only security would still be the veracity of individuals, and there is no reason for supposing that their statements would be more trustworthy on the subject of their expenses than that of their revenues; especially as, the expenditure of most persons being composed of many more items than their income, there would be more scope for concealment and suppression in the detail of expenses than even of receipts.

The taxes on expenditure at present in force, either in this or in other countries, fall only on particular kinds of expenditure, and differ no otherwise from taxes on commodities than in being paid directly by the person who consumes or uses the article, instead of being advanced by the producer or seller, and reimbursed in the price. The taxes on horses and carriages, on dogs, on servants, are all of this nature. They evidently fall on the persons from whom they are levied—those who use the commodity taxed. A tax of a similar description, and more important, is a house-tax; which must be considered at somewhat greater length.

6. THE RENT OF A HOUSE CONSISTS OF TWO PARTS, THE GROUND-RENT, AND WHAT ADAM SMITH CALLS THE BUILDING-RENT The first is determined by the ordinary principles of rent. It is the remuneration given for the use of the portion of land occupied by the house and its appurtenances; and varies from a mere equivalent for the rent which the ground would afford in agriculture to the monopoly rents paid for advantageous situations in populous thoroughfares. The rent of the house itself, as distinguished from the ground, is the equivalent given for the labour and capital expended on the building. The fact of its being received in quarterly or half-yearly payments, makes no difference in the principles by which it is regulated. It comprises the ordinary profit on the builder's capital, and an annuity, sufficient at the current rate of interest, after paying for all repairs chargeable on the proprietor, to replace the original capital by the time the house is worn out, or by the expiration of the usual term of a building lease.

A tax of so much per cent on the gross rent, falls on both those portions alike. The more highly a house is rented, the more it pays to the tax, whether the quality of the situation or that of the house itself is the cause. The incidence, however, of these two portions of the tax must be considered separately.

As much of it as is a tax on building-rent, must ultimately fall on the consumer, in other words the occupier. For as the profits of building are already not above the ordinary rate, they would, if the tax fell on the owner and not on the occupier, become lower than the profits of untaxed employments, and houses would not be built. It is probable, however, that for some time after the tax was first imposed, a great part of it would fall, not on the renter, but on the owner of the house. A large proportion of the consumers either could not afford, or would not choose, to pay their former rent with the tax in addition, but would content themselves with a lower scale of accommodation. Houses therefore would be for a time in excess of the demand. The consequence of such excess, in the case of most other articles, would be an almost immediate diminution of the supply: but so durable a commodity as houses does not rapidly diminish in amount. New buildings indeed, of the class for which the demand had decreased, would cease to be erected, except for special reasons; but in the meantime the temporary superfluity would lower rents, and the consumers would obtain perhaps nearly the same accommodation as formerly for the same aggregate payment, rent and tax together. By degrees, however, as the existing houses wore out, or as increase of population demanded a greater supply, rents would again rise; until it became profitable to recommence building, which would not be until the tax was wholly transferred to the occupier.

In the end, therefore, the occupier bears that portion of a tax on rent which falls on the payment made for the house itself, exclusively of the ground it stands on.

The case is partly different with the portion which is a tax on ground-rent. As taxes on rent, properly so called, fall on the landlord, a tax on ground-rent, one would suppose, must fall on the ground-landlord, at least after the expiration of the building lease. It will not, however, fall wholly on the landlord, unless with the tax on ground-rent there is combined an equivalent tax on agricultural rent. The lowest rent of land let for building is very little above the rent which the same ground would yield in agriculture: since it is reasonable to suppose that land, unless in case of exceptional circumstances, is let or sold for building as soon as it is decidedly worth more for that purpose than for cultivation. If, therefore, a tax were laid on ground-rents without being also laid on agricultural rents, it would, unless of trifling amount, reduce the return from the lowest ground-rents below the ordinary return from land, and would check further building quite as effectually as if it were a tax on building-rents, until either the increased demand of a growing population, or a diminution of supply by the ordinary causes of destruction, had raised the rent by a full equivalent for the tax. But whatever raises the lowest ground-rents, raises all others, since each exceeds the lowest by the market value of its peculiar advantages. If, therefore, the tax on ground-rents were a fixed sum per square foot, the more valuable situations paying no more than those least in request, this fixed payment would ultimately fall on the occupier. Suppose the lowest ground-rent to be 10*l.* per acre, and the highest 1000*l.*, a tax of 1*l.* per acre on ground-rents would ultimately raise the former to 11*l.*, and the latter consequently to 1001*l.*, since the difference of value between the two situations would be exactly what it was before: the annual pound, therefore, would be paid by the occupier. But a tax on ground-rent is supposed to be a portion of a house-tax, which is not a fixed payment, but a percentage on the rent. The cheapest site, therefore, being supposed as before to pay 1*l.*, the dearest would pay 100*l.*, of which only the 1*l.* could be thrown upon the occupier, since the rent would still be only raised to 1001*l.* Consequently, 99*l.* of the 100*l.* levied from the expensive site, would fall on the ground-landlord. A house-tax thus requires to be considered in a double aspect, as a tax on all occupiers of houses, and a tax on ground-rents.

In the vast majority of houses, the ground-rent forms but a small proportion of the annual payment made for the house, and nearly all the tax falls on the occupier. It is only in exceptional cases, like that of the favourite situations in large towns, that the predominant element in the rent of the house is the ground-rent; and among the very few kinds of income which are fit subjects for peculiar taxation, these ground-rents hold the principal place, being the most gigantic example extant of enormous accessions of riches acquired rapidly, and in many cases unexpectedly, by a few families, from the mere accident of their possessing certain tracts of land, without their having themselves aided in the acquisition by the smallest exertion, outlay, or risk. So far therefore as a house-tax falls on the ground-landlord, it is liable to no valid objection.

In so far as it falls on the occupier, if justly proportioned to the value of the house, it is one of the fairest and most unobjectionable of all taxes. No part of a person's expenditure is a better criterion of his means, or bears, on the whole, more nearly the same proportion to them. A house-tax is a nearer approach to a fair income tax than a direct assessment on income can easily be; having the great advantage, that it makes spontaneously all the allowances which it is so difficult to make, and so impracticable to make exactly, in assessing an income tax: for if what a person pays in house-rent is a test of anything, it is a test not of what he possesses, but of what he thinks he can afford to spend. The equality of this tax can only be seriously questioned on two grounds. The first is, that a miser may escape it. This objection applies to all taxes on expenditure: nothing but a direct tax on income can reach a miser. But as misers do not now hoard their treasure, but invest it in productive employments, it not only adds to the national wealth, and consequently to the general means of paying taxes, but the payment claimable from itself is only transferred from the principal sum to the income afterwards derived from it, which pays taxes as soon as it comes to be expended. The second objection is, that a person may require a larger and more expensive house, not from having greater means, but from having a larger family. Of this, however, he is not entitled to complain; since having a large family is at a person's own choice: and, so far as concerns the public interest, is a thing rather to be discouraged than promoted.

A large portion of the taxation of [England] is raised by a house-tax. The parochial taxation of the towns entirely, and of the rural districts partially, consists of an assessment on house-rent. The window-tax, which was also a house-tax, but of a bad kind, operating as a tax on light, and a cause of deformity in building, was exchanged in 1851 for a house-tax properly so called, but on a much lower scale than that which existed previously to 1834. It is to be lamented that the new tax retains the unjust principle on which the old house-tax was assessed, and which contributed quite as much as the selfishness of the middle classes to produce the outcry against the tax. The public were justly scandalized on learning that residences like Chatsworth or Belvoir were only rated on an imaginary rent of perhaps 200*l*. a year, under the pretext that owing to the great expense of keeping them up, they could not be let for more. Probably, indeed, they could not be let even for that, and if the argument were a fair one, they ought not to have been taxed at all. But a house-tax is not intended as a tax on incomes derived from houses, but on expenditure incurred for them. The thing which it is wished to ascertain is what a house costs to the person who lives in it, not what it would bring in if let to some one else. When the occupier is not the owner, and does not hold on a repairing lease, the rent he pays is the measure of what the house costs him: but when he is the owner, some other measure must be sought. A valuation should be made of the house, not at what it would sell for, but at what would be the cost of rebuilding it, and this valuation might be periodically corrected by an allowance for what it had lost in value by time, or gained by repairs and improvements. The amount of the amended valuation would form a principal sum, the interest of which, at the current price of the public funds, would form the annual value at which the building should be assessed to the tax.

As incomes below a certain amount ought to be exempt from income tax, so ought houses below a certain value from house-tax, on the universal principle of sparing from all taxation the absolute necessaries of healthful existence. In order that the occupiers of lodgings, as well as of houses, might benefit, as in justice they ought, by this exemption, it might be optional with the owners to have every portion of a house which is occupied by a separate tenant valued and assessed separately, as is now usually the case with chambers.

PART TWO

The Marxian, Neoclassical, Libertarian, and Chicago Schools

On the Internet . . .

Sites appropriate to Part Two

This Web site lists and provides links to the traditional, revisionist, and modern Marxian economists.

`http://www.econ.jhu.edu/People/fonseca/HET/hethome.htm`

This Web site covers the lives and work of Karl Marx and Friedrich Engels. It offers a comprehensive search engine and includes photos, biographies, and an archive of letters.

`http://www.marx.org`

This Web site provides a brief biography of Milton Friedman and presents his views on consumption theory, expected utility, economic theory, and unemployment versus inflation.

`http://adam.hhss.se/utskott/Friedmans/MILTON.HTM`

This is a list of journal articles by Gary S. Becker.

`http://www.spc.uchicago.edu/users/gsb1/Articles/article2.html`

The Royal Swedish Academy of Sciences provides press releases and biographical information on Friedrich A. Hayek, Milton Friedman, George J. Stigler, Gary S. Becker, and many others.

`http://www.nobel.se/laureates/`

CHAPTER 4 The Marxian School

4.1 KARL MARX

The Rate of Surplus-Value

Karl Marx (1818–1883), was born in Trier, Germany, where he received a classical education. In 1842 he became editor of the *Pheinische Zeitung* at Cologne. The newspaper was suppressed by the government and later ceased publication due to its liberal views. In 1843 Marx moved to Paris, France, where he devoted himself primarily to the study of political economy and the history of the French Revolution. Expelled from France in 1845, he settled in Brussels, Belgium. Marx continued working in journalism intermittently but spent most of his time doing research at the British Museum's library.

Marx's first major work, *The Poverty of Philosophy* (1847), was a critique of the idealistic socialism of J. P. Proudhon. This polemic was followed by *The Communist Manifesto* (1848), which underscored the need for working men to unite in order to liberate themselves from the oppression of capitalism by establishing society's natural progression toward communism and suggesting methods by which this process could be accelerated. In *Das Kapital* (1867), he held that labor is exploited under capitalism, as the value of workers' output is greater than wages paid, the difference being termed surplus-value. In this fashion, the labor time of workers is converted to profits and, in turn, to capital. The accumulated profits are invested in machinery, improving productivity and increasing profits further. Marx held that the rising investments in equipment depress profit rates and that business cycles lead to the acquisition of small companies by large ones, increasing the wealth of the capitalist class. The working class continues to suffer as technological change renders skills obsolete, with skilled workers becoming semiskilled and semiskilled workers joining the growing ranks of the unskilled. According to Marx, this process culminates in a revolution in which the working class overthrows the capitalists to build a socialist society. The scientific aspects of this theory are contained in *A Contribution to the Critique of Political Economy* (1859). The following selection has been taken from *Capital: A Critique of Political Economy* (Vintage Books, 1977), a translation of volume 1 of *Das Kapital.* In it, Marx describes the rate of surplus-value, viewing it as the source of capitalist exploitation in the factory.

Key Concept: the rate of surplus-value

THE DEGREE OF EXPLOITATION OF LABOUR-POWER

The surplus-value generated in the production process by C, the capital advanced, i.e. the valorization of the value of the capital C, presents itself to us first as the amount by which the value of the product exceeds the value of its constituent elements.

The capital C is made up of two components, one the sum of money c laid out on means of production, and the other the sum of money v expended on labour-power; c represents the portion of value which has been turned into constant capital, v that turned into variable capital. At the beginning, then, $C = c + v$: for example, if £500 is the capital advanced, its components may be such that the £500 = £410 constant + £90 variable. When the process of production is finished, we get a commodity whose value = $(c + v) + s$, where s is the surplus-value; or, taking our former figures, the value of this commodity is (£410 constant + £90 variable) + £90 surplus. The original capital has now changed from C to C′, from £500 to £590. The difference is s, or a surplus-value of £90. Since the value of the constituent elements of the product is equal to the value of the capital advanced, it is a mere tautology to say that the excess of the value of the product over the value of its constituent elements is equal to the valorization of the value of the capital advanced, or to the surplus-value produced.

Nevertheless, we must examine this tautology a little more closely. The equation being made is between the value of the product and the value of its constituents consumed in the process of production.... [T]hat portion of the constant capital which consists of the instruments of labour transfers to the product only a fraction of its value, while the remainder of that value continues in its old form of existence. Since this remainder plays no part in the formation of value, we may at present leave it on one side. To introduce it into the calculation would make no difference. For instance, taking our former example, $c =$ £410: assume that this sum consists of £312 value of raw material, £44 value of auxiliary material and £54 value of the machinery worn away in the process; and assume that the total value of the machinery employed is £1,054. Out of this latter sum, then, we reckon as advanced for the purpose of turning out the product the sum of £54 alone, which the machinery loses by wear and tear while performing its function, and therefore parts with to the product. Now if we also reckoned the remaining £1,000, which continues to exist in its old form in the machinery, as transferred to the product, we would also have to reckon it as part of the value advanced, and thus make it appear on both sides of our calculation. We should, in this way, get £1,500 on one side and £1,590 on the other. The difference between these two sums, or the surplus-value, would still be £90. When we refer, therefore, to constant capital advanced for the production of value, we always mean the value of the means of production actually consumed in the course of production, unless the context demonstrates the reverse.

This being so, let us return to the formula $C = c + v$, which we saw was transformed into $C' = (c + v) + s$, C becoming C′. We know that the value of the constant capital is transferred to the product, and merely re-appears in it. The new value actually created in the process, the 'value-product', is therefore not the same as the value of the product; it is not, as it would at first sight appear, $(c + v) + s$ or £140 constant + £90 variable + £90 surplus, but rather $v + s$ or £90 variable + £90 surplus. In other words, not £590 but £180. If c, the constant capital, = O, in other words if there were branches of industry in which the capitalist could dispense with all means of production made by previous labour, whether raw material, auxiliary material, or instruments, employing only labour-power and materials supplied by nature, if that were the case, there would be no constant capital to transfer to the product. This component of the value of the product, i.e. the £410 in our example, would be eliminated, but the sum of £180, the amount of new value created, or the value produced, which contains £90 of surplus-value, would remain just as great as if c represented the highest value imaginable. We should have $C = (O + v) = v$, and C′ the valorized capital $= v + s$, and therefore $C' - C = s$ as before. On the other hand, if $s =$ O, in other words if the labour-power whose value is advanced in the form of variable capital were to produce only its equivalent, we should have $C = c + v$, and C′ (the value of the product) $= (c + v) + O$, hence $C = C'$. In this case the capital advanced would not have valorized its value.

From what has gone before we know that surplus-value is purely the result of an alteration in the value of v, of that part of the capital which was converted into labour-power; consequently, $v + s = v + \Delta v$ (v plus an increment of v). But the fact that it is v alone that varies, and the conditions of that variation, are obscured by the circumstance that in consequence of the increase in the variable component of the capital, there is also an increase in the sum total of the capital advanced. It was originally £500 and becomes £590. Therefore, in order that our investigation may lead to accurate results, we must make abstraction from that portion of the value of the product in which constant capital alone appears, and thus posit the constant capital as zero or make $c =$ O. This is merely an application of a mathematical rule, employed whenever we operate with constant and variable magnitudes, related to each other only by the symbols of addition and subtraction.

A further difficulty is caused by the original form of the variable capital. In our example, C′ = £410 constant + £90 variable + £90 surplus; but £90 is a given and therefore a constant quantity and hence it appears absurd to treat it as variable. In fact, however, the £90 variable is here merely a symbol for the process undergone by this value. The portion of the capital invested in the purchase of labour-power is a definite quantity of objectified labour, a constant value like the value of the labour-power purchased. But in the process of production the place of the £90 is taken by labour-power which sets itself in motion, dead labour is replaced by living labour, something stagnant by something flowing, a constant by a variable. The result is the reproduction of v plus an increment of v. From the point of view of capitalist production, therefore, the whole process appears as the independent motion of what was originally constant value, but has now been transformed into labour-power. Both the process and its result are ascribed to this independent motion of value. If, therefore, such expression as '£90 variable capital' or 'such and such a quantity of self-valorizing value' appear to contain contradictions, this is only because they express a contradiction immanent in capitalist production.

At first sight it appears strange to equate the constant capital to zero. But we do this every day. If, for example, we want to calculate the amount of profit gained by England from the cotton industry, we first of all deduct the sums paid for cotton to the United States, India, Egypt and various other countries, i.e. we posit the value of the capital that merely re-appears in the value of the product as a zero magnitude.

Of course, the ratio of surplus-value not only to that portion of the capital from which it directly arises, and whose change in value it represents, but also to the sum total of the capital advanced, is economically of very great importance.... In order to enable one portion of capital to realize its value by being converted into labour-power, it is necessary that another portion be converted into means of production. In order that variable capital may perform its function, constant capital must be advanced to an adequate proportion, the proportion appropriate to the special technical conditions of each labour process. However, the fact that retorts and other vessels are necessary to a chemical process does not prevent the chemist from ignoring them when he undertakes his analysis of the results. If we look at the creation and the alteration of value for themselves, i.e. in their pure form, then the means of production, this physical shape taken on by constant capital, provides only the material in which fluid, value-creating labour-power has to be incorporated. Neither the nature nor the value of this material is of any importance. All that is needed is a sufficient supply of material to absorb the labour expended in the process of production. That supply once given, the material may rise or fall in value, or even be without any value in itself, like the land and the sea; but this will have no influence on the creation of value or on the variation in the quantity of value.

In the first place, therefore, we equate the constant part of capital with zero. The capital advanced is consequently reduced from $c + v$ to v, and instead of the value of the product $(c + v) + s$ we now have the value produced $(v + s)$. Given that the new value produced = £180, a sum which consequently represents the whole of the labour expended during the process, if we subtract £90 from it, being the value of the variable capital, we have £90 left, the amount of the surplus-value. This sum of £90, or s, expresses the absolute quantity of surplus-value produced. The relative quantity produced, or the ratio in which the variable capital has valorized its value, is plainly determined by the ratio of the surplus-value to the variable capital, and expressed by *s/v*. In our example, this ratio is 90/90, or 100 per cent. This relative increase in the value of the variable capital, or the relative magnitude of the surplus-value, is called here the rate of surplus-value.

We have seen that the worker, during one part of the labour process, produces only the value of his labour-power, i.e. the value of his means of subsistence. Since his work forms part of a system based on the social division of labour, he does not directly produce his own means of subsistence. Instead of this, he produces a particular commodity, yarn for example, with a value equal to the value of his means of subsistence, or of the money for it. The part of his day's labour devoted to this purpose will be greater or less, in proportion to the value of his average daily requirements or, what amounts to the same thing, in proportion to the labour-time required on average to produce them. If the value of his daily means of subsistence represents an average of 6 hours' objectified labour, the worker must work an average of 6 hours to produce that value. If, instead of working for the capitalist, he worked independently on his own account, he would, other things being equal, still be obliged to work for the same number of hours in order to produce the value of his labour-power, and thereby to gain the means of subsistence necessary for his own preservation or continued reproduction. But as we have seen, during that part of his day's labour in which he produces the value of his labour-power, say 3 shillings, he produces only an equivalent for the value of his labour-power already advanced by the capitalist; the new value created only replaces the variable capital advanced. It is owing to this fact that the production of the new value of 3 shillings has the appearance of a mere reproduction. I call the portion of the working day during which this reproduction takes place necessary labour-time, and the labour expended during that time necessary labour; necessary for the worker, because independent of the particular social form of his labour; necessary for capital and the capitalist world, because the continued existence of the worker is the basis of that world.

During the second period of the labour process, that in which his labour is no longer necessary labour, the worker does indeed expend labour-power, he does work, but his labour is no longer necessary labour, and he creates no value for himself. He creates surplus-value which, for the capitalist, has all the charms of something created out of nothing. This part of the working day I call surplus labour-time, and to the labour expended during that time I give the name of surplus labour. It is just as important for a correct understanding of surplus-value to conceive it as merely a congealed quantity of surplus labour-time, as nothing but objectified surplus labour, as it is for a proper comprehension of value in general to conceive it as merely a congealed quantity of so many hours of labour, as nothing but objectified labour. What distinguishes the various economic formations of society—the distinction between for example a society based on slave-labour and a society based on wage-labour—is the form in which this surplus làbour is in each case extorted from the immediate producer, the worker.

Since, on the one hand, the variable capital and the labour-power purchased by that capital are equal in value, and the value of this labour-power determines the necessary part of the working day; and since, on the other hand, the surplus-value is determined by the surplus part of the working day, it follows that surplus-value is in the same ratio to variable capital as surplus labour is to necessary labour. In other words, the rate of surplus value, $\frac{s}{v} = \frac{surplus\ labour}{necessary\ labour}$. Both ratios, $\frac{s}{v}$ and $\frac{surplus\ labour}{necessary\ labour}$, express the same thing in different ways; in the one case in the form of objectified labour, in the other in the form of living, fluid labour.

The rate of surplus-value is therefore an exact expression for the degree of exploitation of labour-power by capital, or of the worker by the capitalist.

We assumed in our example that the value of the product = £410 constant + £90 variable = £90 surplus, and that the capital advanced = £500. Since the surplus-value = £90, and the capital advanced = £500, we should, according to the usual way of reckoning, get 18 per cent as the rate of surplus-value (because it is generally confused with the rate of profit), a rate so low it might well cause a pleasant surprise to Mr Carey and other harmonizers.[1] But in fact the rate of surplus-value is not equal to $\frac{s}{C}$ or $\frac{s}{c+v}$ but to $\frac{s}{v}$; thus it is not $\frac{90}{500}$ but $\frac{90}{90}$ = 100 per cent, which is more than five times the apparent degree of exploitation. Although, in the case we have supposed, we do not know the actual length of the working day, or the duration in days and weeks of the labour process, or the number of workers set in motion simultaneously by the variable capital of £90, the rate of surplus-value $\frac{s}{v}$ accurately discloses to us, by means of its equivalent expression, $\frac{surplus\ labour}{necessary\ labour}$, the relation between the two parts of the working day. This relation is here one of equality, being 100 per cent. Hence the worker in our example works one half of the day for himself, the other half for the capitalist.

The method of calculating the rate of surplus-value is therefore, in brief, as follows. We take the total value of the product and posit the constant capital which merely re-appears in it as equal to zero. What remains is the only value that has actually been created in the process of producing the commodity. If the amount of surplus-value is given, we have only to deduct it from this remainder to find the variable capital. And *vice versa* if the later is given and we need to find the surplus-value. If both are given, we have only to perform the concluding operation, namely calculate $\frac{s}{v}$, the ratio of the surplus-value to the variable capital.

Simple as the method is, it may not be amiss, by means of a few examples, to exercise the reader in the application of the novel principles underlying it.

First we will take the case of a spinning mill containing 10,000 mule spindles, spinning No. 32 yarn from American cotton, and producing 1 lb. of yarn weekly per spindle. We assume the waste to be 6 per cent: accordingly 10,600 lb. of cotton are consumed weekly, of which 600 lb. go to waste. The price of the cotton in April 1871 was $7\frac{3}{4}$d. per lb.; the raw material therefore costs approximately £342. The 10,000 spindles, including machinery for preparation and motive power, cost, we will assume, £1 per spindle, amounting to a total of £10,000. Depreciation we put at 10 per cent, or £1,000 a year = £20 a week. The rent of the building we suppose to be £300 a year, or £6 a week. The amount of coal consumed (for 100 h.p. indicated, at 4 lb. of coal per horse-power per hour during 60 hours, and including coal consumed in heating the mill) is 11 tons a week at 8s. 6d. a ton, and therefore comes to about £$4\frac{1}{2}$ a week; gas, £1 a week,

TABLE 1

Value Produced Per Acre

Seed	£1	9	0	Tithes, rates and taxes	£1	1	0
Manure	£2	10	0	Rent	£1	8	0
Wages	£3	10	0	Farmer's profit and interest	£1	2	0
Total	£7	9	0	Total	£3	11	0

oil etc., £4$\frac{1}{2}$ a week. Total cost of the above auxiliary materials, £10 a week. Therefore the constant part of the value of the week's product is £378. Wages amount to £52 a week. The price of the yarn is 12$\frac{1}{4}$d. per lb., which gives, for the value of 10,000 lb., the sum of £150. The surplus-value is therefore in this case £510 − £430 = £80. We put the constant part of the value of the product equal to zero, as it plays no part in the creation of value. There remains £132 as the weekly value created, which = £52 variable + £80 surplus. The rate of surplus-value is therefore $\frac{80}{52} = 153\frac{11}{13}$ per cent. In a working day of 10 hours with average labour the result is: necessary labour = $3\frac{31}{33}$ hours and surplus labour = $6\frac{2}{33}$.

One more example. Jacob gives the following calculation for the year 1815. Owing to the previous adjustment of several items it is very imperfect; nevertheless it is sufficient for our purpose. In it he assumes that the price of wheat is 8s. a quarter, and that the average yield per acre is 22 bushels.

Here the assumption is always made that the price of the product is the same as its value, and, moreover, surplus-value is distributed under the various headings of profit, interest, rent etc. To us these headings are irrelevant. We simply add them together, and the sum is a surplus-value of £3 11s. 0d. The sum of £3 19s. 0d. paid for seed and manure is constant capital, and we put it equal to zero. There is left the sum of £3 10s. 0d., which is the variable capital advanced, and we see that a new value of £3 10s. 0d. + £3 11s. 0d. has been produced in its place. Therefore $\frac{s}{v} = \frac{£3\ 11s.\ 0d.}{£3\ 10s.\ 0d.}$ i.e. more than 100 per cent. The worker employs more than half his working day in producing the surplus-value, which different persons then share amongst themselves, on different pretexts.

THE REPRESENTATION OF THE VALUE OF THE PRODUCT BY CORRESPONDING PROPORTIONAL PARTS OF THE PRODUCT

Let us now return to the example which showed us how the capitalist converts money into capital. The necessary labour of his spinning worker amounted to 6 hours, surplus labour was the same, the degree of exploitation of labour-power was therefore 100 per cent.

The product of a working day of 12 hours is 20 lb. of yarn, having a value of 30s. No less than eight-tenths of this value, or 24s., is formed by the mere re-appearance in it of the value of the means of production (20 lb. of cotton, value 20s., and the worn part of the spindle, 4s.). In other words, this part consists of constant capital. The remaining two-tenths, or 6s., is the new value created during the spinning process; one half of this replaces the value of the day's labour-power, or the variable capital, the remaining half constitutes a surplus-value of 3s. The total value of the 20 lb. of yarn is thus made up as follows:

30s. value of yarn = 24s.constant + 3s. variable + 3s. surplus.

Since the whole of this value is contained in the 20 lb. of yarn produced, it follows that the various component parts of this value can be represented as being contained respectively in proportional parts of the product.

If the value of 30s. is contained in 20 lb. of yarn, then eight-tenths of this value, or the 24s. that forms its constant part, is contained in eight-tenths of the product, or in 16 lb. of yarn. Of the latter, $13\frac{1}{3}$ lb. represent the value of the raw material, the 20s. worth of cotton spun, and $2\frac{2}{3}$ lb. represent the 4s. worth of spindle etc. worn away in the process.

Hence the whole of the cotton used up in spinning the 20 lb. of yarn is represented by $13\frac{1}{3}$ lb. of yarn. This latter weight of yarn admittedly contains by weight no more than $13\frac{1}{3}$ lb. of cotton, worth $13\frac{1}{3}$s.; but the $6\frac{2}{3}$s. additional value contained in it is the equivalent for the cotton consumed in spinning the remaining $6\frac{2}{3}$ lb. of yarn. The effect is the same as if these $6\frac{2}{3}$ lb. of yarn contained no cotton at all, and the whole 20 lb. of cotton were concentrated in the $13\frac{1}{3}$ lb. of yarn. The latter weight, on the other hand, does not contain an atom of the value of the auxiliary materials and instruments of labour, or of the value newly created in the process.

In the same say, the $2\frac{2}{3}$ lb. of yarn in which the 4s., the remainder of the constant capital, is embodied represent nothing but the value of the auxiliary materials and instruments of labour consumed in producing the 20 lb. of yarn.

We have therefore arrived at this result: although eight-tenths of the product, or 16 lb. of yarn, seen in its physical existence as a use-value, is just as much the fabric of the spinner's labour as the remainder of the same product, yet when viewed in this connection it does not contain and has not absorbed any labour expended during the process of spinning. It is just as if the cotton had converted itself into yarn without any help, it is just as if the shape it had assumed was mere trickery and deceit. In fact, when the capitalist has sold it for 24s. and, with the money, replaced his means of production it becomes evident that the 16 lb. of yarn is nothing more than cotton, spindle-waste and coal in disguise.

On the other hand, the remaining two-tenths of the product, or 4 lb. of yarn, represent nothing but the new value of 6s. created during the 12 hours' spinning process. All the value transferred to those 4 lb. from the raw material and instruments of labour consumed was so to speak intercepted in order to be incorporated in the 16 lb. first spun. In this case, it is as if the spinner had spun

4 lb. of yarn out of air, or as if he had spun it with the aid of cotton and spindles which were available in nature, without human intervention, and therefore transferred no value to the product.

Of this 4 lb. of yarn, in which the whole of the value created in the daily process of spinning is condensed, one half represents the equivalent for the value of the labour consumed, or the 3s. of variable capital, the other half represents the 3s. of surplus-value.

Since 12 hours' labour put in by the spinner are objectified in 6s., it follows that 60 hours' labour are objectified in yarn of the value of 30s. And this quantity of labour-time does in fact exist in the 20 lb. of yarn; for eight-tenths of the yarn, or 16 lb., is a materialization of the 48 hours' labour expended before the beginning of the spinning process on the means of production; the other two-tenths, or 4 lb., is a materialization of the 12 hours' labour expended during the process itself.

... [T]he value of the yarn is equal to the new value created during the production of that yarn plus the value previously existing in the means of production. It has now been shown how the different constitutents of the value of the product, distinguished according to their function or according to their concept, may be represented by corresponding proportional parts of the product itself.

In this way,the product, i.e. the result of the process of production, is split up into different parts, one part representing only the labour previously spent on the means of production, or the constant capital, another part only the necessary labour spent during the process of production, or the variable capital, and another and last part only the surplus labour expended during the process, or the surplus-value. The decomposition of the product is as simple a task as it is important; this will be seen later when we apply it to complex and hitherto unsolved problems.

So far we have treated the total product as the final result, ready for use, of a working day of 12 hours. We can, however, also follow this total product through all the stages of its production; and in this way we shall arrive at the same result as before if we represent the partial products, precipitated at different stages, as functionally distinct parts of the final or total product.

The spinner produces 20 lb. of yarn in 12 hours. Hence he produces $1\frac{2}{3}$ lb. in 1 hour, and $13\frac{1}{3}$ lb. in 8 hours, or a partial product equal in value to all the cotton that is spun in a whole day. Similarly, the partial product of the next period of 1 hour and 36 minutes is $2\frac{2}{3}$ lb. of yarn. This represents the value of the instruments of labour that are consumed in 12 hours. In the following hour and 12 minutes the spinner produces 2 lb. of yarn worth 3s., a value equal to the whole value he creates in his 6 hours of necessary labour. Finally, in the last hour and 12 minutes he produces another 2 lb. of yarn, whose value is equal to the surplus-value created by his surplus labour in the course of half a day. This method of calculation serves the English manufacturer for everyday use; it shows, he will say, that in the first 8 hours, or $\frac{2}{3}$ of the working day, he gets back the value of his cotton; and so on for the remaining hours. It is also a perfectly correct method, since it is in fact the first method given above, only transferred from the spatial sphere, in which the different parts of the completed product lie side by side, to the temporal sphere, in which those parts are produced in succession. But it can also be accompanied by very barbaric notions, especially in the heads of people who are as much interested, practically, in the valorization process, as they are, theoretically, in misunderstanding it. It may be imagined, for instance, that our spinner produces or replaces in the first 8 hours of the working day the value of the cotton, in the following hour and 36 minutes the value of the deterioration in the instruments of labour, in the next hour and 12 minutes the value of his wages, and finally that he devotes only the famous 'last hour' to the production of surplus-value for the factory-owner. In this way the spinner is made to perform the twofold miracle not only of producing cotton, spindles, steam-engine, coal, oil, etc., at the same time as he is using them to spin, but also of turning one working day of a given level of intensity into five similar days. For, in the example we are considering, the production of the raw material and the instruments of labour requires 24 divided by 6 = 4 working days of 12 hours each, and their conversion into yarn requires another such day. That the love of profit induces an easy belief in such miracles, and that there is no lack of sycophantic doctrinaries to prove their existence is demonstrated by the following famous historical example.

SENIOR'S 'LAST HOUR'

One fine morning, in the year 1836, Nassau W. Senior, who may be called the Clauren of the English economists, a man famed both for his economic science and his beautiful style, was summoned from Oxford to Manchester, to learn in the latter place the political economy he taught in the former. The manufacturers chose him as their prize-fighter, not only against the newly passed Factory Act but against the Ten Hours' Agitation which aimed to go beyond it. With their usual practical acuteness they had realized that the learned professor 'wanted a good deal of finishing'; that is why they invited him to Manchester. For his part, the professor has embodied the lecture he received from the Manchester manufacturers in a pamphlet entitled *Letters on the Factory Act, as it Affects the Cotton Manufacture* (London, 1937). Here we find, amongst other things, the following edifying passage:

'Under the present law, no mill in which persons under 18 years of age are employed... can be worked more than $11\frac{1}{2}$ hours a day, that is, 12 hours for 5 days in the week, and 9 on Saturday. Now the following analysis (!) will show that in a mill so worked, the whole net profit is derived from the last hour. I will suppose a manufacturer to invest £100,000—£80,000 in his mill and machinery, and £20,000 in raw material and wages. The annual return of that mill, supposing the capital to be turned once a year, and gross profits to be 15 per cent, ought to be goods worth £115,000... Of this £115,000 each of the twenty-three half-hours of work produces five 115ths, or one 23rd. Of these twenty-three 23rds (constituting the whole £115,000), twenty, that is to say £100,000 out of the £115,000, simply replace the capital; one 23rd (of £5,000 out of the £115,000) makes up for the deterioration of the mill and machinery. The remaining two 23rds, that is the last two of the twenty-three half-hours of every day, produce the net profit of 10 per cent. If, therefore (prices remaining the same), the factory could be kept at work 13 hours instead of $11\frac{1}{2}$, with an addition of about £2,600 to the circulating capital, the net profit would be more than doubled. On the other hand, if the hours of working were reduced by one hour per day (prices remaining the same), the net profit would be destroyed—if they were reduced by one hour and a half, even the gross profit would be destroyed.'

And the professor calls this an 'analysis'! If he believed the outcries of the manufacturers to the effect that the workers spent the best part of the day in the production, i.e. the reproduction or replacement, of the value of the buildings, machinery, cotton, coal, etc., then his analysis was superfluous. His answer could simply have been this: 'Gentlemen! If you work your mills for 10 hours instead of $11\frac{1}{2}$, then, other things being equal, the daily consumption of cotton, machinery etc. will decrease in proportion. You gain just as much as you lose. Your workpeople will in future spend one hour and a half less time in reproducing or replacing the capital advanced.' If, on the other hand, he did not take them at their word but, being an expert in such matters, considered it necessary to undertake an analysis, then he ought, in a question which turns exclusively on the relation of the net profit to the length of the working day, above all to have asked the manufacturers to be careful not to lump together machinery, workshops, raw material and labour, but to be good enough to place the constant capital, invested in buildings, machinery, raw material etc., on one side of the account and the capital advanced in wages on the other side. If it then turned out that, according to the calculations of the manufacturers, the worker reproduced or replaced his wages in 2 half hours, in that case, he should have continued his analysis as follows: 'According to your figures, the workman produces his wages in the last hour but one, and your surplus-value, or net profit, in the last hour. Now, since in equal periods he produces equal values, the product of the last hour but one must have the same value as that of the last hour. Further, it is only while he works that he produces any value at all, and the quantity of work he does is measured by his labour-time. This you say amounts to $11\frac{1}{2}$ hours a day. He employs one portion of these $11\frac{1}{2}$ hours in producing or replacing his wages, and the remaining portion in producing your net profit. Beyond this he does absolutely nothing. But since, on your assumption, his wages and the surplus-value he provides are of equal value, it is clear that he produces his wages in $5\frac{3}{4}$ hours, and your net profit in the other $5\frac{3}{4}$ hours. Again, since the value of the yarn produced in 2 hours is equal to the sum of the value of his wages and of your net profit, the measure of the value of this yarn must be $11\frac{1}{2}$ working hours, of which $5\frac{3}{4}$ hours measure the value of the yarn produced in the last hour but one, and $5\frac{3}{4}$ hours the value of the yarn produced in the last hour of all. We now come to a ticklish point, so watch out! The last working hour but one is, like the first, an ordinary working hour, neither more nor less. How then can the spinner produce in one hour, in the shape of yarn, a value that embodies $5\frac{3}{4}$ hours' labour? The truth is that he does not perform any such miracle. The use-value produced by him in one hour is a definite quantity of yarn. The value of this yarn is measured by $5\frac{3}{4}$

working hours, of which $4\frac{3}{4}$ were, without any assistance from him, previously embodied in the means of production, in the cotton, the machinery, and so on; the remaining one hour alone is added by him. Therefore, since his wages are produced in $5\frac{3}{4}$ hours, and the yarn produced in one hour also contains $5\frac{3}{4}$ hours' work, there is no witchcraft in the result that the value created by his $5\frac{3}{4}$ hours of spinning is equal to the value of the product spun in one hour. You are altogether on the wrong track, if you think that he loses a single moment of his working day in reproducing or replacing the values of the cotton, the machinery and so on. On the contrary, it is because his labour converts the cotton and the spindles into yarn, because he spins, that the values of the cotton and spindles go over to the yarn of their own accord. This is a result of the quality of his labour, not its quantity. It is true that he will transfer to the yarn more value, in the shape of cotton, in one hour than he will in half an hour. But that is only because in one hour he spins up more cotton than in half an hour. You see then that your assertion that the workman produces, in the last hour but one, the value of his wages, and in the last hour your net profit, amounts to no more than this, that in the yarn produced by him in 2 working hours, whether they are the 2 first or the 2 last hours of the working day, there are incorporated $11\frac{1}{2}$ working hours, i.e. precisely as many hours as there are in his working day. And my assertion that in the first $5\frac{3}{4}$ hours he produces his wages, and in the last $5\frac{3}{4}$ hours your net profit, amounts only to this, that you pay him for the former, but not for the latter. In speaking of payment of labour, instead of payment of labour-power, I am only using your own slang expression. Now gentlemen, if you compare the working time you pay for with the working time you do not pay for, you will find that they are related to each other as half a day is to half a day; this gives a rate of 100 per cent, and a very pretty percentage it is. Further, there is not the least doubt that if you make your "hands" toil for 13 hours instead of $11\frac{1}{2}$, and as may be expected from you, if you treat the work done in that extra one hour and a half as pure surplus labour, then the latter will be increased from $5\frac{3}{4}$ hours' labour to $7\frac{1}{4}$ hours' labour, and the rate of surplus-value will go up from 100 per cent to $126\frac{2}{23}$ per cent. So that you are altogether too sanguine in expecting that by such an addition of $1\frac{1}{2}$ hours to the working day the rate will rise from 100 per cent to 200 per cent and more, in other words that it will be "more than doubled". On the other hand—the heart of man is a wonderful thing, especially when it is carried in his wallet—you take too pessimistic a view when you fear that a reduction of the hours of labour from $11\frac{1}{2}$ to 10 will sweep away the whole of your net profit. Not at all. All other conditions remaining the same, the surplus labour will fall from $5\frac{3}{4}$ hours to $4\frac{3}{4}$ hours, a period that still gives a very profitable rate of surplus-value, namely $82\frac{14}{23}$ per cent. But this fateful "last hour" about which you have invented more stories than the millenarians about the Day of Judgement, is "all bosh". If it goes, it will not coast you your "pure profit", nor will it cost the boys and girls you employ their "pure minds". Whenever your "last hour" strikes in earnest, think of the Oxford professor. And now, gentlemen, farewell, and may we meet again in a better world, but not before.' ... The battle-cry of the 'last hour', invented by Senior in 1836, was raised once again in the London *Economist* of 15 April 1848 by James Wilson, an economic mandarin of high standing, in a polemic against the Ten Hours' Bill.

THE SURPLUS PRODUCT

We call the portion of the product that represents surplus-value (i.e. one-tenth of the 20 lb., or 2 lb. of yarn, in the example given above) by the name of 'surplus product' (*Mehrprodukt, produit net*). Just as the rate of surplus-value is determined by its relation, not to the sum total of the capital, but to its variable part, in the same way, the relative amount of the surplus product is determined by its ratio, not to the remaining part of the total product, but to that part of it in which necessary labour is incorporated. Since the production of surplus-value is the determining purpose of capitalist production, the size of a given quantity of wealth must be measured, not by the absolute quantity produced, but by the relative magnitude of the surplus product.

The sum of the necessary labour and the surplus labour, i.e. the sum of the periods of time during which the worker respectively replaces the value of his labour-power and produces the surplus-value, constitutes the absolute extent of his labour-time, i.e. the working day.

NOTES

1. Exponents of the view that the relations of production within bourgeois society are inherently harmonious, and that the antagonisms described by the classical political economists are superficial and accidential rather than intrinsic to the system. Marx devoted a section of the *Grundrisse* (English edition, pp. 883–93) to a critique of the 'harmonizers'.

4.2 FRIEDRICH ENGELS

Barbarism and Civilization

Friedrich Engels (1820–1895) was born in Barmen, the Rhine Province of the Kingdom of Prussia. In 1838, he was forced by family circumstances to enter a commercial house in Bremen as a clerk. In 1842, Engels moved to Manchester, England. Shortly after, he started corresponding with Karl Marx, meeting him for the first time in 1842. From 1845 to 1847 Engels lived in Brussels, Belgium, and Paris, France, combining scientific work with practical activities among the German workers there. After Marx's death in 1883, Engels continued his work on *Das Kapital* and completed it in 1894. He continued to popularize Marx's views, arranging new editions of his works and routinely defending them, while acting as an adviser to several socialist parties.

In 1845, Engels wrote *The Condition of the Working Class in England,* which described the deep poverty in which the proletariat was mired and the need for emancipation. It was a terrible indictment of capitalism and the bourgeoisie. *The Communist Property and the State* (1884) researched the lines of human progress from barbarism to civilization. His other work included *The Peasant War in Germany,* which exhorted peasants to be mindful of their revolutionary traditions by rising up in revolt. In the following excerpt from *The Origin of the Family, Private Property and the State* (1884), Engels makes the case for a return to a more barbaric form of existence, in which workers own the means of production, by tracing the development of man from his most primitive state to that of modern civilization.

Key Concept: barbarism and civilization

[After tracing] the dissolution of the gentile constitution in the three great instances of the Greeks, the Romans, and the Germans,... let us examine the general economic conditions which already undermined the gentile organization of society at the upper stage of barbarism and with the coming of civilization overthrew it completely....

Arising in the middle stage of savagery, further developed during its upper stage, the gens [a group of actual and fictive kinsmen related through one parental line only] reaches its most flourishing period, so far as our sources enable us to judge, during the lower stage of barbarism. We begin therefore with this stage.

Here—the American Indians must serve as our example—we find the gentile constitution fully formed. The tribe is now grouped in several gentes [kinship organizations], generally two. With the increase in population, each of these original gentes splits up into several daughter gentes, their mother gens now appearing as the phratry [brotherhood]. The tribe itself breaks up into several tribes, in each of which we find again, for the most part, the old gentes. The related tribes, at least in some cases, are united in a confederacy. This simple organization suffices completely for the social conditions out of which it sprang. It is nothing more than the grouping natural to those conditions, and it is capable of settling all conflicts that can arise within a society so organized. War settles external conflicts; it may end with the annihilation of the tribe but never with its subjugation. It is the greatness but also the limitation of the gentile constitution that it has no place for ruler and ruled. Within the tribe there is as yet no difference between rights and duties; the question whether participation in public affairs, in blood revenge or atonement, is a right or a duty, does not exist for the Indian; it would seem to him just as absurd as the question whether it was a right or a duty to sleep, eat, or hunt. A division of the tribe or of the gens into different classes was equally impossible. And that brings us to the examination of the economic basis of these conditions.

The population is extremely sparse; it is dense only at the tribe's place of settlement, around which lie in a wide circle first the hunting grounds and then the protective belt of neutral forest which separates the tribe from others. The division of labour is purely primitive, between the sexes only. The man fights in the wars, goes hunting and fishing, procures the raw materials of food and the tools necessary for doing so. The woman looks after the house and the preparation of food and clothing, cooks, weaves, sews. They are each master in their own sphere: the man in the forest, the woman in the house. Each is owner of the instruments which he or she makes and uses: the man of the weapons, the hunting and fishing implements; the woman of the household gear. The housekeeping is communal among several and often many families. What is made and used in common is common property—the house, the garden, the long boat. Here therefore, and here alone, there still exists in actual fact that 'property created by the owner's labour' which in civilized society is an ideal fiction of the jurists and economists, the last lying legal pretense by which modern capitalist property still bolsters itself up.

But humanity did not everywhere remain at this stage. In Asia they found animals which could be tamed and, when once tamed, bred. The wild buffalo cow had to be hunted; the tame buffalo cow gave a calf yearly and milk as well. A number of the most advanced tribes—the Aryans, Semites, perhaps already also the Turanians—now made their chief work first the taming of cattle, later their breeding and tending only. Pastoral tribes separated themselves from the mass of the rest of the barbarians—*the first great social division of labour.* The pastoral tribes produced not only more necessities of life than the other barbarians, but different ones. They possessed the advantage over them of having not only milk, milk products and greater supplies of meat, but also skins, wool, goat hair, and spun and woven fabrics, which became more common as the amount of raw material increased. Thus for the first time regular exchange became possible. At the earlier stages only occasional exchanges can take place; particular skill in the making of weapons and tools may lead to a temporary division of labour. Thus in many places undoubted remains of workshops for the making of stone tools have been found dating from the later Stone Age. The artists who here perfected their skill probably worked for the whole community, as each special handicraftsman still does in the gentile communities in India. In no case could exchange arise at this stage except within the tribe itself, and then only as an exceptional event. But now, with the differentiation of pastoral tribes, we find all the conditions ripe for exchange between branches of different tribes and its development into a regular established institution. Originally tribe exchanged with tribe through the respective chiefs of the gentes; but as the herds began to pass into private ownership, exchange between individuals became more common, and, finally, the only form. Now the chief article which the pastoral tribes exchanged with their neighbors was cattle; cattle became the commodity by which all other commodities were valued and which was everywhere willingly taken in exchange for them—in short, cattle acquired a money function and already at this stage did the work of money. With such necessity and speed, even at the very beginning of commodity exchange, did the need for a money commodity develop.

Horticulture, probably unknown to Asiatic barbarians of the lower stage, was being practised by them in the middle stage at the latest, as the forerunner of agriculture. In the climate of the Turanian plateau, pastoral life is impossible without supplies of fodder for the long and severe winter. Here, therefore, it was essential that land should be put under grass and corn cultivated. The same is true of the steppes north of the Black Sea. But when once corn had been grown for the cattle, it also soon became food for men. The cultivated land still remained tribal property; at first it was allotted to the gens, later by the gens to the household communities and finally to individuals for use. The users may have had certain rights of possession, but nothing more.

Of the industrial achievements of this stage, two are particularly important. The first is the loom, the second the smelting of metal ores and the working of metals. Copper and tin and their alloy, bronze, were by far the most important. Bronze provided serviceable tools and weapons though it could not displace stone tools; only iron could do that, and the method of obtaining iron was not yet understood. Gold and silver were beginning to be used for ornament and decoration and must already have acquired a high value as compared with copper and bronze.

The increase of production in all branches—cattle raising, agriculture, domestic handicrafts—gave human labour-power the capacity to produce a larger product than was necessary for its maintenance. At the same time it increased the daily amount of work to be done by each member of the gens, household community or single family. It was now desirable to bring in new labour forces. War provided them; prisoners of war were turned into slaves. With its increase of the productivity of labour, and therefore of wealth, and its extension of the field of production, the first great social division of labour was bound, in the general historical conditions prevailing, to bring slavery in its train. From the first great social division of labour arose the first great cleavage of society into two classes: masters and slaves, exploiters and exploited.

As to how and when the herds passed out of the common possession of the tribe or the gens into the ownership of individual heads of families, we know nothing at present. But in the main it must have occurred during this stage. With the herds and the other new riches, a revolution came over the family. To procure the necessities of life had always been the business of the man; he produced and owned the means of doing so. The herds were the new means of producing these necessities; the taming of the animals in the first instance and their later tending were the man's work. To him, therefore, belonged the cattle, and to him the commodities and the slaves received in exchange for cattle. All the surplus which the acquisition of the necessities of life now yielded fell to the man; the woman shared in its enjoyment, but had no part in its ownership. The 'savage' warrior and hunter had been content to take second place in the house, after the woman; the 'gentler' shepherd, in the arrogance of his wealth, pushed himself forward into the first place and the woman down into the second. And she could not complain. The division of labour within the family had regulated the division of property between the man and the woman. That division of labour had remained the same; and yet it now turned the previous domestic relation upside down simply because the division of labour outside the family had changed. The same cause which had ensured to the woman her previous supremacy in the house—that her activity was confined to domestic labour—this same cause now ensured the man's supremacy in the house. The domestic labour of the woman no longer counted beside the acquisition of the necessities of life by the man; the latter was everything, the former an unimportant extra. We can already see from this that to emancipate woman and make her the equal of the man is and remains an impossibility so long as the woman is shut out from social productive labour and restricted to private domestic labour. The emancipation of woman will only be possible when woman can take part in production on a large, social scale, and domestic work no longer claims anything but an insignificant amount of her time. And only now has that become possible through modern large-scale industry, which does not merely permit the employment of female labour over a wide range, but positively demands it, while it also tends towards ending private domestic labour by changing it more and more into a public industry.

The man now being actually supreme in the house, the last barrier to his absolute supremacy had fallen. This autocracy was confirmed and perpetuated by the overthrow of mother right, the introduction of father right, and the gradual transition of the pairing marriage into monogamy. But this tore a breach in the old gentile order; the single family became a power, and its rise was a menace to the gens.

The next step leads us to the upper stage of barbarism, the period when all civilized peoples have their heroic age: the age of the iron sword, but also of the iron ploughshare and axe. Iron was now at the service of man, the last and most important of all the raw materials which played a historically revolutionary role—until the potato. Iron brought about the tillage of large areas, the clearing of wide tracts of virgin forest; iron gave to the handicraftsman tools so hard and sharp that no stone, no other known metal, could resist them. All this came gradually; the first iron was often even softer than bronze. Hence stone weapons only disappeared slowly; not merely in the *Hildebrandslied,* but even as late as the battle of Hastings in 1066, stone axes were still used for fighting. But progress could not now be stopped; it went forward with fewer checks and greater speed. The town, with its houses of stone or brick encircled by stone walls, towers and ramparts, became the central seat of the tribe or the confederacy of tribes—an enormous architectural advance, but also a sign of growing danger and need for protection. Wealth increased rapidly, but as the wealth of individuals. The products of weaving, metalwork and the other handicrafts, which were becoming more and more differentiated, displayed growing variety and skill. In addition to corn, leguminous plants and fruits, agriculture now provided wine and oil, the preparation of which had been learned. Such manifold activities were no longer within the scope of one and the same individual; the *second great division of labour* took place—handicraft separated from agriculture. The continuous increase of production and simultaneously of the productivity of labour heightened the value of human labour power. Slavery, which during the preceding period was still in its beginnings and sporadic, now becomes an essential constituent part of the social system; slaves no longer merely help with production—they are driven by dozens to work in the fields and the workshops. With the splitting up of production into the two great main branches, agriculture and handicrafts, arises production directly for exchange, commodity production; with it came commerce, not only in the interior and on the tribal boundaries, but also already overseas. All this, however, was still very undeveloped; the precious metals were beginning to be the predominant and general money commodity, but still uncoined, exchanging simply by their naked weight.

The distinction of rich and poor appears beside that of freemen and slaves —with the new division of labour, a new cleavage of society into classes. The inequalities of property among the individual heads of families break up the old communal household communities wherever they had still managed to survive, and with them the common cultivation of the soil by and for these communities. The cultivated land is allotted for use to single families, at first temporarily, later permanently. The transition to full private property is gradually accomplished, parallel with the transition of the pairing marriage into monogamy. The single family is becoming the economic unit of society.

The denser population necessitates closer consolidation both for internal and external action. The confederacy of related tribes becomes everywhere a necessity, and soon also their fusion, involving the fusion of the separate tribal territories into one territory of the nation. The military leader of the people—*rex, basileus, thiudans*—becomes an indispensable, permanent official. The assembly of the people takes form wherever it did not already exist. Military leader, council, assembly of the people are the organs of gentile society developed into military democracy—military, since war and organization for war have now become regular functions of national life. Their neighbours' wealth excites the greed of peoples who already see in the acquisition of wealth one of the main aims of life. They are barbarians: they think it easier and in fact more honourable to get riches by pillage than by work. War, formerly waged only in revenge for injuries or to extend territory that had grown too small, is now waged simply for plunder and becomes a regular industry. Not without reason the bristling battlements stand menacingly about the new fortified towns; in the moat at their foot yawns the grave of the gentile constitution, and already they rear their towers into civilization. Similarly in the interior, the wars of plunder increase the power of the supreme military leader and the subordinate commanders; the customary election of their successors from the same families is gradually transformed, especially after the introduction of father right, into a right of hereditary succession, first tolerated, then claimed, finally usurped; the foundation of the hereditary monarchy and the hereditary nobility is laid. Thus the organs of the gentile constitution gradually tear themselves loose from their roots in the people, in gens, phratry, tribe, and the whole gentile constitution changes into its opposite: from an organization of tribes for the free ordering of their own affairs it becomes an organization for the plundering and oppression of their neighbours; and correspondingly its organs change from instruments of the will of the people into independent organs for the domination and oppression of the people. That, however, would never have been possible if the greed for riches had not split the members of the gens into rich and poor, if 'the property differences within one and the same gens had not transformed its unity of interest into antagonism between its members' (Marx), if the extension of slavery had not already begun to make working for a living seem fit only for slaves and more dishonourable than pillage.

We have now reached the threshold of civilization. Civilization opens with a new advance in the division of labour. At the lowest stage of barbarism men produced only directly for their own needs; any acts of exchange were isolated occurrences, the object of exchange merely some fortuitous surplus. In the middle stage of barbarism we already find among the pastoral peoples a possession in the form of cattle which, once the herd has attained a certain size, regularly produces a surplus over and above the tribe's own requirements, leading to a division of labour between pastoral peoples and backward tribes without herds, and hence to the existence of two different levels of production side by side with one another and the conditions necessary for regular exchange. The upper stage of barbarism brings us the further division of labour between agriculture and handicrafts, hence the production of a continually increasing portion of the products of labour directly for exchange, so that exchange between individual producers assumes the importance of a vital social function. Civilization consolidates and intensifies all these existing divisions of labour, particularly by sharpening the opposition between town and country (the town may economically dominate the country, as in antiquity, or the country the town, as in the Middle Ages), and it adds a third division of labour, peculiar to itself and of decisive importance. It creates a class which no longer concerns itself with production, but only with the exchange of the products—the *merchants*. Hitherto whenever classes had begun to form, it had always been exclusively in the field of production; the persons engaged in production were separated into those who directed and those who executed or else into large-scale and small-scale producers. Now for the first time a class appears which, without in any way participating in production, captures the direction of production as a whole and economically subjugates the producers; which makes itself into an indispensable middleman between any two producers and exploits them both. Under the pretext that they save the producers the trouble and risk of exchange, extend the sale of their products to distant markets and are therefore the most useful class of the population, a class of parasites comes into being, genuine social sycophants, who, as a reward for their actually very insignificant services, skim all the cream off production at home and abroad, rapidly amass enormous wealth and correspondingly social influence, and for that reason receive under civilization ever higher honours and ever greater control of production until at last they also bring forth a product of their own—the periodical trade crises.

At our stage of development, however, the young merchants had not even begun to dream of the great destiny awaiting them. But they were growing and making themselves indispensable, which was quite sufficient. And with the formation of the merchant class came also the development of *metallic money,* the minted coin, a new instrument for the domination of the non-producer over the producer and his production. The commodity of commodities had been discovered, that which holds all other commodities hidden in itself, the magic power which can change at will into everything desirable and desired. The man who had it ruled the world of production, and who had more of it than anybody else?—the merchant. The worship of money was safe in his hands. He took good care to make it clear that, in face of money, all commodities and hence all producers of commodities must prostrate themselves in adoration in the dust. He proved practically that all other forms of wealth fade into mere semblance beside this incarnation of wealth as such. Never again has the power of money shown itself in such primitive brutality and violence as during these days of its youth. After commodities had begun to sell for money, loans and advances in money came also, and with them interest and usury. No legislation of later times so utterly and ruthlessly delivers over the debtor to the usurious creditor as the legislation of ancient Athens and ancient Rome—and in both cities it arose spontaneously as customary law without any compulsion other than the economic.

Alongside wealth in commodities and slaves, alongside wealth in money, there now appeared wealth in land also. The individuals' rights of possession in the pieces of land originally allotted to them by gens or tribe had now become so established that the land was their hereditary property. Recently they had striven above all to secure their freedom against the rights of the gentile community over these lands since these rights had become for them a fetter. They got rid of the fetter—but soon afterwards of their new landed property also. Full, free ownership of the land meant not only power, uncurtailed and unlimited, to possess the land; it meant also the power to alienate it. As long as the land belonged to the gens, no such power could exist. But when the new landed proprietor shook off once and for all the fetters laid upon him by the prior right of gens and tribe, he also cut the ties which had hitherto inseparably attached him to the land. Money, invented at the same time as private property in land, showed him what that meant. Land could now become a commodity; it could be sold and pledged. Scarcely had private property in land been introduced than the mortgage was already invented. As hetaerism and prostitution dog the heels of monogamy, so from now onward mortgage dogs the heels of private land ownership. You asked for full, free alienable ownership of the land and now you have got it—*'tu l'as voulu, Georges Dandin.'*

With trade expansion, money and usury, private property in land and mortgages, the concentration and centralization of wealth in the hands of a small class rapidly advanced, accompanied by an increasing impoverishment of the masses and an increasing mass of impoverishment. The new aristocracy of wealth, in so far as it had not been identical from the outset with the old hereditary aristocracy, pushed it permanently into the background (in Athens, in Rome, among the Germans). And simultaneous with this division of the citizens into classes according to wealth, there was an enormous increase, particularly in Greece, in the number of slaves whose forced labour was the foundation on which the superstructure of the entire society was reared.

Let us now see what had become of the gentile constitution in this social upheaval. Confronted by the new forces in whose growth it had had no share, the gentile constitution was helpless. The necessary condition for its existence was that the members of a gens or at least of a tribe were settled together in the same territory and were its sole inhabitants. That had long ceased to be the case. Every territory now had a heterogeneous population belonging to the most varied gentes and tribes; everywhere slaves, protected persons and aliens lived side by side with citizens. The settled conditions of life which had only been achieved towards the end of the middle stage of barbarism were broken up by the repeated shifting and changing of residence under the pressure of trade, alteration of occupation and changes in the ownership of the land. The members of the gentile bodies could no longer meet to look after their common concerns; only unimportant matters, like the religious festivals, were still perfunctorily attended to. In addition to the needs and interests with which the gentile bodies were intended and fitted to deal, the upheaval in productive relations and the resulting change in the social structure had given rise to new needs and interests, which were not only alien to the old gentile order, but ran directly counter to it at every point. The interests of the groups of handicraftsmen which had arisen with the division of labour, the special needs of the town as opposed to the country, called for new organs. But each of these groups was composed of people of the most diverse gentes, phratries, and tribes, and even included aliens. Such organs had therefore to be formed outside the gentile constitution, alongside of it, and hence in opposition to it. And this conflict of interests was at work within every gentile body, appearing in its most extreme form in the association of rich and poor, usurers and debtors, in the same gens and the same tribe. Further, there was the new mass of population outside the gentile bodies, which, as in Rome, was able to become a power in the land and at the same time was too numerous to be gradually absorbed into the kinship groups and tribes. In relation to this mass, the gentile bodies stood opposed as closed, privileged corporations; the primitive natural democracy had changed into a malign aristocracy. Lastly, the gentile constitution had grown out of a society which knew no internal contradictions, and it was only adapted to such a society. It possessed no means of coercion except public opinion. But here was a society which by all its economic conditions of life had been forced to split itself into freemen and slaves, into the exploiting rich and the exploited poor; a society which not only could never again reconcile these contradictions, but was compelled always to intensify them. Such a society could only exist either in the continuous open fight of these classes against one another or else under the rule of a third power, which, apparently standing above the warring classes, suppressed their open conflict and allowed the class struggle to be fought out at most in the economic field, in so-called legal form. The gentile constitution was finished. It had been shattered by the division of labour and its result, the cleavage of society into classes. It was replaced by the *state*.

The three main forms in which the state arises on the ruins of the gentile constitution have been examined in detail above. Athens provides the purest, classic form; here the state springs directly and mainly out of the class oppositions which develop within gentile society itself. In Rome, gentile society becomes a closed aristocracy in the midst of the numerous *plebs* who stand outside it and have duties but no rights; the victory of *plebs* breaks up the old constitution based on kinship and erects on its ruins the state, into which both the gentile aristocracy and the *plebs* are soon completely absorbed. Lastly, in the case of the German conquerors of the Roman Empire, the state springs directly out of the conquest of large foreign territories which the gentile constitution provides no means of governing. But because this conquest involves neither a serious struggle with the original population nor a more advanced division of labour; because conquerors and conquered are almost on the same level of economic development, and the economic basis of society remains therefore as before—for these reasons the gentile constitution is able to survive for many centuries in the altered, territorial form of the mark constitution and even for a time to rejuvenate itself in a feebler shape in the later noble and patrician families, and indeed in peasant families. . . .

The state is therefore by no means a power imposed on society from without; just as little is it 'the reality of the moral idea', 'the image and the reality of reason'. . . . Rather, it is a product of society at a particular stage of development; it is the admission that this society has involved itself in insoluble self-contradiction and is cleft into irreconcilable antagonisms which it is powerless to exorcise. But in order that these antagonisms, classes with conflicting economic interests, shall not consume themselves and society in fruitless struggle, a power, apparently standing above society, has become necessary to moderate the conflict and keep it within the bounds of 'order'; and this power, arisen out of society but placing itself above it and increasingly alienating itself from it, is the state.

In contrast to the old gentile organization, the state is distinguished firstly by the grouping of its members *on a territorial basis*. The old gentile bodies, formed and held together by ties of blood had, as we have seen, become inadequate largely because they presupposed that the gentile members were bound to one particular locality, whereas this had long ago ceased to be the case. The territory was still there, but the people had become mobile. The territorial division was therefore taken as the starting point and the system introduced by which citizens exercised their public rights and duties where they took up residence, without regard to gens or tribe. This organization of the citizens of the state according to domicile is common to all states. To us, therefore, this organization seems natural; but, as we have seen, hard and protracted struggles were necessary before it was able in Athens and Rome to displace the old organization founded on kinship.

The second distinguishing characteristic is the institution of a *public force* which is no longer immediately identical with the people's own organization of themselves as an armed power. This special public force is needed because a self-acting armed organization of the people has become impossible since their cleavage into classes. The slaves also belong to the population; as against the 365,000 slaves, the 90,000 Athenian citizens constitute only a privileged class.

The people's army of the Athenian democracy confronted the slaves as an aristocratic public force and kept them in check; but to keep the citizens in check as well, a police force was needed as described above. This public force exists in every state; it consists not merely of armed men but also of material appendages, prisons and coercive institutions of all kinds, of which gentile society knew nothing. It may be very insignificant, practically negligible, in societies with still undeveloped class antagonisms and living in remote areas, as at times and in places in the United States of America. But it becomes stronger in proportion as the class antagonisms within the state become sharper and as adjoining states grow larger and more populous. It is enough to look at Europe today, where class struggle and rivalry in conquest have brought the public power to such a pitch that it threatens to devour the whole of society and even the state itself.

In order to maintain this public power, contributions from the state citizens are necessary—*taxes*. These were completely unknown to gentile society. We know more than enough about them today. With advancing civilization, even taxes are not sufficient; the state draws drafts on the future, contracts loans —*state debts*. Our old Europe can tell a tale about these, too.

In possession of the public power and the right of taxation, the officials now present themselves as organs of society standing *above* society. The free, willing respect accorded to the organs of the gentile constitution is not enough for them, even if they could have it. Representatives of a power which estranges them from society, they have to be given prestige by means of special decrees which invest them with a peculiar sanctity and inviolability. The lowest police officer of the civilized state has more 'authority' than all the organs of gentile society put together; but the mightiest prince and the greatest statesman or general of civilization might envy the humblest of the gentile chiefs the unforced and unquestioned respect accorded to him. For the one stands in the midst of society; the other is forced to pose as something outside and above it.

As the state arose from the need to keep class antagonisms in check, but also arose in the thick of the fight between the classes, it is normally the state of the most powerful, economically dominant class, which by its means becomes also the politically dominant class and so acquires new means of holding down and exploiting the oppressed class. The ancient state was, above all, the state of the slave owners for holding down the slaves, just as the feudal state was the organ of the nobility for holding down the peasant serfs and bondsmen, and the modern representative state is the instrument for exploiting wage labour by capital. Exceptional periods, however, occur when the warring classes are so nearly equal in forces that the state power, as apparent mediator, acquires for the moment a certain independence in relation to both. This applies to the absolute monarchy of the seventeenth and eighteenth centuries, which balanced the nobility and the bourgeoisie against one another; and to the Bonapartism of the First and particularly of the Second French Empire, which played off the proletariat against the bourgeoisie and the bourgeoisie against the proletariat. The latest achievement in this line, in which ruler and ruled look equally comic, is the new German Empire of the Bismarckian nation; here the capitalists and the workers are balanced against one another and both of them fleeced for the benefit of the decayed Prussian cabbage Junkers [a class of aristocrats who dominated Germany from the Middle Ages through the end of the nineteenth century].

Further, in most historical states the rights conceded to citizens are graded on a property basis whereby it is directly admitted that the state is an organization for the protection of the possessing class against the non-possessing class. This is already the case in the Athenian and Roman property classes; similarly in the medieval feudal state in which the extent of political power was determined by the extent of land-ownership; similarly, also, in the electoral qualifications in modern parliamentary states. This political recognition of property differences is, however, by no means essential. On the contrary, it marks a low stage in the development of the state. The highest form of the state, the democratic republic, which in our modern social conditions becomes more and more an unavoidable necessity and is the form of state in which alone the last decisive battle between proletariat and bourgeoisie can be fought out—the democratic republic no longer officially recognizes differences of property. Wealth here employs its power indirectly, but all the more surely. It does this in two ways: by plain corruption of officials, of which America is the classic example; and by an alliance between the government and the stock exchange, which is effected all the more easily the higher the state debt mounts and the more the joint-stock companies concentrate in their hands not only transport but also production itself, and themselves have their own centre in the stock exchange. In addition to America, the latest French republic illustrates this strikingly, and honest little Switzerland has also given a creditable performance in this field. But that a democratic republic is not essential to this brotherly bond between government and stock exchange is proved not only by England but also by the new German Empire, where it is difficult to say who scored most by the introduction of universal suffrage, Bismarck or the Bleichröder bank. And lastly the possessing class rules directly by means of universal suffrage. As long as the oppressed class—in our case, therefore, the proletariat—is not yet ripe for its self-liberation, so long will it in its majority recognize the existing order of society as the only possible one and remain politically the tail of the capitalist class, its extreme left wing. But in the measure in which it matures towards its self-emancipation, in the same measure it constitutes itself as its own party and votes for its own representatives, not those of the capitalists. Universal suffrage is thus the gauge of the maturity of the working class. It cannot and never will be anything more in the modern state; but that is enough. On the day when the thermometer of universal suffrage shows boiling point among the workers, they as well as the capitalists will know where they stand.

The state, therefore, has not existed from all eternity. There have been societies which have managed without it, which had no notion of the state or state power. At a definite stage of economic development, which necessarily involved the cleavage of society into classes, the state became a necessity because of this cleavage. We are now rapidly approaching a stage in the development of production at which the existence of these classes has not only ceased to be a necessity but becomes a positive hindrance to production. They will fall as inevitably as they once arose. The state inevitably falls with them. The society which organizes production anew on the basis of free and equal association of the producers will put the whole state machinery where it will then belong—into the museum of antiquities, next to the spinning wheel and the bronze axe.

Civilization is, therefore, according to the above analysis, the stage of development in society at which the division of labour, the exchange between individuals arising from it, and the commodity production which combines them both come to their full growth and revolutionize the whole of previous society.

At all earlier stages of society, production was essentially collective, just as consumption proceeded by direct distribution of the products within larger or smaller communistic communities. This collective production was very limited; but inherent in it was the producers' control over their process of production and their product. They knew what became of their product: they consumed it; it did not leave their hands. And so long as production remains on this basis, it cannot grow above the heads of the producers nor raise up incorporeal alien powers against them, as in civilization is always and inevitably the case.

But the division of labour slowly insinuates itself into this process of production. It undermines the collectivity of production and appropriation, elevates appropriation by individuals into the general rule, and thus creates exchange between individuals—how it does so, we have examined above. Gradually commodity production becomes the dominating form.

With commodity production, production no longer for use by the producers but for exchange, the products necessarily change hands. In exchanging his product, the producer surrenders it; he no longer knows what becomes of it. When money, and with money the merchant, steps in as intermediary between the producers, the process of exchange becomes still more complicated, the final fate of the products still more uncertain. The merchants are numerous, and none of them knows what the other is doing. The commodities already pass not only from hand to hand; they also pass from market to market; the producers have lost control over the total production within their own spheres, and the merchants have not gained it. Products and production become subjects of chance.

But chance is only the one pole of a relation whose other pole is named 'necessity'. In the world of nature, where chance also seems to rule, we have long since demonstrated in each separate field the inner necessity and law asserting itself in this chance. But what is true of the natural world is true also of society. The more a social activity, a series of social processes, becomes too powerful for men's conscious control and grows above their heads, and the more it appears a matter of pure chance, then all the more surely within this chance the laws peculiar to it and inherent in it assert themselves as if by natural necessity. Such laws also govern the chances of commodity production and exchange. To the individuals producing or exchanging, they appear as alien, at first often unrecognized, powers, whose nature must first be labouriously investigated and established. These economic laws of commodity production are modified with the various stages of this form of production; but in general the whole period of civilization is dominated by them. And still to this day the product rules the producer; still to this day the total production of society is regulated, not by a jointly devised plan, but by blind laws, which manifest themselves with elemental violence in the final instance in the storms of the periodical trade crises.

We saw above how at a fairly early stage in the development of production, human labour power obtains the capacity of producing a considerably greater product than is required for the maintenance of the producers, and how this stage of development was in the main the same as that in which division of labour and exchange between individuals arise. It was not long then before the great 'truth' was discovered that man also can be a commodity, that human energy can be exchanged and put to use by making a man into a slave. Hardly had men begun to exchange than already they themselves were being exchanged. The active became the passive, whether the men liked it or not.

With slavery, which attained its fullest development under civilization, came the first great cleavage of society into an exploiting and an exploited class. This cleavage persisted during the whole civilized period. Slavery is the first form of exploitation, the form peculiar to the ancient world; it is succeeded by serfdom in the Middle Ages, and wage labour in the more recent period. These are the three great forms of servitude characteristic of the three great epochs of civilization; open, and in recent times disguised, slavery always accompanies them.

The stage of commodity production with which civilization begins is distinguished economically by the introduction of (1) metal money and with it money capital, interest and usury, (2) merchants, as the class of intermediaries between the producers, (3) private ownership of land and the mortgage system, (4) slave labour as the dominant form of production. The form of family corresponding to civilization and coming to definite supremacy with it is monogamy, the domination of the man over the woman and the single family as the economic unit of society. The central link in civilized society is the state, which in all typical periods is without exception the state of the ruling class and in all cases continues to be essentially a machine for holding down the oppressed, exploited class. Also characteristic of civilization is the establishment of a permanent opposition between town and country as the basis of the whole social division of labour; and further, the introduction of wills whereby the owner of property is still able to dispose over it even when he is dead. This institution, which is a direct affront to the old gentile constitution, was unknown in Athens until the time of Solon; in Rome it was introduced early, though we do not know the date; among the Germans it was the clerics who introduced it in order that there might be nothing to stop the pious German from leaving his legacy to the Church.

With this as its basic constitution, civilization achieved things of which gentile society was not even remotely capable. But it achieved them by setting in motion the lowest instincts and passions in man and developing them at the expense of all his other abilities. From its first day to this, sheer greed was the driving spirit of civilization; wealth and again wealth and once more wealth, wealth, not of society but of the single scurvy individual—here was its one and final aim. If at the same time the progressive development of science and a repeated flowering of supreme art dropped into its lap, it was only because without them modern wealth could not have completely realized its achievements.

Since civilization is founded on the exploitation of one class by another class, its whole development proceeds in a constant contradiction. Every step forward in production is at the same time a step backwards in the position of the oppressed class, that is, of the great majority. Whatever benefits some necessarily injures the others; every fresh emancipation of one class is necessarily a new oppression for another class. The most striking proof of this is provided by the introduction of machinery, the effects of which are now known to the whole world. And if among the barbarians, as we saw, the distinction between rights and duties could hardly be drawn, civilization makes the difference and antagonism between them clear even to the dullest intelligence by giving one class practically all the rights and the other class practically all the duties.

But that should not be: what is good for the ruling class must also be good for the whole of society with which the ruling class identifies itself. Therefore the more civilization advances, the more it is compelled to cover the evils it necessarily creates with the cloak of love and charity, to palliate them or to deny them—in short, to introduce a conventional hypocrisy which was unknown to earlier forms of society and even to the first stages of civilization, and which culminates in the pronouncement: the exploitation of the oppressed class is carried on by the exploiting class simply and solely in the interests of the exploited class itself; and if the exploited class cannot see it and even grows rebellious, that is the basest ingratitude to its benefactors, the exploiters.

And now, in conclusion, [early anthropologist Lewis H.] Morgan's judgement of civilization:

> Since the advent of civilization, the outgrowth of property has been so immense, its forms so diversified, its uses so expanding and its management so intelligent in the interests of its owners, that it has become, on the part of the people, *an unmanageable power. The human mind stands bewildered in the presence of its own creation.* The time will come, nevertheless, when human intelligence will rise to the mastery over property, and define the relations of the state to the property it protects, as well as the obligations and the limits of the rights of its owners. The interests of society are paramount to individual interests, and the two must be brought into just and harmonious relations. A mere property career is not the final destiny of mankind, if progress is to be the law of the future as it has been of the past. The time which has passed away since civilization began is but a fragment of the past duration of man's existence; and but a fragment of the ages yet to come. The dissolution of society bids fair to become the termination of a career of which property is the end and aim; because such a career contains the elements of self-destruction. Democracy in government, brotherhood in society, equality in rights and privileges, and universal education, foreshadow the next higher plane of society to which experience, intelligence and knowledge are steadily tending. *It will be a revival, in a higher form, of the liberty, equality and fraternity of the ancient gentes* [pp. 561–2; Engels's italics].

CHAPTER 5 The Neoclassical School

5.1 ALFRED MARSHALL

Equilibrium of Normal Demand and Supply

Alfred Marshall (1842–1924), the originator of partial equilibrium analysis, was born in London, England. At the University of Cambridge, he became mentor and professor to John Maynard Keynes, who described him as the greatest economist of his time.

Marshall is credited with introducing concepts that remain part of our economic vocabulary to this day. They include the price elasticity of demand, economies of scale, variation in cost industries, the ceteris paribus assumption, and partial equilibrium analysis. The ceteris paribus assumption frees economists from having to monitor multiple variables simultaneously. By assuming that all other variables are being held constant, they can focus on the relationships between a few variables and gradually relax this restriction as new knowledge becomes available. When applied to demand, this method results in partial equilibrium analysis in which price-volume relationships are studied in isolation while other variables that influence price and volume, including income and tastes and prices of complementary and substitute goods, are held constant.

Marshall's principal contribution was his ability to reconcile supply-side and demand-oriented economics. His predecessors included supply-side economists who maintained that the value of a good is determined by its cost of labor, land, and capital. They heatedly debated the demand-oriented school, which upheld the notion that value is determined by the price that buyers are willing to pay for a good. Marshall integrated the two positions by stating that both supply and demand determine prices. In the following excerpt from *Principles of Economics* (1890), he demonstrates that in the short run demand influences the value of a product. However, in the long run the cost of production determines the value of a product. Consequently, in the long run prices will tend towards the lowest possible cost of production to provide the necessary quantities demanded by consumers.

Key Concept: the relative influence of demand and cost of production on value

1. Even in the corn-exchange of a country town on a market-day the equilibrium price is affected by calculations of the future relations of production and consumption; while in the leading corn-markets of America and Europe dealings for future delivery already predominate and are rapidly weaving into one web all the leading threads of trade in corn throughout the whole world. Some of these dealings in "futures" are but incidents in speculative manoeuvres; but in the main they are governed by calculations of the world's consumption on the one hand, and of the existing stocks and coming harvests in the Northern and Southern hemispheres on the other. Dealers take account of the areas sown with each kind of grain, of the forwardness and weight of the crops, of the supply of things which can be used as substitutes for grain, and of the things for which grain can be used as a substitute. Thus, when buying or selling barley, they take account of the supplies of such things as sugar, which can be used as substitutes for it in brewing, and again of all the various feeding stuffs, a scarcity of which might raise the value of barley for consumption on the farm. If it is thought that the growers of any kind of grain in any part of the world have been losing money, and are likely to sow a less area for a future harvest; it is argued that prices are likely to rise as soon as that harvest comes into sight, and its shortness is manifest to all. Anticipations of that rise exercise an influence on present sales for future delivery, and that in its turn influences cash prices; so that these prices are indirectly affected by estimates of the expenses of producing further supplies.

[Here] we are specially concerned with movements of price ranging over still longer periods than those for which the most far-sighted dealers in futures generally make their reckoning: we have to consider the volume of production adjusting itself to the conditions of the market, and the normal price being thus determined at the position of stable equilibrium of normal demand and normal supply.

2. In this discussion we shall have to make frequent use of the terms *cost* and *expenses* of production; and some provisional account of them must be given before proceeding further.

We may revert to the analogy between the supply price and the demand price of a commodity. Assuming for the moment that the efficiency of production depends solely upon the exertions of the workers, we saw that "the price required to call forth the exertion necessary for producing any given amount of a commodity may be called the supply price for that amount, with reference of course to a given unit of time." But now we have to take account of the fact that the production of a commodity generally requires many different kinds of labour and the use of capital in many forms. The exertions of all the different kinds of labour that are directly or indirectly involved in making it; together with the abstinences or rather the waitings required for saving the capital used in making it: all these efforts and sacrifices together will be called the *real cost of production* of the commodity. The sums of money that have to be paid for these efforts and sacrifices will be called either its *money cost of production*, or, for shortness, *its expenses of production*; they are the prices which have to be paid in order to call forth an adequate supply of the efforts and waitings that are required for making it; or, in other words, they are its supply price.

The analysis of the expenses of production of a commodity might be carried backward to any length; but it is seldom worth while to go back very far. It is for instance often sufficient to take the supply prices of the different kinds of raw materials used in any manufacture as ultimate facts, without analysing these supply prices into the several elements of which they are composed; otherwise indeed the analysis would never end. We may then arrange the things that are required for making a commodity into whatever groups are convenient, and call them its *factors of production.* Its expenses of production when any given amount of it is produced are thus the supply prices of the corresponding quantities of its factors of production. And the sum of these is the supply price of that amount of the commodity.

3. The typical modern market is often regarded as that in which manufacturers sell goods to wholesale dealers at prices into which but few trading expenses enter. But taking a broader view, we may consider that the supply price of a commodity is the price at which it will be delivered for sale to that group of persons whose demand for it we are considering; or, in other words, in the market which we have in view. On the character of that market will depend how many trading expenses have to be reckoned to make up the supply price. For instance, the supply price of wood in the neighbourhood of Canadian forests often consists almost exclusively of the price of the labour of lumber men: but the supply price of the same wood in the wholesale London market consists in a large measure of freights; while its supply price to a small retail buyer in an English country town is more than half made up of the charges of the railways and middlemen who have brought what he wants to his doors, and keep a stock of it ready for him. Again, the supply price of a certain kind of labour may for some purposes be divided up into the expenses of rearing, of general education and of special trade education. The possible combinations are numberless; and though each may have incidents of its own which will require separate treatment in the complete solution of any problem connected with it, yet all such incidents may be ignored, so far as the general reasonings [here] are concerned.

In calculating the expenses of production of a commodity we must take account of the fact that changes in the amounts produced are likely, even when there is no new invention, to be accompanied by changes in the relative quantities of its several factors of production. For instance, when the scale of production increases, horse or steam power is likely to be substituted for manual labour; materials are likely to be brought from a greater distance and in greater quantities, thus increasing those expenses of production which correspond to the work of carriers, middlemen and traders of all kinds.

As far as the knowledge and business enterprise of the producers reach, they in each case choose those factors of production which are best for their purpose; the sum of the supply prices of those factors which are used is, as a rule, less than the sum of the supply prices of any other set of factors which could be substituted for them; and whenever it appears to the producers that this is not the case, they will, as a rule, set to work to substitute the less expensive method. And further on we shall see how in a somewhat similar way society substitutes one undertaker for another who is less efficient in proportion to his charges. We may call this, for convenience of reference, *The principle of substitution.*

The applications of this principle extend over almost every field of economic inquiry.

4. The position then is this: we are investigating the equilibrium of normal demand and normal supply in their most general form; we are neglecting those features which are special to particular parts of economic science, and are confining our attention to those broad relations which are common to nearly the whole of it. Thus we assume that the forces of demand and supply have free play; that there is no close combination among dealers on either side, but each acts for himself, and there is much free competition; that is, buyers generally compete freely with buyers, and sellers compete freely with sellers. But though everyone acts for himself, his knowledge of what others are doing is supposed to be generally sufficient to prevent him from taking a lower or paying a higher price than others are doing. This is assumed provisionally to be true both of finished goods and of their factors of production, of the hire of labour and of the borrowing of capital. We have already inquired to some extent, and we shall have to inquire further, how far these assumptions are in accordance with the actual facts of life. But meanwhile this is the supposition on which we proceed; we assume that there is only one price in the market at one and the same time; it being understood that separate allowance is made, when necessary, for differences in the expense of delivering goods to dealers in different parts of the market; including allowance for the special expenses of retailing, if it is a retail market.

In such a market there is a demand price for each amount of the commodity, that is, a price at which each particular amount of the commodity can find purchasers in a day or week or year. The circumstances which govern this price for any given amount of the commodity vary in character from one problem to another; but in every case the more of a thing is offered for sale in a market the lower is the price at which it will find purchasers; or in other words, the demand price for each bushel or yard diminishes with every increase in the amount offered.

The unit of time may be chosen according to the circumstances of each particular problem: it may be a day, a month, a year, or even a generation: but in every case it must be short relatively to the period of the market under discussion. It is to be assumed that the general circumstances of the market remain unchanged throughout this period; that there is, for instance, no change in fashion or taste, no new substitute which might affect the demand, no new invention to disturb the supply.

The conditions of normal supply are less definite; and a full study of them... will [find them] to vary in detail with the length of the period of time to which the investigation refers; chiefly because both the material capital of machinery and other business plant, and the immaterial capital of business skill and ability and organization, are of slow growth and slow decay.

Let us call to mind the "representative firm," whose economies of production, internal and external, are dependent on the aggregate volume of production of the commodity that it makes, and, postponing all further study of the nature of this dependence, let us assume that the normal supply price of any amount of that commodity may be taken to be its normal expenses of production (including *gross* earnings of management) by that firm. That is, let us assume that this is the price the expectation of which will just suffice to maintain the existing aggregate amount of production; some firms meanwhile rising and increasing their output, and others falling and diminishing theirs; but the aggregate production remaining unchanged. A price higher than this would increase the growth of the rising firms, and slacken, though it might not arrest, the decay of the falling firms; with the net result of an increase in the aggregate production. On the other hand, a price lower than this would hasten the decay of the falling firms, and slacken the growth of the rising firms; and on the whole diminish production: and a rise or fall of price would affect in like manner though perhaps not in an equal degree those great joint-stock companies which often stagnate, but seldom die.

5. To give definiteness to our ideas let us take an illustration from the woollen trade. Let us suppose that a person well acquainted with the woollen trade sets himself to inquire what would be the normal supply price of a certain number of millions of yards annually of a particular kind of cloth. He would have to reckon (i) the price of the wool, coal, and other materials which would be used up in making it, (ii) wear-and-tear and depreciation of the buildings, machinery and other fixed capital, (iii) interest and insurance on all the capital, (iv) the wages of those who work in the factories, and (v) the gross earnings of management (including insurance against loss), of those who undertake the risks, who engineer and superintend the working. He would of course estimate the supply prices of all these different factors of production of the cloth with reference to the amounts of each of them that would be wanted, and on the supposition that the conditions of supply would be normal; and he would add them all together to find the supply price of the cloth.

Let us suppose a list of supply prices (or a supply schedule) made on a similar plan to that of our list of demand prices: the supply price of each amount of the commodity in a year, or any other unit of time, being written against that amount. As the flow, or (annual) amount of the commodity increases, the supply price may either increase or diminish; or it may even alternately increase and diminish. For if nature is offering a sturdy resistance to man's efforts to wring from her a larger supply of raw material, while at that particular stage there is no great room for introducing important new economies into the manufacture, the supply price will rise; but if the volume of production were greater, it would perhaps be profitable to substitute largely machine work for hand work and steam power for muscular force; and the increase in the volume of production would have diminished the expenses of production of the commodity of our representative firm. But those cases in which the supply price falls as the amount increases involve special difficulties of their own....

6. When therefore the amount produced (in a unit of time) is such that the demand price is greater than the supply price, then sellers receive more than is sufficient to make it worth their while to bring goods to market to that amount; and there is at work an active force tending to increase the amount brought forward for sale. On the other hand, when the amount produced is such that the demand price is less than the supply price, sellers receive less than is sufficient to make it worth their while to bring goods to market on that scale; so that those who were just on the margin of doubt as to whether to go on producing are decided not to do so, and there is an active force at work tending to diminish the amount brought forward for sale. When the demand price is equal to the supply price, the amount produced has no tendency either to be increased or to be diminished; it is in equilibrium.

When demand and supply are in equilibrium, the amount of the commodity which is being produced in a unit of time may be called the *equilibrium-amount*, and the price at which it is being sold may be called the *equilibrium-price.*

Such an equilibrium is *stable*; that is, the price, if displaced a little from it, will tend to return, as a pendulum oscillates about its lowest point; and it will be found to be a characteristic of stable equilibria that in them the demand price is greater than the supply price for amounts just less than the equilibrium amount, and *vice versâ*. For when the demand price is greater than the supply price, the amount produced tends to increase. Therefore, if the demand price is greater than the supply price for amounts just less than an equilibrium amount; then, if the scale of production is temporarily diminished somewhat below that equilibrium amount, it will tend to return; thus the equilibrium is stable for displacements in that direction. If the demand price is greater than the supply price for amounts just less than the equilibrium amount, it is sure to be less than the supply price for amounts just greater: and therefore, if the scale of production is somewhat increased beyond the equilibrium position, it will tend to return; and the equilibrium will be stable for displacements in that direction also.

When demand and supply are in stable equilibrium, if any accident should move the scale of production from its equilibrium position, there will be instantly brought into play forces tending to push it back to that position; just as, if a stone hanging by a string is displaced from its equilibrium position, the force of gravity will at once tend to bring it back to its equilibrium position. The movements of the scale of production about its position of equilibrium will be of a somewhat similar kind.

But in real life such oscillations are seldom as rhythmical as those of a stone hanging freely from a string; the comparison would be more exact if the string were supposed to hang in the troubled waters of a mill-race, whose stream was at one time allowed to flow freely, and at another partially cut off. Nor are these complexities sufficient to illustrate all the disturbances with which the economist and the merchant alike are forced to concern themselves. If the person holding the string swings his hand with movements partly rhythmical and partly arbitrary, the illustration will not outrun the difficulties of some very real and practical problems of value. For indeed the demand and supply schedules do not in practice remain unchanged for a long time together, but are constantly being changed; and every change in them alters the equilibrium amount and the equilibrium price, and thus gives new positions to the centres about which the amount and the price tend to oscillate.

These considerations point to the great importance of the element of time in relation to demand and supply, to the study of which we now proceed. We shall gradually discover a great many different limitations of the doctrine that the price at which a thing can be produced represents its real cost of production, that is, the efforts and sacrifices which have been directly and indirectly devoted to its production. For, in an age of rapid change such as this, the equilibrium of normal demand and supply does not thus correspond to any distinct relation of a certain aggregate of pleasures got from the consumption of the commodity and an aggregate of efforts and sacrifices involved in producing it: the correspondence would not be exact, even if normal earnings and interest were exact measures of the efforts and sacrifices for which they are the money payments. This is the real drift of that much quoted, and much-misunderstood doctrine of Adam Smith and other economists that the normal, or "natural," value of a commodity is that which economic forces tend to bring about *in the long run*. It is the average value which economic forces would bring about if the general conditions of life were stationary for a run of time long enough to enable them all to work out their full effect.

But we cannot foresee the future perfectly. The unexpected may happen; and the existing tendencies may be modified before they have had time to accomplish what appears now to be their full and complete work. The fact that the general conditions of life are not stationary is the source of many of the difficulties that are met with in applying economic doctrines to practical problems.

Of course Normal does not mean Competitive. Market prices and Normal prices are alike brought about by a multitude of influences, of which some rest on a moral basis and some on a physical; of which some are competitive and some are not. It is to the persistence of the influences considered, and the time allowed for them to work out their effects that we refer when contrasting Market and Normal price, and again when contrasting the narrower and the broader use of the term Normal price.

7.... We might as reasonably dispute whether it is the upper or the under blade of a pair of scissors that cuts a piece of paper, as whether value is governed by utility or cost of production. It is true that when one blade is held still, and the cutting is effected by moving the other, we may say with careless brevity that the cutting is done by the second; but the statement is not strictly accurate, and is to be excused only so long as it claims to be merely a popular and not a strictly scientific account of what happens.

In the same way, when a thing already made has to be sold, the price which people will be willing to pay for it will be governed by their desire to have it, together with the amount they can afford to spend on it. Their desire to have it depends partly on the chance that, if they do not buy it, they will be able to get another thing like it at as low a price: this depends on the causes that govern the supply of it, and this again upon cost of production. But it may so happen that the stock to be sold is practically fixed. This, for instance, is the case with a fish market, in which the value of fish for the day is governed almost exclusively by the stock on the slabs in relation to the demand: and if a person chooses to take the stock for granted, and say that the price is governed by demand, his brevity may perhaps be excused so long as he does not claim strict accuracy. So again it may be pardonable, but it is not strictly accurate to say that the varying prices which the same rare book fetches, when sold and resold at Christie's auction room, are governed exclusively by demand.

Taking a case at the opposite extreme, we find some commodities which conform pretty closely to the law of constant return; that is to say, their average cost of production will be very nearly the same whether they are produced in small quantities or in large. In such a case the normal level about which the market price fluctuates will be this definite and fixed (money) cost of production. If the demand happens to be great, the market price will rise for a time above the level; but as a result production will increase and the market price will fall: and conversely, if the demand falls for a time below its ordinary level.

In such a case, if a person chooses to neglect market fluctuations, and to take it for granted that there will anyhow be enough demand for the commodity to insure that some of it, more or less, will find purchasers at a price equal to this cost of production, then he may be excused for ignoring the influence of demand, and speaking of (normal) price as governed by cost of production —provided only he does not claim scientific accuracy for the wording of his doctrine, and explains the influence of demand in its right place.

Thus we may conclude that, *as a general rule*, the shorter the period which we are considering, the greater must be the share of our attention which is given to the influence of demand on value; and the longer the period, the more important will be the influence of cost of production on value. For the influence of changes in cost of production takes as a rule a longer time to work itself out than does the influence of changes in demand. The actual value at any time, the market value as it is often called, is often more influenced by passing events and by causes whose action is fitful and short lived, than by those which work persistently. But in long periods these fitful and irregular causes in large measure efface one another's influence; so that in the long run persistent causes dominate value completely. Even the most persistent causes are however liable to change. For the whole structure of production is modified, and the relative costs of production of different things are permanently altered, from one generation to another.

When considering costs from the point of view of the capitalist employer, we of course measure them in money; because his direct concern with the efforts needed for the work of his employees lies in the money payments he must make. His concern with the real costs of their effort and of the training required for it is only indirect, though a monetary assessment of his own labour is necessary for some problems, as will be seen later on. But when considering costs from the social point of view, when inquiring whether the cost of attaining a given result is increasing or diminishing with changing economic conditions, then we are concerned with the real costs of efforts of various qualities, and with the real cost of waiting. If the purchasing power of money, in terms of effort has remained about constant, and if the rate of remuneration for waiting has remained about constant, then the money measure of costs corresponds to the real costs: but such a correspondence is never to be assumed lightly.

Income and Capital

Irving Fisher (1867–1947) was born in Saugerties, New York. He graduated from York University with a B.A. (1888) and a Ph.D. (1891) in mathematics. He joined Yale University as assistant professor of mathematics in 1892 and transferred to the department of political economy in 1895. He was promoted to full professor in 1898 and remained there until his retirement in 1935.

Fisher pioneered the application of mathematics to economic theory. His equation of exchange has become a standard. Taking the standard accounting equation of MV + M′V′ = PT, with M as the quantity of currency, V as the velocity of money, M′ as the quantity of demand deposits, V′ as the velocity of demand deposits, P as the price level, and T as the total transactions in the economy, Fisher demonstrated that the stability of V and V′ could be tested as M, P, and T were directly observable. His works include *The Nature of Capital and Income* (1906), *The Theory of Indices* (1911), and *The Theory on Taxation* (1942). The following is an excerpt from *The Theory of Interest as Determined by Impatience to Spend Income and Opportunity to Invest It* (1907). Here Fisher distinguishes between nominal and real rates of interest. Nominal rates include real rates and inflationary expectations. He views the interest rate as the bridge between income and capital, distinguishes between the concepts of interest and the rate of interest, and emphasizes the importance of considering the time value of money.

Key Concept: income and capital

The Nature of Capital and Income *(first published in 1906) was primarily intended to serve as a foundation for* The Rate of Interest *which immediately followed it. It was my expectation that the student would read the former before reading the latter.*

But now, for the convenience of those who do not wish to take the time to read The Nature of Capital and Income, *I have written this [summarization]. I have availed myself of this opportunity to redistribute the emphasis and to make those amendments in statement which further study has indicated to be desirable.*

Irving Fisher

1. SUBJECTIVE, OR ENJOYMENT, INCOME

Income is a series of events.

According to the modern theory of relativity the elementary reality is not matter, electricity, space, time, life or mind, but events.

For each individual only those events which come within the purview of his experience are of direct concern. It is these events—the psychic experiences of the individual mind—which constitute ultimate income for that individual. The outside events have significance for that individual only in so far as they are the means to these inner events of the mind. The human nervous system is, like a radio, a great receiving instrument. Our brains serve to transform into the stream of our psychic life those outside events, which happen to us and stimulate our nervous system.

But the human body is not ordinarily regarded as an owned object, and only those events in consciousness traceable to owned objects other than the human body are generally admitted to be psychic income. However, the human machine still plays a rôle in so far as, through its purposeful activities, it produces, or helps produce, other owned objects which are material sources of desirable events—food, houses, tools, and other goods, which in their turn set in motion a chain of operations whose ultimate effect is registered in our stream of consciousness. The important consideration from this point of view is that human beings are ever striving to control the stream of their psychic life by appropriating and utilizing the materials and forces of Nature.

In Man's early history he had little command over his environment. He was largely at the mercy of natural forces—wind and lightning, rain and snow, heat and cold. But today Man protects himself from these by means of those contrivances called houses, clothing, and furnaces. He diverts the lightning by means of lightning rods. He increases his food supply by means of appropriated land, farm buildings, plows, and other implements. He then refashions the food by means of mills, grinding machinery, cook-stoves and other agencies, and by the labor of human bodies, including his own.

Neither these intermediate processes of creation and alteration nor the money transactions following them are of significance except as they are the necessary or helpful preliminaries to psychic income—human enjoyment. We must be careful lest, in fixing our eyes on such preliminaries, especially money transactions, we overlook the much more important enjoyment which it is their business to yield.

Directors and managers providing income for thousands of people sometimes think of their corporation merely as a great money-making machine. In their eyes, its one purpose is to earn money dividends for the stockholders, money interest for the bondholders, money wages and money salaries for the employees. What happens after these payments are made seems too private a matter to concern them. Yet that is the nub of the whole arrangement. It is only what we carry out of the market place into our homes and private lives which really counts. Money is of no use to us until it is spent. The ultimate wages are not paid in terms of money but in the enjoyments it buys. The dividend check becomes income in the ultimate sense only when we eat the food, wear the clothes, or ride in the automobile which are bought with the check.

2. OBJECTIVE, OR REAL, INCOME (OUR "LIVING")

Enjoyment income is a psychological entity and cannot be measured directly. We can approximate it indirectly, however, by going one step back of it to what is called real income. Real wages, and indeed real income in general, consist of those final physical events in the *outer* world which give us our *inner* enjoyments.

This real income includes the shelter of a house, the music of a victrola or radio, the use of clothes, the eating of food, the reading of the newspaper and all those other innumerable events by which we make the world about us contribute to our enjoyments. Metaphorically we sometimes refer to this, our real income, as our "bread and butter."

These finals in the stream of outer events are what we call our "living," as implied in the phrases cost of living and earning a living. The final outer events and the inner events which they entail run closely parallel, or, rather, the inner events generally follow closely in time on the outer. The enjoyment of music is felt almost instantaneously as the piano or singer produces it. The enjoyment of food is experienced with the eating or soon after the eating.

These outer events, such as the use of food, or clothes, etc., are like the resultant inner events in not being very easily measured. They occur largely in the privacy of the home; they are often difficult to express in any standard units. They have no common denominator. Even the individual who experiences them cannot weigh and measure them directly. All he can do is to measure the money he paid to get them.

3. COST OF LIVING, A MEASURE OF REAL INCOME

So, just as we went back of an individual's enjoyment income to his real income, we now go back of his real income, or his living, to his *cost* of living, the money measure of real income. You cannot measure in dollars either the inner event of your enjoyment while eating your dinner or the outer event of eating it, but you can find out definitely how much money that dinner cost you. In the same way, you cannot measure your enjoyment at moving picture theater, but you do know what you paid for your ticket; you cannot measure exactly what your house shelter is really worth to you, but you can tell how much you pay for your rent, or what is a fair equivalent for your rent if you happen to live in your own house. You cannot measure what it is worth to wear an evening suit, but you can find out what it costs to hire one, or a fair equivalent of its hire if, perchance, the suit belongs to you. Deducing such equivalents is an accountant's job.

The total cost of living, in the sense of money payments, is a negative item, being outgo rather than income; but it is our best practical measure of the positive items of real income for which those payments are made. For from this total valuation of positive real income may be subtracted the total valuation of the person's labor pain during the same period, if we wish to compare a laborer's income with that of a man who does no labor but lives on his income from capital (other than himself), a "rentier."

Enjoyment income, real income, and the cost of living are merely three different stages of income. All three run closely parallel to each other, although they are not exactly synchronous in time. These discrepancies, as has been intimated, are negligible as between real and enjoyment income. So also the time elapsing between the cost of living and the living is usually brief. There is a little delay between the spending of money at the box office and the seeing of the entertainment, or between paying board or rent and making use of the food or housing facilities. In many cases, the money payment follows rather than precedes the enjoyment.

4. COST OF AN ARTICLE VS. COST OF ITS USE

The only time discrepancy worth careful noting is that which occurs when the money spent is not simply for the temporary use of some object but for the whole object, which means merely for all its possible future uses. If a house is not rented but bought, we do not count the purchase price as all spent for this year's shelter. We expect from it many more years of use. Hence out of the entire purchase price, we try to compute a fair portion of the purchase price to be charged up to this year's use. In like manner, the statisticians of cost of living should distribute by periods the cost of using a person's house furnishings, clothing, musical instruments, automobiles and other durable goods, and not charge the entire cost against the income of the year of purchase. To any given year should be charged only that year's upkeep and replacement, which measures, at least roughly, the services rendered by the goods in question during that particular year. The true real annual income from such goods is the equivalent approximately of the cost of the services given off by those goods each year.

Strictly speaking, then, in making up our income statistics, we should always calculate the value of *services,* and never the value of the objects rendering those services. It is true that, in the case of short-lived objects like food, we do not ordinarily need, in practice, to go to the trouble of distinguishing their total cost from the cost of their use. A loaf of bread is worth ten cents because its use is worth ten cents. We cannot rent food; we can only buy it outright. Yet there is some discrepancy in time in the case of foods that keep, such as flour, preserved foods and canned goods. These we may buy in one year but not use until a later year, and in such cases the money given for the food might almost be said to be invested rather than spent, like the money given for a house. A man who buys a basket of fruit and eats it within an hour is certainly spending his money for the enjoyment of eating the fruit. But, if he buys a barrel of apples in the fall to be eaten during the winter, is he spending his money or is he investing it for a deferred enjoyment? Theoretically, the barrel of apples is an investment comparable to a house or any other durable good. Practically it is classed as expenditure, although it is a border-line case.

Spending and investing differ only in degree, depending on the length of time elapsing between the expenditure and the enjoyment. To spend is to pay money for enjoyments which come very soon. To invest is to pay money for enjoyments which are deferred to a later time. We spend money for our daily bread and butter or for a seat at the theater, but we invest money in the purchase of bonds, farms, dwellings, or automobiles, or even of suits of clothes.

5. MEASURING AT THE DOMESTIC THRESHOLD

In practice, we can estimate with fair accuracy in all ordinary cases how much of what we pay is for this year's use. That is to say, we can find out pretty nearly our cost of living for the year. We need only reckon what is spent on personal articles and services—on everything which enters our dwellings (or enters us), food, drink, clothes, furniture, household rent, fuel and light, amusements, and so on, our "bread and butter"—exclusive of what is left over for future years, such as what we pay for securities, machinery, or real estate, or what we put into the savings bank. The domestic threshold is, in general, a pretty good line of division. The cost of almost every object which crosses it measures a portion of our real income, and few other expenditures do.

Thus, at the end of production economics, or business economics, we find home economics. It is the housekeeper, the woman who spends, who takes the final steps through the cost of living toward getting the real income of the family, so that the family's enjoyment income may follow.

6. MONEY INCOME

We have just been dealing with money payments for consumption goods, or money *outgo.* We may now go back one further step to money received by the individual spender, or money income. Money income includes all money *received* which is not obviously, and in the nature of the case, to be devoted to reinvestment—or, as the expression is, "earmarked" for reinvestment. In other words, all money received and readily available and intended to be used for spending is money income. It sometimes differs from real income considerably. For instance, if you more than "earn your living" of $6,000 with a salary of $10,000, you voluntarily put by the $4,000 remaining as savings. This part of your money income is saved from being turned immediately into real income.

That is, instead of spending all your salary for this year's living you invest $4,000 of it to help toward the cost of living of future years. And so, the $4,000 is not only credited as income but debited as outgo. With it you buy durable objects such as land or buildings, or part rights in these, such as stocks or bonds. Your money income is in this case your salary (or it may be dividends, rent, interest, or profits) and it exceeds real income by the amount of your savings. On the other hand, you may be living beyond your (money) income. This means, expressed in terms of the concepts here used, that your real income for the year is greater than your money income.

That all one spends on his living measures real income, even when he "lives beyond his income" (beyond his *money* income), may be a hard saying to some who have never attempted to work out consistent definitions of economic concepts which will not only satisfy the requirements of economic theory but which will also bring these economic concepts into conformity with the theory and practice of accountancy. But a definition of income which satisfies both theory and practice, in both economics and accountancy, *must* reckon as income in the most basic sense all those uses, services, or living for which the cost of living is expended even though such expenditure may exceed the money income.

Thus we have a picture of three successive stages, or aspects, of a man's income:

Enjoyment or psychic income, consisting of agreeable sensations and experiences;

Real income *measured* by the cost of living;

Money income, consisting of the money received by a man for meeting his costs of living;

The last—money income—is most commonly called income; and the first —enjoyment income—is the most fundamental. But, for accounting purposes, real income, as measured by the cost of living, is the most practical.

To recapitulate, we have seen that the enjoyment income is a psychological matter, and hence cannot be measured directly. So we look to real income instead; but even real income is a heterogeneous jumble. It includes quarts of milk, visits to the moving picture house, etc., and in that form cannot be measured easily or as a whole. Here is where the cost of living comes in. It is the practical, homogeneous measure of real income. As the cost of living is expressed in terms of dollars it may, therefore, be taken as our best measure of income *in place of* enjoyment income, or real income. Between it and real income there are no important discrepancies as there are between money income and real income. Money income practically never conforms exactly to real income because either savings raise money income above real income, or deficits push money income below real income.

7. CAPITAL VALUE

Savings bring us to the nature of capital. Capital, in the sense of capital *value,* is simply future income discounted or, in other words, capitalized. The value of any property, or rights to wealth, is its value *as a source of income* and is found by discounting that expected income. We may, if we so choose, for logical convenience, include as property the ownership in ourselves, or we may, conformably to custom, regard human beings as in a separate category.

I define wealth as consisting of material objects owned by human beings (including, if you please, human beings themselves). The ownership may be divided and parcelled out among different individuals in the form of partnership rights, shares of stock, bonds, mortgages, and other forms of property rights. In whatever ways the ownership be distributed and symbolized in documents, the entire group of property rights are merely means to an end—income. Income is the alpha and omega of economics.

8. THE RATE OF INTEREST

The bridge or link between income and capital is the *rate of interest*. We may define the *rate of interest as the per cent of premium* paid on money at one date in terms of money to be in hand one year later. Theoretically, of course, we may substitute for money in this statement wheat or any other sort of goods.... But practically, it is only money which is traded as between present and future. Hence, the rate of interest is sometimes called the price of money; and the market in which present and future money are traded for that price, or premium, is called the money market. If $100 today will exchange for $105 to be received one year hence, the premium on present money in terms of future money is $5 and this, as a percentage of the $100, or the rate of interest, is five per cent. That is to say, the price of today's money in terms of next year's money is five per cent above par. It should always be remembered *that interest and the rate of interest are not identical.* Interest is computed by multiplying capital value by the rate of interest.

The aim [here] is to show how the *rate* of interest is caused or determined. Some writers have chosen, for purposes of exposition, to postulate two questions involved in the theory of the rate of interest, viz., (1) why any rate of interest exists and (2) how the rate of interest is determined. This second question, however, embraces also the first, since to explain how the rate of interest is determined involves the question of whether the rate can or cannot be zero, i.e., whether a positive rate of interest must necessarily exist.

9. DISCOUNTING IS FUNDAMENTAL

But although the rate of interest may be used either way—for computing from present to future values, or from future to present values—the latter process (discounting) is by far the more important of the two. Accountants, of course, are constantly computing in both directions; for they have to deal with both sets of problems. But the basic problem of time valuation which Nature sets us is always that of translating the future into the present, that is, the problem of

FIGURE 1

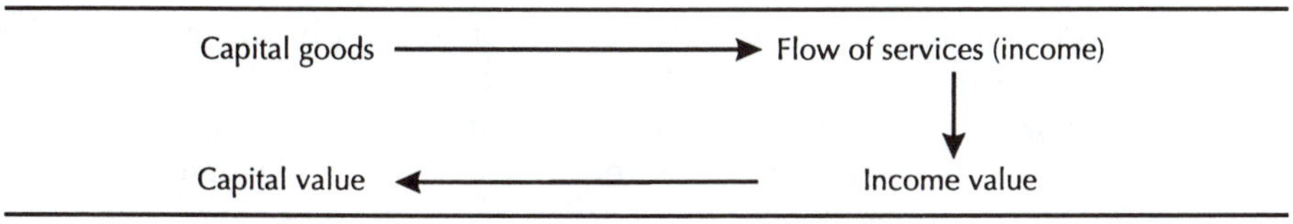

Capital goods →	Flow of services (income)
	↓
Capital value ←	Income value

ascertaining the capital value of future income. The value of capital must be computed from the value of its estimated future net income, not *vice versa.*

This statement may at first seem puzzling, for we usually think of causes and effects as running forward not backward in time. It would seem then that income must be derived from capital; and, in a sense, this is true. Income *is* derived from capital *goods.* But the *value* of the income is not derived from the *value* of the capital goods. On the contrary, the value of the capital is derived from the value of the income. Valuation is a human process in which foresight enters. Coming events cast their shadows before. Our valuations are always anticipations.

These relations are shown in [Figure 1], in which the arrows represent the order of sequence—(1) from capital goods to their future services, that is, income; (2) from these services to their value; and (3) from their value back to capital value.

Not until we know how much income an item of capital will probably bring us can we set any valuation on that capital at all. It is true that the wheat crop depends on the land which yields it. But the value of the crop does not depend on the value of the land. On the contrary, the value of the land depends on the expected value of its crops.

The present worth of any article is what buyers are willing to give for it and sellers are ready to take for it. In order that each man may logically decide what he is willing to give or take, he must have: (1) some idea of the value of the future benefits which that article will yield, and (2) some idea of the rate of interest by which these future values may be translated into present values by discounting.

10. COSTS, OR NEGATIVE INCOME

Cost of production of durable agents or capital goods has its influence included in the preceding formulation, since any cost is simply a negative item of income. Future negative items are to be discounted exactly as future positive items. It is to be remembered that at the given point of time when the value is being computed only *future* costs can enter into the valuation of any good. Past costs have no *direct* influence on value. Only indirectly do they enter to the extent that they have determined the existing supply of goods and have thus either raised or lowered the value of the services of these goods.

In this indirect way, past costs can determine present values temporarily and until the prices of goods available are brought into conformity with the present costs of production through the operation of supply and demand. For example, the cost of producing woolen cloth declined very sharply after the close of the World War, but the price did not decline for many months because the new cloth made at less expense was not sufficient to meet the demand, hence the price remained above the new costs of production for a time. Again, the cost of making shoes advanced rapidly during the early years of the twentieth century, but the price of shoes did not advance *pari passu* [at an equal rate or pace] with increased costs, because the supply of more cheaply made shoes was still large and for a time controlled the market price. In the same indirect way, many other influences affect the value of the services of any good, especially any alternative to those services. But none of these considerations affects the principle that the value of the good itself is the discounted value of the value (however determined) of its future services.

11. THE DISCOUNT PRINCIPLE APPLIED

The principles which have been explained for obtaining the present value of a future sum apply very definitely to many commercial transactions, such as to the valuation of bank assets, which indeed exist largely in the form of discount paper, or short time loans of some other kinds. The value of a note is always the discounted value of the future payment to which it entitles the holder.

Elaborate mathematical tables have been calculated and are used by brokers for informing their customers what price should be paid for a five per cent bond in order that the purchaser may realize 5 per cent, 4 per cent, or any other rate of interest on the prices to be paid. The price of the bond is calculated from two items, the rate of interest to be realized and the series of sums or other benefits which the bond is going to return to the investor. Aside from risk, there can never be any other factors in the calculation except these two. Of course, an investor may refuse to buy a bond at the market price because he has, as an alternative, the opportunity to buy another bond cheaper so that he can realize a higher rate on his purchase price. But that fact does not alter the principle that market prices represent discounted benefits. The only market effect of this man's refusal will be a slight tendency to lower the market price of the first bond and raise that of its rival, that is, to alter the rate of interest realized.... Here we are concerned only to note that the price of the bond is dependent solely on two factors; (1) its benefits and (2) the interest rate by which these are discounted.

The principle is, of course, not confined to bonds. It applies in any market to all property and wealth—stocks, land (which has a discounted capital value just as trùly as any other capital), buildings, machinery, or anything whatsoever. Risk aside, each has a market value dependent solely on the same two factors, the benefits, or returns, expected by the investor and the market rate of interest by which those benefits are discounted.

The income which he expects may be a perpetual income (flowing uniformly or in recurring cycles) or it may be any one of innumerable other types. If we assume that five per cent is the rate of interest, any one of the following income streams will have a present value of $1000: a perpetual annuity of $50 per year; or an annuity of $50 a year for ten years; together with $1000 at the end of the period; or $100 a year for fourteen years, after which nothing at all; or $25 a year for ten years, followed by $187.50 a year for ten years, after which nothing at all.

5.3 JOAN ROBINSON

Vicissitudes of a Developing Economy

Joan Robinson (1903–1983) was born into a middle-class English family. She graduated from Girton College, Cambridge, in 1925 and later joined the Cambridge University faculty as an assistant lecturer in economics after a brief spell in India. She became full professor in 1965, retiring in 1971. Robinson is regarded as one of the leading defenders of Keynesian economic theory. She breathed fresh air into John Maynard Keynes's analysis, noting that Keynes confined himself to short periods in which decisions are made about expectations for the future. Robinson criticized attempts to ignore the inherent uncertainty in expectations for the future by assuming the existence of equilibrium.

Robinson attacked the neoclassical theory of capital in a paper published in 1954 entitled *The Production Function and the Theory of Capital.* Her other works include *The Economics of Imperfect Competition* (Macmillan, 1933), a popular textbook at many universities, and *Introduction to the Theory of Employment* (Macmillan, 1969). She ignited controversy by challenging neoclassical economics in its depiction of the role of capital in production. Neoclassical economists held that producers minimize the costs of production. But the costs of production depend on the price of capital goods as inputs, and the value of capital goods themselves depends upon the value of the final products that they produce. A circular relationship results, with the cost of capital goods depending on the final product and the final product deriving its price from prices of capital goods. As production takes place over time, a firm must place a value upon capital goods used in production before it can determine the market price of its final products. The solution to this dilemma was provided by Marxism, which views capital as an intermediate product between labor inputs and final outputs. Essentially, Robinson shifted the analysis from market adjustments in neoclassical economics to the use of capital goods in technology-dependent production processes. The following excerpt is taken from *The Rate of Interest and Other Essays* (Macmillan, 1954). In it Robinson applies Keynesian economics to a developing economy. She explores the impact of a rise in thriftiness and the balance between capital accumulation, the supply of labor, and population growth rates.

Key Concept: challenges of a developing economy

I. THRIFTINESS

An important feature in our picture of the golden age of steady progress is that saving represents an unchanging proportion of total income, to which the stock of productive equipment and its distribution between the sectors of industry are appropriate. We must now consider what happens if thriftiness increases (the proportion of income consumed falls), and what influences are likely to make thriftiness alter.

An increase in thriftiness may be induced by an increase in investment plans—in the large, when a society begins to develop habits of enterprise and of thrift together, or in detail, when entrepreneurs limit family expenditure or dividend payments in order to have more funds to plough back into their businesses. Then greater thrift makes possible a greater rate of accumulation. But here we wish to consider the effect of an increase in thriftiness in itself, not induced by some other change in the situation.

(a) Effect of a Rise in Thriftiness

Suppose that the system has been expanding at a steady geometrical rate, in the manner of the golden age, up to a certain moment, and that then thriftiness increases, so that the ratio of consumption to income falls. This means that the increment of demand for consumption goods falls short of the increment of supply made possible by the addition to equipment which took place over the immediate past. Surplus capacity emerges in the consumption-good industries, orders for new capital goods consequently fail to be placed, and the rate of investment falls off (or fails to increase at its former rate). If the change is foreseen before it occurs, investment in the consumption-good industries is curtailed appropriately, and surplus capacity does not appear in them, but this only means that investment falls all the sooner.

If the change came about gradually, instead of in a sudden burst, the effect would be no better. It is true that the system could accommodate itself smoothly to a gradual change if there were some force causing the proportion of investment to income to rise as the proportion of consumption fell off. But an increase in thriftiness, whether sudden or gradual, provides no such force, for it does nothing to induce an increase in investment plans, or (except to the very minor extent that it releases capacity suitable for investment industries) to make possible the speeding up of the rate at which plans are carried out.

It seems, then, that a rise in thriftiness above the level to which the system has become adjusted slows up the rate of capital accumulation.

Here it is necessary to [address] the controversy about the rate of interest.... "Classical economics" is usually represented as denying the above proposition and as showing that an increase in thriftiness is a cause of increased accumulation, the causal links being the behaviour of the rate of interest, and the behaviour of money-wage rates. But "classical economics", in this sense, is a somewhat artificial construction. It is derived by asking questions suggested by the General Theory and then patching together answers from the implicit assumptions, the asides and the *obiter dicta* made, for instance by [Alfred] Marshall, in the course of answering quite different questions. In particular,... the supposed classical theory of the rate of interest will not survive being transplanted into the setting of an analysis of historical development. The view that a rising value of money is favourable to accumulation I do not think has ever seriously been maintained, outside the context of pure static theory. Thus so far as "classical economics" is concerned, there does not seem to be any case to answer.

(b) Causes of Changes in Thriftiness

Granted that increasing thriftiness unaccompanied by increasing investment opportunities is inimical to accumulation, the next question to be asked is in what conditions thriftiness is likely to increase.

[John Maynard] Keynes, formalising a long tradition of "under-consumptionist" theory, argued that the mere increase of wealth increases thriftiness. This point of view appears at first sight to be supported by the fact that, over the up and down of the trade cycle, consumption increases in a smaller proportion than income (investment bears a higher ratio to income in the boom than in the slump) so that, when national income increases, the increment of saving may be as high as fifty per cent. of the increment of income, while total net saving is only, say, ten per cent. of total income. If this relationship holds good as income per head increases over the long run, the ratio of saving to income must be continuously increasing.

But there is a great deal of difference between an increase in real national income which comes about in the upswing of a boom and an increase due to capital accumulation and technical progress. In a boom, the increase of income goes too fast for consumption habits to be fully adjusted to it, and it is confined to small sectors of the community, whereas the long-run increase in income is gradual and widely diffused. Boom incomes may not be expected to last, so that prudence dictates the building up of reserves.

Moreover, the proportion of profits to national income rises, as a boom develops, above its long-run average, because prices rise relatively to money costs, and the propensity to save which applies to profits is markedly higher than that for wages, or even for rentier incomes. The question can be treated in terms of Marshall's short and long-period supply price: when demand increases, given capital equipment, prices rise relatively to money-wage rates and abnormal profits are earned. When the consequent stimulus to investment has led to an appropriate expansion of capacity, profits fall back to normal. And super-normal thriftiness disappears with super-normal profits.

It is therefore impossible to argue from the high short-run marginal propensity to save to a secular rise in thriftiness.

Nor is there much force in the argument that as real income rises material human wants become progressively more fully satisfied, for wants increase with the power to meet them, especially in a stratified society, where the upper income groups are continually putting ideas into the heads of those below, and where artful salesmanship is continually creating new wants in order to exploit them.

But the "under-consumptionist" case does not rest mainly on the idea that thriftiness must rise with average income, rather that it must increase with growing inequality of incomes, and that inequality tends to grow as capitalism develops, because the discovery of ever more ways of substituting power and mechanical devices for human muscle and skill is continuously reducing the share in the product of industry received by labour.

We have seen, however, that *a priori* there is no particular reason to expect technical progress to be "favourable to capital" in the sense that it raises the ratio of capital to output, and statistical investigation, as far as it has gone, suggests that the ratio tends to be fairly constant over the long run.

Moreover, as technique grows more complex it increases the amount of professional and administrative services which industry requires, so that the number of families supported by the non-wage share of total proceeds grows relatively to the number of workers in the narrow sense. Thus even when the share of wages falls, thriftiness does not necessarily increase.

(Technical progress has a further equalising tendency in that it raises the purchasing power incomes mainly spent upon mass-produced commodities faster than those devoted to personal services and the products of individual craftsmen, but to pursue this point would take us too deeply into index-number problems.)

Another major influence upon distribution is the prevalence of monopoly. Here we must beware of double counting, for, if the degree of monopoly is measured simply by the ratio of gross margins to prime costs, it will appear to rise as a result of a mere increase in the ratio of capital costs to output due to capital-favouring changes in technique. Moreover, a prevalent type of quasi-monopoly limits competition in price while allowing it free play in salesmanship of all sorts (a part of which, indeed, may be genuine improvements in the quality of commodities) so that costs, instead of profits, are raised by it. The type of monopoly which is relevant here is that which raises the average rate of profit because it puts obstacles in the way of the process... by which an excess of price over costs is competed away.

It may be that the prospect of enjoying a monopoly, at least for a certain time, is required to induce many innovations, and in so far as this is true, there is an element of monopoly profit in the "necessary supply price" of some commodities. But all the same a growth in the rate of profit due, for instance, to an increase in the minimum investment required by new techniques (which increases risk and reduces the number of entrepreneurs who can command the necessary finance) reduces the share of wages in net output just as much as a rise in profits brought about by nefarious means.

There are reasons apart from the nature of technical change why we should expect monopoly to increase as time goes by. In many industries a few firms, escaping the degeneration described by Marshall, gradually grow and swallow up the smaller fry. And in many an amalgamation or cartel formed in mere self-defence during a period of surplus capacity persists for ever after (though some breakdown when prosperity returns).

But even if there is a tendency for monopoly to increase as time goes by, there is a powerful counter-acting force in the development of Trade Unions, which persuade the monopolists to pass back a part of their profits to the workers, in the form of wages and amenities, in order to avoid industrial strife.

From all this it appears that, although there is much to support the underconsumptionist view that the share of wages in income must fall as capital accumulates, and thriftiness increase, yet it is also possible that the counteracting forces may be sufficiently powerful to reverse the result.

II. THE SUPPLY OF LABOUR

The conditions which make the golden age of steady accumulation possible entail that total output increases at the same proportional rate as the stock of capital measured in terms of product. The demand for labour is increasing or shrinking according as the rise in output per man-hour, due to technical progress, goes on at a slower or a faster pace than the increase in total output. When output per man-hour rises faster than total output there is a continually growing amount of technological unemployment, or a continual fall in hours worked per man-year. When output per man-hour is rising more slowly, the demand for labour is increasing.

We must now consider the inter-action between the demand for labour and the growth of population.

There are many complicated and important questions connected with the age, class and sex composition of a population which are bound up with changes in its rate of growth, and with the length of past time that any given pattern of growth has been experienced. All this group of problems we shall ignore, setting out only a crude argument in terms of absolute numbers of "men". The two aspects of the problem which are most germane to our argument are (*a*) the cessation of population growth after it has been going on for some time and (*b*) the continuance of population growth at an excessive rate.

(a) Cessation of Growth in Numbers

First consider an economy which has been enjoying steady progress, in the manner of the golden age, in which technical progress is raising output per man-hour less fast than capital is accumulating. This has been possible because population has been growing, and every year more hands are producing and more mouths consuming than the year before.

Let us suppose that, by a fortunate accident, accumulation of capital and growth of population are in harmony so that the rate of growth in the numbers of workers required to operate the ever-growing stock of capital at normal capacity is just about equal to the rate of growth in the number of available workers. So long as slumps are avoided, unemployment is a small and fairly steady proportion of the ever-growing total of employment.

Since the growth of real income per head is insufficient to keep demand expanding at the same rate as capacity output, the system, so to say, relies upon the increase in population to keep it running. What would happen if the growth of population slowed down?

As soon as entrepreneurs, each in his own line, foresee that the market for commodities will cease to expand at its former rate, they curtail investment plans, a slump sets in and profits fall below normal. If they fail to observe what is happening and go blindly on with investment plans at the rate appropriate to the former situation, excess capacity emerges and consequently the slump, by being delayed, is so much the worse when it comes.

This decline in investment would be offset if there were a corresponding decline in propensity to save. The change in the pattern of life entailed by a change in the rate of growth of population must certainly affect every aspect of the economy, but there is no presumption that any change in thriftiness which results from it will be sufficient to offset the decline in investment; or even that it will be in the right direction.

Assuming that (in the absence of conscious interference with the *laisser faire* economy) the propensity to consume is no greater than it was when population was increasing faster, the economy has fallen into a slump. The community, now, is suffering from "underconsumption" in the purest sense. It has a propensity to save appropriate to a higher rate of accumulation than now appears profitable to its entrepreneurs.

Though the trouble is due to failure of its numbers to increase, it is in no sense suffering from a "scarcity of labour", for, quite apart from the unemployment caused by the slump conditions, there is redundant labour in the investment industries. If consumption were to increase above its former level, there would be labour available to meet demand. Lack of mobility, it is true, may be an impediment to transfers of labour from one sector to another, but the question of mobility fails to arise, for in fact, far from increasing, total consumption falls as a result of the fall in incomes derived from investment activity, and there is general unemployment of the all-too familiar kind.

(Though this situation can properly be described as "underconsumption" it does not follow that, if the community were to depart from pure *laisser faire* and try to deal with the position by a conscious policy, an increase in consumption would be the best policy to adopt—that is quite another story.)

(b) Over-population

Now consider a case with steady accumulation and neutral progress as before, but with the population growing at a faster rate than the demand for labour. Let us assume first of all that there are no opportunities for employment except those offered by capitalist enterprise, and let us compare the position at two points of time divided by an interval during which the population has increased.

Does the existence of available labour tend to increase the amount of employment? Clearly it increases human needs, but does it increase effective demand?

In so far as State or individual charity provides consumption for the unemployed at the expense of saving that would otherwise be made—that is, in so far as consumption of the recipient of charity is additional to and not in substitution for the consumption of the givers (or tax payers)—the level of consumption (at a given level of investment) has been raised and consequently the total level of employment in consumption industries is greater. But this cannot have eliminated unemployment, for if it did it would not. As soon as the unemployed were off their conscience the rest of the community would return to a higher rate of saving. It requires a growing amount of unemployment to keep employment increasing this way.

Moreover, the contribution which "doles" make to the consumption of the unemployed may be very small. "It's the poor what helps the poor", and most of what the unemployed consume is not additional demand. If the unemployed are supported by friends and relations who in any case have no margin for saving, an addition to the number of mouths to be fed has no effect upon total consumption, and therefore no effect upon output and employment at all.

(It may seem unduly pessimistic to argue that both an excess and a deficiency in population growth causes unemployment, but we should look at employment, rather than unemployment, to see what is happening. In the first case, a fall in the rate of growth of numbers causes a fall in the rate of growth of employment; in the second case employment increases at its former rate, but it increases by less than available labour, so that unemployment increases also.)

The existence of the "reverse army" of unemployed workers reacts upon employment in another way. It weakens the bargaining position of labour and makes it impossible for Trade Unions to keep monopoly profits in check. Thus prices tend to be higher relatively to money-wage rates than they are where full employment and full capacity coincide. In consequence, the competitive advantage to be gained by finding labour-saving techniques is weakened. Moreover, since the price of equipment (as of other commodities) is raised relatively to wage rates by the high rate of profit, capital-saving techniques are likely to be sought for even if they are actually labour-using. Consequently employment per unit of output is kept high. This is the reverse of technological unemployment. Thus compared to an economy which has developed without redundant labour, an economy with a large reserve army of unemployed workers may have a reserve of productive capacity, which more capital would release, also within the labour force which it does employ.

There is another channel through which some of the redundant workers may get themselves into employment, and that is through the demand for housing. A growth in the numbers supported by a given family income deflects demand from consumption goods in general to demand for housing (a man would rather wear clogs in his own house than leather boots in his mother-in-law's). We shall not consider a country where the unemployed can build themselves hovels of mud, but one where housing is provided by capitalist enterprise. Now, the industry whose output is room-years of living space employs exceptionally little current wage-labour, so that more of the flow of expenditure on house-rent goes to capital than is the case with almost any other kind of outlay. Thus a deflection of demand from things in general to housing has the same effect as a bout of innovations "favourable to capital" and tends to promote investment in the same way. (This cannot, of course, provide a permanent cure for unemployment due to an excessive rate of growth of population, for it requires a given rate of growth to maintain given employment in building.) The effect of an increase in house building is powerfully reinforced if the society concerned has certain standards of public health so that, if not housing itself, at least the auxiliary services of drainage, etc. are provided at public expense.

Thus it is an exaggeration to say that the existence of available labour has no influence at all on the amount of employment.

The assumption that all employment is given by capitalist enterprise is also exaggerated. No society is so completely specialised as to make self-employment quite impossible. The reserve army can usually produce some kind of output, for its own use or for trade with the capitalist sector. Industries may be built upon material salvaged from capitalist rubbish heaps (petrol tins in Syria). Personal services are pressed upon whoever has a copper to spare (shoe-blacks in Spain) and layers of middlemen squeeze themselves into every gap between cost and demand-price (traders in Africa).

The distinction between employment and "disguised unemployment" in a slump, though not absolutely clear cut, is a straightforward conception. Workers have been expelled from jobs that they were recently holding, and will return as soon as they are sent for. In a developing economy the line is not so easy to draw, for the self-supporting members of the reserve army are tiny capitalists (even a couple of old petrol tins is a stock of capital goods if they are in process of being made into saucepans), and may even employ each other for wages. The "kulaks" [wealthy peasant farmers] among them approximate to capitalist employers. However, the distinguishing characteristic of their industry is that it has a very marked inferiority in productive efficiency to regular employment, and that their propensity to consume is markedly higher than that of regular capitalists, because they are living very near the minimum subsistence.

The whole picture is radically different when there is land available to be taken into cultivation outside the capitalist sphere. Where the workers who are not offered employment by capitalists can set off into hitherto unpeopled territory where they can support their families by their own labour, their departure relieves the situation in three ways: first, they find themselves a less wretched means of life; second, by removing the enervating influence of redundant labour, they stimulate the capitalists at home to improve technique; and third, their trade, in due course, with the centres they have left, causes the total of effective demand to expand at a faster rate, and so sets up an inducement to invest in capitalist industries which export to them.

(The safety valve of migration to the New World from areas of surplus population was an essential part of the mechanism of nineteenth-century capitalism, and now that it is choked up we begin to realise how much it contributed to the working of the machine.)

CHAPTER 6 The Libertarian School

6.1 CARL MENGER

The Nature and Origin of Value

Carl Menger (1840–1921), founder of the Austrian school of economics, was born in Neu-Sandez, Galicia, Austria. After completing his formal education in Prague, Czechoslovakia; Cracow, Poland; and Vienna; Austria, he became a professor of economics at the University of Vienna in 1883. After a 30-year tenure at the university, Menger retired to concentrate his energies on economic research.

The following selection has been taken from Menger's most famous work, originally published in 1871 and translated as *Principles of Economics.* In this book, working along the same lines as William Stanley Jevons (1835–1882) in England and Léon Walras (1834–1910) in France, he formulates his marginal theory of utility and a subjective theory of value. According to Menger, if every person maximizes benefits, then society will maximize its benefits. The following selection explains his concept of value, which holds that value is fundamental to economic activity. There is a hierarchy of needs with the need for goods of higher order being satisfied before goods of lower order. The value of the last good is the marginal utility, or the last amount spent by the consumer, which gives no more or less satisfaction than the last amount spent on any other good.

Key Concept: marginal utility

If the requirements for a good, in a time period over which the provident activity of men is to extend, are greater than the quantity of it available to them for that time period, and if they endeavor to satisfy their needs for it as completely as possible in the given circumstances, men feel impelled to engage in the activity... designated *economizing.* But their perception of this relationship gives rise to another phenomenon, the deeper understanding of which is of decisive importance for our science. I refer to the value of goods.

If the requirements for a good are larger than the quantity of it available, and some part of the needs involved must remain unsatisfied in any case, the available quantity of the good can be diminished by no part of the whole amount, in any way practically worthy of notice, without causing some need, previously provided for, to be satisfied either not at all or only less completely than would otherwise have been the case. The satisfaction of some one human need is therefore dependent on the availability of each concrete, practically significant, quantity of all goods subject to this quantitative relationship. If economizing men become aware of this circumstance (that is, if they perceive that the satisfaction of one of their needs, or the greater or less completeness of its satisfaction, is dependent on their command of each portion of a quantity of goods or on each individual good subject to the above quantitative relationship) these goods attain for them the significance we call *value.* Value is thus the importance that individual goods or quantities of goods attain for us because we are conscious of being dependent on command of them for the satisfaction of our needs.

The value of goods, accordingly, is a phenomenon that springs from the same source as the economic character of goods—that is, from the relationship, explained earlier, between requirements for and available quantities of goods. But there is a difference between the two phenomena. On the one hand, perception of this quantitative relationship stimulates our provident activity, thus causing goods subject to this relationship to become objects of our economizing (i. e. economic goods). On the other hand, perception of the same relationship makes us aware of the significance that command of each concrete unit of the available quantities of these goods has for our lives and well-being, thus causing it to attain *value* for us. Just as a penetrating investigation of mental processes makes the cognition of external things appear to be merely our consciousness of the impressions made by the external things upon our persons, and thus, in the final analysis, merely the cognition of states of our own persons, so too, in the final analysis, is the importance that we attribute to things of the external world only an outflow of the importance to us of our continued existence and development (life and well-being). Value is therefore nothing inherent in goods, no property of them, but merely, the importance that we first attribute to the satisfaction of our needs, that is, to our lives and well-being, and in consequence carry over to economic goods as the exclusive causes of the satisfaction of our needs.

From this, it is also clear why only economic goods have value to us, while goods subject to the quantitative relationship responsible for non-economic character cannot attain value at all. The relationship responsible for the non-economic character of goods consists in requirements for goods being smaller than their available quantities. Thus there are always portions of the whole supply of non-economic goods that are related to no unsatisfied human need, and which can therefore lose their goods-character without impinging in any way on the satisfaction of human needs. Hence no satisfaction depends on our control of any one of the units of a good having non-economic character, and from this it follows that definite quantities of goods subject to this quantitative relationship (non-economic goods) also have no value to us.

If an inhabitant of a virgin forest has several hundred thousand trees at his disposal while he needs only some twenty a year for the full provision of his requirements for timber, he will not consider himself injured in any way, in the satisfaction of his needs, if a forest fire destroys a thousand or so of the trees, provided he is still in a position to satisfy his needs as completely as before with the rest. In such circumstances, therefore, the satisfaction of none of his needs depends upon his command of any single tree, and for this reason a tree also has no value to him.

But suppose there are also in the forest ten wild fruit trees whose fruit is consumed by the same individual. Suppose too, that the amount of fruit available to him is not larger than his requirements. Certainly then, not a single one of these fruit trees can be burned in the fire without causing him to suffer hunger as a result, or without at least causing him to be unable to satisfy his need for fruit as completely as before. For this reason each one of the fruit trees has value to him.

If the inhabitants of a village need a thousand pails of water daily to meet their requirements completely, and a brook is at their disposal with a daily flow of a hundred thousand pails, a concrete portion of this quantity of water, one pail for instance, will have no value to them, since they could satisfy their needs for water just as completely if this partial amount were removed from their command, or if it were altogether to lose its goods-character. Indeed, they will let many thousands of pails of this good flow to the sea every day without in any way impairing satisfaction of their need for water. As long as the relationship responsible for the non-economic character of water continues, therefore, the satisfaction of none of their needs will depend upon their command of any one pail of water in such a way that the satisfaction of this need would not take place if they were not in a position to use that particular pail. For this reason a pail of water has no value to them.

If, on the other hand, the daily flow of the brook were to fall to five hundred pails daily due to an unusual drought or other act of nature, and the inhabitants of the village had no other source of supply, the result would be that the total quantity then available would be insufficient to satisfy their full needs for water, and they could not venture to lose any part of that quantity, one pail for instance, without impairing the satisfaction of their needs. Each concrete portion of the quantity at their disposal would certainly then have value to them.

Non-economic goods, therefore, not only do not have exchange value, as has previously been supposed in the literature of our subject, but no value at all, and hence no use value. . . . For the time being, let it be observed that exchange value and use value are two concepts subordinate to the general concept of value, and hence coordinate in their relations to each other. All that I have already said about value in general is accordingly as valid for use value as it is for exchange value.

If then, a large number of economists attribute use value (though not exchange value) to non-economic goods, and if some recent English and French economists even wish to banish the concept use value entirely from our science and see it replaced with the concept utility, their desire rests on a misunderstanding of the important difference between the two concepts and the actual phenomena underlying them.

Utility is the capacity of a thing to serve for the satisfaction of human needs, and hence (provided the utility is *recognized*) it is a general prerequisite of goods-character. Non-economic goods have utility as well as economic goods, since they are just as capable of satisfying our needs. With these goods also, their capacity to satisfy needs must be *recognized* by men, since they could not otherwise acquire goods-character. But what distinguishes a non-economic good from a good subject to the quantitative relationship responsible for economic character is the circumstance that the satisfaction of human needs does not depend upon the availability of concrete quantities of the former but does depend upon the availability of concrete quantities of the latter. For this reason the former possesses utility, but only the latter, in addition to utility, possesses also that significance for us that we call value.

Of course the error underlying the confusion of utility and use value has had no influence on the practical activity of men. At no time has an economizing individual attributed value under ordinary circumstances to a cubic foot of air or, in regions abounding in springs, to a pint of water. The practical man distinguishes very well the capacity of an object to satisfy one of his needs from its value. But this confusion has become an enormous obstacle to the development of the more general theories of our science.

The circumstance that a good has value to us is attributable, as we have seen, to the fact that command of it has for us the significance of satisfying a need that would not be provided for if we did not have command of the good. Our needs, at any rate in part, at least as concerns their origin, depend upon our wills or on our habits. Once the needs have come into existence, however, there is *no further arbitrary element* in the value goods have for us, for their value is then the necessary consequence of our knowledge of their importance for our lives or well-being. It would be impossible, therefore, for us to regard a good as valueless when we know that the satisfaction of one of our needs depends on having it at our disposal. It would also be impossible for us to attribute value to goods when we know that we are not dependent upon them for the satisfaction of our needs. The value of goods is therefore nothing arbitrary, but always the necessary consequence of human knowledge that the maintenance of life, of well-being, or of some ever so insignificant part of them, depends upon control of a good or a quantity of goods.

Regarding this *knowledge,* however, men can be in error about the value of goods just as they can be in error with respect to all other objects of human knowledge. Hence they may attribute value to things that do not, according to economic considerations, possess it in reality, if they mistakenly assume that the more or less complete satisfaction of their needs depends on a good, or quantity of goods, when this relationship is really non-existent. In cases of this sort we observe the phenomenon of *imaginary* value.

The value of goods arises from their relationship to our needs, and is not inherent in the goods themselves. With *changes in this relationship,* value arises and disappears. For the inhabitants of an oasis, who have command of a spring that abundantly meets their requirements for water, a certain quantity of water at the spring itself will have no value. But if the spring, as the result of an earthquake, should suddenly decrease its yield of water to such an extent that the satisfaction of the needs of the inhabitants of the oasis would no longer be fully provided for, each of their concrete needs for water would become dependent upon the availability of a definite quantity of it, and such a quantity would immediately attain value for each inhabitant. This value would, however, suddenly disappear if the old relationship were reëstablished and the spring regained its former yield of water. A similar result would ensue if the population of the oasis should increase to such an extent that the water of the spring would no longer suffice for the satisfaction of all needs. Such a change, due to the increase of consumers, might even take place with a certain regularity at such times as the oasis was visited by numerous caravans.

Value is thus nothing inherent in goods, no property of them, nor an independent thing existing by itself. It is a judgment economizing men make about the importance of the goods at their disposal for the maintenance of their lives and well-being. Hence value does not exist outside the consciousness of men. It is, therefore, also quite erroneous to call a good that has value to economizing individuals a "value," or for economists to speak of "values" as of independent real things, and to objectify value in this way. For the entities that exist objectively are always only particular things or quantities of things, and their value is something fundamentally different from the things themselves; it is a judgment made by economizing individuals about the importance their command of the things has for the maintenance of their lives and well-being. Objectification of the value of goods, which is entirely *subjective* in nature, has nevertheless contributed very greatly to confusion about the basic principles of our science.

6.2 WILLIAM STANLEY JEVONS

Brief Account of a General Mathematical Theory of Political Economy

William Stanley Jevons (1835–1882) was born in Liverpool, England. At the age of 16, he entered University College in London, where he studied botany and chemistry and cultivated an interest in social issues. His academic appointments included tutor at Owens College in Manchester (1863–1876) and chair of the economics department at University College in London (1876–1880). He died in a drowning accident in 1882, leaving his greatest work, "Brief Account of a General Mathematical Theory of Political Economy," *Journal of the Royal Statistical Society* (June 1866), from which the following selection has been taken, unfinished.

Jevons's early contribution was in the area of monetary statistics. In a series of papers, including "A Serious Fall in the Value of Gold Ascertained, and Its Social Effects Set Forth" (1863), he pioneered a highly accurate method of estimation of the decline in the value of gold, which later came to be known as price index numbers. In this selection, Jevons presents his theory of utility and value. He considers the utility of a commodity to be related to that commodity only. The more one has of a commodity, the less the satisfaction obtained from consuming an additional unit of it. It follows, concludes Jevons, that inferior goods such as bread will have less marginal utility because their abundance reduces the satisfaction from consuming an additional unit. In contrast, consumption of an additional unit of a scarce commodity like precious stones yields great satisfaction. In other words, it has greater marginal utility because of its high price and limited availability.

Key Concept: the coefficient of utility

1. The following paper briefly describes the nature of a Theory of Economy which will reduce the main problem of this science to a mathematical form. Economy, indeed, being concerned with quantities, has always of necessity been mathematical in its subject, but the strict and general statement, and the easy comprehension of its quantitative laws has been prevented by a

neglect of those powerful methods of expression which have been applied to most other sciences with so much success. It is not to be supposed, however, that because economy becomes mathematical in form, it will, therefore, become a matter of rigorous calculation. Its mathematical principles may become formal and certain, while its individual data remain as inexact as ever.

2. A true theory of economy can only be attained by going back to the great springs of human action—the feelings of pleasure and pain. A large part of such feelings arise periodically from the ordinary wants and desires of body or mind, and from the painful exertion we are continually prompted to undergo that we may satisfy our wants.

Economy investigates the relations of ordinary pleasures and pains thus arising, and it has a wide enough field of inquiry. But economy does not treat of all human motives. There are motives nearly always present with us, arising from conscience, compassion, or from some moral or religious source, which economy cannot and does not pretend to treat. These will remain to us as outstanding and disturbing forces; they must be treated, if at all, by other appropriate branches of knowledge.

3. We always treat feelings as being capable of more or less, and I now hold that they are quantities capable of scientific treatment.

Our estimation of the comparative amounts of feeling is performed in the act of choice or volition. Our choice of one course out of two or more proves that, in our estimation, this course promises the greatest balance of pleasure. When there is a large overbalancing force on one side, indeed, the estimation of the amount of this balance is no doubt very rude; but all the critical points of the theory will depend on that nice estimation of the opposing motives which we make when these are nearly equal, and we hesitate between them.

4. As several writers have previously remarked, feelings have two dimensions, intension and duration. A pleasure or a pain may be either weak or intense in any indivisible moment; it may also last a long or a short time. If the intensity remains uniform, the quantity of feeling generated is found by multiplying the units of intensity into the units of duration. But if the intensity, as is usually the case, varies as some function of the time, the quantity of feeling is got by infinitesimal summation or integration.

Thus, if the duration of a feeling be represented by the abscissa of a curve, the intensity will be the ordinate, and the quantity of feeling will be the area.

5. Pleasure and pain, of course, are opposed as positive and negative quantities.

6. A principle of the mind which any true theory must take into account is that of foresight. Every expected future pleasure or pain affects us with similar feelings in the present time, but with an intensity diminished in some proportion to its uncertainty and its remoteness in time. But the effects of foresight merely complicate without altering the other parts of the theory.

7. Such are the main principles of feeling on which economy is founded. A second part of the theory proceeds from feelings to the useful objects or utilities by which pleasurable feeling is increased or pain removed.

An object is useful when it either affects the senses pleasurably in the present moment, or when, by foresight, it is expected that it will do so at some future time. Thus we must carefully distinguish actual utility in present use from estimated future utility, which yet, by allowing for the imperfect force of anticipation, and for the uncertainty of future events, gives a certain present utility.

8. Amount of utility corresponds to amount of pleasure produced. But the continued uniform application of a useful object to the senses or the desires will not commonly produce uniform amounts of pleasure. Every appetite or sense is more or less rapidly satiated. A certain quantity of an object received, a further quantity is indifferent to us, or may even excite disgust. Every successive application will commonly excite the feelings less intensely than the previous application. The utility of the last supply of an object, then, usually decreases in some proportion, or as some function of the whole quantity received. This variation theoretically existing even in the smallest quantities, we must recede to infinitesimals, and what we shall call the coefficient of utility, is the ratio between the last increment or infinitely small supply of the object, and the increment of pleasure which it occasions, both, of course, estimated in their appropriate units.

9. The coefficient of utility is, then, some generally diminishing function of the whole quantity of the object consumed. Here is the most important law of the whole theory.

This function of utility is peculiar to each kind of object, and more or less to each individual. Thus, the appetite for dry bread is much more rapidly satisfied than that for wine, for clothes, for handsome furniture, for works of art, or, finally, for money. And every one has his own peculiar tastes in which he is nearly insatiable.

10. A third part of the theory now treats of labor; which, although the means by which we seek pleasure, is always accompanied by a certain painful exertion, rapidly increasing as some function of the intensity or the duration of the labor. Thus, labor will be exerted both in intensity and duration until a further increment will be more painful than the increment of produce thereby obtained is pleasurable. Here labor will stop, but up to this point it will always be accompanied by an excess of pleasure.

It is obvious that the final point of labor will depend upon the final ratio of utility of the object produced.

11. I assume, as obviously true, that the abilities of men are infinitely varied, whether by nature or by education, so that both the same person may vary in his power of producing different objects, and any two persons may vary in respect of the same object.

This, indeed, is in direct opposition to the erroneous simplification of the science effected by [David] Ricardo, when he assumed that all laborers have a certain uniform power; the higher classes of mechanics and other skilled or learned producers being treated as mere exceptions to the rule.

12. The theory of rent, which here comes in, is not materially different from that of Dr. [James] Anderson and later writers.

13. We now arrive at the theory of exchange, which is a deduction from the laws of utility.

If a person has any useful object, but an object belonging to another person would have greater utility, he will be glad to give the one in return for the other.

But it is a necessary condition that the other person will likewise gain, or at least not lose by the exchange.

Whether the exchange will take place or not can only be ascertained by estimating the utility of the objects on either side, which is done by integrating the appropriate functions of utility up to the quantity of each object as limits. A balance of utility on both sides will lead to an exchange.

14. Suppose, however, that the useful objects on either side are commodities of which more or less may be given, and this even down to infinitely small quantities. Such is substantially the case in ordinary commercial sales. There are now no definite amounts of utility to be balanced against each other, but the one person will now give to the other so much of his commodity, and at such a ratio of exchange, that if he gave an infinitely small quantity, either more or less, but at the same rate, he would not gain in utility by it. The increments of utility lost and gained at the limits of the quantities exchanged must be equal, otherwise further exchange would take place.

The ratio of the increments of the commodities, however, would be indeterminate but for the existence of a law that all quantities of the same commodity, being uniform in kind, must be exchanged at the same rate. The last increments, then, must be exchanged, in the ratio of the whole quantities exchanged. To explain in ordinary words how the adjustment takes place under this condition is almost impossible. But light is at once thrown on the whole matter by stating that in every such exchange we have two unknown quantities and two equations by which to determine them. The unknown quantities are the quantities of commodity given and received. The known quantities are those of the commodities previously possessed. We have also the functions of utility of the commodities with the respect to the persons. An equation may thus be established on either side between the utility gained and sacrificed at the ratio of exchange of the whole commodities, upon the last increments exchanged.

15. When the useful object on one side only is infinitely divisible, we shall have only one unknown quantity, namely, that of the divisible commodity given for the indivisible object, and also one equation to determine it by, namely, that on the part of the person holding the divisible commodity, and able to give more or less for it. But this does not apply to unique objects, like a statue, a rare book, or gem, which do not admit of the conception of more or less.

When both commodities are indivisible, . . . we have neither unknown quantities nor equations.

16. The equations in an exchange may prove impossible, or without solutions. This will indicate either that no exchange of commodity can take place at all, or that at least one of the parties to the exchange is not satisfied even with the whole of the commodity formerly belonging to the other.

17. The principle of exchange thus deduced in the case of two persons and two commodities, applies to any number of persons and commodities. It, therefore, applies not only to the general inland trade of a country, but to the trade between aggregates of men or nations—international trade.

The number of equations is very rapidly increased according to the simple law of combinations.

18. Of course such equations as are here spoken of are merely theoretical. Such complicated laws as those of economy cannot be accurately traced in individual cases. Their operation can only be detected in aggregates and by the method of averages. We must think under the forms of these laws in their theoretic perfection and complication; in practice we must be content with approximate and empirical laws.

19. Let it be remarked, that though the exchanges be regulated by equations, there cannot be equality in the whole utilities gained and lost, which are found by integrating the functions of utility of the respective commodities before and after exchange.

The balance is the gain of utility, and from the nature of exchange there must be a gain on one side at least.

20. Combining the theory of exchanges with that of labor and production, the quantity which each person produces will be dependant upon the result of the exchanges; for this may greatly modify the conditions of utility.

A new set of unknown quantities are thus introduced; but it will be found that just as many new equations to determine them may be established. Each such equation is between the utility of the last increment of produce and the increment of labor necessary to produce it.

21. The only further part of the theory which I will here at all attempt to explain is that referring to capital. I shall give a definition of capital different from the established one, and much simpler. Mr. J. S. Mill says (*Principles*, 3rd edition, vol. i, p. 67), "What capital does for production is to afford the shelter, protection, tools and materials which the work requires, and to feed and otherwise maintain the laborers during the process."

To understand capital properly, we must omit all but the last enumerated part. Thus, I define capital as consisting of all useful objects which, in supplying a laborer's ordinary wants and desires, enable him to undertake works of which the result will be deferred for a greater or less space of time. Capital, in short, is nothing but maintenance of laborers.

It is, of course, perfectly true that buildings, tools, materials, &c., are a necessary means of production; but they are already the product of labor assisted by capital or maintenance. They are the results of the application of capital to labor at an imperfect stage.

Without capital a person must have immediate returns, or else he perishes. With capital he may sow in the spring that he may reap in the autumn; or he may undertake labor-saving enterprises, such as roads and railways, which will not make a full return for many years. Most improved modes of applying labor require that the enjoyment of the result shall be deferred.

22. While amount of capital is estimated by the amount of utility of which the enjoyment is deferred, amount of employment of capital is the amount of utility multiplied by the number of units of time during which its enjoyment is deferred.

23. The interest of all capital in a market is of one rate only, and that, therefore, the lowest rate; because capital consists only in maintenance, and may therefore be applied indifferently to any branch of industry. Buildings, tools, &c., which have hitherto been classed with capital, are, on the contrary, usually applicable only to the single purpose for which they were designed. The profit

they bring, therefore, in no way follows the laws of the interest of capital, but rather those of rent, or the produce of natural agents. This has been already remarked by Professor Newman, in his Lectures on Political Economy, and by other writers.

24. As labor must be supposed to be aided with some capital, the rate of interest is always determined by the ratio which a new increment of produce bears to the increment of capital by which it was produced. As the interest of all capital must be uniform, the benefit which the mass of capital already available confers upon the laborer goes for nothing in determining the rate of interest, which depends solely upon the portion last added, or which may be added.

25. We can now easily explain the known fact, that the interest of capital always tends to fall very rapidly as its amount increases, in proportion to the labor it supports. It is because for equal increments of time the necessary increments of capital increase with the time. Thus, if I undertake a work which I can finish in one year, I have to await the result on an average only half a year. If, however, I work a second year before getting the result, I wait a whole year for the former year's work and half a year for the second year's work. Thus I employ at least three times as much capital in the second year as in the first. In the third year I should employ at least five times as much capital, in the fourth year at least seven times, and so on. Unless, then, the advantages of the successive deferments increase in the arithmetical series 3, 5, 7, 9, &c., the proportional profit from the new additions must fall, and, as was said before, the lowest rate for which capital may be had governs the rate of all other capital.

26. It is the accepted opinion of writers of the present day, that the rate of interest tends to fall because the soil does not yield proportionate returns as its cultivation is pushed. But I must hold that this decrease in the proportionate returns would chiefly fall upon the wages of the laborer. The interest of capital has no relation to the absolute returns to labor, but only to the increased return which the last increment of capital allows.

27. Having thus explained some of the principal features of the theory, I shall close without venturing into the higher complications of the subject, where the effects of money, of credit, of combination of labor, of the risk or uncertainty of undertakings, and of bankruptcy, are taken into account.

The last result of the theory will be to give a determination of the rates of wages, or the produce of labour after deduction of rent, interest, profit, insurance and taxation, which are so many payments which the labourer makes for advantages enjoyed.

6.3 FRIEDRICH A. HAYEK

Consumers' and Producers' Goods

Friedrich A. Hayek (1899–1992) was born in Vienna, Austria. The publication of a collection of lectures on business cycles earned him a faculty position at the London School of Economics from 1931 until 1950, when he moved to the University of Chicago. In 1962, Hayek left the University of Chicago for the University of Frieburg, Germany, and later, the University of Salzburg, Austria. After nine years at the University of Salzburg, where he found little interest in his methods, Hayek returned to Frieburg. In 1974, he was awarded the Nobel Prize for his work on the theory of capital and his analysis of economic fluctuations.

Hayek is best known for his monetarist approach to trade cycle theory and his theory of capital. His trade cycle theory is contained in *Prices and Production* (Routledge & Kegan Paul, 1931), from which the following selection has been excerpted. Hayek presents an economic boom as a period of overinvestment. Following excessive investment over savings, prices become distorted, causing economic collapse. According to Hayek, the Great Depression was preceded by overconsumption, which reduced the money supply, and in turn, the demand for labor, which sharply raised unemployment. The mechanism of the free market was the only means by which equilibrium could be restored. In the following selection, Hayek uses the Austrian theory of capital to explain the relationship between intermediate and consumer goods in the production process. As savings rise, the demand for capital goods rises over that for consumer goods, causing a lengthening of the period of production. The amount spent on earlier stages of production increases, that which is spent on later stages of production decreases, and the total spent on intermediate products increases as well.

Key Concept: profits as determinants of reinvestment

I find it convenient to represent the successive applications of the original means of production which are needed to bring forth the output of consumers' goods accruing at any moment of time, by the hypotenuse of a right-angled triangle, such as the triangle in Fig. 1. The value of these original means of production is expressed by the horizontal projection of the hypotenuse, while the vertical dimension, measured in arbitrary periods from the top to the bottom, expresses the progress of time, so that the inclination of the line representing the amount of original means of production used means that these original means of production are expended continuously during the whole process of production. The bottom of the triangle represents the value of the current output of consumers' goods. The area of the triangle thus shows the totality of the successive stages through which the several units of original means of production pass before they become ripe for consumption. It also shows the total amount of intermediate products which must exist at any moment of time in order to secure a continuous output of consumers' goods. For this reason we may conceive of this diagram not only as representing the successive stages of the production of the output of any given moment of time, but also as representing the processes of production going on simultaneously in a stationary society. To use a happy phrase of J. B. Clark's, it gives a picture of the "synchronised process of production".

Now it should be clear without further explanation that the proportion between the amount of intermediate products (represented by the area of the triangle) which is necessary at any moment of time to secure a continuous output of a given quantity of consumers' goods, and the amount of that output, must grow with the length of the roundabout process of production. As the average time interval between the application of the original means of production and the completion of the consumers' goods increases, production becomes more capitalistic, and *vice versa.* In the case we are contemplating in which the original means of production are applied at a constant rate throughout the whole process of production, this average time is exactly half as long as the time which elapses between the application of the first unit of original means of production and the completion of the process. Accordingly, the total amount of intermediate products may also be represented by a rectangle half as high as the triangle, as indicated by the dotted line in the diagram. The areas of the two figures are necessarily equal, and it sometimes assists the eye to have a rectangle instead of a triangle when we have to judge the relative magnitude represented by the area of the figure. Furthermore, it should be noticed that, as the figure represents values and not physical production, the surplus return obtained by the roundabout methods of production is not represented in the diagram.... I have intentionally neglected interest [here. For now] we may assume that the intermediate products remain the property of the owners of the original means of production until they have matured into consumers' goods and are sold to consumers. Interest is then received by the owners of the original means of production together with wages and rent.

A perfectly continuous process of this sort is somewhat unwieldy for theoretical purposes: moreover such an assumption is not perhaps sufficiently realistic. It would be open to us to deal with the difficulties by the aid of higher mathematics. But I, personally, prefer to make it amenable to a simpler method by dividing the continuous process into distinct periods, and by substituting for the concept of a continuous flow the assumption that goods move intermit-

FIGURE 1

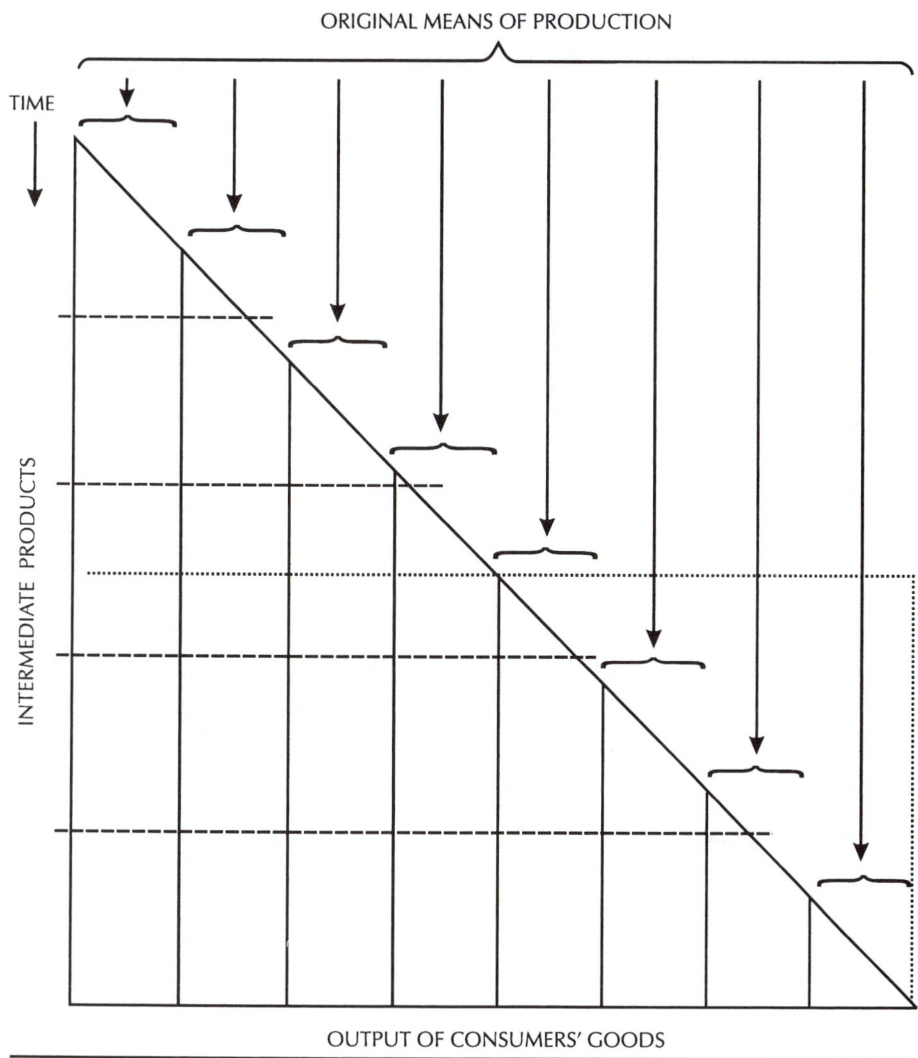

tently in equal intervals from one stage of production to the next. In this way, in my view, the loss in precision is more than compensated by the gain in lucidity.

Probably the simplest method of transforming the picture of the continuous process into a picture of what happens in a given period is to make cross sections through our first figure at intervals corresponding to the periods chosen, and to imagine observers being posted at each of these cross cuts who watch and note down the amount of goods flowing by. If we put these cross sections, as indicated by the broken lines in Fig. 1, at the end of each period, and represent the amount of goods passing these lines of division in a period

FIGURE 2

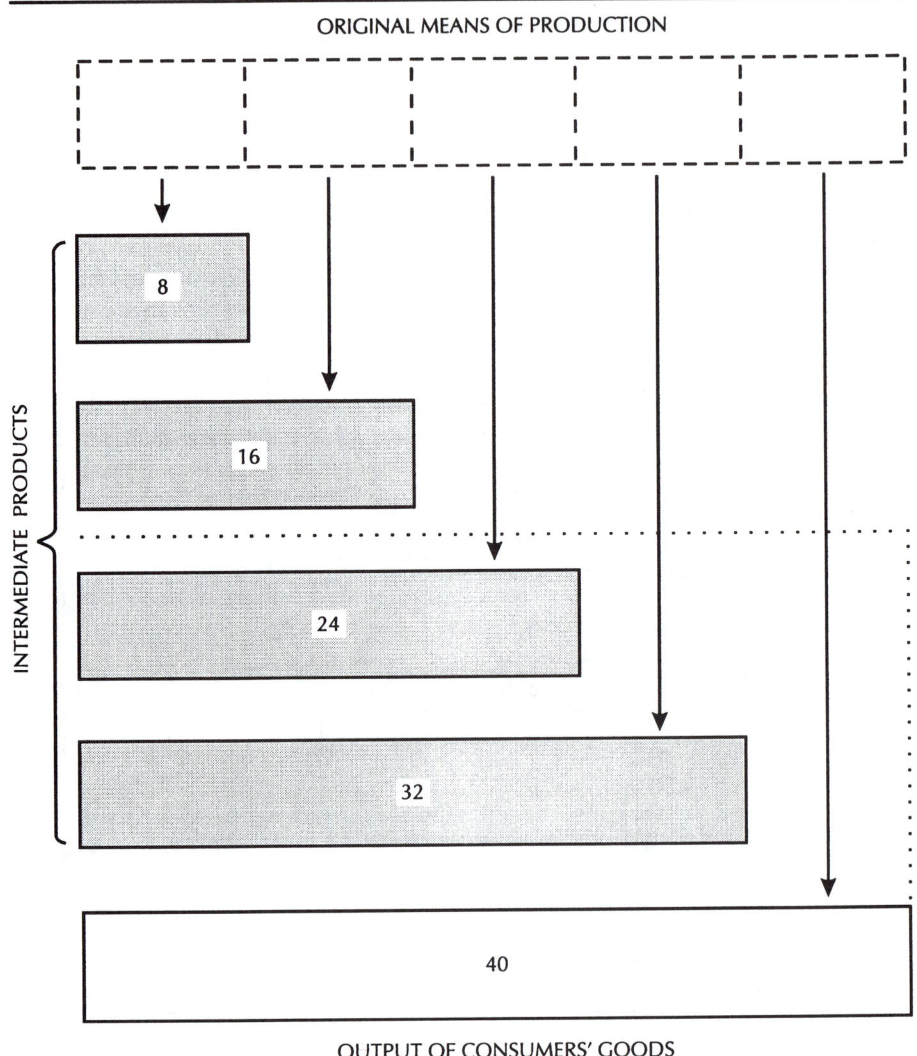

by a rectangle of corresponding size, we get the new illustration of the same process given in Fig. 2.

It is convenient for the purposes of exposition to count only that part of the total process of production which is completed during one of these periods, as a separate stage of production. Each of the successive shaded blocks in the diagram will then represent the product of the corresponding stage of production as it is passed on to the next while the differences in the length of the successive blocks correspond to the amount of original means of production used in the succeeding stage. The white block at the bottom represents the output of consumers' goods during the period. In a stationary state, which is still the only state I am considering, this output of consumers' goods is necessarily equal to the total income from the factors of production used, and is exchanged for this income. The proportion of the white area to the shaded area, in this diagram 40:80 or 1:2, expresses the proportion between the output of consumers' goods and the output of intermediate products (or between the amount of consumption and the amount of new and renewed investment during any period of time).

So far, I have used this schematic illustration of the process of production only to represent the movements of goods. It is just as legitimate to use it as an illustration of the movement of money. While goods move downwards from the top to the bottom of our diagram, we have to conceive of money moving in the opposite direction, being paid first for consumers' goods and thence moving upwards until, after a varying number of intermediary movements, it is paid out as income to the owners of the factors of production, who in turn use it to buy consumers' goods. But in order to trace the relation between actual money payments, or the proportional quantities of money used in the different stages of production, and the movements of goods, we need a definite assumption in regard to the division of the total process among different firms, which alone makes an exchange of goods against money necessary. For this does not by any means necessarily coincide with our division into separate stages of production of equal length. I shall begin with the simplest assumption, that these two divisions do coincide, that is to say that goods moving towards consumption do change hands against money in equal intervals which correspond to our unit production periods.

In such a case, the proportion of money spent for consumers' goods and money spent for intermediate products is equal to the proportion between the total demand for consumers' goods and the total demand for the intermediate products necessary for their continuous production; and this, in turn, must correspond, in a state of equilibrium, to the proportion between the output of consumers' goods during a period of time and the output of intermediate products of all earlier stages during the same period. Given the assumptions we are making, all these proportions are accordingly equally expressed by the proportion between the area of the white rectangle and the total shaded area. It will be noticed that the same device of the dotted line as was used in the earlier figure is employed to facilitate the comparison of the two areas. The dotted rectangle shows that, in the kind of production represented by Fig. 2, which actually takes four successive stages, the average length of the roundabout process is only two stages, and the amount of intermediate products is therefore twice as great as the output of customers' goods.

Now if we adopt this method of approach, certain fundamental facts at once become clear. The first fact which emerges is that the amount of money spent on producers' goods during any period of time may be far greater than the amount spent for consumers' goods during the same period. It has been computed, indeed, that in the United States, payments for consumers' goods amount only to about one-twelfth of the payments made for producers' goods of all kinds.

Nevertheless, this fact has not only very often been overlooked, it was even expressly denied by no less an authority than Adam Smith. According to Smith: "The value of goods circulated between the different dealers never can exceed the value of those circulated between dealers and consumers; whatever is bought by the dealer being ultimately destined to be sold to the consumers." This proposition clearly rests upon a mistaken inference from the fact that the total expenditure made in production must be covered by the return from the sale of the ultimate products; but it remained unrefuted, and quite recently in our own day it has formed the foundation of some very erroneous doctrines. The solution of the difficulty is, of course, that most goods are exchanged several times against money before they are sold to the consumer, and on the average exactly as many times as often as the total amount spent for producers' goods is larger than the amount spent for consumers' goods.

Another point which is of great importance for what follows, and which, while often overlooked in current discussions, is quite obvious if we look at our diagram, is the fact that what is generally called the capital equipment of society —the total of intermediate products in our diagram—is not a magnitude which, once it is brought into existence, will necessarily last for ever independently of human decisions. Quite the contrary: whether the structure of production remains the same depends entirely upon whether entrepreneurs find it profitable to re-invest the usual proportion of the return from the sale of the product of their respective stages of production in turning out intermediate goods of the same sort. Whether this is profitable, again, depends upon the prices obtained for the product of this particular stage of production on the one hand and on the prices paid for the original means of production and for the intermediate products taken from the preceding stage of production on the other. The continuance of the existing degree of capitalistic organisation depends, accordingly, on the prices paid and obtained for the product of each stage of production and these prices are, therefore, a very real and important factor in determining the direction of production.

The same fundamental fact may be described in a slightly different way. The money stream which the entrepreneur representing any stage of production receives at any given moment is always composed of net income which he may use for consumption without disturbing the existing method of production, and of parts which he must continuously re-invest. But it depends entirely upon him whether he re-distributes his total money receipts in the same proportions as before. And the main factor influencing his decisions will be the magnitude of the profits he hopes to derive from the production of his particular intermediate product.

And now at last we are ready to commence to discuss the main problem of this [selection], the problem of how a transition from less to more capitalistic methods of production, or *vice versa*, is actually brought about, and what conditions must be fulfilled in order that a new equilibrium may be reached. The first question can be answered immediately: a transition to more (or less) capitalistic methods of production will take place if the total demand for producers' goods (expressed in money) increases (or decreases) relatively to the demand

FIGURE 3

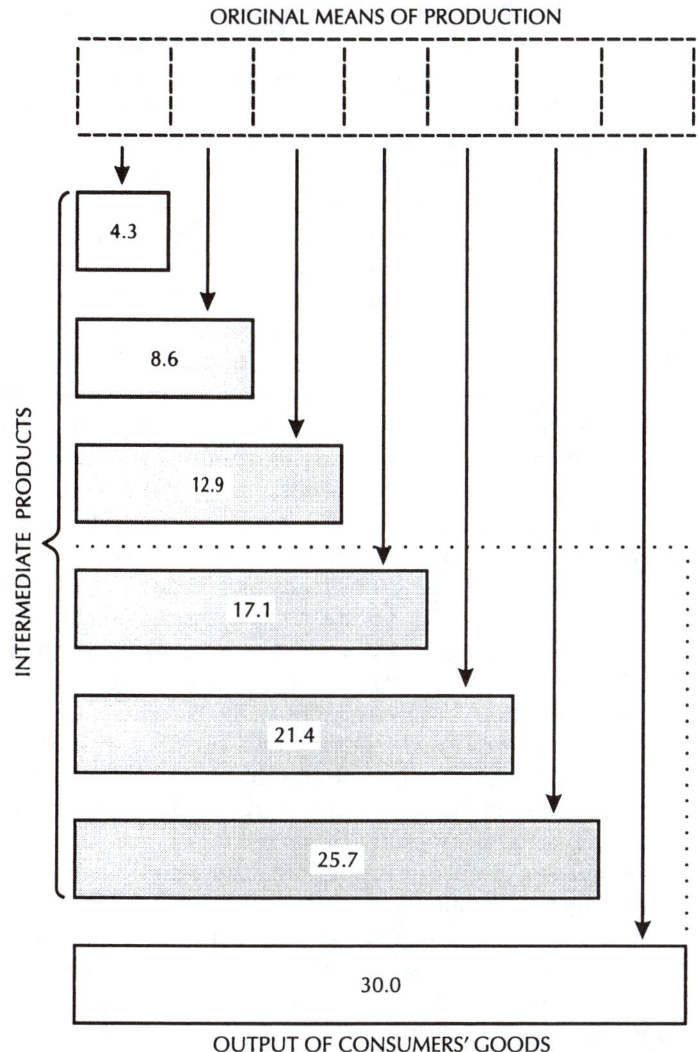

for consumers' goods. This may come about in one of two ways: either as a result of changes in the volume of voluntary saving (or its opposite), or as a result of a change in the quantity of money which alters the funds at the disposal of the entrepreneurs for the purchase of producers' goods. Let us first consider the case of changes in voluntary saving, that is, simple shifts of demand between consumers' goods and producers' goods.

As a starting point, we may take the situation depicted in Fig. 2, and suppose that consumers save and invest an amount of money equivalent to one fourth of their income of one period. We may assume further that these savings are made continuously, exactly as they can be used for building up the new process of production. The proportion of the demand for consumers' goods to the demand for intermediate products will then ultimately be changed from 40:80 to 30:90, or 1:2 to 1:3. The additional amounts of money available for the purchase of intermediate products must now be so applied that the output of consumers' goods may be sold for the reduced sum of thirty now available for that purpose. It should now be sufficiently clear that this will only be the case if the average length of the roundabout processes of production and, therefore, in our instance, also the number of successive stages of production, is increased in the same proportion as the demand for intermediate products has increased relatively to the demand for consumers' goods, i.e., from an average of two to an average of three (or from an actual number of four to an actual number of six) stages of production. When the transition is completed, the structure of production will have changed from that shown in Fig. 2 to the one shown in Fig. 3. (It should be remembered that the relative magnitudes in the two figures are values expressed in money and not physical quantities, that the amount of original means of production used has remained the same, and that the amount of money in circulation and its velocity of circulation are also supposed to remain unchanged.)

If we compare the two diagrams, we see at once that the nature of the change consists in a stretching of the money stream flowing from the consumers' goods to the original means of production. It has, so to speak, become longer and narrower. Its breadth at the bottom stage, which measures the amount of money spent during a period of time on consumers' goods and, at the same time, the amount of money received as income in payment for the use of the factors of production, has permanently decreased from forty to thirty. This means that the price of a unit of the factors of production, the total amount of which (if we neglect the increase of capital) has remained the same, will fall in the same proportion, and the price of a unit of consumers' goods, the output of which has increased as a consequence of the more capitalistic methods of production, will fall in still greater proportion. The amount of money spent in each of the later stages of production has also decreased, while the amount used in the earlier stages has increased, and the total spent on intermediate products has increased also because of the addition of a new stage of production.

Now it should be clear that to this change in the distribution of the amounts of money spent in the different stages of production there will correspond a similar change in the distribution of the total amount of goods existing at any moment. It should also be clear that the effect thus realised,—given the assumptions we are making,—is one which fulfils the object of saving and investing, and is identical with the effect which would have been produced if the savings were made in kind instead of in money. Whether it has been brought about in the most expeditious way, and whether the price changes which follow from our assumptions provide a suitable stimulus to the readjustment are not questions with which we need concern ourselves at this juncture. Our present purpose is fulfilled if we have established, that under the assumptions we have made, the initial variation in the proportional demand for consumers' goods and for intermediate products respectively becomes permanent, that a new equilibrium may establish itself on this basis, and that the fact that the amount of money remains unchanged, in spite of the increase of the output of

FIGURE 4

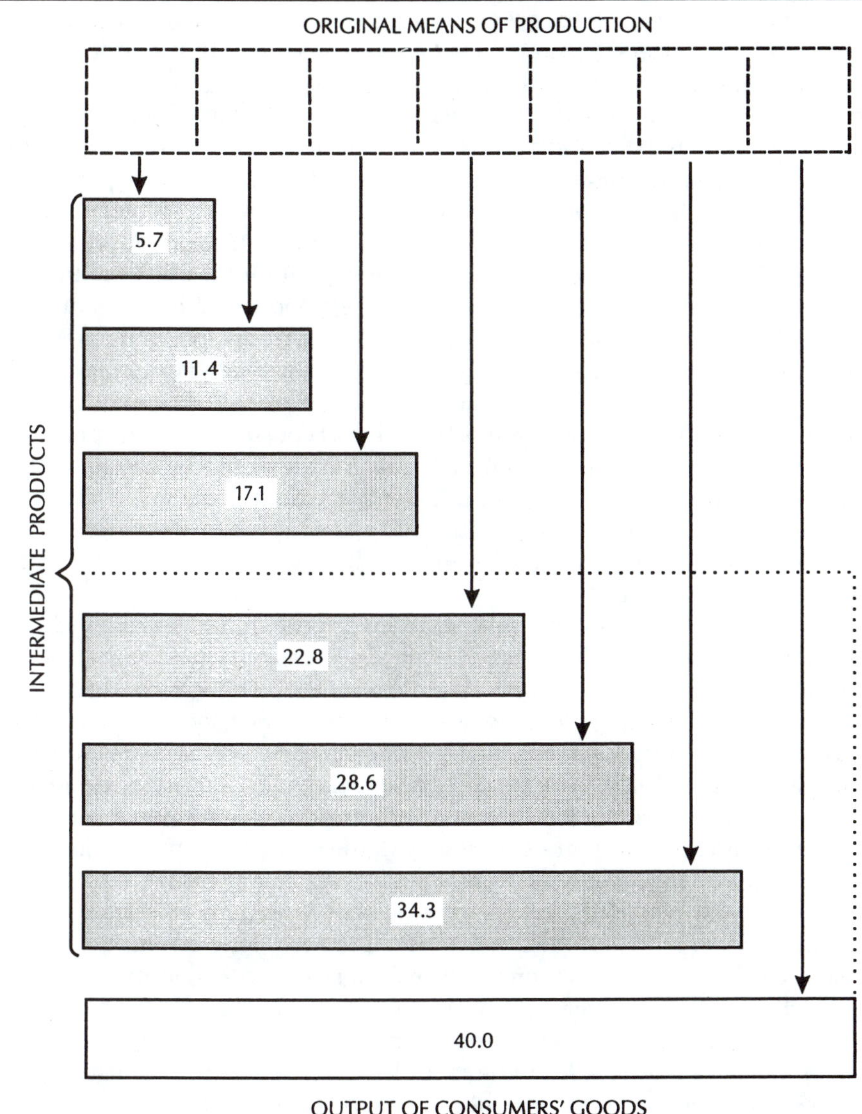

consumers' goods and of the still greater increase of the total turnover of goods of all kinds and stages, offers no fundamental difficulties to such an increase of production, since total expenditure on the factors of production, or total costs, will still be covered by the sums received out of the sales of consumers' goods.

But now the question arises: does this remain true if we drop the assumptions that the amount of money remains unchanged and that, during the process of production, the intermediate products are exchanged against money at equal intervals of time?

Let us begin by investigating the effects of a change in the amount of money in circulation. It will be sufficient if we investigate only the case most frequently to be encountered in practice: the case of an increase of money in the form of credits granted to producers. Again we shall find it convenient to start from the situation depicted in Fig. 2 and to suppose that the same change in the proportion between the demand for consumers' goods and the demand for intermediate products, which, in the earlier instance, was supposed to be produced by voluntary saving, is now caused by the granting of additional credits to producers. For this purpose, the producers must receive an amount of forty in additional money. As will be seen from Fig. 4, the changes in the structure of production which will be necessary in order to find employment for the additional means which have become available will exactly correspond to the changes brought about by saving. The total services of the original means of production will now be expended in six instead of in four periods; the total value of intermediate goods produced in the different stages during a period will have grown to three times instead of twice as large as the value of consumers' goods produced during the same period; and the output of each stage of production, including the final one, measured in physical units will accordingly be exactly as great as in the case represented in Fig. 3. The only difference at first apparent is that the money values of these goods have grown by one-third compared with the situation depicted in Fig. 3.

There is, however, another and far more important difference which will become apparent only with the lapse of time. When a change in the structure of production was brought about by saving, we were justified in assuming that the changed distribution of demand between consumers' goods and producers' goods would remain permanent, since it was the effect of voluntary decisions on the part of individuals. Only because a number of individuals had decided to spend a smaller share of their total money receipts on consumption and a larger share on production was there any change in the structure of production. And since, after the change had been completed, these persons would get a greater proportion of the increased total real income, they would have no reason again to increase the *proportion* of their money receipts spent for consumption. There would accordingly exist no inherent cause for a return to the old proportions.

In the same way, in the case we are now considering, the use of a larger proportion of the original means of production for the manufacture of intermediate products can only be brought about by a retrenchment of consumption. But now this sacrifice is not voluntary, and is not made by those who will reap the benefit from the new investments. It is made by consumers in general who, because of the increased competition from the entrepreneurs who have received the additional money, are forced to forego part of what they used to consume. It comes about not because they want to consume less, but because they get less goods for their money income. There can be no doubt that, if their money receipts should rise again, they would immediately attempt to expand consumption to the usual proportion.... [For now, let us assume that] in time, their receipts will rise as a consequence of the increase of money in circulation.... But if it [happens], then at once the money stream will be re-distributed between consumptive and productive uses according to the wishes of the individual concerned, and the artificial distribution, due to the injection of the new

FIGURE 5

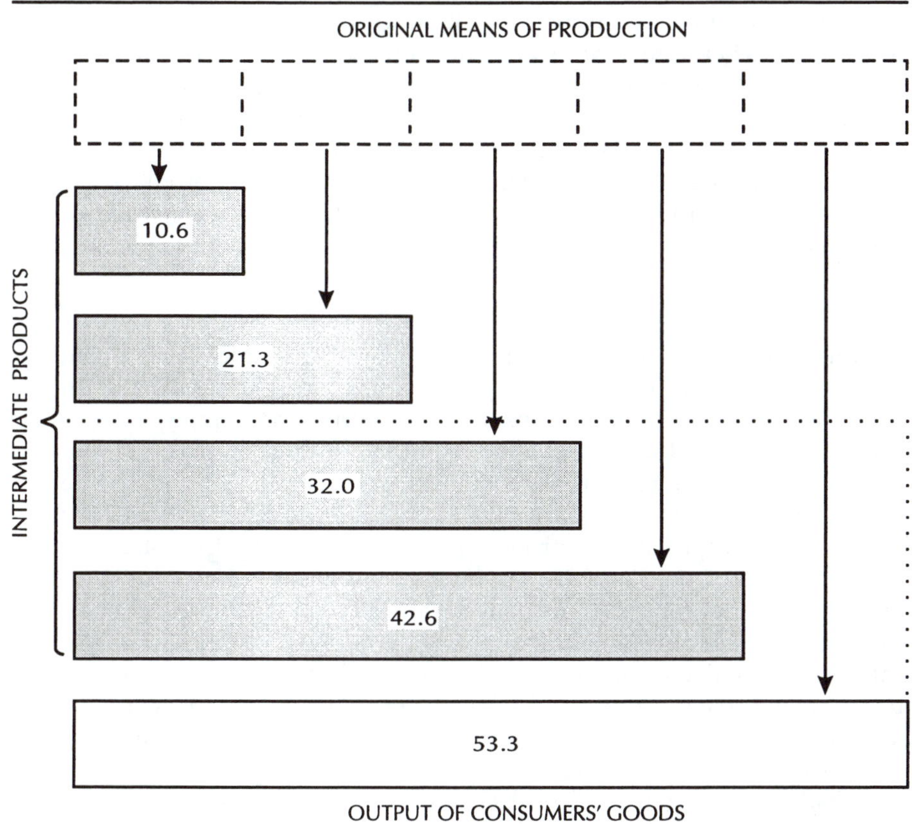

money, will, partly at any rate, be reversed. If we assume that the old proportions are adhered to, then the structure of production too will have to return to the old proportion, as shown in Fig. 5. That is to say production will become less capitalistic, and that part of the new capital which was sunk in equipment adapted only to the more capitalistic processes will be lost.... [S]uch a transition to less capitalistic methods of production necessarily takes the form of an economic crisis.

But it is not necessary that the proportion between the demand for consumers' goods and the demand for intermediate products should return exactly to its former dimensions as soon as the injection of new money ceases. In so far as the entrepreneurs have already succeeded, with the help of the additional money, in completing the new processes of longer duration, they will, perhaps, receive increased money returns for their output which will put them in a position to continue the new processes, i.e., to expend permanently a larger share of their money receipts upon intermediate products without, reducing their own consumption. It is only in consequence of the price changes caused by the increased demand for consumers' goods that, as we shall see, these processes too become unprofitable.

But for the producers who work on a process where the transition to longer roundabout processes is not yet completed when the amount of money ceases to increase the situation is different. They have spent the additional money which put them in a position to increase their demand for producers' goods and in consequence it has become consumers' income; they will, therefore, no longer be able to claim a larger share of the available producers' goods, and they will accordingly have to abandon the attempt to change over to more capitalistic methods of production.

All this becomes easier to follow if we consider the simpler case in which an increase in demand for consumers' goods of this sort is brought about directly by additional money given to consumers. In recent years, in the United States, Messrs. Foster and Catchings have urged that, in order to make possible the sale of an increased amount of consumers' goods produced with the help of new savings, consumers must receive a proportionately larger money income. What would happen if their proposals were carried out? If we start with the situation which would establish itself as a consequence of new savings if the amount of money remained unchanged (as shown in Fig. 3), and then assume that consumers receive an additional amount of money sufficient to compensate for the relative increase of the demand for intermediate products caused by the savings (i.e., an amount of 15) and spend it on consumers' goods, we get a situation in which the proportion between the demand for consumers' goods, and the demand for producers' goods, which, in consequence of the new savings, had changed from 40:80 to 30:90 or from 1:2 to 1:3 would again be reduced to 45:90 or 1:2. That this would mean a return to the less capitalistic structure of production which existed before the new savings were made, and that the only effect of such an increase of consumers' money incomes would be to frustrate the effect of saving follows clearly from Fig. 6. (The difference from the original situation depicted in Fig. 2 is again only a difference in money values and not a difference in the physical quantities of goods produced or in their distribution to the different stages of production.)

It is now time to leave this subject and to pass on to the last problem with which I have to deal [here]. I wish now to drop the second of my original assumptions, the assumption, namely, that during the process of production the intermediate products are exchanged against money between the firms at successive stages of production in equal intervals. Instead of this very artificial assumption, we may consider two possible alternatives: we may suppose (*a*) that in any line of production the whole process is completed by a single firm, so that no other money payments take place than the payments for consumers' goods and the payments for the use of the factors of production: or we may suppose (*b*) that exchanges of intermediate products take place, but at very irregular intervals, so that in some parts of the process the goods remain for several periods of time

FIGURE 6

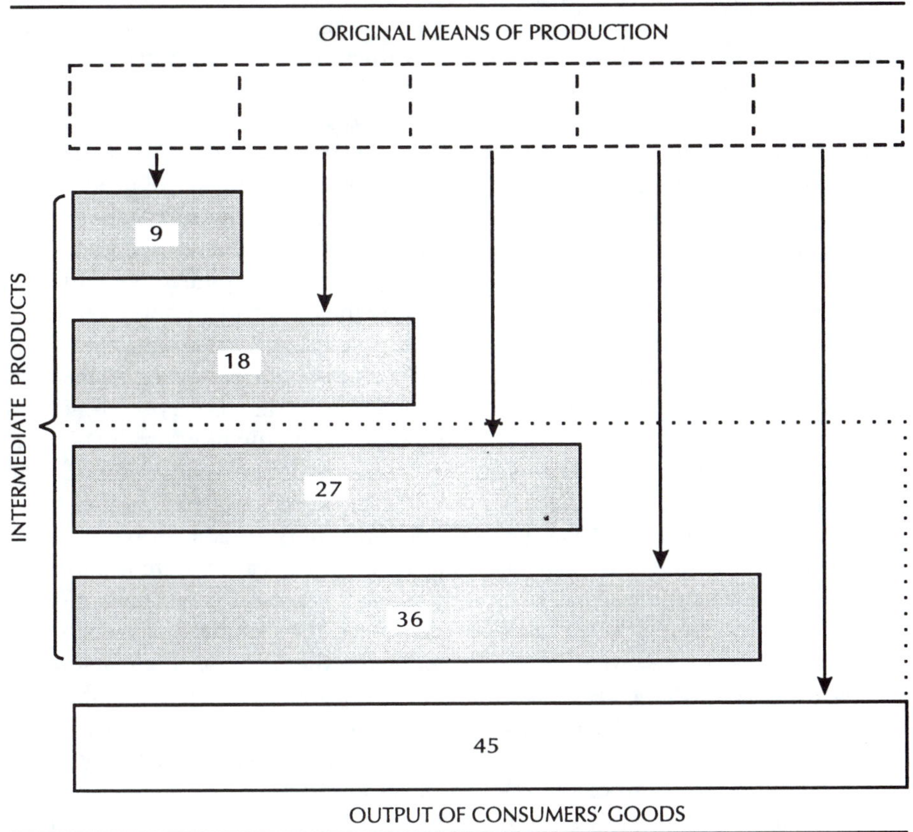

in the possession of one and the same firm, while in other parts of the process they are exchanged once or several times during each period.

(*a*) Let us consider first the case in which the whole process of production in any line of production is completed by a single firm. Once again we may use Fig. 1 to illustrate what happens. In this case the base of the triangle represents the total payments for consumers' goods and the hypotenuse (or, more correctly, its horizontal projection) represents the amounts of money paid for the original means of production used. No other payments would be made and any amount of money received from the sale of consumers' goods could immediately be spent for original means of production. It is of fundamental importance to remember that we can assume only that any *single* line of production is in this way integrated into one big firm. It would be entirely inappropriate in this connection to suppose that the production of *all* goods is concentrated in one enterprise. For, if this were the case, of course the manager of this firm could, like the economic dictator of a communistic society, arbitrarily decide what part of the available means of production should be applied to the production of consumers' goods and what part to the production of producers' goods. There would exist for him no reason to borrow and, for individuals, no opportunity to invest savings. Only if *different* firms compete for the available means of production will saving and investing in the ordinary sense of the word take place, and it is therefore such a situation which we must make the starting point of our investigation.

Now, if any of these integrated industries decides to save and invest part of its profits in order to introduce more capitalistic methods of production, it must not immediately pay out the sums saved for original means of production. As the transition to more capitalistic methods of production means that it will be longer until the consumers' goods produced by the new process are ready, the firm will need the sums saved to pay wages, etc., during the interval of time between the sale of the last goods produced by the old process, and the getting ready of the first goods produced by the new process. So that, during the whole period of transition, it must pay out less to consumers than it receives in order to be able to bridge the gap at the end of this period, when it has nothing to sell but has to continue to pay wages and rent. Only when the new product comes on the market and there is no need for further saving will it again currently pay out all its receipts.

In this case, therefore, the demand for consumers' goods, as expressed in money, will be only temporarily reduced, while in the case where the process of production was divided between a number of independent stages of equal length, the reduction of the amount available for the purchase of consumers' goods was a permanent one. In the present case, the prices of the consumers' goods will, accordingly, fall only in inverse proportions as their quantity has increased, while the total paid as income for the use of the factors of production will remain the same. These conclusions are, however, only provisional as they do not take account of the relative position of the one firm considered to all other firms which will certainly be affected by a change of relative prices and interest rates which are necessarily connected with such a process. Unfortunately, these influences are too complicated to allow of treatment within the scope of [this selection], and I must ask you, therefore, to suspend judgment upon the ultimate effects of the price changes which will take place under these conditions.

But there is one point to which I must particularly direct your attention: The reason in this case why the unchanged amount of money used in production remains sufficient, in spite of the fact that a larger amount of intermediate products now exists, whereas in the former case, the use of an increased amount of intermediate products required the use of an increased quantity of money is this. In the former case the intermediate products passed from one stage of production to the next by an exchange against money. But in the present case this exchange is replaced by internal barter, which makes money unnecessary. Of course, our division of the continuous process of production into separate stages of equal length is entirely arbitrary: it would be just as natural to divide it into stages of different lengths and then speak of these stages as exhibiting so many more or less instances of internal barter. But the procedure which has been adopted serves to bring out ... the concept of the relative volume of the flow of goods during any period of time, as compared with the amount of goods exchanged against money in the same period. If we divide the path traversed by the elements of any good from the first expenditure of original means of production until it gets in the hands of the final consumer into unit periods, and then measure the quantities of goods which pass each of these lines of division during a period of time, we secure a comparatively simple measure of the flow of goods without having recourse to higher mathematics. Thus, we may say that, in the instance we have been considering, money has become more efficient in moving goods, in the sense that a given amount of exchanges against money has now become sufficient to make possible the movement of a greater volume of goods than before.

(*b*) Perhaps this somewhat difficult concept becomes more intelligible if I illustrate it by supposing that two of the independent firms which we have supposed to represent the successive stages of production in our diagrams 2 and 6 are combined into one firm. This is the second of the alternative possibilities I set out to consider. Once this has happened, the passage of the intermediate products from the one to the next stage of production will take place without money payments being necessary, and the flow of goods from the moment they enter the earlier of the two stages until they leave the later will be effected by so much less money. A corresponding amount of money will thus be released and may be used for other purposes. The reverse effect will, of course, be witnessed if the two firms separate again. An increased amount of money payments will be required to effect the same movement of goods and the proportion of money payments to the flow of goods advancing towards consumption will have increased.

Unfortunately, all names which might be used to designate this kind of monetary effectiveness have already been appropriated for designating different concepts of the velocity of money. Until somebody finds a fitting term, therefore, we shall have to speak somewhat clumsily of the proportion between the amount of goods exchanged against money and the total flow of goods or of the proportion of the total movements of goods which is effected by exchange against money.

Now this proportion must on no account be confused with the proportion of the volume of money payments to the physical volume of trade. The proportion I have in mind may remain the same while the volume of trade increases relatively to the total of money payments and the price level falls, if only the same proportion of the total flow of goods is exchanged against money, and it may change though the proportion of the total of money payments to the physical volume of trade remains the same. It is, therefore, not necessarily influenced either by changes in the amount of money or by changes in the physical volume of trade; it depends only upon whether, in certain phases of the process of production, goods do or do not change hands.

So far I have illustrated this concept only by instances from the sphere of production. It may be applied also to the sphere of consumption. Here, too, sometimes a larger and sometimes a smaller share of the total output of consumers' goods is exchanged for money before it is consumed. Accordingly, here, too, we may speak about the proportion which the total output of consumers' goods in a period of time bears to the output which is sold for money. And this proportion may be different in the different stages of production. But in its effect upon the structure of production, the efficiency of a given amount of money spent in any stage of production (including the last stage—consumption) is determined by the proportion in that stage; and any change in that proportion has the same effects as an alteration in the amount of money spent in this particular stage of production.

So much for the complications which arise when we drop the assumption that production is carried on in independent stages of equal length. It has been necessary to discuss them here at some length in order to clear the way for an investigation... in connection with the arguments for and against an elastic money supply. But for the tasks which I shall have to face tomorrow, it will be expedient again to make use of the simplest assumption and to suppose that production is carried on in independent stages of equal length, as we did in our schematic representations, and that this proportion is not only the same in all stages of production, but also that it remains constant over time.

CHAPTER 7 The Chicago School

7.1 FRANK H. KNIGHT

Enterprise and Profit

Frank H. Knight (1885–1972), founder of the Chicago school of economics, was born in White Oak, Illinois. He held teaching positions at Cornell University and the University of Iowa before joining the University of Chicago in 1928, where he remained until his retirement in 1952. His work lives on in that of his students, most notably Milton Friedman and James Buchanan.

Knight believed that a laissez-faire system is more efficient in managing uncertainty than a socialist system. A laissez-faire system assigns production decisions to private entrepreneurs whose reward is determined by the market in terms of the success of the business. They also are held responsible for the failure of the business. In contrast, a socialist system lacks a market mechanism for determining profits, leading to an inability to select and reward employees on the basis of their accomplishments.

In the following selection, taken from *Risk, Uncertainty and Profit,* originally published in 1921, Knight distinguishes between risk and uncertainty. He perceives risk as one of the normal costs of business as it can be predicted with a high degree of certainty. Examples include the risk of fire or accidents. Uncertainty, on the other hand, is so unpredictable that accurate forecasting is inconceivable. To cope with uncertainty, the entrepreneur evaluates incomplete information and uses subjective judgments to make decisions. Accordingly, the entrepreneur is compensated both for providing management services and for managing uncertainty.

Key Concept: profit as the reward for managing uncertainty

To secure the minimum degree of uncertainty and at the same time keep the discussion as close to reality as possible, it is necessary to exercise some care in defining the assumptions with which we are working. The most obvious initial requirement is to eliminate the factors of social progress from consideration and consider first a static society. But this postulate calls for discrimination in handling. In an *absolutely* unchanging social life there would . . . be no uncertainty whatever. . . . Such conditions are thoroughly incompatible with the most fundamental facts of the world in which we live, but their study serves the analytic purpose of isolating the effects of uncertainty. For different kinds of change and different degrees of change are real facts, and it will therefore involve less abstraction to study hypothetical conditions under which change is restricted to the most fundamental and ineradicable kind and amount. Societies may be and have been nearly *unprogressive,* and the obvious simplification to make is therefore the elimination of progressive change.

After abstracting all the elements of general progressive change . . . a large amount of uncertainty will be left in human life, due to changes of the character of *fluctuations* which cannot be thought away without violence to material possibility. Strictly accurate formulation of conditions involving a realistic minimum of uncertainty cannot be made, but are not necessary; it is sufficient to indicate in a rough way the situation we propose to discuss. Several factors affect the amount of uncertainty to be recognized, and have to be taken into account. The first to be noted is the time length of the production process, for the longer it is, the more uncertainty will naturally be involved. Of very great importance also is the general level of economic life. The lower wants of man, those having in the greatest degree the nature of necessities, are the most stable and predictable. The higher up the scale we go, the larger the proportion of the aesthetic element and of social suggestion there is involved in motivation, the greater becomes the uncertainty connected with foreseeing wants and satisfying them. On the production side, on the other hand, most manufacturing processes are more controllable and calculable as to outcome than are agricultural operations under usual conditions. We must notice also the development of science and of the technique of social organization. Greater ability to forecast the future and greater power to control the course of events manifestly reduce uncertainty, and of still greater importance is the status of . . . various devices . . . for reducing uncertainty by consolidation.

All these perplexities about which some more or less definite assumption must be made can be disposed of by being as realistic as possible. Let us say simply that we are talking about the United States in the early years of the twentieth century, but with abstraction made of progressive changes. That is, we assume a population static in numbers and composition and without the mania of change and advance which characterizes modern life. Inventions and improvements in technology and organization are to be eliminated, leaving the general situation as we know it to-day to remain stationary. Similarly in regard to the saving of new capital, development of new natural resources, redistribution of population over the soil or redistribution of ownership of goods, education, etc., among the people. But we shall not assume that men are omniscient and immortal or perfectly rational and free from caprice as individuals.

We shall neglect natural catastrophes, epidemics, wars, etc., but take for granted the "usual" uncertainties of the weather and the like, along with the "normal" vicissitudes of mortal life, and uncertainties of human choice.

[With regard to] social organization... let us inquire as to what will be the effects of introducing the minimum degree of uncertainty into the situation. The essential features of the hypothetical society as thus far constructed need to be kept clearly in mind. Acting as individuals under absolute freedom but without collusion, men are supposed to have organized economic life with primary and secondary division of labor, the use of capital, etc., developed to the point familiar in present-day America. The principal fact which calls for exercise of the imagination is the internal organization of the productive groups or establishments. With uncertainty entirely absent, every individual being in possession of perfect knowledge of the situation, there would be no occasion for anything of the nature of responsible management or control of productive activity. Even marketing operations in any realistic sense would not be found. The flow of raw materials and productive services through productive processes to the consumer would be entirely automatic.

We do not need to strain the imagination by supposing supernatural powers of prescience on the part of men. We can think of the adjustment as the result of a long process of experimentation, worked out by trial-and-error methods alone. If the conditions of life and the people themselves were entirely unchanging a definite organization would result, perfect in the sense that no one would be under an incentive to change. So in the organization of the productive groups, it is not necessary to imagine every worker doing exactly the right thing at the right time in a sort of "preëstablished harmony" with the work of others. There might be managers, superintendents, etc., for the purpose of coördinating the activities of individuals. But under conditions of perfect knowledge and certainty such functionaries would be laborers merely, performing a purely routine function, without responsibility of any sort, on a level with men engaged in mechanical operations.

With the introduction of uncertainty—the fact of ignorance and necessity of acting upon opinion rather than knowledge—into this Eden-like situation, its character is completely changed. With uncertainty absent, man's energies are devoted altogether to doing things; it is doubtful whether intelligence itself would exist in such a situation; in a world so built that perfect knowledge was theoretically possible, it seems likely that all organic readjustments would become mechanical, all organisms automata. With uncertainty present, doing things, the actual execution of activity, becomes in a real sense a secondary part of life; the primary problem or function is deciding what to do and how to do it. The two most important characteristics of social organization brought about by the fact of uncertainty have already been noticed. In the first place, goods are produced for a market, on the basis of an entirely impersonal prediction of wants, not for the satisfaction of the wants of the producers themselves. The producer takes the responsibility of forecasting the consumers' wants. In the second place, the work of forecasting and at the same time a large part of the technological direction and control of production are still further concentrated upon a very narrow class of the producers, and we meet with a new economic functionary, the entrepreneur.

When uncertainty is present and the task of deciding what to do and how to do it takes the ascendancy over that of execution, the internal organization of the productive groups is no longer a matter of indifference or a mechanical detail. Centralization of this deciding and controlling function is imperative, a process of "cephalization," such as has taken place in the evolution of organic life, is inevitable, and for the same reasons as in the case of biological evolution. Let us consider this process and the circumstances which condition it. The order of attack on the problem is suggested by the classification... of the elements in uncertainty in regard to which men may in large measure differ independently.

In the first place, occupations differ in respect to the kind and amount of knowledge and judgment required for their successful direction as well as in the kind of abilities and tastes adapted to the routine operations. Productive groups or establishments now compete for managerial capacity as well as skill, and a considerable rearrangement of personnel is the natural result. The final adjustment will place each producer in the place where his particular combination of the two kinds of attributes seems to be most effective.

But a more important change is the tendency of the groups themselves to specialize, finding the individuals with the greatest managerial capacity of the requisite kinds and placing them in charge of the work of the group, submitting the activities of the other members to their direction and control. It need hardly be mentioned explicitly that the organization of industry depends on the fundamental fact that the intelligence of one person can be made to direct in a general way the routine manual and mental operations of others. It will also be taken into account that men differ in their powers of effective control over other men as well as in intellectual capacity to decide what should be done. In addition, there must come into play the diversity among men in degree of confidence in their judgment and powers and in disposition to act on their opinions, to "venture." This fact is responsible for the most fundamental change of all in the form of organization, the system under which the confident and venturesome "assume the risk" or "insure" the doubtful and timid by guaranteeing to the latter a specified income in return for an assignment of the actual results.

Uncertainty thus exerts a fourfold tendency to select men and specialize functions: (1) an adaptation of men to occupations on the basis of kind of knowledge and judgment; (2) a similar selection on the basis of degree of foresight, for some lines of activity call for this endowment in a very different degree from others; (3) a specialization within productive groups, the individuals with superior managerial ability (foresight and capacity of ruling others) being placed in control of the group and the others working under their direction; and (4) those with confidence in their judgment and disposition to "back it up" in action specialize in risk-taking. The close relations obtaining among these tendencies will be manifest. We have not separated confidence and venturesomeness at all, since they act along parallel lines and are little more than phases of the same faculty—just as courage and the tendency to minimize danger are proverbially commingled in all fields, though they are separable in thought. In addition the tendencies numbered (3) and (4) operate together. With human nature as we know it it would be impracticable or very unusual for one man to guarantee to another a definite result of the latter's actions without being given power to direct his work. And on the other hand the second party would not place himself under the direction of the first without such a guaranty. The result is a "double contract" of the type famous in the history of the evasion of usury laws. It seems evident also that the system would not work at all if good judgment were not in fact generally associated with confidence in one's judgment on the part both of himself and others. That is, men's judgment of their own judgment and others' judgment as to both kind and grade must in the large be much more right than wrong.

The result of this manifold specialization of function is *enterprise and the wage system of industry.* Its existence in the world is a direct result of the fact of uncertainty; our task in the remainder of this study is to examine this phenomenon in detail in its various phases and divers relations with the economic activities of man and the structure of society. It is not necessary or inevitable, not the only conceivable form of organization, but under certain conditions has certain advantages, and is capable of development in different degrees. The essence of enterprise is the specialization of the function of *responsible direction* of economic life, the neglected feature of which is the inseparability of these *two* elements, *responsibility* and *control.* Under the enterprise system, a special social class, the business men, direct economic activity; they are in the strict sense the producers, while the great mass of the population merely furnish them with productive services, placing their persons and their property at the disposal of this class; the entrepreneurs *also* guarantee to those who furnish productive services a fixed remuneration. Accurately to define these functions and trace them through the social structure will be a long task, for the specialization is never complete; but at the end of it we shall find that in a free society the two are essentially inseparable. Any degree of effective exercise of judgment, or making decisions, is in a free society coupled with a corresponding degree of uncertainty-bearing, of taking the responsibility for those decisions.

With the specialization of function goes also a differentiation of reward. The produce of society is similarly divided into *two kinds of income,* and two only, contractual income, which is essentially *rent,* as economic theory has described incomes, and residual income or *profit.* But the differentiation of contractual income, like that of profit, is never complete; neither variety is ever met with in a pure form, and every real income contains elements of both rent and profit. And with uncertainty present (the condition of the differentiation itself) it is not possible even to determine just how much of any income is of one kind and how much of the other; but a partial separation can be made, and the causal distinction between the two kinds is sharp and clear.

We may imagine a society in which uncertainty is absent transformed on the introduction of uncertainty into an enterprise organization. The readjustments will be carried out by the same trial-and-error methods under the same motives, the effort of each individual to better himself, which we have already described. The ideal or limiting condition constantly in view would still be the equalization of all available alternatives of conduct by each individual through the distribution of efforts and of expenditure of the proceeds of effort among the lines open. Under the new system labor and property services actually come into the market, become commodities and are bought and sold. They are thus brought into the comparative value scale and reduced to homogeneity in price terms with the fund of values made up of the direct means of want satisfaction.

Another feature of the new adjustment is that a condition of perfect equilibrium is no longer possible. Since productive arrangements are made on the basis of anticipations and the results actually achieved do not coincide with these as a usual thing, the oscillations will not settle down to zero. For all changes made by individuals relate to the established value scale and this price-system will be subject to fluctuations due to unforeseen causes; consequently individual changes in arrangements will continue indefinitely to take place. The experiments by which alone the value of human judgment is determined involve a proportion of failures or errors, are never complete, and in view of human mortality have constantly to be recommenced at the beginning.

We turn now to consider in broad outline the two types of individual income implied in the enterprise system of organization, contractual income and profit. We shall try as hitherto to explain events by placing ourselves in the actual positions of the men acting or making decisions and interpreting their acts in terms of ordinary human motives. The setting of the problem is a free competitive situation in which all men and material agents are competing for employment, including all men at the time engaged as entrepreneurs, while all entrepreneurs are competing for productive services and at the same time all men are competing for positions as entrepreneurs. The essential fact in understanding the reaction to this situation is that men are acting, competing, on the basis of what they *think* of the *future.* To simplify the picture and make it concrete we shall as before assume that there exists some sort of grouping of men and things under the control of other men as entrepreneurs (a random grouping will do as a start) and that entrepreneurs and others are in competition as above stated.

The production-distribution system is worked out through offers and counter-offers, made on the basis of anticipations, of two kinds. The laborer asks what he thinks the entrepreneur will be able to pay, and in any case will not accept less than he can get from some other entrepreneur, or by turning entrepreneur himself. In the same way the entrepreneur offers to any laborer what he thinks he must in order to secure his services, and in any case not more than he thinks the laborer will actually be worth to him, keeping in mind what he can get by turning laborer himself. The whole calculation is in the future; past and even present conditions operate only as grounds of prediction as to what may be anticipated.

Since in a free market there can be but one price on any commodity, a general wage rate must result from this competitive bidding. The rate established may be described as the socially or competitively anticipated value of the laborer's product, using the term "product" in the sense of specific contribution, as already explained. It is not the opinion of the future held by either party to an employment bargain which determines the rate; these opinions merely set maximum and minimum limits outside of which the agreement cannot take place. The mechanism of price adjustment is the same as in any other market. There is always an established uniform rate, which is kept constantly at the point which equates the supply and demand. If at any moment there are more bidders willing to employ at a higher rate than there are employees willing to accept the established rate, the rate will rise accordingly, and similarly if there is a balance of opinion in the opposite direction. The final decision by any individual as to what to do is based on a comparison of a momentarily existing price with a subjective judgment of significance of the commodity. The judgment in this case relates to the indirect significance derived from a twofold estimate of the future, involving both technological and price uncertainties. The employer in deciding whether to offer the current wage, and the employee in deciding whether to accept it, must estimate the technical or physically measured product (specific contribution) of the labor and the price to be expected for that product when it comes upon the market. The estimation may involve two sorts of calculation or estimate of probability. The venture itself may be of the nature of a gamble, involving a large proportion of inherently unpredictable factors. In such a case the decision depends upon an "estimate" of an "objective probability" of success, or of a series of such probabilities corresponding to various degrees of success or failure. And normally, in the case of intelligent men, account will be taken of the probable "true value" of the estimates in the case of all estimated factors.

The meaning of the term "social" or "competitive" anticipation will now be clear. The question in the mind of either party to an employment agreement relates simply to the fact of a difference between the current standard of remuneration for the services being bargained for and his own estimate of their worth, discounted by probability allowances. The magnitude of the difference is altogether immaterial. The prospective employer may know absolutely that the service has a value to him ever so much greater than the price he is paying, but he will have to pay only the competitively established rate, and his purchase will affect this rate no more than if he were ever so hesitant about the bargain, just so he makes it. It is the general estimate of the magnitudes involved, in the sense of a "marginal" demand price, which fixes the actual current rate.

... The value of a laborer or piece of material equipment to a particular productive group is determined by the specific physical contribution to output under the principle of diminishing returns with increase in the proportion of that kind of agency in the combination, and on the price of this contribution under the principle of diminishing utility with increase in the proportion of productive energy devoted to making the particular product turned out by the establishment in question. But the facts upon which the working-out of the organization depends can no longer be objectively determined with accuracy by experiment; all the data in the case must be *estimated,* subject to a larger or smaller margin of error, and this fact causes differences more fundamental than the resemblances in the two situations. The function of making these estimates and of "guaranteeing" their value to the other participating members of the group falls to the responsible entrepreneur in each establishment, producing a new type of activity and a new type of income entirely unknown in a society where uncertainty is absent....

When... the managerial function comes to require the exercise of judgment involving *liability to error,* and when in consequence the assumption of *responsibility* for the correctness of his opinions becomes a condition prerequisite to getting the other members of the group to submit to the manager's direction, the nature of the function is revolutionized; the manager becomes an entrepreneur. He may, and typically will, to be sure, continue to perform the old mechanical routine functions and to receive the old wages; but in addition he makes responsible decisions, and his income will normally contain in addition to wages a pure *differential* element designated as "profit" by the economic theorist. This profit is simply the difference between the market price of the productive agencies he employs, the amount which the competition of other entrepreneurs forces him to guarantee to them as a condition of securing their services, and the amount which he finally realizes from the disposition of the product which under his direction they turn out.

The character of the entrepreneur's income is evidently complex, and the relations of its component elements subtle. It contains an element which is ordinary contractual income, received on the ground of routine services performed by the entrepreneur personally for the business (wages) or earned by property which belongs to him (rent or capital return). And the differential element is again complex, for it is clear that there is an element of calculation and an element of luck in it. An adequate examination and analysis of this phenomenon requires time and careful thinking. The background of the problem should now be clear: the uncertainty of all life and conduct which call for the exercise of judgment in business, the economy of division of labor which compels men to work in groups and to delegate the function of control as other functions are specialized, the facts of human nature which make it necessary for one who directs the activities of others to assume responsibility for the results of the operations, and finally the competitive situation which pits the judgment of each entrepreneur against that of the extant business world in adjusting the contractual incomes which he must pay before he gets anything for himself.

The first step in attacking the problem is to inquire into the meaning of entrepreneur ability and its conditions of demand and supply. In regard to the first main division of the entrepreneur's income, the ordinary wage for the routine services of labor and property furnished to the business, no comment is necessary. This return is merely the competitive rate of pay for the grade of ability or kind of property in question. To be sure, it may not be possible in practice to say exactly what this rate is. Not merely is perfect standardization of things and services unattainable under the fluctuating conditions of real life, but in addition the conditions of the entrepreneur specialization may well bring it about that the same things are not done under closely comparable conditions by entrepreneurs and non-entrepreneurs. Hence the separation between the pure wage or rent element and the elements arising out of uncertainty cannot generally be made with complete accuracy. The serious difficulty comes with the attempt to deal with the relation between judgment and luck in determining that part of the entrepreneur's income which is associated with the performance of his peculiar twofold function of (a) exercising responsible control and (b) securing the owners of productive services against uncertainty and fluctuation in their incomes. Clearly this special income is also connected with a sort of effort and sacrifice and into the nature and conditions of supply and demand of the capacities and dispositions for these efforts and sacrifices it must be pertinent to inquire.

It is unquestionable that the entrepreneur's activities effect an enormous saving to society, vastly increasing the efficiency of economic production. Large-scale operations, highly organized industry, and minute division of labor would be impossible without specialization of the managerial function, and human nature being as it is, the guaranteeing function must apparently go along with that of control; indeed, in the ultimate sense of control the two are not even theoretically separable. Thus there would be a large saving even outside of any question of the superior abilities of certain individuals over other individuals for the performance of this function. And there is still another gain of large magnitude through the reduction of uncertainty by the principle of consolidation, which also is independent of the personal attributes of the entrepreneur. But these economies, due to the system as such, and not to activities of the individuals performing a special function, accrue to society; no cause can be discovered in this connection alone which would give rise to a special distributive share.

7.2 MILTON FRIEDMAN AND ANNA JACOBSON SCHWARTZ

Independence of Monetary Changes

Milton Friedman, considered the foremost advocate of monetary policy of the twentieth century, was born in 1912 in Brooklyn, New York. In 1946, after a one-year sojourn at the University of Minnesota, he returned to the University of Chicago. Since his retirement from the university in 1977, Friedman has occupied the position of senior research associate at the Hoover Institution at Stanford University. Since 1937 he has been associated with the National Bureau of Economic Research, which has supported both his early work on monopoly practices in the medical profession and his decades-long investigation of monetary policy.

Anna Jacobson Schwartz, the economic historian, was born in 1915 in New York. A graduate of Columbia University (M.S., Ph.D., 1935, 1964), she held research positions at the National Bureau of Economic Research and Columbia University as well as several faculty positions at Hunter College, Baruch College, New York University, and the City University Business School in London. Heavily influenced by Friedman, Schwartz regarded her early scholarly work, *The Growth and Fluctuation of the British Economy, 1790–1850,* to be deficient in its failure to assign a central role of monetary policy through its interpretation of the behavior of interest rates and price level, rather than relative price changes. She rectified this omission in *A Monetary History of the United States, 1867–1960* (1963), *Monetary Statistics of the United States* (1970), and *Monetary Trends in the United States and United Kingdom: Their Relation to Income, Prices, and Interest Rates, 1867–1975* (1982) by showing that changes in the growth rate of money affect the growth rate of nominal income, instability in the growth rate of money is associated with the instability in the growth of nominal income, a sustained change in the growth rate of money tends to be followed by a change in the inflation rate in the same direction after a lag of several years, and short-run changes in the growth rate of money tend to be followed by changes in the same direction of real output after a lag of several quarters.

In *A Theory of the Consumption Function* (Princeton University Press, 1957), Friedman described the basic tenets of his permanent income hypothesis of consumption. In a departure from John Maynard Keynes's theory of current consumption being dependent on current income, Friedman postulated that consumers base consumption decisions on permanent or long-term income. He went on to demonstrate that long-term changes in demand for money are caused by changes in permanent income. His calculations of permanent income as a weighted average of past incomes have been extensively employed in econometrics. Historical validation of his theories is provided by *A Monetary History of the United States 1867–1960* (Princeton University Press, 1963) in which Friedman and Schwartz have compiled monetary data from the 1860s onward to demonstrate that changes in the money supply act as principal sources of inflation or deflation and that consumption shows a stronger relationship with the money supply than government spending. In the following selection taken from this work, Friedman and Schwartz describe the sharp reduction in the money supply in the 1930s, which prolonged America's Great Depression. They view this as further evidence of the powerful effect of changes in the money supply on the economy.

Key Concept: the independence of monetary changes

The close relation between changes in the stock of money and changes in other economic variables, alone, tells nothing about the origin of either or the direction of influence. The monetary changes might be dancing to the tune called by independently originating changes in the other economic variables; the changes in income and prices might be dancing to the tune called by independently originating monetary changes; the two might be mutually interacting, each having some elements of independence; or both might be dancing to the common tune of still a third set of influences. A great merit of the examination of a wide range of qualitative evidence, so essential in a monetary history, is that it provides a basis for discriminating between these possible explanations of the observed statistical covariation. We can go beyond the numbers alone and, at least on some occasions, discern the antecedent circumstances whence arose the particular movements that become so anonymous when we feed the statistics into the computer.

One thing is abundantly clear from our narrative. Monetary changes have in fact often been independent, in the sense that they have often not been an immediate or necessary consequence of contemporaneous changes in business conditions.

The clearest example is perhaps the monetary expansion from 1897 to 1914, which was worldwide and reflected an increased output of gold. The increased output of gold was partly a consequence of earlier decades of declining prices, which encouraged gold production, and so speaks also for a mutual interaction between monetary and economic changes. But clearly the monetary expansion cannot be attributed to the contemporary rise in money income and prices. By itself, the rise in money income and prices made for a reduced output of gold in the world at large and for an outflow of gold from any single country in a gold-standard world. If the common movement of money and income was not purely coincidental, the direction of influence must run from money to income.

The two major rises in the stock of money during World Wars I and II are about equally clear. In the early stages of both wars, the rise reflected an inflow of gold into the United States, as belligerent nations used the resources they could readily mobilize to purchase war material in the United States. The inflows of gold were not by-products of contemporary changes in economic activity in this country or abroad, as gold flows had been in the years before 1914. They were a consequence of the outbreak of the two wars and the deliberate policy decisions of the political authorities in the countries at war. In the later stages of both wars, the rise reflected political decisions of U.S. authorities about the financing of war expenditures. Those decisions involved a major expansion in high-powered money which continued the work begun by gold inflows. Again, if the common movement of the stock of money and of money income and prices is not coincidental or the consequence of a common cause, the direction of influence must run from money to income.

The resumption and silver episodes display a substantial independence in the monetary changes that occurred and also a rather complex action and interaction between monetary and business changes. The pressures for and against resumption in the 1870's and the drive for free silver in the 1890's were major elements that shaped the course of events. Both were in some measure independent of the contemporary course of economic activity, though not of course of longer-run economic developments. Both were also much affected by the course of events, the pressures against resumption and for free silver being greatly strengthened by a slowing down or decline in the pace of business activity or a decline in agricultural prices. More important, such contemporaneous events as the state of the harvests at home and abroad, developments in the railroad industry in the 1870's and in the London money market in the 1890's had important effects on the particular dates at which those political pressures produced monetary disturbances, which in their turn reacted on business conditions and political attitudes.

The establishment of the Federal Reserve System provides the student of money a closer substitute for the controlled experiment to determine the direction of influence than the social scientist can generally obtain. The System was at times simply a means through which other forces operated—as during the two world wars, and much of the thirties when it followed a largely passive course, and after World War II when its policy of supporting the prices of government securities left it little independent initiative. But the establishment of the System gave a small body of individuals the power, which they exercised from time to time, to alter the course of events in significant and identifiable ways through a deliberative process—a sequence parallel with the conduct of a controlled experiment. True, the actions of the monetary authorities were greatly affected by the climate of opinion and knowledge in which they operated. Their attitudes, the experiments they undertook, and the interpretation they placed on the results were to a large extent determined by the contemporary course of events and the contemporary state of knowledge about monetary phenomena. This has also been true of physical scientists in deciding what experiments to undertake and in interpreting the results in light of preceding experiments and the contemporary body of knowledge. In either case, such dependence on the existing state of knowledge does not alter the scientific independence from the prior or contemporary course of events of the changes introduced into the controlled variables. What it means in both cases is simply that later students may reinterpret the results of the experiments in light of the changed body of knowledge and draw conclusions that are different from those drawn by the original experimenters.

True, also, it is often impossible and always difficult to identify accurately the effects of the actions of the monetary authorities. Their actions are taken amidst many other circumstances, and it may not be at all clear whether their actions or some of the other circumstances produced the results observed. This is equally true of the experiments of physical scientists. No experiment is completely controlled, and most experiments add little to tested and confirmed knowledge about the subject of experiment. It is the rare crucial experiment that throws a flood of light on its subject—a light that blinds us to many less important experiments that were necessary before the one crucial experiment could be made.

Three counterparts of such crucial experiments stand out in the monetary record since the establishment of the Federal Reserve System. On three occasions the System deliberately took policy steps of major magnitude which cannot be regarded as necessary or inevitable economic consequences of contemporary changes in money income and prices. Like the crucial experiments of the physical scientist, the results are so consistent and sharp as to leave little doubt about their interpretation. The dates are January–June 1920, October 1931, and July 1936–January 1937. These are the three occasions—and the only three—when the Reserve System engaged in acts of commission that were sharply restrictive: in January 1920, by raising the rediscount rate from 4¾ per cent to 6 per cent and then in June 1920, to 7 per cent, at a time when member banks were borrowing from the Reserve Banks more than the total of their reserve balances; in October 1931, by raising the rediscount rate from 1½ per cent to 3½ per cent within a two-week period, at a time when a wave of failures was engulfing commercial banks, as in the preceding year, and indebtedness to the System was growing; in July 1936 and January 1937, by announcing the doubling of reserve requirements in three stages, the last effective on May 1, 1937, at a time when the Treasury was engaged in gold sterilization, which was the equivalent of a large-scale restrictive open market operation. There is no other occasion in Federal Reserve history when it has taken explicit restrictive measures of comparable magnitude—we cannot even suggest possible parallels.

The strictly monetary changes associated with those actions were equally sharp and distinctive. The actions were followed after some months in 1920 and 1936–37, immediately in 1931, by sharp declines in the stock of money, the three sharpest declines within a twelve-month period in the history of the Reserve System; declines of 9 per cent (1920), 14 per cent (1931), and 3 per cent (1937), respectively. And for the first and third declines, the numbers understate the severity of the monetary reaction. In 1919 and again in 1936, the money stock was growing at a rapid rate, so the subsequent declines represented a deceleration from an unusually high rate of growth to an unusually high rate of decline.

The 1931 decline—the severest absolute decline of the three—was the mildest in terms of deceleration; the money stock in the preceding year had been falling at a slightly lower rate, so the increase in the rate of decline in the year beginning October 1931 was only about one percentage point.

The economic changes associated with those monetary actions were equally sharp and equally distinctive. Each was followed by sharp contractions in industrial production, after some months in 1920 and 1936–37, and immediately in 1931: declines within a twelve-month period of 30 per cent (1920), 24 per cent (1931), and 34 per cent (1937), respectively. There are only two other comparably severe declines in industrial production: during 1929–31, dealt with further below; and 1945, when the sharp decline represented a shift in the composition of output away from military products after the end of the war, rather than a general contraction in economic activity, as at the other four dates. Other indicators confirm the story told by industrial production. Whether one looks at wholesale prices, freight car loadings, common stock prices, or department stores sales, the downturns that followed the three monetary actions are the severest by a wide margin in the history of the Federal Reserve System, except only the 1929 to 1931 decline.

The strength of the evidence furnished by those three quasi-controlled experiments can perhaps be made clearer by an analogy. Suppose we had medical records of 42 married couples (to match the 42 years of Federal Reserve history from 1919 to 1960, excluding World War I because the System was not effectively in control). Suppose 3 men and 4 women were found to have a specified illness; suppose that 3 of the 4 women turned out to be the wives of the 3 men with the same illness. The presumption that the illness was contagious would certainly be very strong—especially so, if it were discovered that the husband of the fourth woman was the only remaining man to have a biologically related but not identical illness. Similarly, the three episodes described above establish a comparably strong presumption that the economic changes were the consequence of the deliberately undertaken monetary actions, and hence that our finding of a close covariation between the stock of money and income reflects the existence of an influence running from money to income. Indeed, in one respect the analogy seriously understates the strength of the evidence. It takes no account of the time sequence of events.

The presumption that the economic changes were the consequence of the monetary changes is greatly strengthened by examination of the one sharp economic contraction not associated with explicit restrictive measures by the Federal Reserve System—the 1929 to 1931 contraction, which was the first part of the great contraction from 1929 to 1933. That contraction has served perhaps more than any other experience to strengthen the view that money dances to the tune of business. The reason is that the Reserve System did not, in fact, stem the decline of one-third in the stock of money—by far the largest in the course of a cyclical contraction at least since 1893–43—or the accompanying contraction in economic activity. The System pleaded impotence, arguing explicitly that the nonmonetary forces making for contraction were so strong and violent that it was powerless to stem the tide, and implicitly that the depth of the decline in the money stock was due to the depth of the decline in business activity, rather than, as the evidence cited above suggests, the reverse. Many others, recognizing the good intentions of the monetary authorities and the ability of many individuals in the System, while independently holding a wide variety of views about the role of money in economic affairs, accepted the System's plea. In addition, a revolution in economic theory, having quite different origins and by no means necessarily implying the impotence of monetary policy, offered a theoretical structure that at one and the same time could rationalize the impotence of monetary policy and provide an intellectually satisfying alternative explanation on the economic debacle.

There is one sense—and, so far as we can see, only one—in which a case can be made for the proposition that the monetary decline was a consequence of the economic decline. That sense is not relevant to our main task of seeking to understand economic interrelations, since it involves relying primarily on psychological and political factors. The System was operating in a climate of opinion that in the main regarded recessions and depressions as curative episodes, necessary in order to purge the body economic of the aftereffects of its earlier excesses. The prevailing opinion also confused money and credit; confused the elasticity of one component of the money stock relative to another with the elasticity of the total stock; regarded it as desirable that the stock of money should respond to the "needs of trade," rising in expansions and falling in contractions; and attached much greater importance to the maintenance of the gold standard and the stability of exchanges than to the maintenance of internal stability. Most of those attitudes characterized the public at large and not merely the financial community or the Reserve System in particular. Given that milieu, it can be argued that the System followed an inevitable policy; that it could not have been expected to prevent the appreciable decline in the stock of money during 1930, because it and others as well regarded the decline as a desirable offset to earlier speculative excess; and that its failure to react vigorously, after banks began failing on a large scale in late 1930 and the public sought to convert deposits into currency, reflected the attitude that it was desirable to liquidate "bad" banks, to let "nature take its course" rather than to support the financial system "artificially." Certainly, the assignment of priority to the maintenance of the gold standard was in a proximate sense the reason for the sharp rise in discount rates in October 1931 following Britain's departure from gold and a gold outflow from the United States—the restrictive action described above as one of the System's crucial experiments.

This account portrays accurately an important part of the situation. It helps to explain how able and public-spirited men could have acted in a manner which in retrospect appears misguided, why there was so notable an absence of economic statesmanship outside the System and hence no steady informed pressure on the System for different action. But even on that level, the account is seriously incomplete. We are inclined to believe that the particular course of action followed by the Reserve System owed less to the climate of opinion—though it was certainly a necessary condition—than to a sequence of more or less accidental events and the running conflict for power within the System. [Federal Reserve Bank of New York governor] Benjamin Strong's death in 1928 unleashed an active phase of conflict which dominated policy throughout 1929, producing a deadlock between the Board and the New York Bank—acting as leader of all the Banks—about the proper policy to adopt in face of the stock market boom. The result was a policy that, in our view, was too easy to break the bull market and too tight to permit vigorous business expansion. The conflict plus the reaction by the rest of the System to the New York Bank's independent (and effective) operations in the wake of the stock market crash in October 1929 indirectly led to a shift of power over open market operations. A 5-man committee, dominated by the New York Bank, was replaced by a 12-man committee of the 12 Federal Reserve Bank governors in which New York played a less important role. That shift stacked the cards heavily in favor of a policy of inaction and drift.

We share the view expressed by Carl Snyder, for many years associated with the New York Bank as a statistician and economist, that if Benjamin Strong could "have had twelve months more of vigorous health, we might have ended the depression in 1930, and with this the long drawn out world crisis that so profoundly affected the ensuing political developments." As it was, Strong's successor at New York, George L. Harrison, vigorously advocated expansionary action in 1930, but was unable to prevail over the combined opposition of the Board and the other Bank governors. Harrison was in favor of expansionary action in 1931, that time with the support of the new governor of the Board, Eugene Meyer, but the pattern of deadlock and inaction had been set, to be broken only temporarily in 1932 under the pressure of Congressional prodding. Despite the general climate of opinion, the technical personnel of the New York Bank—and it must be recalled that under Strong the New York Bank dominated System policy almost completely—were consistently in favor of the policies which seem to us in retrospect the ones that should have followed.

In any event, what is relevant to our present purpose is neither praise nor blame, nor even a full understanding of the reasons for the System's behavior under the difficult and trying circumstances it faced. Even if its behavior was psychologically or politically inevitable under the circumstances, that would explain only why the quasi-controlled experiment was conducted. It would not explain the results of the experiment. The question would remain whether the monetary changes were the inevitable result of the economic changes, so that, if the System had not been the intermediary, some other mechanism would have enforced the same monetary changes; or whether the monetary changes can be regarded as an economically independent factor which accounted in substantial measure for the economic changes. There is little doubt about the answer. At all times throughout the 1929–33 contraction, alternative policies were available to the System by which it could have kept the stock of money from falling, and indeed could have increased it at almost any desired rate. Those policies did not involve radical innovations. They involved measures of a kind the System had taken in earlier years, of a kind explicitly contemplated by the founders of the System to meet precisely the kind of banking crisis that developed in late 1930 and persisted thereafter. They involved measures that were actually proposed and very likely would have been adopted under a slightly different bureaucratic structure or distribution of power, or even if the men in power had had somewhat different personalities. Until late 1931—and we believe not even then—the alternative policies involved no conflict with the maintenance of the gold standard. Until September 1931, the problem that recurrently troubled the System was how to keep the gold inflows under control, not the reverse.

To consider still another alternative: if the pre-1914 banking system rather than the Federal Reserve System had been in existence in 1929, the money stock almost certainly would not have undergone a decline comparable to the one that occurred. Comparison of the 1907 banking panic under the earlier system and the closely similar liquidity crisis which began in the late 1930 offers strong evidence for this judgment. If the earlier system had been in operation, and if everything else had proceeded as it did up to December 1930, the experience of 1907 strongly suggests that there would have been a more severe initial reaction to the bank failures than there was in 1930, probably involving concerted restriction by banks of the convertibility of deposits into currency. The restriction might have had more severe initial effects toward deepening the economic contraction than the persistent pressure on the banking system that characterized late 1930 and early 1931 had. But it also would have cut short the spread of the crisis, would have prevented cumulation of bank failures, and would have made possible, as it did in 1908, economic recovery after a few months.

While, therefore, the actions of the Reserve System in 1929–33 may be understandable under the circumstances, even psychologically and politically inevitable, the contraction is additional strong evidence for the economic independence of monetary changes from the contemporary course of income and prices, even during the early phase of the contraction, from 1929 to 1931, when the decline in the stock of money was not the result of explicit restrictive measures taken by the System. It can indeed be regarded as a fourth crucial experiment, making the matching of independent monetary decline and subsequent economic decline 4 to 4.

The existence of an important independent influence running from money to income explains the contrast we have noted between the variability in monetary arrangements during the near-century we have studied and the stability of the relation between changes in money and in other economic variables. The variability of monetary arrangements has produced, as we have seen, a corresponding variation in the movements of money itself. But, given that the major channel of influence is from money to business, there is no reason the changes in monetary arrangements should have altered the relation between movements in money and in business. That relation is determined primarily by the channels through which money affects business. So long as they remain the same, as apparently they have, so also should the relation between money and business.

Suppose, however, the major channel of influence had been from business to money. Changes in monetary institutions would then have affected not only the behavior of money but also the relation between money and other economic variables, since a change in business would have had different effects on the stock of money under the different monetary arrangements. Under the pre-1914 gold standard, for example, a business expansion in the United States tended to generate a deficit in the balance of payments, which in turn tended to produce an outflow of gold and hence downward pressure on the stock of money. That particular link in the sequence was largely severed by the gold-sterilization policy followed by the Federal Reserve in the 1920's and by the Treasury in part of the 1930's, and was greatly weakened by the change in the character of the gold standard during the rest of the period after 1914. Both before and after 1914, business expansion raised interest rates and stimulated banks to expand. However, before 1914, a rise in interest rates could raise the stock of money only through a rise in the deposit-reserve ratio or through the attraction of capital and thereby gold from abroad. After 1914, a rise in interest rates could also raise the stock of money by inducing banks to borrow more heavily from the Federal Reserve System. If the predominant direction of influence had been from business to money, these and other changes in the links between business and money would very likely have produced an appreciably different relation between movements in the two before and after 1914, and perhaps also for further subdivisions of those periods.

While the influence running from money to economic activity has been predominant, there have clearly also been influences running the other way, particularly during the shorter-run movements associated with the business cycle. The cyclical pattern of the deposit-reserve ratio is one example. The resumption and silver episodes, the 1919 inflation, and the 1929–33 contraction reveal clearly other aspects of the reflex influence of business on money. Changes in the money stock are therefore a consequence as well as an independent source of change in money income and prices, though, once they occur, they produce in their turn still further effects on income and prices. Mutual interaction, but with money rather clearly the senior partner in longer-run movements and in major cyclical movements, and more nearly an equal partner with money income and prices in shorter-run and milder movements—this is the generalization suggested by our evidence.

7.3 GARY S. BECKER

Underinvestment in College Education?

Gary S. Becker was born in Pottsville, Pennsylvania, in 1930. He became professor of economics at Columbia University in 1960 and later joined the University of Chicago in 1970, where he remains a professor. In 1967 Becker won the distinguished John Bates Clark medal of the American Economic Association and also served as its president in 1974. He received the Nobel Prize in economics for extending the concept of human capital, which orginated in the work of Theodore W. Schultz, Greg Lewis, and George J. Stigler.

Becker believes that personal decisions are inherently rational. His doctoral dissertation on discrimination defined it as an act in which the individual is willing to incur economic cost in order to avoid entering into a contract with others not of his own gender or race. These views were enshrined in his first major work, *The Economics of Discrimination* (University of Chicago Press, 1971), which extended the concept of self-defeating discrimination into an analysis of the effects of prejudice on the earnings, employment, and occupations of minorities. In the following selection from his second book, *Human Capital: A Theoretical and Empirical Analysis, With Special Reference to Education,* 2d ed. (National Bureau of Economic Research, 1975), Becker indicates that schooling and labor training provide the impetus for human capital formation. He concludes that to the extent that all forms of capital yield income and other productive outputs over a long period of time, expenditures on education, training, health care, and the promotion of ethical conduct are investments in human capital.

Key Concept: private money gains and social productivity gains

This [selection] adds several dimensions to the evaluation of the effects of college education on earnings and productivity by comparing private and social gains from college education with those from other investments. These comparisons permit a determination of how much is gained or lost by individuals and society from investing in the former rather than the latter, and are essential to determine whether there is underinvestment in college education; they also help determine whether the capital market difficulties, the lack of knowledge and liquidity, etc.,... have been serious impediments to the flow of resources into college education.

1. PRIVATE MONEY GAINS

In discussing whether the private gain from college exceeds that on other investments, a distinction must be made between the typical college graduate and the typical high-school graduate. [Evidence] indicated that the former gains more from college than the latter would, that he comes from a much higher socioeconomic background, and that he very likely finances his education with resources that would otherwise (in part at least) have been invested elsewhere, while the latter often would have to borrow, live frugally as a student, or work overtime (after school). For the sake of brevity, the discussion is limited to white male graduates, although interesting comparisons could be made with dropouts, nonwhites, and women.

The private rate of return after adjusting for differential "ability" seems to be more than 12 per cent to the cohort of white male college graduates. When comparing the rate on college with rates that would have been obtained if the resources spent on college had been invested elsewhere, there has been a rather surprising tendency to select rates on liquid investments bearing little risk, such as government bonds or savings accounts. [Evidence] indicates, however, that an investment in college education is subject to considerable risk, and is obviously extremely illiquid. Consequently, the gain from education should be compared with that on investments with equally large risk and illiquidity.

[E]arlier analysis indicated that the variation in the rate of return from corporate manufacturing investments is of the same order of magnitude as that from college education. [George J.] Stigler estimated the average rate of return on the former at a little over 7 per cent, several percentage points higher than that on riskless assets, but still much lower than the 12+ per cent received by white male college graduates. Although this difference of some 5 percentage points might be explained by compensating differences in liquidity and taxation, a more reasonable inference would be that the private money gain from college to the typical white male graduate is greater than what could have been obtained by investing elsewhere.

An estimate of the money gain could be found by discounting the adjusted income differentials between college and high-school graduates at a rate measuring alternative opportunities. If the 4 per cent riskless rate were used, the present value of the gain to the 1949 cohort of white males would be more than $30,000; the more appropriate rate of 6 per cent would cut the gain to under $20,000, and the possibly still more appropriate rate of 10 per cent would cut it to under $4000. Although all these estimates are very much under the $100,000 figure often bandied about, they are not insignificant. For example, even if the gain were "only" $3500 (a 10 per cent rate), average tuition and fees in 1949 could have been raised by more than 300 per cent without wiping it out.

The typical high-school graduate is another story. Instead of more than 12 per cent, he would receive 10 to 11 per cent if he went to college. Moreover, instead of investing resources that could have been invested elsewhere he would have to finance much of his college education by borrowing from friends or relatives, by living frugally, or by working after school and during vacations. Since households regularly pay from 8 to 18 per cent on bank and instalment credit loans and even more on others, the cost of borrowing and/or the preference for present consumption must be considered substantial. Consequently, even an 11 per cent rate of return from college would not bulk very large, especially when it is recognized that liquidity considerations would be important here because these persons presumably have a limited command of liquid assets.

So while a college education seems to yield a net money gain to the typical white male college graduate, it may not to the typical white male high-school graduate. One should note, however, that the rapid growth in recent years of low-interest student loans subsidized by state and federal governments certainly must increase the attractiveness of a college education. A study of the demand for these loans should shed considerable light on the conclusions reached here, and especially on the capital market impediments to investment in college education.

2. SOCIAL PRODUCTIVITY GAINS

The social economic gain from education, the gain to society as opposed to individuals, could differ from the private gain because of differences between social and private costs and returns. Economists (and others) have generally had little success in estimating the social effects of different investments, and, unfortunately, education is no exception. One can, however, develop some lower and upper limits that effectively rule out many of the more fanciful assertions about the effects of education.

Total social as well as private costs would be the sum of direct and indirect costs. Direct costs are clearly greater to society than to students because some of the expenditures on students are paid out of public and private subsidies. Obviously, "free" state and municipal colleges use scarce resources and are not free to society. Indirect costs, on the other hand, would be greater to society only if the output of students foregone by society exceeded the earnings foregone by students, which is not so obviously true.

Direct social costs would be the sum of educational expenditures by colleges and the social cost of books and additional living expenses. While the latter can be approximated by their private cost, an estimate of educational expenditures is not obtained as easily since colleges spend money on athletic competitions, room and board, adult education, research, medical care, etc., as well as on education proper. In other words, they are multiproduct "firms" with a total expenditure much greater than that on the single product education. I have tried to approximate educational expenditures by eliminating expenditures on "noneducational activities," extension services, research, and "specialized instruction" from the total.

Although social costs should obviously include capital as well as current costs, the fraction of educational expenditures paid by fees has usually been overestimated because only current expenditures have been considered. Since educational institutions are quite capital-intensive, expenditures are substantially raised and the fraction attributed to fees lowered when physical capital is included. For example, in 1950 the use value of capital in colleges was about 26 per cent of current expenditures, so that although fees were 42 per cent of current expenditures, they were only about 33 per cent of all expenditures. The full private contribution to all social costs has, however, been greatly underestimated because indirect costs are generally ignored, and they are mostly a private cost. If, for example, foregone earnings were used to represent indirect social costs, college students would be paying through tuition, fees, and foregone earnings almost three-quarters of all social costs.

Social and private economic returns from college would differ if a college education had different effects on earnings and productivity. A student generally must only determine the effect of a college education on his earnings, but society needs to determine its effect on national income. Thus if college graduates earn more partly because their productivity was systematically overestimated, private returns would tend to be larger than social ones. A more common criticism, however, is that earnings greatly understate the social productivity of college graduates (and other educated persons) because they are (allegedly) only partly compensated for their effect on the development and spread of economic knowledge. In technical language, social returns are said to be larger than private returns because of the external economies produced by college graduates.

As a first approximation, social returns will be measured by the before-tax earnings differentials, tax payments being one kind of external economy, and indirect social costs will be measured by the before-tax earnings foregone. The social rate of return, unadjusted for differential ability, would then be about 13 per cent to the 1939 cohort of urban, native white, male college graduates and 12.5 per cent to the 1949 cohort of white male college graduates. These are only slightly less than the private rates because differential tax payments almost offset the subsidies to college education. Similar results would be found for dropouts and for nonwhite, female, and rural college graduates. Adjustments for IQ, grades, and other ability factors would have about the same effect on the social rates as they did on the private rates: relatively little for the typical college person, and a few percentage points for the typical high-school graduate (if he had gone to college).

The development of a more sophisticated estimate of the social gain is not easy because other external effects are very difficult to measure. The absence of any direct measurements forced me to use an indirect and not very reliable method. E. Denison estimated the contribution of physical capital, labor, increasing returns, and many other factors to economic growth in the United States. After deducting these contributions, a residual is left over that he calls the contribution of "advancement in knowledge." By attributing all of the residual to education, an upper limit to the social effect of education can be developed.

According to Denison, about .58 percentage points of the 1.60 per cent average annual growth from 1929 to 1957 in national income per person employed is explained by the growth in knowledge, and about .67 percentage points by the growth in education. If the growth in knowledge was considered an indirect effect of the growth in education, the share attributed to education would almost double. This in turn implies that the estimated average rate of return on education would also almost double.

If the contribution of different educational levels to the advance in knowledge were proportionate to their direct effects on earnings—possibly college graduates had a disproportionately large contribution—the unadjusted social rate of return to white male graduates would be estimated at close to 25 per cent. The initial estimate of the social rate, 13 per cent, and the 25 per cent provide a lower and an admittedly rough upper limit to the true rate, the difference between them measuring the ignorance of external effects. Although this difference is embarrassingly large, it does suggest that, contrary to many assertions, the private economic gain from education is much of the social economic gain. For the private gain is more than half of the apparent upper limit, and presumably a good deal more than half of the true social rate.

In recent years the federal government has been subsidizing investment in education through scholarships and loans, and investment in business capital through accelerated depreciation, tax credits, and other means. Somehow the limited funds available must be allocated between these different kinds of investment. One determinant clearly should be, and hopefully is, their relative contribution to national income, a topic that will now be discussed briefly.

A first approximation to the social rate of return on business capital can be found by relating profits to capital, with profits including the corporate income and other direct taxes. The before-tax rate of return on corporate manufacturing capital averaged about 12 per cent for both 1938–1947 and 1947–1957, compared to an after-tax rate of 7 per cent. If the before-tax rate on all corporations were between 10 and 13 per cent and that on unincorporated firms between 4 and 8 per cent, almost the same as the after-tax rate on corporations, the rate on all business capital would be between 8 and 12 per cent. The first approximation to the social rate of return to white male college graduates would be between 10 and 13 per cent after adjustment for differential ability. Since the rates to dropouts, women, and nonwhites would be a few percentage points lower, the rate to all college entrants would be between 8 and 11 per cent. The rates on business capital and college education seem, therefore, to fall within the same range.

A fuller treatment of external effects could, however, change the picture entirely. It has been seen that if all the unexplained residual for 1929–1957 were attributed to education, its estimated social rate would almost double; if, on the other hand, all was attributed to business capital, its estimated social rate would much more than double. Consequently, depending on the allocation of the residual, that is, the "advance in knowledge," the estimated social rate on college education could be as much as twice and as little as less than half of that on business capital. Ignorance about the "residual," therefore, precludes at present any firm judgment about the relative social rates on business capital and college education.

TABLE 1

Investment in College Education Relative to Physical Capital for Selected Years

	Ratio of Investment in College to Gross Physical Investment	*Ratio of Foregone Earnings to Gross Physical Investment*
1920	.026	.016
1930	.076	.037
1940	.082	.040
1950	.103	.062
1956	.121	.071

Source: The numerators from T. W. Schultz "Capital Formation by Education," *Journal of Political Economy,* December 1960, Table 6; the denominators from Simon Kuznets, *Capital in the American Economy: Its Formation and Financing,* Princeton for NBER, 1961, Table R-4, p. 490.

3. PRIVATE REAL RATES

A treatment of the full, as opposed to the economic, social rate of return on college education would involve a consideration of cultural advance, democratic government, etc., and is clearly far beyond the scope of this study. Even a treatment of the full private rate is exceedingly difficult and I shall be content simply to raise some questions and suggest a few very tentative answers.

In deciding whether to go to college, attitudes toward college life and studying, the kind of work college graduates do, and other psychic factors are relevant as well as the gain in earnings. Full or real returns and costs would be the sum of monetary and psychic ones, and the real gain would depend on the relation between these real returns and costs. The psychic gain from college, like the monetary gain, probably differs considerably between the typical college and high-school graduate. For presumably the former does and the latter does not go to college partly because of a difference in expected psychic gains. Or to use more direct evidence, lack of interest is usually a major reason cited by high-school seniors in explaining why they were not going to college, and by college dropouts in explaining why they never finished.

Quantitative estimates of psychic gains are never directly available and are usually computed residually as the difference between independent estimates of monetary and real gains. Unfortunately, independent estimates of the real gains to college graduates are not available. For example, they could not be measured by the monetary gains from other capital because there may also be psychic gains from such capital, and, more importantly, because the real gains from college and other capital may differ owing to differences in access to the capital market or to other factors. One can use actual behavior to test whether real gains do differ. For if, say, college education were an unusually attractive investment, pressure would develop to invest more there, and while it could be offset in the short run by financing and other difficulties, these could be at least partially surmounted in the long run.

Table 1 indicates that the gross investment in college education rose from about 2.5 per cent of that in physical capital in 1920 to about 8 per cent in 1940 and 12 per cent in 1956. Foregone earnings, which are a rough measure of private investment, rose no less rapidly. So the private real rate of return has apparently been higher on college education than on physical capital. Since the money rate has probably also been higher (see section 1), the evidence on real rates does not necessarily mean that the psychic rate has been higher on college education than on physical capital, but only that it could not have been much lower.

7.4 GEORGE J. STIGLER

Can Regulatory Agencies Protect the Consumer?

George J. Stigler (1911–1991) was born in Seattle, Washington. After prewar appointments at Iowa State University and the University of Minnesota, followed by wartime service at the Office of Price Administration in Washington, D.C. during World War II, he filled faculty positions at several universities, including the University of Minnesota, Brown University, Columbia University, and the University of Chicago. In 1982 Stigler was awarded the Nobel Prize in economics for his work on the theory of economic regulation.

Stigler's work has focused on the areas of pure theory and economic regulation. In pure theory, he extended Adam Smith's contention that the size of the firm is affected by transportation costs and population density; defined the survivorship principle, whereby he devised a minimum efficient scale for the smallest plant remaining in operation after changes in technology or markets; and provided a model for analyzing informational issues in economics. In the following excerpt from *The Citizen and the State: Essays on Regulation* (University of Chicago Press, 1975), Stigler rejects the prevailing notion that regulatory agencies work on behalf of consumers, suggesting that they shield industries from new competition instead. He concludes that defenses available to individuals and small groups afford better protection to the consumer than state regulation.

Key Concept: the inability of the state to protect consumers

The consumer—and the investor and the laborer—have always been subjected to vicissitudes arising out of chance, ignorance, neglect, and fraud. Some are essentially inescapable: no sovereign has discovered a way to insure that everything taught in school is correct. Some are largely avoidable, but sometimes at costs more onerous than the vicissitudes: consider how much time would be required thoroughly to test ten competing brands of a product. That may very well be the reason there is no business which supplies leading brands of goods for experiment by the prospective buyer.

For the long centuries during which the state concerned itself little with such problems, the consumer had two main resources in dealing with the possible vicissitudes of purchasing, lending, working, and living. The first resource was his own intelligence, enshrined in the doctrine of *caveat emptor.* That phrase poorly describes the situation, and for at least three reasons:

1. The consumer did not have to beware of everything: he could contract with the seller for express warranties with respect to the commodity, and these warranties were and are enforceable.
2. There were implied warranties that the goods were of merchantable quality: the seller was required to reveal defects which would not be discoverable with ordinary examination.
3. The seller then, as now, had a good deal to beware of too. Anyone who thinks that there are more careless, irresponsible, or dishonest sellers than buyers obviously has never been a seller.

There was a second resource of the consumer to deploy against the vicissitudes of inferior performance, and that was the great engine of competition. It is widely assumed that if company A produces shoddy goods, rival B must also lower the quality of its goods to compete in price. That is exactly the opposite of the typical sequence: it is usually profitable to compete by improving quality, reliability, and safety. Consider just two types of evidence for the protective function of competition:

1. It is commonplace that there has been a strong secular trend in the improvement of the quality of manufactured goods. Tires last longer and seldom blow out; food is cleaner; antibiotics are more effective. To quote the National Bureau of Economic Research's Committee on Price Statistics:

   > If a poll were taken by professional economists and statisticians they would designate (and by a wide majority) the failure of the price indexes to take full account of quality changes as the most important defect in these indexes. And by almost as large a majority, they would believe that this failure introduces a systematic upward bias in the price indexes—that quality changes on average have been quality improvements.

2. The great merchandising dynasties—the Marshall Fields, the Macys, the Lazarus companies, Sears Roebuck, and Ward—are famous for their standards of reliability, not for the skill with which they ignore a customer's complaints. Their main asset, and the source of their economic prosperity, is their reputation for fair and careful dealing. Similarly with manufacturers: Henry Ford became enormously richer than Lydia Pinkham.

Of course, neither the diligence of ordinary mortals nor the competitive energies of an extraordinary economy will detect and prevent or correct all the mishaps and negligences and frauds of life. In Barnum's time a sucker may have been born every minute: now the population is three times as big and surely even (or especially?) in America at least several rogues are born every hour. So it is natural to turn to that center of authority, that depository of virtue and benevolence, that fountain of justice, the state, to provide further and fuller protection to the consumer. We are now well launched upon a luxuriously prolific regime of laws and agencies to protect the consumer. Any underestimate which the state may have made in the past of the need for protecting the individual in economic (and social) life is being more than corrected by the vigor and extravagance of its belated efforts.

The question before the house is what the government can do to help the consumer. Discussion of this question can proceed at either of two levels.

The first, and overwhelmingly popular, level of discourse is deductive and horatory. Appoint to a commission seven highly intelligent men who have unflagging zeal to serve the public interest, and only the public interest, equip them with the resources to find out what to do, and give them the legal power to do it. Then automobiles will be safe, stock exchanges will charge reasonable commissions, and mutual funds will not spend too much on selling costs. If on occasion a commissioner is less than superb, replace him; if on occasion the commission does something wrong, reprimand it; if the commission does too little, enlarge its powers and fatten its appropriations. With at most an occasional searching glance from the legislature, the agency will take care of monopolistic railroads, or profit-grubbing television, or deceptively quoted interest rates, or whatever. In this easy world we would need only listen to the demands of a Mr. Ralph Nader each day and fashion a new agency to solve his problem: one agency = one problem solved. The only suitable word to terminate such a discussion is "Amen": have not five or seven apostles been dealt off the top?

There is a second level of discourse, and I shall be so stubborn as to refuse to leave it during the remainder of this paper. It proceeds rather differently. The state has been protecting consumers for quite a time: for example, it is eighty-three years [1971] since the Interstate Commerce Commission (ICC) was created to assure safety of trains, adequacy of service, and reasonableness of rates. For fifty-six years the Federal Trade Commission (FTC) has been stamping out unfair methods of competition; for sixty-four years food and drug products have been under federal control; and even the Securities and Exchange Commission (SEC) is thirty-six years old, and no longer able to sprint. The vast body of actual experience, not the prospectuses of reformers, must be the basis upon which we appraise the role of the government in protecting the consumer.

If commissioners have often been lazy or timid, or deeply subservient to the industry they purport to regulate, it is inexcusably romantic to assume that all future appointments will be regulatory saints. If, whatever the quality of commissioners, quite often the law dictates inherently anticonsumer policies, what purpose is there in unctuously demanding better laws from better Congresses? Or perhaps we should have a commission to regulate Congress? The regulatory experience is now sufficiently varied and lengthy so that we can isolate the essential characteristics of the regulatory process, characteristics which determine what, in fact, the consumer may expect from regulation.

I shall illustrate much of the subsequent discussion from the regulation of the security markets, but this is simply quixotic chivalry in meeting Mr. [Manuel] Cohen on his own field. Whatever the regulatory area of special interest, let me emphasize that our task is to ascertain the basic character of public regulation, not its incidental scandals or triumphs. I shall assume, what I believe to be true, that usually the regulators are honest and conscientious, and that in particular the SEC's members, and especially its past chairmen, are paragons of virtue. Our concern is with the logic and basic forces of regulation, and they not only transcend fluctuations in personnel and events but basically dictate what type of men (or rather, of that subset of men called lawyers) will typically be appointed.

And now to the main thesis: public regulation weakens the defenses the consumer has in the market and often imposes new burdens upon him, without conferring corresponding protections. The doctrine of *caveat emptor* has not lost its force: the only change is that now the consumer must beware of different threats, and threats which he is less well equipped to defend against. The thesis will be developed with special reference to the SEC and the security markets.

We start with four important examples of the impairment of traditional consumer defenses by the SEC (acting often in collaboration with the New York Stock Exchange):

1. The New York Stock Exchange (NYSE) has imposed and enforced a minimum commission structure which is highly discriminatory against higher-priced stocks and larger-volume transactions and against nonmember brokers. No economist believes that it costs brokers ten times as much to sell 1,000 shares as 100 shares, or that a share selling for $100 costs substantially more to handle than one selling for $25, or that it is economically desirable that nonmember brokers share the work but not the commission. This discriminatory structure of commissions has been set with the tacit and more recently explicit approval of the SEC, and this approval is the only defense of this flagrant cartel-determined price structure against attack under the antitrust laws.
2. In the sale of mutual fund shares, the costs of the initial sale are much higher than the costs of collecting subsequent payments, and the mutuals have accordingly made a larger charge against the first-year contributions of a customer than against contributions in later years—a practice called "front-end loading." The SEC has now obtained legislation controlling front-end loading. Now the buyers of a mutual fund who do *not* withdraw from the fund will be permitted to bear the fund's costs in dealing with buyers who soon withdraw and are not charged the full costs of their temporary participation—a perverse incentive structure which must increase withdrawals. One could also raise some question of the equity of taxing the prudent to subsidize the impetuous. This SEC position stems from economic error, not industry pressure (as in the case of the commission structure).
3. Again, in the sale of mutual fund shares, a statutory provision (section 22[d] of the Investment Company Act) compels all sellers of the shares to observe the offering price—a special and unusually rigid instance of

resale price maintenance. The SEC explicitly refrained from requesting repeal of this extreme form of price-fixing by private enterprises.

4. The SEC has obtained legislation to regulate the selling expenses of mutual funds. The regulation of rates is of course a traditional regulatory weapon to defend the consumer, and in the case of railroad passengers has achieved almost 100 percent protection against both accidents and service. The SEC ceilings will make it more difficult for new funds to be launched and thus will reduce the competition which is the investor's main defense against excessive costs. The large, established mutual funds are naturally agreeable to this legislation.

These are examples of policies inimical to the investor's welfare which have been instituted or supported by the regulatory agency charged with protecting the investor. One could cite instances of nonfeasance as well: perhaps the most contemporary has been the practice of stock brokerage houses of operating on miserly capital bases, so that a moderate break in the market has led to a large number of failures. The SEC and its ally, the NYSE, have effectively delayed the brokerage houses which sought to go public and acquire an adequate volume of permanent capital not subject to partnership withdrawals—but I must add that most individual investors presumably are not so naive as to believe that the SEC's extensive regulation of this industry has increased the safety of its enterprises.

Competition, like other therapeutic forms of hardship, is by wide and agelong consent, highly beneficial to society when imposed upon—other people. Every industry that can afford a spokesman has emphasized both its devotion to the general principle and the overriding need for reducing competition within its own markets because this is the one area in which competition works poorly. The doctors must protect their patients against (unlicensed) quacks, and the medical profession must be right because Heaven has rewarded its benevolence with the highest earnings of any profession. Farmers must protect the consumer against famine, and this is best done by the subtle path of restrictions upon output and subsidies to producers.

Regulatory bodies are remarkably loyal in their acceptance of this two-edged philosophy—as indeed they should be, since they owe their existence to it. There may be instances in which the SEC, for example, has actually fostered competition in the industries for which it must answer to God, if not to man, and I hope that Mr. Cohen with his unrivaled knowledge can produce at least one. For every (or any) genuine instance that may be supplied, however, it will be ridiculously easy to supply five instances of the suppression of competition. Regulation and competition are rhetorical friends and deadly enemies: over the doorway of every regulatory agency save two should be carved: "Competition Not Admitted." The Federal Trade Commission's doorway should announce, "Competition Admitted in Rear," and that of the Antitrust Division, "Monopoly Only by Appointment."

Against the charge that public regulation imposes large costs, particularly by suppressing competition, the friends of public regulation will make three answers:

1. Some of the neglects—such as the monopolistic setting of commission rates and the inadequate capital requirements for stock exchange members—are about to be mended. One must make two decisive criticisms of this reply: (1) if evils persist for thirty-six years before they are mended, this is a grave criticism of the regulatory process; and (2) there is not the slightest assurance that the forthcoming reforms, if indeed they come forth, will remedy the past deficiencies. What historical justification is there for reverting to the theological level of discourse?
2. Some of the evils of the industry—such as the minimum commission on mutual fund share sales—are set by statute and hence are beyond the reach of the regulators. Observe: the effects of a regulation are to be judged not by the statutes actually passed by legislatures, but by those the friends of regulation would wish to see enacted.
3. There have been offsetting benefits of regulation, so that even if for argument's sake the complaints were accepted, the net balance would still be with regulation.

   This third response is of course the crucial one, and it invites more extensive comment.

I am not prepared either to deny or to accept the proposition that the SEC has accomplished much good along with whatever harm to the investor it has fostered or supported. Like every other regulatory body, it has been virtually free of any objective measure of its economic effects, and indeed *effects* are seldom considered explicitly in its statements. For example, some years ago it won a case against an advisory service which bought and sold stocks prior to advising its subscribers to do the same. Did the SEC ask whether the subscribers were injured by the practice? Certainly not, for its concern was only with legalistic concepts of conflict of interest and economic substance was irrelevant. In fact, the subscribers to the service would have profited if they had followed, with a lag, the advice of the service....

Yet one test of the achievements of regulation in this area can be cited. Six years ago I made a study of the effects of the SEC's review of the prospectuses for new stock issues. The procedure consisted basically of two steps:

1. A thousand dollars was hypothetically invested in each new issue of common stock (above a certain minimum issue size) from 1923 to 1927 and from 1949 to 1955—thus before and after the SEC began to review prospectuses to ensure a measure of accurate information.
2. The performance in each case was compared with the movement of the stock market, as measured by the comprehensive Standard and Poor Index, in the same period.

The main finding was that in both periods the purchaser of new stock issues lost about 11 percent after one year and 21 percent after two years relative to buying the Standard and Poor stocks.... One cannot claim utter precision for such a finding, but my conclusion is surely conservative: the SEC did not appreciably improve the experience of investors in the new issues market by its expensive review of prospectuses.

The record of regulation of the securities markets is wholly typical of regulatory programs. Consider the regulation of transportation. What does the consumer owe to the ICC? He owes for certain only two things: the support of a compulsory noncompetitive rate structure in the motor trucking industry, which, if not regulated, would be a highly competitive industry, and the imposition of a nonviable rigidity upon the railroad industry which is helping to destroy it before our eyes. What does the consumer owe the Civil Aeronautics Board (CAB)? Again, as with the ICC, very high barriers to the entry of new firms, and the support of a rate structure seriously in conflict with competition. What does the consumer owe to the regulation of television? Mainly such things as an extraordinary campaign to prevent and hamper pay television—although the main channel of this obstructive influence by commercial TV and movie theatre industries has been through the Congress, acting upon the Federal Communications Commission (FCC).

I have neither inclination nor evidence to deny the regulatory process occasional triumphs. The delay in introducing thalidomide* in the United States presumably was a splendid success, and should receive full credit. But we must base public policy not upon signal triumphs or scandalous failures but upon the regular, average performance of the policy. If the policies which delayed thalidomide would delay a new penicillin at least as long—as seems highly probable—we must reckon this in the costs of the program.

The ultimate, inescapable fact of life for the consumer is that he must beware—as much today as in the past. I began by saying that, under the earlier regime of *caveat emptor,* the consumer was protected basically by his own care and intelligence and by the most powerful of allies, competition. Public regulation weakens and sometimes destroys these defenses against fraud and negligence, without replacing the protections they used to afford.

Consider a regulatory activity—perhaps the federal milk marketing boards which have so carefully cartelized the production and distribution of milk in the United States, to the substantial economic detriment of the consumer. If one milk company exploits or misleads its customers, each consumer has an incentive to seek out a more reliable or more efficient supplier. The larger the misdeeds of this company, and the larger the consumption of milk by the consumer, the greater his rewards if he can uncover a new source of supply. Profit-seeking outsiders will strive mightily to respond to this demand for lower but profitable prices. These incentives provide a strong sanction even on a monopolist. (There is a widespread view that a monopolist profits by lowering the quality of goods compared to what competition would provide, and this view is simply erroneous economic theory. There is an equally popular view —often held by the very same people!—that competition leads to continuous reductions of quality and it is equally erroneous.)

* [Thalidomide is the morning-sickness drug responsible for severe birth defects from 1956 to 1961. —Eds.]

What is the consumer's recourse if he is being exploited by a federal marketing order which either neglects his interests or, as is the case at present in the United States, positively arms and protects a cartel in exploiting this consumer? His sole defense is to organize a political campaign to change or eliminate that marketing scheme. For the individual consumer this is a bleak prospect. The costs—in time, effort, and money—to change legislation are large; the reward to any one consumer from joining a consumer lobby is negligible. The milk marketing board in Chicago, according to a competent economist's analysis, raised the price of milk at least two cents per quart in the mid-1960s—or perhaps $10 to $20 per family per year. If a family were to devote a sum such as this to stirring up opposition to the marketing order, and even if the battle could be restricted to Chicago (the underlying legislation is federal), it would be a wretched option: the family would receive negligible benefits from its own activity.

The sheltered farmers, milk companies, and laborers in the industry have much larger stakes, and they can and do mount the legislative drives which create and dominate such legislation. The individual consumer has no real defense, given the nature of our political process, which allows compact groups with substantial per capita interests to win out over diffused masses of consumers, no one of whom can effectively combat special interest legislation.

Occasionally the consumer will be protected in the legislature by another industry which happens to share the consumer's goal but not his impotence. This fortuitous and uncommon circumstance aside, he is the victim without recourse of our political system which is inaccessible to groups that may be large but whose members as individuals have only small stakes in a controversy.

We are now going through a new period of salvation by public reform, similar in scale, and in the comparative roles assigned to emotion and to knowledge, to the muckraking period preceding World War I. Then we had Upton Sinclair and Ida Tarbell and a host of others; now we have Ralph Nader and his graduate and prep school students. In both periods the intellectual quality of the reform literature is, on all except its very best pages, rankly deplorable. Allegations are facts, villainy is ubiquitous, costs of reforms are not the rational prices which keep a sensible society from going overboard in one direction but the shallow, cynical excuses of the vested interests, and the federal political and administrative machinery is easily perfected in motive and achievement, once we replace the louts who have distorted and perverted it for many years! Even in the superior examples of this literature, such as the so-called Nader report (by Robert Fellmeth) on the Interstate Commerce Commission, utter disillusionment with past regulation leads to a demand for better regulation! On this wave of sentiment, no doubt, a few pieces of reform—bad and good—will be brought in, but they will not amount to much.

They will not amount to much because there is no durable, effective political basis to support—or direct—the efforts of professional (to say nothing of amateur) reformers. Mr. Nader must flit from automobiles to drugs to local property assessments, cognizant that the public's interests and sympathies are not forever captureable by his vendetta against the Corvair. Recitals of ancient evil bore even a punctilious saint, so a constant supply of new charges against new villains must be uncovered or fabricated, and suitably printed in the hot ink of outrage. The self-appointed savior and his colleagues and legislative allies may get an occasional law. But they will not, year in and year out, attend the appropriation hearings, and the unending sequence of hearings on new appointments, which in the long run determine the direction and personnel of the regulatory agency.

The superiority of the traditional defenses of the individual—reliance upon his own efforts and the power of competition—lie precisely in the characteristics which distinguish them from public regulation. Each of the traditional defenses is available and working at all times—self-interest and competition are never passing fads. Each of the traditional defenses is available to individuals and small groups—changes in policy and adaptation to new circumstances do not require changes in the ponderous, expensive, insensitive machinery of a great state. It is of regulation that the consumer must beware.

PART THREE

The Keynesian and Institutionalist Schools

On the Internet . . .

Sites appropriate to Part Three

A note on the life and work of John Maynard Keynes.

```
http://www.blupete.com/Literature/
  Biographies/Philosophy/Keynes.htm
```

Provided by "The Memory Hole," a publishing project intended to make accessible politically controversial materials, this Web site provides the text of Keynes's *The Economic Consequences of the Peace.*

```
http://www.borg.com/~akoontz/tmh/books/
  keynes0.html
```

This is a listing of 190 book citations by Keynes and post-Keynesian economists.

```
http://www.mala.bc.ca/~mcneil/cit/
  citlckeynes.htm
```

The International Thorstein Veblen Association's Web site contains essays and information on Veblen.

```
http://clear.lakes.com/~eltechno/
  TVbase.html
```

CHAPTER 8 The Keynesian School

8.1 JOHN MAYNARD KEYNES

The Principle of Effective Demand

John Maynard Keynes (1883–1946) was born in Cambridge, England, to a relatively affluent home. He received his undergraduate and graduate education at King's College in Cambridge, where he studied philosophy and economics. Keynes was one of Alfred Marshall's favorite students at Cambridge. He worked with the government on problems of Indian finance in addition to lecturing at Cambridge. Keynes was the U.K. Treasury's chief representative at the Versailles peace conference in 1919. In addition, he was an executive of two finance companies, an active member of the Liberal Party, and a contributor of articles to various journals and newspapers.

The following selection has been taken from *The General Theory of Employment, Interest, and Money* (Harcourt Brace Jovanovich, 1964), originally published in 1936. In it Keynes attacks classical economics by positing that the level of employment depends on the level of demand, which consists of the propensities to invest and consume. He asserts that in a fully employed economy if the propensity to save exceeds the propensity to invest, total demand will be unable to sustain full employment, which will lead to recession. Conversely, if in a fully employed economy the amount of savings is less than that required for investment, inflation will result.

Key Concept: the principle of effective demand

I

We need, to start with, a few terms which will be defined precisely later. In a given state of technique, resources and costs, the employment of a given volume of labour by an entrepreneur involves him in two kinds of expense: first of all, the amounts which he pays out to the factors of production (exclusive of other entrepreneurs) for their current services, which we shall call the *factor cost* of the employment in question; and secondly, the amounts which he pays out to other entrepreneurs for what he has to purchase from them together with the sacrifice which he incurs by employing the equipment instead of leaving it idle, which we shall call the *user cost* of the employment in question. The excess of the value of the resulting output over the sum of its factor cost and its user cost is the profit or, as we shall call it, the *income* of the entrepreneur. The factor cost is, of course, the same thing, looked at from the point of view of the entrepreneur, as what the factors of production regard as their income. Thus the factor cost and the entrepreneur's profit make up, between them, what we shall define as the *total income* resulting from the employment given by the entrepreneur. The entrepreneur's profit thus defined is, as it should be, the quantity which he endeavours to maximise when he is deciding what amount of employment to offer. It is sometimes convenient, when we are looking at it from the entrepreneur's standpoint, to call the aggregate income (*i.e.* factor cost *plus* profit) resulting from a given amount of employment the *proceeds* of that employment. On the other hand, the aggregate supply price[1] of the output of a given amount of employment is the expectation of proceeds which will just make it worth the while of the entrepreneurs to give that employment.

It follows that in a given situation of technique, resources and factor cost per unit of employment, the amount of employment, both in each individual firm and industry and in the aggregate, depends on the amount of the proceeds which the entrepreneurs expect to receive from the corresponding output. For entrepreneurs will endeavour to fix the amount of employment at the level which they expect to maximise the excess of the proceeds over the factor cost.

Let Z be the aggregate supply price of the output from employing N men, the relationship between Z and N being written $Z = \phi(N)$, which can be called the *Aggregate Supply Function*. Similarly, let D be the proceeds which entrepreneurs expect to receive from the employment of N men, the relationship between D and N being written $D = f(N)$, which can be called the *Aggregate Demand Function*.

Now if for a given value of N the expected proceeds are greater than the aggregate supply price, *i.e.* if D is greater than Z, there will be an incentive to entrepreneurs to increase employment beyond N and; if necessary, to raise costs by competing with one another for the factors of production, up to the value of N for which Z has become equal to D. Thus the volume of employment is given by the point of intersection between the aggregate demand function and the aggregate supply function; for it is at this point that the entrepreneurs' expectation of profits will be maximised. The value of D at the point of the aggregate demand function, where it is intersected by the aggregate supply function, will be called *the effective demand*. . . . [T]his is the substance of the General Theory of Employment. . . .

The classical doctrine, on the other hand, which used to be expressed categorically in the statement that "Supply creates its own Demand" and continues to underlie all orthodox economic theory, involves a special assumption as to the relationship between these two functions. For "Supply creates its own Demand" must mean that $f(N)$ and $\phi(N)$ are equal for *all* values of N, *i.e.* for all levels of output and employment; and that when there is an increase in $Z(= \phi(N))$ corresponding to an increase in N, $D(=f(N))$ necessarily increases by the same amount as Z. The classical theory assumes, in other words, that the aggregate demand price (or proceeds) always accommodates itself to the aggregate supply price; so that, whatever the value of N may be, the proceeds D assume a value equal to the aggregate supply price Z which corresponds to N. That is to say, effective demand, instead of having a unique equilibrium value, is an infinite range of values all equally admissible; and the amount of employment is indeterminate except in so far as the marginal disutility of labour sets an upper limit.

If this were true, competition between entrepreneurs would always lead to an expansion of employment up to the point at which the supply of output as a whole ceases to be elastic, i.e. where a further increase in the value of the effective demand will no longer be accompanied by any increase in output. Evidently this amounts to the same thing as full employment.... [W]e have [defined] full employment in terms of the behaviour of labour. An alternative, though equivalent, criterion is that at which we have now arrived, namely a situation in which aggregate employment is inelastic in response to an increase in the effective demand for its output. Thus Say's law, that the aggregate demand price of output as a whole is equal to its aggregate supply price for all volumes of output, is equivalent to the proposition that there is no obstacle to full employment. If, however, this is not the true law relating the aggregate demand and supply functions, there is a vitally important chapter of economic theory which remains to be written and without which all discussions concerning the volume of aggregate employment are futile.

II

...In this summary we shall assume that the money-wage and other factor costs are constant per unit of labour employed. But this simplification, with which we shall dispense later, is introduced solely to facilitate the exposition. The essential character of the argument is precisely the same whether or not money-wages, etc., are liable to change.

The outline of our theory can be expressed as follows. When employment increases, aggregate real income is increased. The psychology of the community is such that when aggregate real income is increased aggregate consumption is increased, but not by so much as income. Hence employers would make a loss if the whole of the increased employment were to be devoted to satisfying the increased demand for immediate consumption. Thus, to justify any given amount of employment there must be an amount of current investment sufficient to absorb the excess of total output over what the community chooses to consume when employment is at the given level. For unless there is this amount of investment, the receipts of the entrepreneurs will be less than is required to induce them to offer the given amount of employment. It follows, therefore, that, given what we shall call the community's propensity to consume, the equilibrium level of employment, *i.e.* the level at which there is no inducement to employers as a whole either to expand or to contract employment, will depend on the amount of current investment. The amount of current investment will depend, in turn, on what we shall call the inducement to invest; and the inducement to invest will be found to depend on the relation between the schedule of the marginal efficiency of capital and the complex of rates of interest on loans of various maturities and risks.

Thus, given the propensity to consume and the rate of new investment, there will be only one level of employment consistent with equilibrium; since any other level will lead to inequality between the aggregate supply price of output as a whole and its aggregate demand price. This level cannot be *greater* than full employment, *i.e.* the real wage cannot be less than the marginal disutility of labour. But there is no reason in general for expecting it to be *equal* to full employment. The effective demand associated with full employment is a special case, only realised when the propensity to consume and the inducement to invest stand in a particular relationship to one another. This particular relationship, which corresponds to the assumptions of the classical theory, is in a sense an optimum relationship. But it can only exist when, by accident or design, current investment provides an amount of demand just equal to the excess of the aggregate supply price of the output resulting from full employment over what the community will choose to spend on consumption when it is fully employed.

This theory can be summed up in the following propositions:

(1) In a given situation of technique, resources and costs, income (both money-income and real income) depends on the volume of employment N.

(2) The relationship between the community's income and what it can be expected to spend on consumption, designated by D_1, will depend on the psychological characteristic of the community, which we shall call its *propensity to consume.* That is to say, consumption will depend on the level of aggregate income and, therefore, on the level of employment N, except when there is some change in the propensity to consume.

(3) The amount of labour N which the entrepreneurs decide to employ depends on the sum (D) of *two* quantities, namely D_1, the amount which the community is expected to spend on consumption, and D_2, the amount which it is expected to devote to new investment. D is what we have called above the *effective demand.*

(4) Since $D_1 + D_2 = D = \phi(N)$, where ϕ is the aggregate supply function, and since, as we have seen in (2) above, D_1 is a function of N, which we may write $\chi(N)$, depending on the propensity to consume, it follows that $\phi(N) - \chi(N) = D_2$.

(5) Hence the volume of employment in equilibrium depends on (i) the aggregate supply function, ϕ, (ii) the propensity to consume, χ, and (iii) the volume of investment, D_2. This is the essence of the General Theory of Employment.

(6) For every value of N there is a corresponding marginal productivity of labour in the wage-goods industries; and it is this which determines the real wage. (5) is, therefore, subject to the condition that N cannot *exceed* the value which reduces the real wage to equality with the marginal disutility of labour. This means that not all changes in D are compatible with our temporary assumption that money-wages are constant. Thus it will be essential to a full statement of our theory to dispense with this assumption.

(7) On the classical theory, according to which $D = \phi(N)$ for *all* values of N, the volume of employment is in neutral equilibrium for all values of N less than its maximum value; so that the forces of competition between entrepreneurs may be expected to push it to this maximum value. Only at this point, on the classical theory, can there be stable equilibrium.

(8) *When employment increases,* D_1 *will increase, but not by so much as* D; since when our income increases our consumption increases also, but not by so much. The key to our practical problem is to be found in this psychological law. For it follows from this that the greater the volume of employment the greater will be the gap between the aggregate supply price (Z) of the corresponding output and the sum (D_1) which the entrepreneurs can expect to get back out of the expenditure of consumers. Hence, if there is no change in the propensity to consume, employment cannot increase, unless at the same time D_2, is increasing so as to fill the increasing gap between Z and D_1. Thus—except on the special assumptions of the classical theory according to which there is some force in operation which, when employment increases, always causes D_2 to increase sufficiently to fill the widening gap between Z and D_1—the economic system may find itself in stable equilibrium with N at a level below full employment, namely at the level given by the intersection of the aggregate demand function with the aggregate supply function.

Thus the volume of employment is not determined by the marginal disutility of labour measured in terms of real wages, except in so far as the supply of labour available at a given real wage sets a *maximum* level to employment. The propensity to consume and the rate of new investment determine between them the volume of employment, and the volume of employment is uniquely related to a given level of real wages—not the other way round. If the propensity to consume and the rate of new investment result in a deficient effective demand, the actual level of employment will fall short of the supply of labour potentially available at the existing real wage, and the equilibrium real wage will be *greater* than the marginal disutility of the equilibrium level of employment.

This analysis supplies us with an explanation of the paradox of poverty in the midst of plenty. For the mere existence of an insufficiency of effective demand may, and often will, bring the increase of employment to a standstill *before* a level of full employment has been reached. The insufficiency of effective demand will inhibit the process of production in spite of the fact that the marginal product of labour still exceeds in value the marginal disutility of employment.

Moreover the richer the community, the wider will tend to be the gap between its actual and its potential production; and therefore the more obvious and outrageous the defects of the economic system. For a poor community will be prone to consume by far the greater part of its output, so that a very modest measure of investment will be sufficient to provide fill employment;

whereas a wealthy community will have to discover much ampler opportunities for investment if the saving propensities of its wealthier members are to be compatible with the employment of its poorer members. If in a potentially wealthy community the inducement to invest is weak, then, in spite of its potential wealth, the working of the principle of effective demand will compel it to reduce its actual output, until, in spite of its potential wealth, it has become so poor that its surplus over its consumption is sufficiently diminished to correspond to the weakness of the inducement to invest.

But worse still. Not only is the marginal propensity to consume weaker in a wealthy community, but, owing to its accumulation of capital being already larger, the opportunities for further investment are less attractive unless the rate of interest falls at a sufficiently rapid rate; which brings us to the theory of the rate of interest and to the reasons why it does not automatically fall to the appropriate level. . . .

Thus the analysis of the Propensity to Consume, the definition of the Marginal Efficiency of Capital and the theory of the Rate of Interest are the three main gaps in our existing knowledge which it will be necessary to fill. When this has been accomplished, we shall find that the Theory of Prices falls into its proper place as a matter which is subsidiary to our general theory. We shall discover, however, that Money plays an essential part in our theory of the Rate of Interest; and we shall attempt to disentangle the peculiar characteristics of Money which distinguish it from other things.

III

The idea that we can safely neglect the aggregate demand function is fundamental to the Ricardian economics, which underlie what we have been taught for more than a century. [Thomas] Malthus, indeed, had vehemently opposed [David] Ricardo's doctrine that it was impossible for effective demand to be deficient; but vainly. For, since Malthus was unable to explain clearly (apart from an appeal to the facts of common observation) how and why effective demand could be deficient or excessive, he failed to furnish an alternative construction; and Ricardo conquered England as completely as the Holy Inquisition conquered Spain. Not only was his theory accepted by the city, by statesmen and by the academic world. But controversy ceased; the other point of view completely disappeared; it ceased to be discussed. The great puzzle of Effective Demand with which Malthus had wrestled vanished from economic literature. You will not find it mentioned even once in the whole works of [Alfred] Marshall, [Francis Ysidro] Edgeworth and [A. C.] Pigou, from whose hands the classical theory has received its most mature embodiment. It could only live on furtively, below the surface, in the underworlds of Karl Marx, Silvio Gesell or Major Douglas.

The completeness of the Ricardian victory is something of a curiosity and a mystery. It must have been due to a complex of suitabilities in the doctrine to the environment into which it was projected. That it reached conclusions quite different from what the ordinary uninstructed person would expect, added, I suppose, to its intellectual prestige. That its teaching, translated into practice, was austere and often unpalatable, lent it virtue. That it was adapted to carry a vast and consistent logical superstructure, gave it beauty. That it could explain much social injustice and apparent cruelty as an inevitable incident in the scheme of progress, and the attempt to change such things as likely on the whole to do more harm than good, commended it to authority. That it afforded a measure of justification to the free activities of the individual capitalist, attracted to it the support of the dominant social force behind authority.

But although the doctrine itself has remained unquestioned by orthodox economists up to a late date, its signal failure for purposes of scientific prediction has greatly impaired, in the course of time, the prestige of its practitioners. For professional economists, after Malthus, were apparently unmoved by the lack of correspondence between the results of their theory and the facts of observation;—a discrepancy which the ordinary man has not failed to observe, with the result of his growing unwillingness to accord to economists that measure of respect which he gives to other groups of scientists whose theoretical results are confirmed by observation when they are applied to the facts.

The celebrated *optimism* of traditional economic theory, which has led to economists being looked upon as Candides, who, having left this world for the cultivation of their gardens, teach that all is for the best in the best of all possible worlds provided we will let well alone, is also to be traced, I think, to their having neglected to take account of the drag on prosperity which can be exercised by an insufficiency of effective demand. For there would obviously be a natural tendency towards the optimum employment of resources in a Society which was functioning after the manner of the classical postulates. It may well be that the classical theory represents the way in which we should like our Economy to behave. But to assume that it actually does so is to assume our difficulties away.

NOTES

1. Not to be confused (*vide infra*) with the supply price of a unit of output in the ordinary sense of this term.

8.2 ALVIN H. HANSEN

Notes on Early Economic Thinking and on Social Philosophy

Alvin H. Hansen (1887–1975) was born in Viburg, South Dakota. He taught at the University of Minnesota and in 1937 joined Harvard University as professor of political economy. After retirement from Harvard in 1957, Hansen continued to work as visiting professor at many universities in the United States and abroad. He also served in various positions in government. Hansen was appointed in 1933 as director of research for President Roosevelt's Committee of Inquiry on National Policy in International Economic Relations. In 1937, he worked as a member of the President's Advisory Council on Social Security. Hansen also served for one year as special economic adviser to the Board of Governors of the Federal Reserve System.

Many agree that Hansen did more than any other economist to bring the Keynesian Revolution to America. His *Fiscal Policy and Business Cycles* (1941) was the first work to support the whole of Keynes's analysis of the causes of the Great Depression. He extended Keynes's liquidity preference analysis, which upheld the notion that the growth of liquid assets could increase consumption and employment. This notion suggested that if the wealthy held most of the liquid assets, consumption would rise, minimally fueling unemployment. Accordingly, the correct policy to stimulate demand, and in turn, growth was a mixed public-private economy. In the following selection, taken from *A Guide to Keynes* (McGraw-Hill, 1953), Hansen discusses mercantilism and the role of money, as well as private enterprise and the welfare state. Although a staunch Keynesian, he takes issue with Keynes's assertions that a large accumulated stock of capital reduces investment and that the propensity to consume is falling. Hansen observes that capital is only one determinant of investment (technology and population growth being the others) and maintains that the propensity to consume has remained stable over time.

Key Concept: mercantilism, the role of money, and the welfare state

[GENERAL THEORY, CHAPTERS 23, 24]

These chapters are brilliantly written and highly entertaining. Here Keynes lets himself go. Many would say that he threw caution to the winds and allowed his fancy to roam in an irresponsible manner. Still, a careful reading will disclose the fact that, while flying his kite, he has his feet on the ground at least a good deal of the time! He wrote while the world was still at peace and one could daydream and speculate about Utopia. Things have changed.

All the elements of his theoretical system had already been expounded in earlier chapters, and these two concluding chapters add nothing of substance to the analytical arsenal in which we are primarily interested. But apart from his fascinating flights of fancy, something can be gleaned from penetrating sidelights into his general system of thinking.

Mercantilism and the Role of Money

The section on mercantilism harks back to the preoccupation of the *Treatise*—the role of money. The *General Theory* has the effect of relegating money to a place of less prominence than that assigned to it in the *Treatise.* Chapter 23 appears to be a reversion, in a measure, to his former enthusiasm concerning the importance of money. The mercantilists are praised for the emphasis they placed on money. Home investment is governed (as they saw it) by the domestic rate of interest, and this in turn is governed by the quantity of money. The balance of trade is, they thought, rightly a chief concern of economic policy because, in the absence of domestic gold production, it controls a country's money supply. All this is a throwback to earlier views.

In the many quotations which he gives from the mercantilists, based on [Eli F.] Heckscher, Keynes seems to give unqualified approval to a purely monetary theory of the rate of interest. Here and elsewhere he is not quite fair to his own system, which, taken in its entirety, is certainly not purely, or even mainly, monetary. In the complete Keynesian system the determinates of the rate of interest are not only the quantity of money and liquidity preference but also the investment-demand schedule and the consumption function. Here, perhaps even more than elsewhere, Keynes opens wide the door to the criticism that he is satisfied with a primitive and indefensible *monetary* theory of interest.

Some interesting brief comments on large issues are offered here and there. Thus, it is suggested (footnote, p. 340) that all human history discloses, as we should expect from a knowledge of human nature, a long-run tendency for money wages to rise. Increasing wages, rising productivity, and a growing labor force could scarcely fail, more or less, to create a need for more money. "Thus, apart from progress and increasing population, a gradually increasing stock of money has proved imperative" in view of the tendency for the wage unit to rise over long periods of time.

The problems and actual experiences encountered in the mercantilist literature point, Keynes believed, to the conclusion "that there has been a chronic tendency throughout human history for the propensity to save to be stronger than the inducement to invest" (p. 347). He further suggests that the weakness of the inducement to invest may today lie in the extent of existing accumulations of capital goods, whereas in the mercantilist period the main explanation could perhaps be found in the great risks and hazards of that period (p. 348). Again on page 349 he refers to "the growth of wealth and the diminishing marginal propensity to consume."

Two points with respect to Keynes's statement are to be noted here, (1) that a large accumulated *stock* of capital tends per se to reduce investment opportunities, and (2) that the secular propensity to consume is falling.

With respect to the former it should be noted that the extent of future investment opportunities in any country depends partly on the degree to which capital accumulation has already been built up in relation to the prevailing technique and to the expanse and richness of its territory and resources, partly on the prospect of technological progress, and partly on population growth. The accumulation of a large stock of capital is indeed, as Keynes suggests, an important and relevant factor, but only one among several. The year 1800 found England equipped with primitive tools; by the end of the century she had accumulated a vast stock of fixed capital. Thus nineteenth-century England is an example of the "exuberance of the greatest age of the inducement to investment" (p. 353). With respect to the secular propensity to consume, my own view has always been that it is reasonable to assume it to be stable over time, as indeed [Simon] Kuznets' data appear to show.

Keynes credits the mercantilists with fragments of practical wisdom (p. 340) which later economists ignored. The "unrealistic abstractions of Ricardo" created a "cleavage between the conclusions of economic theory and those of common sense" (pp. 340, 350).

Chapter 23 ends with an appraisal of the strength and weakness of the analysis of saving, consumption, and investment in [Bernard] Mandeville, [Thomas] Malthus, and [John] Hobson. These views need no comment here except to say that it is now possible, in view of the theoretical system developed in the *General Theory,* to appraise the good and bad points in these authors in a manner that was formerly not possible. One has only to contrast the literature dealing with these writers prior to and after 1936 to see how inadequate the work of these forerunners was in contrast with the theoretical structure erected by Keynes.

Private Enterprise, the Welfare State, and Socialism

The issues raised in Chap. 23 are carried forward in Chap. 24 with special reference to the broader social implications of the *General Theory.* Does the Keynesian analysis lead to socialism, or is it a means of saving capitalism and individualism? Does it lead to autarchy in trade, or to freer trade? Is "full employment" the goal, or is "full investment" the goal? Is main reliance to be placed on reducing the rate of interest, on raising the consumption function, or on enlarging the scope of public and private investment?

Merely to mention these issues is enough to show why the *General Theory* has aroused so much opposition. Keynes attacked dominant orthodox theories; he attacked conventional dogmas with respect to practical policy; and he attacked the doctrine that reliance can be placed on automatic adjustment processes. He labeled as outstanding faults of the modern economy, failure to provide full employment and an inequitable distribution of wealth and income.

He contended that his analysis leads to directly opposite conclusions from those reached by orthodox economics with respect to the effect of measures (*e.g.*, taxation) designed to lessen the existing inequality of income. Greater equality will raise the consumption function; and an increase in the propensity to consume will serve to increase the inducement to invest (p. 373). Yet he states, as part of his faith, a belief in the "social and psychological justification for significant inequalities of incomes and wealth," though not as large as those which existed in 1936 (p. 374).

Similarly his analysis leads, he thought, to diametrically opposite conclusions from those reached by classical theory with respect to capital formation. According to the classicals, a high propensity to save is the source of high capital formation; and a high volume of saving was thought to be promoted by (1) a low propensity to consume and (2) a high rate of interest. As Keynes saw it, the opposite is true: a high level of investment is promoted by a low rate of interest and by a high propensity to consume. Basically, of course, the explanation for these different conclusions must be sought in the fact that the classicals were thinking of full-employment conditions, while Keynes had in mind the condition of underemployment.

Keynes explicitly pointed out that a system of highly progressive taxes might reduce the net rate of return, after taxes, sufficiently to cause a low level of investment even though the rate of interest were low. "I must not be supposed to deny the possibility, or even the probability, of this outcome" (p. 377). Thus steeply progressive taxes might have the effect of preventing the optimum volume of capital formation. Here as so often in economics one encounters a dilemma: highly progressive taxes are favorable to a high level of consumption since such taxes promote greater equality of income, but they tend to have a deterrent effect on investment.

Keynes expressed forcibly the view that a program of continuous full employment would provide so high a rate of capital formation, assuming no radical change in the consumption function, that, within a generation or so, the marginal efficiency of capital would be driven down to zero (*i.e.*, the capital stock would increase until the condition of *full investment* is reached). Necessary conditions for this eventuality to occur would be (1) a fairly inelastic marginal efficiency schedule and (2) relatively small upward shifts in the schedule (*i.e.*, inadequate investment outlets due to a sluggish technology and a slow rate of population growth).

In line with his faith, often expressed, in the virtues of active enterprise (in contrast with the passive virtues of thrift) he unfurled the banner for the intelligence, determination, and executive skill of the entrepreneur (p. 376) while complacently foreseeing the gradual euthanasia of the *rentier* class.

He affirmed his faith in individual initiative and private enterprise. He was opposed to a system of state socialism. Nevertheless, the role of the State must, he thought, be greatly increased. "The State will have to exercise a guiding influence on the propensity to consume partly through its scheme of taxation, partly by fixing the rate of interest, and partly, perhaps, in other ways"

(p. 378). Banking policy alone, via a low rate of interest, will not provide sufficient investment, he thought, for full employment. Public investment (but Keynes did not go into details) will be needed. Mixed companies—public authority combined with private initiative—have already played an important role in many countries, and such ventures may be expanded. State control of investment in housing—low-cost public housing, lending, insurance, and guaranteeing operations—have become standard policies in all advanced countries. State action to ensure adequate investment, public and private, together with a tax policy designed to raise the consumption function—these are the types of measures which seemed promising. "It is not the ownership of the instruments of production which it is important for the State to assume" (p. 378). What is needed is "an adjustment between the propensity to consume and the inducement to invest" (p. 379). It is no more necessary, he thought, to socialize economic life now than formerly.

Once sustained full employment is achieved, classical theory comes into its own. At full employment, the price system can be expected to direct productive resources, economically and wisely, into the right channels. What we suffer from is not misdirected employment but underemployment. The "free play of economic forces" can be trusted to give us efficient use of the factors of production (p. 379). In support of Keynes's position, one may cite the miraculous productivity and efficiency which the American economy has displayed ever since 1941 under the stimulus of a high level of Aggregate Demand.

Keynes was keenly aware of the advantages of individualism and free enterprise—the play of self-interest, the safeguard of personal liberty, the exercise of personal choice, and the variety of life which these institutions encourage. Indeed Keynes averred that he defended the enlargement of the functions of government (designed "to adjust the propensity to consume to the inducement to invest") as the "only practicable means of avoiding the destruction of existing economic forms" and promoting the "successful functioning of individual initiative" (p. 380). The world will not continue to tolerate unemployment. What is needed is a "right analysis . . . to cure the disease whilst preserving efficiency and freedom" (p. 381).

Did Keynes Cease to Be a Keynesian?

It has frequently of late been asserted that, toward the end of his life, the views of Keynes with respect to policy matters had substantially changed, indeed had reverted in large measure to the classical position. That Keynes's theoretical and policy conceptions would have developed along new lines, had he lived a decade or two longer, is highly probable. His was not a static mind. That his ideas would revert to the old conceptions is, however, more doubtful. Apart from hearsay, which is often conflicting and at best undependable, there is the interesting article, published after his death, in the June, 1946, issue of the *Economic Journal*. This article, while dealing with the balance of payments of the United States, raises some larger issues with respect to the role of automatic forces and governmental intervention.

I have studied this article carefully, but I cannot find support for the thesis that it indicates a change in his fundamental thinking, let alone a "recantation," as has on occasion been suggested. Keynes always laid stress on the important role of automatic forces in economic life. Indeed, this could not be otherwise, since such State interventionism as he advocated (mainly in respect to monetary and fiscal policy) was designed to affect Aggregate Demand; beyond that, the automatic forces were assumed to be in control.

If we "succeed in establishing an aggregate volume of output corresponding to full employment as nearly as is practicable, *the classical theory comes into its own again* from this point onward" (p. 378, italics mine). Keynes was never an advocate of authoritarian government. In the *General Theory* he declared that his theory is "moderately conservative in its implications" (p. 377). No "obvious case is made out for a system of State Socialism which would embrace most of the economic life of the community" (p. 378). Again he sees "no reason to suppose that the existing system seriously misemploys the factors of production which are in use" (p. 379). There "will still remain a wide field for the exercise of private initiative and responsibility. Within this field the traditional advantages of individualism will still hold good" (p. 380). These advantages he details as those of "efficiency," "decentralization," and the "play of self-interest" (p. 380). The "reaction against the appeal to self-interest may have gone too far" (p. 380). Individualism is the "best safeguard of personal liberty" (p. 380). It is also the "best safeguard of the variety of life," the loss of which is the "greatest of all the losses of the homogeneous or totalitarian state" (p. 380). Individualism "preserves the traditions which embody the most secure and successful choices of former generations" (p. 380). Being the "handmaid of experiment as well as of tradition and of fancy, it is the most powerful instrument to better the future" (p. 380). "The authoritarian state systems of today seem to solve the problem of unemployment at the expense of efficiency and of freedom" (p. 381).

It is well to remember that these phrases are drawn not from the posthumous article but from the *General Theory* of 1936. Had they been written in 1946, many would have jumped at the conclusion that Keynes had "recanted."

In the article of 1946 he said similar things, but certainly no more in defense of individualism or the automatic forces than those I have cited above. The most telling phrases in this last publication are as follows (italics mine):

> In the long run more fundamental forces may be at work, if all goes well, tending toward equilibrium.... I find myself moved, not for the first time, to remind contemporary economists that the classical teaching embodied some permanent truths of great significance, which we are liable today to overlook because *we associate them with other doctrines which we cannot now accept without much qualification.* There are in these matters deep undercurrents at work, natural forces, we can call them, or even the invisible hand, which are operating toward equilibrium. If this were not so we could not have got on even as well as we have for many decades past....
>
> I must not be misunderstood. *I do not suppose that the classical medicine will work by itself or that we can depend on it.* We need quicker and less painful aids of which exchange variation and overall import controls are the most important.... The great virtue of the Bretton Woods and Washington proposals, taken in conjunction, is that *they marry the use of the necessary expedients to the wholesome long-run*

doctrine. It is for this reason that, speaking in the House of Lords, I claimed that "Here is an attempt to use *what we have learnt from modern experience and modern analysis,* not to defeat but to implement, the wisdom of Adam Smith."

There is nothing in any of these statements which even approaches a recantation of the *General Theory.* Indeed the *General Theory,* as we have seen, contains similar statements in defense of individualism and the importance of automatic forces within the framework of a full employment economy.

Since the posthumous article in particular deals with international matters and especially with the joint effort, which Keynes did so much to implement, of the United States and Great Britain to restore multilateral trade to the utmost possible extent, something needs to be said about the alleged change, in later years, in Keynes's thinking along this particular line. Discussions with Keynes about monetary and financial matters, both in Washington and in London during the year 1941, disclosed that he was undergoing a pronounced shift in his attitude toward multilateral trade. This shift related, however, not to any fundamental change in his economic philosophy, but rather to what appeared feasible and realistic in terms of practical policy. Toward the end of 1941, Keynes at long last became convinced that the United States could be sufficiently relied upon to play a positive role in international economic and financial matters to justify risking a program of Anglo-American collaboration designed to promote a multilateral trading world. The isolationist tariff policy of the United States during the twenties had been superseded by the Hull trade agreements and the lend-lease program of President Roosevelt. Keynes had previously been profoundly impressed with the danger of being tied to the American economy. Witness the speculative and feverish foreign investments of the twenties, followed by a swift contraction of lending; the boom; and the "bust" in 1929, with its international repercussions. In this kind of world he was firmly convinced that Britain had better manage her balance of payments along "sterling-area" and "payments-agreements" lines, rather than risk the play of automatic forces in a multilateral world market subjected to violent and seemingly uncontrollable fluctuations.

But by the end of 1941 he became convinced that a new foundation, with Anglo-American cooperation, could be constructed upon which to erect a new multilateral trading world—or at least the thing was worth risking. On one occasion, in the autumn of 1941, when the importance of multilateral trade based upon high levels of employment in the advanced industrial countries and developmental programs in the more backward areas had been urged upon him in private conversation, his instant response was: "Well, on that basis we should all favor multilateral trade."

The above-cited declaration could scarcely be called a recantation. Already in 1936 in the *General Theory* he had said:

> But if nations can learn to provide themselves with full employment by their domestic policy . . . there need be no important economic forces calculated to set the interest of one country against that of its neighbors. . . . International trade would cease to be what it is, namely, a desperate expedient to maintain employment at home by forcing sales on foreign markets and restricting purchases . . . but a

willing and unimpeded exchange of goods and services in conditions of mutual advantage (pp. 382–383).

This point of view he again reiterated in the *Economic Journal* article of 1946. A multilateral trading world is worth striving for. It cannot work without active international collaboration on the part of the United States. But, he declares (italics mine):

> One is entitled to draw some provisional comfort from the present mood of the American Administration and, as I judge it, of the American people also, as embodied in the *Proposals for Consideration of an International Conference on Trade and Employment.* We have here sincere and thoroughgoing proposals, advanced on behalf of the United States, expressly *directed towards creating a system* which allows the classical medicine to do its work.

With respect to his attitude toward the United States in the thirties, to which I have referred above, it may be noted that he here refers to "this magnificent objective approach which a few years ago we should have regarded as offering incredible promise of a better scheme of things."

There is no evidence here of any change in his fundamental economic thinking: what had changed was his view of the role of the United States in international economic affairs. On the basis of the official program of the American government, a multilateral trading world could, he believed, succeed. But if the program is abandoned, or if for other reasons it fails, then "we, and everyone else, will try something different."

In closing, Keynes raised quite frankly the question of whether or not his proposals may have "insufficient roots in the motives which govern the evolution of political society" (p. 383). He did not pretend to know the answer. Yet he offered his belief that, quite apart from the mood for bold ventures engendered by the devastating experiences of the interwar years, "the ideas of economists and political philosophers . . . are more powerful than is commonly understood" (p. 383). The power of vested interests, he thought, is exaggerated compared with the "gradual encroachment of ideas" (p. 383). Ideas, not vested interests, are, in the final analysis, "dangerous for good or evil" (p. 384).

Overfull Employment

Time has run fast since 1936. Had Keynes known how history was so soon to unfold itself, he might well have ended his book on a different note. The Second World War, of a magnitude hitherto undreamed of in terms of percentage of resources devoted to military uses, the vast postwar restocking and reconstruction boom, the cold war with its imperious defense budgets, the welfare demands of labor governments—all this ended for the time being any possibility of underemployment. The problem in most countries became rather that of overfull employment. In Britain, in the Scandinavian countries, in Holland, and elsewhere, governments greatly extended their control over economic life. Full employment was, however, primarily the result of the war and postwar developments, not of conscious policy. There was indeed always the fear that the backlogs of deferred demand and the vast defense and foreign-aid budgets in the United States would some day peter out, throwing the leading industrial country into depression. But in the labor and socialist governments of Europe at any rate there was the firm determination at all costs to maintain full employment and to raise consumption standards.

Not until 1952 did a weakening of demand in any major industry (*e.g.*, textiles) cause serious concern in England. Aggregate Demand remained high, but pockets of unemployment here and there began to appear. This was not the kind of problem envisaged by Keynes, nor indeed is it comparable in seriousness with the general problem of over-all inadequate demand. But it is nonetheless a knotty one. If it is sought to erase sectional unemployment merely by expansion of Aggregate Demand, the result is simply to cause an inflation. True, the maintenance of adequate, but not excessive, Aggregate Demand, aided by retraining and deliberate programs designed to relocate labor (with transportation allowances and housing at the new job sites) can surely do a great deal. But the human instinct is to "stay put," to bolster up declining industries, and not to undertake the hard task of promoting labor mobility.

For most advanced democratic countries, full employment has become a settled policy more quickly than Keynes had believed possible or indeed than would have been possible except for the war and its aftermath. Instead of unemployment, statesmen everywhere are confronted with inflationary pressures and the tough job of maintaining, within the pattern of full employment, a flexible economic system.

Keynesian critics may, however, have exaggerated the dangers of inflation and wage control in a full-employment society. The price inflation of 1946–1947 in the United States was a product of the war, not a test of peacetime full employment. Indeed from January, 1948, to December, 1948, the United States enjoyed full employment without inflation despite the absence of price and wage controls. The wholesale price level stood at 166 in January, 1948, and at only 162 in December, 1948, with an average of 165 for the whole year; in January unemployment was only 2,065,000 and in December, 1,941,000, or 3.1 per cent of the labor force. When Beveridge suggested (*Full Employment in a Free Society*) the goal of only 3 per cent unemployment, there was a general disposition to ridicule the figure as utopian. Now, in fact, the goal of only 3 per cent is, everyone will agree, far more difficult for a country with high seasonal unemployment and rapid regional adjustments like the United States than for a small, compact, and homogeneous country like Great Britain. Nevertheless, the United States actually maintained this goal without price inflation and without controls during the year 1948. In 1949 and the first half of 1950, the inflationary pressure was eased, it is true, by a rise of unemployment to 5.5 per cent. But even this is considerably below the margin of safety suggested by some economists who have stressed the dangers of wage and price inflation in a full-employment society. Moreover, with unemployment averaging well below 3 per cent, wholesale prices fell from 116.5 (new index) to 109.7 during the two-year period from February, 1951, to January, 1953.

Had Keynes lived, we can be sure he would have critically reexamined his whole system of thinking. His was not a mind that stood still. He was always in the vanguard, exploring new ideas and discarding old ones, even though these old ideas were his own. And in particular, he would no doubt have turned his attention to the practical problems of a full-employment society. As he himself said (p. 383) this would require "a volume of a different character... to indicate even in outline the practical measures in which they might be gradually clothed."

NOTES

1. The optimism of the classicals rested on the assumption of unlimited investment opportunities. On this basis, the higher the propensity to save, the greater the *amount* of capital formation.

Real and Nominal Objectives

James Tobin was born in 1918 in Champaign, Illinois. He obtained his education from Harvard University (M.A., A.B., 1939; M.A., 1940; Ph.D., 1947), where he was exposed to a rich intellectual environment created by such luminaries as Joseph Schumpeter, Alvin Hansen, and Wassily Leontief and rising junior faculty and graduate students, including Paul Samuelson, Paul Sweeney, and John Kenneth Galbraith. After a three-year appointment to the Society of Fellows, he accepted a position at Yale University, where he remained until his retirement in 1988. In 1981, he was awarded the Nobel Prize in economics for his portfolio theory of investment.

An ardent supporter of Keynesian policy, Tobin's view of the transmission process by which monetary policies are transmitted into changes in gross domestic product (GDP) expenditures differed from the monetary position that central bank control of the money supply is reflected in income and prices. In the following selection from *Essays in Economics, National and International* (MIT Press, 1996), he proposes limiting central bank control to some short-term money-market interest rates, which would affect other interest rates and GDP expenditures. A long-standing critic of tight Federal Reserve policies to stem inflation, Tobin claims that such policies slow the economy and sharply raise unemployment. Alternatively, he believes, central banks should stimulate the economy sufficiently so that the expected gain from unemployment exceeds the expected loss due to inflation acceleration.

Key Concept: weaknesses in nominalist monetary strategies

Should monetary authorities consider the real economic performance of their economies in setting policies? Should their objectives include real outcomes of national and international performance—production, employment, capital formation, trade—as well as nominal variables—prices, nominal incomes, exchange rates?

Today many economists and central bankers answer no. Monetary authorities' capabilities and responsibilities, they argue, cover only nominal variables. After all, they have only nominal instruments. Dedication of those instruments to real objectives has, they allege, not improved but if anything actually worsened real performance, while destabilizing prices and causing inflation. Chastened by the stagflation of the last fifteen years, central banks should be content to provide a stable, credible, predictable noninflationary nominal path and to accept whatever real outcomes come along that way. Devotees of the new classical macroeconomics assure us that those outcomes will be optimal. Knowing that the central bank will neither confuse them nor rescue them from the consequences of imprudent wage and price increases, private agents in free markets will achieve the natural equilibrium values of real variables, quantities, and relative prices.

The issue is an old one, and the answer has oscillated over the history of central banking. The primacy of nominal objectives was well established before the Great Depression. Central banks and governments were expected to place defense of a fixed parity of their currency with gold or foreign currencies ahead of domestic economic performance. Today some economists, statesmen, and commentators—frustrated by exchange rate instabilities these past ten years—advocate restoration of an international gold standard. They believe that the discipline of gold convertibility, available to individuals as well as to foreign governments, would create and maintain anti-inflationary expectations and behaviors.

Monetarists concur with the objective but prefer the discipline of nominal monetary rules to that of gold. Some would impose such rules by legislative or constitutional mandate. The purpose and effect are the same as intended by advocates of the gold standard. Monetary operations will be, and will be seen to be, independent of actual real economic performance.

I believe that purely nominalist monetary strategies are neither feasible nor desirable, for several reasons.

The first reason is political. The responsibility of the central government for real macroeconomic performance is strongly entrenched in the politics of democratic societies. This has been true at least since the Great Depression of the 1930s and especially after World War II. In the United States, for example, the Employment Act of 1946 and the Full Employment and Balanced Growth Act of 1978 ("Humphrey–Hawkins") commit the federal government, including the Federal Reserve System, to the pursuit of real economic goals. More important realistically, unemployment, real growth, and related variables are significant factors in public opinion and in electoral campaigns.

A purely nominal stance of monetary policy, willfully blindfold to real developments, is not likely to be credible. Sooner or later the central bank of a democracy will rescue the economy from the worst unintended real byproducts of a fixed nominalist line, just as Paul Volcker [former chairman of the Federal Reserve] did last summer. Expectation that this will happen is bound to undermine policies whose effectiveness depends on public belief that it never will.

Central banks cannot stand aloof from objectives highly valued by the societies they serve. Central bankers and their constituencies frequently dismiss the priorities of elected officials, for example, reduction of unemployment, as "political" hence unworthy of respect. The legitimacy of such a value judgment is as doubtful as its welfare economics.

The second point is economic. The dichotomy between real and nominal policy operations, by which monetary instruments are classified as purely nominal, is not valid theoretically or empirically.

Nominal price and wage paths are sluggish, some more sluggish than others. Prices and wages which are administered or negotiated change less rapidly and readily than the prices of financial assets and of commodities traded in auction markets. Because of such inertia, fluctuations in aggregate nominal spending resulting from monetary operations have important real consequences over fairly long short runs. The 1980–83 recession and depression confirm this obvious fact once again. Nor is it confined to downturns. Cyclical recoveries, stimulated or at least accommodated by monetary expansions, generate real as well as nominal gains. It is disingenuous, to say the least, for central bankers to pretend that their actions have no effects on real interest rates, unemployment rates, and other variables of concern to the populace.

The claim that monetary policies, since they necessarily rely on nominal instruments, can have only nominal effects trades on an analogy between altering monetary stocks and changing the unit of account. Switching the unit of account from dollars to half dollars would, everyone agrees, have no real consequences. Why shouldn't doubling the stock of "dollars" by other means be likewise neutral? The analogy is false. Actual central bank operations do not, while units changes do, change the public's stocks of all nominal assets in the same proportion. Actual operations effect exchanges of some assets for others, usually obligations to pay currency on demand for obligations to pay currency in future. Since future currency is not a perfect substitute for present currency, these exchanges are not neutral. They generally affect real interest rates, real exchange rates, saving, investment, and other real variables. Price changes affect private wealth and its distribution. Changes in inflation rates and in the distribution of price expectations necessarily alter real rates of return on currency and other assets with fixed nominal interest, and therefore influence the whole structure of asset prices and returns.

Some of these nonneutral effects vanish, in principle, in long-run steady states. Others do not. Time will eliminate the inertia of price and wage adjustments. But there are no long-run steady states whose properties are independent of the paths by which they are reached. For example, depressions and high real interest rates may interrupt irreversibly the accumulation of physical and human capital.

I am arguing that monetary authorities should not, indeed cannot, escape responsibility for real macroeconomic outcomes. To avoid misunderstanding I stress that I certainly am not advocating that they disregard nominal outcomes, price levels, and inflation rates. Somewhere in the framework of monetary policy objectives and targets there must be nominal anchors that prevent unlimited accommodation and give due weight to the costs of inflation and society's distaste for it. Milton Friedman told us in his famous Presidential Address some fifteen years ago that monetary policy could not *peg* real variables like unemployment and real interest rates and should not try. If "peg" meant to seek a particular unchanging numerical value forever, I think no one wanted or wants to peg. Permanent pegging of unemployment is one thing. Taking account of the state of the labor market is quite another. Trying to move unemployment down in some circumstances, up in others, is not pegging.

We should be careful not to draw the wrong lessons from the 1970s. After 1965 there were three bursts of inflation, each followed by recessions deliberately provoked by anti-inflationary monetary policies. The first acceleration of inflation, associated with the Vietnam war, was a classic demand-pull episode. President Johnson, contrary to the advice of his own economists, loaded his increased war spending on to an already fully employed economy without raising taxes, and in retrospect the Federal Reserve was overaccommodative. The two bursts of inflation in the 1970s were associated with extraordinary supply and price shocks: the first in 1973–74 from food shortages, oil embargo, and OPEC's fourfold increase in the dollar price of oil; the second in 1978–80 from the Iranian revolution, restriction of Middle East oil supplies, and a further tripling of the OPEC price. These events happened to occur in the late stages of cyclical recoveries, to which conscious stimulative and accommodative policies in the United States and other countries had contributed.

The lessons pundits and policymakers commonly draw from these experiences are that recoveries are dangerous, especially if they are promoted by policy. Accordingly central banks are most reluctant now to adopt expansionary policies even when their economies are as severely depressed as they are today. But these are the wrong lessons if the frightening bursts of inflation were due not to recoveries per se or to policies that fostered them, but to the extraordinary exogenous shocks. Vietnam, OPEC, and the Ayatollah Khomeini were not the endogenous consequences of normal policy-assisted business cycle recoveries. Fear of recurrences should not paralyze our governments and central banks and consign our economies to chronic stagnation.

The serious question of macroeconomic policy today is how much unemployment and general economic slack to maintain as insurance against another acceleration of inflation. According to a widely accepted model, there exists at any time a minimum unemployment rate consistent with nonacceleration, sometimes called the natural rate of unemployment or more neutrally the non-accelerating-inflation-rate-of-unemployment (NAIRU). Here the unemployment rate is serving as a barometer of general slack, of the overall pressure of aggregate demand on productive capacity. Unfortunately no one knows what the NAIRU is. Current estimates for the United States vary from 8 percent to 5 percent. For policymakers this doubt is compounded by uncertainty about the translation of their instruments via aggregate demand into unemployment. The decision problem is to balance, given these uncertainties, the costs of unemployment and lost production against the risks and costs of accelerating inflation. Those costs and risks can be made commensurate by estimating the extra unemployment-years necessary to eliminate a bulge of accelerating inflation should it occur.

A conservative solution is to minimize expected unemployment subject to the constraint that the probability of trespassing the NAIRU threshold not exceed some epsilon, perhaps even zero. Thus if there were any non-negligible probability that policies designed to bring expected unemployment down to, say, 9 percent would generate acceleration—either because the NAIRU may be at least that high or because the policies might actually bring a lower unemployment rate—then conservative policymakers would seek to keep unemployment higher than 9 percent. This solution is in the spirit of macroeconomic strategies prevailing today, and it is a recipe and rationale for stagnation.

An optimal cost-benefit solution would not apply so absolute a constraint. A marginal dose of stimulus is justified if and only if the expected gain from reduction in unemployment exceeds the expected loss due to inflation acceleration. The latter is the cost of the unemployment correction necessary to eliminate the acceleration multiplied by the probability that the NAIRU threshold will have been crossed. If, for example, the correction costs two unemployment points for every point by which the threshold was crossed, then the median estimate of NAIRU is the proper target of policy. A higher relative correction cost implies a higher unemployment target, a lower appraisal of the cost a more ambitious unemployment goal.

CHAPTER 9 The Institutionalist School

9.1 THORSTEIN VEBLEN

The Theory of Business Enterprise

Thorstein Veblen (1857–1929) was born in Manitowoc County, Wisconsin, and grew up in rural Minnesota. He received his B.A. from Carleton College in 1880 and his Ph.D. in philosophy from Yale University in 1884. After seven unhappy years spent looking for a teaching position, Veblen eventually succeeded in obtaining one at the University of Chicago in 1892. Fourteen years later, he moved to Stanford University and then on to the University of Missouri. Veblen taught political economy and gained a reputation as a brilliant and innovative teacher. He was a founding member of New York's New School for Social Research.

Veblen perceived a fundamental conflict between profit-seeking owners and industry, which seek to maximize production of goods. He blamed businesses for economic depressions. Veblen believed that the profit motive drives new firms to replace older enterprises and that any actions taken by business to prevent depressions are counterproductive because they include mergers and increase consumption by the elite. These ideas were articulated in his social critique *The Theory of the Leisure Class: An Economic Study of Institutions* (1899) and the more strictly economic works of *The Theory of Business Enterprise* (Charles Scribners Sons, 1904), from which the following selection has been taken, and *Absentee Ownership: Business Enterprise in Recent Times* (B. W. Huebsch, 1923). Veblen held that the threat to profit-oriented business comes from the machine process whose greater productivity challenges monopolistic restrictions of output and orientation toward wasteful consumption. He warned that either the machine process would succeed in eroding business institutions or society would revert to predatory barbarism or totalitarianism. The following selection is devoted to the essence of the machine process.

Veblen's other works include *The Socialist Economics of Karl Marx and His Followers* (1906), *Fisher's Capital and Income* (1908), *The Limitations of Marginal Utility* (1909), *Fisher's Rate of Interest* (1909), *The Higher Learning in America* (B. W. Huebsch, 1918) and *The Vested Interests and the Common Man* (1919). He is occasionally criticized for his rejection of the market system, lack of interest in incremental social change, and for his undue faith in the simplicity of economic planning under the authority of engineers.

Key Concept: the machine process

THE MACHINE PROCESS

In its bearing on modern life and modern business, the "machine process" means something more comprehensive and less external than a mere aggregate of mechanical appliances for the mediation of human labor. It means that, but it means something more than that. The civil engineer, the mechanical engineer, the navigator, the mining expert, the industrial chemist and mineralogist, the electrician,—the work of all these falls within the lines of the modern machine process, as well as the work of the inventor who devises the appliances of the process and that of the mechanician who puts the inventions into effect and oversees their working. The scope of the process is larger than the machine. In those branches of industry in which machine methods have been introduced, many agencies which are not to be classed as mechanical appliances, simply, have been drawn into the process, and have become integral factors in it. Chemical properties of minerals, *e.g.*, are counted on in the carrying out of metallurgical processes with much the same certainty and calculable effect as are the motions of those mechanical appliances by whose use the minerals are handled. The sequence of the process involves both the one and the other, both the apparatus and the materials, in such intimate interaction that the process cannot be spoken of simply as an action of the apparatus upon the materials. It is not simply that the apparatus reshapes the materials; the materials reshape themselves by the help of the apparatus. Similarly in such other processes as the refining of petroleum, oil, or sugar; in the work of the industrial chemical laboratories; in the use of wind, water, or electricity, etc.

Wherever manual dexterity, the rule of thumb, and the fortuitous conjunctures of the seasons have been supplanted by a reasoned procedure on the basis of a systematic knowledge of the forces employed, there the mechanical industry is to be found, even in the absence of intricate mechanical contrivances. It is a question of the character of the process rather than a question of the complexity of the contrivances employed. Chemical, agricultural, and animal industries, as carried on by the characteristically modern methods and in due touch with the market, are to be included in the modern complex of mechanical industry.

No one of the mechanical processes carried on by the use of a given outfit of appliances is independent of other processes going on elsewhere. Each draws upon and presupposes the proper working of many other processes of a similarly mechanical character. None of the processes in the mechanical industries is self-sufficing. Each follows some and precedes other processes in an endless sequence, into which each fits and to the requirements of which each must adapt its own working. The whole concert of industrial operations is to be taken as a machine process, made up of interlocking detail processes, rather than as a multiplicity of mechanical appliances each doing its particular work in severalty. This comprehensive industrial process draws into its scope and turns to account all branches of knowledge that have to do with the material sciences, and the whole makes a more or less delicately balanced complex of sub-processes.

Looked at in this way the industrial process shows two well-marked general characteristics: (*a*) the running maintenance of interstitial adjustments between the several sub-processes or branches of industry, wherever in their working they touch one another in the sequence of industrial elaboration; and (*b*) an unremitting requirement of quantitative precision, accuracy in point of time and sequence, in the proper inclusion and exclusion of forces affecting the outcome, in the magnitude of the various physical characteristics (weight, size, density, hardness, tensile strength, elasticity, temperature, chemical reaction, actinic sensitiveness, etc.) of the materials handled as well as of the appliances employed. This requirement of mechanical accuracy and nice adaptation to specific uses has led to a gradual pervading enforcement of uniformity to a reduction to staple grades and staple character in the materials handled, and to a thorough standardizing of tools and units of measurement. Standard physical measurements are of the essence of the machine's regime.

The modern industrial communities show an unprecedented uniformity and precise equivalence in legally adopted weights and measures. Something of this kind would be brought about by the needs of commerce, even without the urgency given to the movement for uniformity by the requirements of the machine industry. But within the industrial field the movement for standardization has outrun the urging of commercial needs, and has penetrated every corner of the mechanical industries. The specifically commercial need of uniformity in weights and measures of merchantable goods and in monetary units has not carried standardization in these items to the extent to which the mechanical need of the industrial process has carried out a sweeping standardization in the means by which the machine process works, as well as in the products which it turns out.

As a matter of course, tools and the various structural materials used are made of standard sizes, shapes, and gauges. When the dimensions, in fractions of an inch or in millimetres, and the weight, in fractions of a pound or in grammes, are given, the expert foreman or workman, confidently and without reflection, infers the rest of what need be known of the uses to which any given item that passes under his hand may be turned. The adjustment and adaptation of part to part and of process to process has passed out of the category of craftsmanlike skill into the category of mechanical standardization. Hence, perhaps, the greatest, most wide-reaching gain in productive celerity and efficiency through modern methods, and hence the largest saving of labor in modern industry.

Tools, mechanical appliances and movements, and structural materials are scheduled by certain conventional scales and gauges; and modern industry has little use for, and can make little use of, what does not conform to the standard. What is not competently standardized calls for too much of craftsmanlike skill, reflection, and individual elaboration, and is therefore not available for economical use in the processes. Irregularity, departure from standard measurements in any of the measurable facts, is of itself a fault in any item that is to find a use in the industrial process, for it brings delay, it detracts from its ready usability in the nicely adjusted process into which it is to go; and a delay at any point means a more or less far-reaching and intolerable retardation of the comprehensive industrial process at large. Irregularity in products intended for industrial use carries a penalty to the nonconforming producer which urges him to fall into line and submit to the required standardization.

The materials and moving forces of industry are undergoing a like reduction to staple kinds, styles, grades, and gauge. Even such forces as would seem at first sight not to lend themselves to standardization, either in their production or their use, are subjected to uniform scales of measurement; as, *e.g.*, water-power, steam, electricity, and human labor. The latter is perhaps the least amenable to standardization, but, for all that, it is bargained for, delivered, and turned to account on schedules of time, speed, and intensity which are continually sought to be reduced to a more precise measurement and a more sweeping uniformity.

The like is true of the finished products. Modern consumers in great part supply their wants with commodities that conform to certain staple specifications of size, weight, and grade. The consumer (that is to say the vulgar consumer) furnishes his house, his table, and his person with supplies of standard weight and measure, and he can to an appreciable degree specify his needs and his consumption in the notation of the standard gauge. As regards the mass of civilized mankind, the idiosyncrasies of the individual consumers are required to conform to the uniform gradations imposed upon consumable goods by the comprehensive mechanical processes of industry. "Local color" it is said, is falling into abeyance in modern life, and where it is still found it tends to assert itself in units of the standard gauge.

From this mechanical standardization of consumable goods it follows, on the one hand, that the demand for goods settles upon certain defined lines of production which handle certain materials of definite grade, in certain, somewhat invariable forms and proportions; which leads to well-defined methods and measurements in the processes of production, shortening the average period of "ripening" that intervenes between the first raw stage of the product and its finished shape, and reducing the aggregate stock of goods necessary to be carried for the supply of current wants, whether in the raw or in the finished form. Standardization means economy at nearly all points of the process of supplying goods, and at the same time it means certainty and expedition at nearly all points in the business operations involved in meeting current wants. Besides this, the standardization of goods means that the interdependence of industrial processes is reduced to more definite terms than before the mechanical standardization came to its present degree of elaborateness and rigor. The margin of admissible variation, in time, place, form, and amount, is narrowed. Materials, to answer the needs of standardized industry, must be drawn from certain standard sources at a definite rate of supply. Hence any given detail industry depends closely on receiving its supplies from certain, relatively few, industrial establishments whose work belongs earlier in the process of elaboration. And it may similarly depend on certain other, closely defined, industrial establishments for a vent of its own specialization and standardization product. It may likewise depend in a strict manner on special means of transportation.

Machine production leads to a standardization of services as well as of goods. So, for instance, the modern means of communication and the system into which these means are organized are also of the nature of a mechanical process, and in this mechanical process of service and intercourse the life of all civilized men is more or less intimately involved. To make effective use of the modern system of communication in any way or all of its ramifications (streets, railways, steamship lines, telephone, telegraph, postal service, etc.), men are required to adapt their needs and their motions to the exigencies of the process whereby this civilized method of intercourse is carried into effect. The service is standardized, and therefore the use of it is standardized also. Schedules of time, place, and circumstance rule throughout. The scheme of everyday life must be arranged with a strict regard to the exigencies of the process whereby this range of human needs is served, if full advantage is to be taken of this system of intercourse, which means that, in so far, one's plans and projects must be conceived and worked out in terms of those standard units which the system imposes.

For the population of the towns and cities, at least, much the same rule holds true of the distribution of consumable goods. So, also, amusements and diversions, much of the current amenities of life, are organized into a more or less sweeping process to which those who would benefit by the advantages offered must adapt their schedule of wants and the disposition of their time and effort. The frequency, duration, intensity, grade, and sequence are not, in the main, matters for the free discretion of the individuals who participate. Throughout the scheme of life of that portion of mankind that clusters about the centres of modern culture the industrial process makes itself felt and enforces a degree of conformity to the canon of accurate quantitative measurement. There comes to prevail a degree of standardization and precise mechanical adjustment of the details of everyday life, which presumes a facile and unbroken working of all those processes that minister to these standardized human wants.

As a result of this superinduced mechanical regularity of life, the livelihood of individuals is, over large areas, affected in an approximately uniform manner by any incident which at all seriously affects the industrial process at any point. . . .

BUSINESS ENTERPRISE

. . . In current economic theory the business man is spoken of under the name of "entrepreneur" or "undertaker," and his function is held to be the coördinating of industrial processes with a view to economics of production and heightened serviceability. The soundness of this view need not be questioned. It has a great sentimental value and is useful in many ways. There is also a modicum of truth in it as an account of facts. In common with other men, the business man is moved by ideals of serviceability and an aspiration to make the way of life easier for his fellows. Like other men, he has something of the instinct of workmanship. No doubt such aspirations move the great business man less urgently than many others, who are, on that account, less successful in business affairs. Motives of this kind detract from business efficiency, and an undue yielding to them on the part of business men is to be deprecated as an infirmity. Still, throughout men's dealing with one another and with the interests of the community there runs a sense of equity, fair dealing, and workmanlike integrity; and in an uncertain degree this bent discountenances gain that is got at an undue cost to others, or without rendering some colorable equivalent. Business men are also, in a measure, guided by the ambition to effect a creditable improvement in the industrial processes which their business traffic touches. These sentimental factors in business exercise something of a constraint, varying greatly from one person to another, but not measurable in its aggregate results. The careers of most of the illustrious business men show the presence of some salutary constraint of this kind. Not infrequently an excessive sensitiveness of this kind leads to a withdrawal from business, or from certain forms of business which may appeal to a vivid fancy as peculiarly dishonest or peculiarly detrimental to the community. Such grounds of action, and perhaps others equally genial and equally unbusinesslike, would probably be discovered by a detailed scrutiny of any large business deal. Probably in many cases the business strategist, infected with this human infirmity, reaches an agreement with his rivals and his neighbors in the industrial system without exacting the last concession that a ruthless business strategy might entitle him to. The result is, probably, a speedier conclusion and a smoother working of the large coalitions than would follow from the unmitigated sway of business principles.

But the sentiment which in this way acts in constraint of business traffic proceeds on such grounds of equity and fair dealing as are afforded by current business ethics; it acts within the range of business principles, not in contravention of them; it acts as a conventional restraint upon pecuniary advantage, not in abrogation of it. This code of business ethics consists, after all, of mitigations of the maxim, *Caveat emptor*. It touches primarily the dealings of man with man, and only less directly and less searchingly inculcates temperance and circumspection as regards the ulterior interests of the community at large. Where this moral need of a balance between the services rendered the community and the gain derived from a given business transaction asserts itself at all, the balance is commonly sought to be maintained in some sort of pecuniary terms; but pecuniary terms afford only a very inadequate measure of serviceability to the community.

Great and many are the items of service to be set down to the business man's account in connection with the organization of the industrial system, but when all is said, it is still to be kept in mind that his work in the correlation of industrial processes is chiefly of a permissive kind. His furtherance of industry is at the second remove, and is chiefly of a negative character. In his capacity as business man he does not go creatively into the work of perfecting mechanical processes and turning the means at hand to new or larger uses. That is the work of the men who have in hand the devising and oversight of mechanical processes. The men in industry must first create the mechanical possibility of such new and more efficient methods and correlations, before the business man sees the chance, makes the necessary business arrangements, and gives general directions that the contemplated industrial advance shall go into effect. The period between the time of earliest practicability and the effectual completion of a given consolidation in industry marks the interval by which the business man retards the advance of industry. Against this are to be offset the cases, comparatively slight and infrequent, where the business men in control push the advance of industry into new fields and prompt the men concerned with the mechanics of the case to experiment and exploration in new fields of mechanical process.

When the recital is made, therefore, of how the large consolidations take place at the initiative of the business men who are in control, it should be added that the fact of their being in control precludes industrial correlations from taking place except by their advice and consent. The industrial system is organized on business principles and for pecuniary ends. The business man is at the centre; he holds the discretion and he exercises it freely, and his choice falls out now on one side, now on the other. The retardation as well as the advance is to be set down to his account.

As regards the economies in cost of production effected by these consolidations, there is a further characteristic feature to be noted, a feature of some significance for any theory of modern business. In great measure the saving effected is a saving of the costs of business management and of the competitive costs of marketing products and services, rather than a saving in the prime costs of production. The heightened facility and efficiency of the new and larger business combinations primarily affect the expenses of office work and sales, and it is in great part only indirectly that this curtailment and consolidation of business management has an effect upon the methods and aims of industry proper. It touches the pecuniary processes immediately, and the mechanical processes indirectly and in an uncertain degree. It is of the nature of a partial neutralization of the wastes due to the presence of pecuniary motives and business management,—for the business management involves waste wherever a greater number of men or transactions are involved than are necessary to the effective direction of the mechanical processes employed. The amount of "business" that has to be transacted per unit of product is much greater where the various related industrial processes are managed in severalty than where several of them are brought under one business management. A pecuniary discretion has to be exercised at every point of contact or transition, where the process or its product touches or passes the boundary between different spheres of ownership. Business transactions have to do with ownership and changes of ownership. The greater the parcelment in point of ownership, the greater the amount of business work that has to be done in connection with a given output of goods or services, and the slower, less facile, and less accurate on the whole, is the work. This applies both to the work of bargain and contract, wherein pecuniary initiative and discretion are chiefly exercised, and to the routine work of accounting, and of gathering and applying information and misinformation.

The standardization of industrial processes, products, services, and consumers... very materially facilitates the business man's work in reorganizing business enterprises on a larger scale; particularly does this standardization serve his ends by permitting a uniform routine in accounting, invoices, contracts, etc., and so admitting a large central accounting system, with homogeneous ramifications, such as will give a competent conspectus of the pecuniary situation of the enterprise at any given time.

The great, at the present stage of development perhaps the greatest, opportunity for saving by consolidation, in the common run of cases, is afforded by the ubiquitous and in a sense excessive presence of business enterprise in the economic system. It is in doing away with unnecessary business transactions and industrially futile manoeuvring on the part of independent firms that the promoter of combinations finds his most telling opportunity. So that it is scarcely an overstatement to say that probably the largest, assuredly the securest and most unquestionable, service rendered by the great modern captains of industry is this curtailment of the business to be done—this sweeping retirement of business men as a class from the service and the definitive cancelment of opportunities for private enterprise.

So long as related industrial units are under different business managements, they are, by the nature of the case, at cross-purposes, and business consolidation remedies this untoward feature of the industrial system by eliminating the pecuniary element from the interstices of the system as far as may be. The interstitial adjustments of the industrial system at large are in this way withdrawn from the discretion of rival business men, and the work of pecuniary management previously involved is in large part dispensed with, with the result that there is a saving of work and an avoidance of that systematic mutual hindrance that characterizes the competitive management of industry. To the community at large the work of pecuniary management, it appears, is less serviceable the more there is of it. The heroic rôle of the captain of industry is that of a deliverer from an excess of business management. It is a casting out of business men by the chief of business men.

9.2 JOHN KENNETH GALBRAITH

The Dependence Effect

John Kenneth Galbraith was born in 1908 in Ontario, Canada. He started his teaching career at Harvard University, spent a year at the University of Cambridge (1937), and taught again at Harvard and later at Princeton University before the outbreak of World War II. From 1938 to 1943, Galbraith was head of the price section of the Office of Price Administration. After leaving government, he worked as a member of the editorial board of *Fortune* magazine and director of the U.S. Strategic Bombing Survey. In the 1960s Galbraith was an adviser to the Kennedy administration and U.S. ambassador to India.

A Keynesian, Galbraith supported government spending to reduce unemployment and recommended spending on social programs over private consumption. He viewed economic history as a progression from free markets to monopolies. Galbraith maintained that this concentration of corporate power (political and economic) brings powerful buyers into play as well as sellers, large retailing firms offset the power of oligopolist producers, and consumer power is given greater voice through state intervention. In the following selection, taken from *The Affluent Society* (Houghton Mifflin, 1958), Galbraith views modern consumers as being caught in the grip of dependence on material possessions. He states that the abundance of goods in modern society coupled with artificial demand created by advertising and salesmanship leads to insatiable consumer demand for new products, which continually raises production. Galbraith concludes that higher production arouses greater consumer demand, thereby fostering dependence.

Key Concept: the dependence effect

The notion that wants do not become less urgent the more amply the individual is supplied is broadly repugnant to common sense. It is something to be believed only by those who wish to believe. Yet the conventional wisdom must be tackled on its own terrain. Intertemporal comparisons of an individual's state of mind do rest on doubtful grounds. Who can say for sure that the deprivation which afflicts him with hunger is more painful than the deprivation which afflicts him with envy of his neighbor's new car? In the time that has passed since he was poor his soul may have become subject to a new and deeper searing. And where a society is concerned, comparisons between marginal satisfactions when it is poor and those when it is affluent will involve not only the same individual at different times but different individuals at different times. The scholar who wishes to believe that with increasing affluence there is no reduction in the urgency of desires and goods is not without points for debate. However plausible the case against him, it cannot be proven. In the defense of the conventional wisdom this amounts almost to invulnerability.

However, there is a flaw in the case. If the individual's wants are to be urgent they must be original with himself. They cannot be urgent if they must be contrived for him. And above all they must not be contrived by the process of production by which they are satisfied. For this means that the whole case for the urgency of production, based on the urgency of wants, falls to the ground. One cannot defend production as satisfying wants if that production creates the wants.

Were it so that a man on arising each morning was assailed by demons which instilled in him a passion sometimes for silk shirts, sometimes for kitchenware, sometimes for chamber pots, and sometimes for orange squash, there would be every reason to applaud the effort to find the goods, however odd, that quenched this flame. But should it be that his passion was the result of his first having cultivated the demons, and should it also be that his effort to allay it stirred the demons to ever greater and greater effort, there would be question as to how rational was his solution. Unless restrained by conventional attitudes, he might wonder if the solution lay with more goods or fewer demons.

So it is that if production creates the wants it seeks to satisfy, or if the wants emerge *pari passu* [at an equal rate or pace] with the production, then the urgency of the wants can no longer be used to defend the urgency of the production. Production only fills a void that it has itself created.

II

The point is so central that it must be pressed. Consumer wants can have bizarre, frivolous, or even immoral origins, and an admirable case can still be made for a society that seeks to satisfy them. But the case cannot stand if it is the process of satisfying wants that creates the wants. For then the individual who urges the importance of production to satisfy these wants is precisely in the position of the onlooker who applauds the efforts of the squirrel to keep abreast of the wheel that is propelled by his own efforts.

That wants are, in fact, the fruit of production will now be denied by few serious scholars. And a considerable number of economists, though not always in full knowledge of the implications, have conceded the point.... [John Maynard] Keynes noted that needs of "the second class," i.e., those that are the result of efforts to keep abreast or ahead of one's fellow being "may indeed be insatiable; for the higher the general level the higher still are they." And emulation has always played a considerable role in the views of other economists of want creation. One man's consumption becomes his neighbor's wish. This already means that the process by which wants are satisfied is also the process by which wants are created. The more wants that are satisfied the more new ones are born.

However, the argument has been carried farther. A leading modern theorist of consumer behavior, Professor [James S.] Duesenberry, has stated explicitly that "ours is a society in which one of the principal social goals is a higher standard of living.... [This] has great significance for the theory of consumption... the desire to get superior goods takes on a life of its own. It provides a drive to higher expenditure which may even be stronger than that arising out of the needs which are supposed to be satisfied by that expenditure." The implications of this view are impressive. The notion of independently established need now sinks into the background. Because the society sets great store by ability to produce a high living standard, it evaluates people by the products they possess. The urge to consume is fathered by the value system which emphasizes the ability of the society to produce. The more that is produced the more that must be owned in order to maintain the appropriate prestige. The latter is an important point, for, without going as far as Duesenberry in reducing goods to the role of symbols of prestige in the affluent society, it is plain that his argument fully implies that the production of goods creates the wants that the goods are presumed to satisfy.

III

The even more direct link between production and wants is provided by the institutions of modern advertising and salesmanship. These cannot be reconciled with the notion of independently determined desires, for their central function is to create desires—to bring into being wants that previously did not exist. This is accomplished by the producer of the goods or at his behest. A broad empirical relationship exists between what is spent on production of consumers' goods and what is spent in synthesizing the desires for that production. A new consumer product must be introduced with a suitable advertising campaign to arouse an interest in it. The path for an expansion of output must be paved by a suitable expansion in the advertising budget. Outlays for the manufacturing of a product are not more important in the strategy of modern business enterprise than outlays for the manufacturing of demand for the product. None of this is novel. All would be regarded as elementary by the most retarded student in the nation's most primitive school of business administration. The cost of this want formation is formidable. In 1956 total advertising expenditure—though, as noted, not all of it may be assigned to the synthesis of wants—amounted to about ten billion dollars. For some years it had been increasing at a rate in excess of a billion dollars a year. Obviously, such outlays must be integrated with the theory of consumer demand. They are too big to be ignored.

But such integration means recognizing that wants are dependent on production. It accords to the producer the function both of making the goods and of making the desires for them. It recognizes that production, not only passively through emulation, but actively through advertising and related activities, creates the wants it seeks to satisfy.

The businessman and the lay reader will be puzzled over the emphasis which I give to a seemingly obvious point. The point is indeed obvious. But it is one which, to a singular degree, economists have resisted. They have sensed, as the layman does not, the damage to established ideas which lurks in these relationships. As a result, incredibly, they have closed their eyes (and ears) to the most obtrusive of all economic phenomena, namely modern want creation.

This is not to say that the evidence affirming the dependence of wants on advertising has been entirely ignored. It is one reason why advertising has so long been regarded with such uneasiness by economists. Here is something which cannot be accommodated easily to existing theory. More pervious scholars have speculated on the urgency of desires which are so obviously the fruit of such expensively contrived campaigns for popular attention. Is a new breakfast cereal or detergent so much wanted if so much must be spent to compel in the consumer the sense of want? But there has been little tendency to go on to examine the implications of this for the theory of consumer demand and even less for the importance of production and productive efficiency. These have remained sacrosanct. More often the uneasiness has been manifested in a general disapproval of advertising and advertising men, leading to the occasional suggestion that they shouldn't exist. Such suggestions have usually been ill received.

And so the notion of independently determined wants still survives. In the face of all the forces of modern salesmanship it still rules, almost undefiled, in the textbooks. And it still remains the economist's mission—and on few matters is the pedagogy so firm—to seek unquestioningly the means for filling these wants. This being so, production remains of prime urgency. We have here, perhaps, the ultimate triumph of the conventional wisdom in its resistance to the evidence of the eyes. To equal it one must imagine a humanitarian who was long ago persuaded of the grievous shortage of hospital facilities in the town. He continues to importune the passers-by for money for more beds and refuses to notice that the town doctor is deftly knocking over pedestrians with his car to keep up the occupancy.

And in unraveling the complex we should always be careful not to overlook the obvious. The fact that wants can be synthesized by advertising, catalyzed by salesmanship, and shaped by the discreet manipulations of the persuaders shows that they are not very urgent. A man who is hungry need never be told of his need for food. If he is inspired by his appetite, he is immune to the influence of Messrs. Batten, Barton, Durstine & Osborn [of the BBDO advertising agency]. The latter are effective only with those who are so far removed from physical want that they do not already know what they want. In this state alone men are open to persuasion.

The general conclusion of these pages is of such importance for this essay that it had perhaps best be put with some formality. As a society becomes increasingly affluent, wants are increasingly created by the process by which they are satisfied. This may operate passively. Increases in consumption, the counterpart of increases in production, act by suggestion or emulation to create wants. Or producers may proceed actively to create wants through advertising and salesmanship. Wants thus come to depend on output. In technical terms it can no longer be assumed that welfare is greater at an all-round higher level of production than at a lower one. It may be the same. The higher level of production has, merely, a higher level of want creation necessitating a higher level of want satisfaction. There will be frequent occasion to refer to the way wants depend on the process by which they are satisfied. It will be convenient to call it the Dependence Effect.

We may now contemplate briefly the conclusions to which this analysis has brought us.

Plainly the theory of consumer demand is a peculiarly treacherous friend of the present goals of economics. At first glance it seems to defend the continuing urgency of production and our preoccupation with it as a goal. The economist does not enter into the dubious moral arguments about the importance or virtue of the wants to be satisfied. He doesn't pretend to compare mental states of the same or different people at different times and to suggest that one is less urgent than another. The desire is there. That for him is sufficient. He sets about in a workmanlike way to satisfy desire, and accordingly he sets the proper store by the production that does. Like woman's his work is never done.

But his rationalization, handsomely though it seems to serve, turns destructively on those who advance it once it is conceded that wants are themselves both passively and deliberately the fruits of the process by which they are satisfied. Then the production of goods satisfies the wants that the consumption of these goods creates or that the producers of goods synthesize. Production induces more wants and the need for more production. So far, in a major *tour de force,* the implications have been ignored. But this obviously is a perilous solution. It cannot long survive discussion.

Among the many models of the good society no one has urged the squirrel wheel. Moreover, as we shall see presently, the wheel is not one that revolves with perfect smoothness. Aside from its dubious cultural charm, there are serious structural weaknesses which may one day embarrass us. For the moment, however, it is sufficient to reflect on the difficult terrain which we are traversing.... [W]e were [deeply] committed to production for reasons of economic security. Not the goods but the employment provided by their production was the thing by which we set ultimate store. Now we find our concern for goods further undermined. It does not arise in spontaneous consumer need. Rather, the dependence effect means that it grows out of the process of production itself. If production is to increase, the wants must be effectively contrived. In the absence of the contrivance the increase would not occur. This is not true of all goods, but that it is true of a substantial part is sufficient. It means that since the demand for this part would not exist, were it not contrived, its utility or urgency, ex contrivance, is zero. If we regard this production as marginal, we may say that the marginal utility of present aggregate output, ex advertising and salesmanship, is zero. Clearly the attitudes and values which make production the central achievement of our society have some exceptionally twisted roots.

Perhaps the thing most evident of all is how new and varied become the problems we must ponder when we break the nexus with the work of [David] Ricardo and face the economics of affluence of the world in which we live. It is easy to see why the conventional wisdom resists so stoutly such change. It is a far, far better thing to have a firm anchor in nonsense than to put out on the troubled seas of thought.

PART FOUR

Welfare, Trade Economics, and Growth and Development

On the Internet . . .

Sites appropriate to Part Four

"The Skeptic's Reward," dated October 26, 1986, written by *Boston Globe* staffer David Walsh, describes James Buchanan's skepticism of the establishment.

http://www.boston.com/globe/search/stories/nobel/1986/1986d.html

This Web site provides career information and links to books, speeches, and newspaper and magazine articles with regard to Thomas Sowell.

http://www.tsowell.com

An economic group at the University of Wisconsin at Madison organizes events and lectures on the subject of John R. Commons.

http://www.ssc.wisc.edu/~vdavis/jrc.htm

CHAPTER 10 Welfare Economics and Economic Decision Making

10.1 VILFREDO PARETO

The Social System and Equilibrium

Vilfredo Pareto (1848–1923) was born in Paris, France, in 1848. His academic preparation consisted of a degree in civil engineering, a field whose mathematical rigor characterized his later work. From 1870 to 1893, while employed as a civil engineer, Pareto wrote several articles on mathematical economics. The popularity of his work led to his succession of Léon Walras as chair of political economy at the University of Lausanne in 1893.

Pareto's earliest work, *Course of Political Economy* (1896), set forth the law of income distribution. Using a complex mathematical proof, he demonstrated that wealth distribution in society fit a consistent pattern throughout history and in all societies. The following selection is from his magnum opus, *Manual of Political Economy* (1906). In the book Pareto lays the foundation for welfare economics by coining the term *pareto optimum,* in which the optimum allocation of resources in a society cannot be attained as long as a single individual is better off with others as well as before. In *Mind and Society* (1916), Pareto posited the regeneration of the upper classes through the process of the circulation of elites, whereby the composition of the elites is constantly in flux, with the descent to the lower classes of the entrenched elites and the ascent to the elites of enterprising members of the lower classes. These sentiments parallel those expressed in *Les Systemes Socialistes,* in which Pareto attacked Marxism as advocating a class struggle, replacing oppressive capitalist elites with equally tyrannical proletarian elites. In this selection from *Manual of Political Economy,* Pareto describes the point at which maximum ophelimity, or power to give economic satisfaction, for a community is reached.

Key Concept: maximum ophelimity

2128. *Maximum of ophelimity* [economic satisfaction] FOR *a community in political economy.* A problem of just that character arose in economics and had to be solved by that science. It will be well to consider it briefly, that we may be the better prepared to solve the more difficult sociological problem. In economics the equilibrium can be determined provided we stipulate that every individual achieves the maximum of ophelimity. The ties can be posited in such a way that the equilibrium will be perfectly determined. If, now, certain ties are suppressed, the perfect determination will come to an end, and the equilibrium will be possible at an infinite number of points at which maxima of individual ophelimities are attained. In the first case, only movements leading to the determined point of equilibrium were possible; in the second, other movements also are possible. These are of two quite distinct types. Movements of a first type, *P*, are such that, beneficial to certain individuals, they are necessarily harmful to others. Movements of a second type, *Q*, are such that they are to the advantage, or to the detriment, of all individuals without exception. The points *P* are determined by equating with zero a certain sum of homogeneous quantities dependent on heterogenous ophelimities.

2129. Consideration of the two types of points, *P* and *Q*, is of great importance in political economy. When the community stands at a point *Q*, that it can leave with resulting benefits to all individuals, procuring greater enjoyments for all of them, it is obvious that from the economic standpoint it is advisable not to stop at that point, but to move on from it as far as the movement away from it is advantageous to all. When, then, the point *P*, where that is no longer possible, is reached, it is necessary, as regards the advisability of stopping there or going on, to resort to other considerations foreign to economics—to decide on grounds of ethics, social utility, or something else, which individuals it is advisable to benefit, which to sacrifice. From the strictly economic standpoint, as soon as the community has reached a point *P* it has to stop. That point therefore plays in the situation a rôle analogous to the rôle of the point where the maximum of individual ophelimity is attained and at which, accordingly, the individual stops. Because of that analogy it has been called *point of maximum ophelimity* FOR *the community. . . .*

2130. If a community could be taken as a single individual, it would have a maximum of ophelimity just as a single individual has; there would, that is, be points at which the ophelimity *of* the community would attain a maximum. These points would not be the same as the points *Q* indicated in §2128. Since, in fact, advances from those points can be made with resulting benefit to all the individuals in a community, it is obvious that the ophelimity of the community might be increased in that fashion. But it cannot be said that such points would coincide with the points *P*. Let us take a community made up of just two persons, *A* and *B*. We can move from a point *P*, adding 5 to *A*'s ophelimity and taking 2 from the ophelimity of *B*, and so reaching a point *s*; or adding 2 to *A*'s ophelimity and taking 1 from *B*'s, so that a point *t* is reached. We cannot know at which of the two points, *s*, *t*, the ophelimity *of* the community will be greater or less until we know just how the ophelimities of *A* and of *B* are to be compared; and precisely because they cannot be compared, since they are heterogeneous quantities, no maximum ophelimity *of* the community exists; whereas a maximum ophelimity *for* the community can exist, since it is determined independently of any comparison between the ophelimities of different individuals.

10.2 A. C. PIGOU

Profit and Technical Efficiency

A. C. Pigou (1877–1959) was born on the Isle of Wight in Britain. At the University of Cambridge, his initial academic preparation consisted of instruction in history and philosophy, which were gradually replaced by economics. In 1901, he started lecturing in economics, rising to prominence as a defender of Marshallian tradition for which he was attacked by both John Maynard Keynes and Ronald Coase. His only foray into public policy making met with little success; as a member of two governmental committees, he advocated a return to the gold standard at the pre-1914 exchange rate—a policy that was ridiculed by Keynes.

In *The Economics of Welfare* (London Macmillan, 1932), Pigou argued that externalities, as observed by Alfred Marshall, provide sufficient cause for government intervention as social costs are higher than private costs for negative externalities. He recommended government intervention through taxes and subsidies. In *Wealth and Welfare* (1912), Pigou set forth the conditions under which private and social product might be different. He stated that maximum satisfaction may not be achieved under private enterprise and recommended the reduction of income inequality by raising the wages of poorer workers. He rejected the notion that the needy were temperamentally different from the affluent, observing that measures to promote equality would, over time, eliminate differences in temperament. In the following selection, taken from *Socialism Versus Capitalism* (Macmillan, 1937), Pigou examines factors that influence technical efficiency in private and socialist enterprises, concluding that neither is more technically efficient than the other.

Key Concept: private versus socialist enterprises

When ownership and control are united in a single hand there is greater freedom of action, more scope for initiative, a greater readiness to attempt untried ways and to take risks, a quicker response to changing conditions, probably more drive, than are to be found either in joint stock companies or in any socialised industrial form. Thus the private business form of industry gives scope for people with a little private capital to start some new method or even new product, which experts consider impracticable and yet which may succeed. The late Lord Melchett, in his book on *Industry and Politics,* gives, from one of his speeches in the House of Commons, a very interesting account of his father's career. "It is now nearly fifty years since two young men got to know each other in business. With the very little money they had saved they decided to start a new enterprise. Their capital was very insufficient; their optimism very great. They adopted a process entirely unknown in this country. They asked people who understood the industry to come into it, but they laughed at it.... Who would have been prepared to take the risk which all the most experienced men in the industry said was an absurd risk to take?... This is only one instance. These two men were my father and the late Sir John Brunner. They did not work 8 hours a day, but 36 hours on end without stopping. They created work for themselves; they created works where thousands of people have been employed. One of the difficulties which I feel with regard to socialism is that I do not see how you can make any progress." For [Alfred] Marshall this was a decisive consideration. He wrote in 1907: "Governmental intrusion into businesses which require ceaseless invention and fertility of resource is a danger to social progress, the more to be feared because it is insidious. It is notorious that, though departments of central and municipal governments employ many thousands of highly paid servants in engineering and other progressive industries, very few inventions of any importance are made by them: and nearly all of those few are the work of men like Sir W. H. Preece who had been thoroughly trained in free enterprise before they entered government service. Government creates scarcely anything. If government control had supplanted that of private enterprise a hundred years ago there is good reason to suppose that our methods of manufacture now would be about as effective as they were fifty years ago, instead of being perhaps four or even six times as efficient as they were then.... A government could print a good edition of Shakespeare's works, but it could not get them written. When municipalities boast of their electric light and power works, they remind me of the man who boasted of 'the genius of *my Hamlet*', when he had but printed a new edition of it. The carcase of municipal electric works belongs to the officials; the genius belongs to free enterprise. I am not urging that municipalities should avoid all such undertakings without exception; for, indeed, when a large use of rights of way, especially in public streets, is necessary, it is doubtless generally best to retain the ownership, if not also the management, of the inevitable monopoly in public hands. I am only urging that every new extension of governmental work in branches of production which need ceaseless creation and initiative is to be regarded as *prima facie* anti-social, because it retards the growth of that knowledge and those ideas which are incomparably the most important form of collective wealth."...

Now, it may be that Marshall's judgment is here over-emphatic. He did not live to see, for example, the enormous progress that has been made since the war in aircraft design, largely through government-controlled research. "A hundred years ago, when great overseas markets were being opened up and huge transformations of economic life were ripe for accomplishment as soon as feudal restrictions (Corn Laws and the like) could be shaken off, the business man was not the man of caution, but the man of adventure. The feudal opposition to business men's plans purposed to do nothing at all, but to maintain the existing order of things in the countryside. To-day, however, the business man for the most part is the opponent of changes. Where great and rapid transformations have been accomplished in the last five years, whether in our own country (the grid, the marketing boards, the sugar industry) or in the other countries (land reclamation in Italy, the Mussel Shoals Scheme in the United States, the Shannon Scheme in Ireland, the Turk-Sib Railway in Russia), not business men but Governments have been the active promoters. The business man's area has been that of existing economic conditions, which he has wished to see maintained in an orderly permanence. Business men who were not conservative in this wide sense have often turned out to be adventurers in the narrow sense." Marshall, were he alive to-day, might, in the light of these facts, have somewhat modified his verdict. None the less, the line of argument on which he relied still constitutes, within its range, a strong case for capitalism as an engine of technical efficiency in individual industries.

Turn to another consideration. The comparative productive efficiency of the capitalist and the socialist forms often depends upon how far, under the two forms, industries are split up or unified geographically. Thus it may happen that under capitalism the railways of a country are operated by a number of companies; that substantial economies would result from unification; that inability to agree on terms prevents the companies from combining voluntarily, and that the State, in fear of creating too powerful a private monopoly, will not compel them to do so. In these circumstances socialisation on a national scale would, other things being equal, promote efficiency. On the other hand, it may happen that the most economical area over which to organise an electrical power system is smaller than the whole area of the country, but larger than the area covered by most local authorities. In these circumstances there is a danger that under socialisation the industry will be partitioned into sections that are economically too small, whereas under private enterprise proper ones would be chosen. Of course, this *need* not happen; *ad hoc* socialised concerns on an appropriate scale may be specially created; but it *may* happen. The comparative advantages under this head of capitalist and socialist forms cannot, therefore, be determined for particular industries until the detailed character of the alternatives that are practically available are known.

This leads up to a further somewhat similar consideration. In some industries average cost of production will be much the same whether the available productive resources are divided up among few or many productive centres—plants or firms. In others, however, it may well be that there is some size of plant or firm that is more economical, *i.e.* produces at lower average cost, than either larger or smaller ones can do. When conditions of this sort prevail, capitalism provides a machinery by which the optimum size of productive unit tends to establish itself. For units that are too large or too small find themselves undersold in the market by firms of the right size. Too large firms, therefore, tend to contract and too small firms to expand, on pain of being driven into bankruptcy. This mechanism does not exist under socialism. Some alternative mechanism is, therefore, needed. It is not very difficult to provide this. The Public Board, which, we may presume, controls the industry, can obtain costs statistics from all the plants included in it. On the basis of these statistics it should be able, not merely to discover, and so to get rid of, relatively inefficient managers, but also to obtain a rough idea of what, with a manager of given competence, is the optimum size of individual plant. In this way it can make deliberately those adjustments, which, under capitalism, are accomplished by the blind forces of competition. We have, of course, been supposing that under capitalism the several plants or firms are independent. If they are combined under the control of a single trust, obviously the people at the head of the trust have exactly the same problem to face, and are in exactly the same position, as a Public Board. In this matter, therefore, capitalism and socialism are, it would seem, much on a level.

Up to this point I have spoken as though efficiency were simply a matter of cost, tacitly assuming that, with capitalism and socialism alike, the proper quality of product is assured. Under perfect competition this might perhaps be so. But in actual life competition is not perfect. However true it may be that shady business practices *in the long run* bring a nemesis, the fact remains that in capitalist industries it often pays to sell bad goods. A consumers' association for providing itself with raspberry jam will be under no temptation to manufacture pips for it out of wood; a capitalist jam-maker may do this. A municipal authority will be under no temptation to slaughter animals for food under insanitary conditions to escape the expense of making them sanitary: a private butchering concern may do this. This is a very important matter, so important, indeed, that in industries closely associated with public health it is customary in [England] to insist on rigorous inspection, and, when, as in the construction and operation of sewers, that is, for technical reasons, difficult, on public ownership and operation.

There is another kindred fact. Not only in industries connected with public health but in many others affected with a public interest—gas, water, electricity and so on,—it is generally agreed that private operation can only be permitted subject to public control. Nobody would suggest, for example, that railway and gas companies should be free to charge whatever prices for their services they choose. The degree and manner of control vary in different cases, but some degree and manner of it there is bound to be. This implies two things. First, the case for private enterprise, so far as it depends upon the existence under it of free and untrammelled initiative, is weakened. An enterprise that is bound by special State-imposed rules is not a completely free enterprise, and does not necessarily possess in full degree those elements of efficiency that freedom is believed to confer. Secondly, the arrangements for exercising control themselves entail cost, and in strict accountancy this cost, even when it is not passed on to the industry's customers, none the less belongs to the industry and ought to be reckoned as a negative element in measurements of its efficiency.

Since we left Marshall's argument the drift of this discussion has, on the whole, been more favourable than adverse to the claims of socialisation from the standpoint of technical efficiency. But there remains an important consideration on the other side. It is widely held that capitalist industries, even in the joint stock form, are likely to be more efficient than similarly situated socialised industries, because with them bad management may entail bankruptcy and transfer to other hands. Socialised concerns, other than co-operative societies, are sheltered against this. The late Lord Melchett wrote: "What keeps this private capitalist system going? I will tell you. If a private capitalistic business is badly managed, it goes into the bankruptcy court. What does that mean? It means you have a method by which inefficiency is automatically weeded out of your industrial system. You have a method by which efficiency is automatically rewarded. It may be a crude system, it may seem a hard system, but it is the only system in the world which has been devised up to the present." But to argue in this way is to oversimplify the facts. First, in many cases the joint-stock concern, which is the alternative to a socialised concern, would not be subject to competition. A gas, water or tramway system, if it is not operated by a municipality, must, for obvious reasons of economy, be in the hands of a single company. Secondly, even outside the public utility field, many important industries are operated, not by competing companies, but by concerns that co-operate together, sometimes in price cartels, sometimes in closer associations. There is no question of competition here. This consideration, therefore, important as it is, covers a narrower field than is sometimes supposed.

The general outcome of the foregoing discussion is indecisive. As regards the technical efficiency of particular industries it is impossible to say *in general terms* that the dominant capitalist form—the joint stock company—is superior or inferior to whatever socialised form would be the most likely alternative to it. The comparison must turn on the detailed circumstances of each several case; particularly on whether the joint stock company is in truth a private business in disguise;—and the balance will probably tip sometimes one way, sometimes the other. It follows that the issue between generalized capitalism and generalized socialism cannot be greatly affected—much less settled—by the class of consideration that has been discussed [here].

10.3 JAMES M. BUCHANAN

Achieving Economic Reform

James M. Buchanan was born in 1919 in Murfreesboro, Tennessee. He received his B.A. from Middle Tennessee State College (1940), his M.S. from the University of Tennessee (1941), and his Ph.D. from the University of Chicago (1948). In 1956 he joined the University of Virginia as professor of economics and founder of the Thomas Jefferson Center of Political Economy. In 1969 he became professor and director of the Center for Study of Public Choice, first at the Virginia Polytechnic Institute and later at George Mason University in Virginia. In 1986 Buchanan was awarded the Nobel Prize in economics for his emphasis on the significance of fundamental rules and his conceptualization of the political system as an exchange process for the achievement of mutual advantage.

Buchanan is considered the world leader in public choice theory. Public choice theory predicts the impact of the behavior of individuals as voters, taxpayers, lobbyists, or members of political parties on the political community. He distinguishes between the constitutional level of choice, which defines the rules of the game, and the postconstitutional level, which develops strategies for playing the game within the rules established. Buchanan's best work is probably *Calculus of Consent, Logical Foundations of Constitutional Democracy* (University of Michigan Press, 1962), written in collaboration with Gordon Tullock. The book poses the question of how exchanges can be organized to provide participants with positive benefits. It also examines the various rules that govern the making of governmental policy choices, including unanimity, qualified majority, vote trading, and the basis of representation. Buchanan expanded these applications in *Public Finance in Democratic Process* (1966) and in *The Demand and Supply of Public Goods* (Rand McNally, 1968). In the following selection, which has been taken from *The Economics and the Ethics of Constitutional Order* (University of Michigan Press, 1991), he demonstrates that the need for economic reform stems from rule by majority whereby the majority earns the right to impose its wishes on others. Buchanan recommends constitutional change requiring the assent of parties other than the majority.

Key Concept: economic reform

Economists, along with others, agree that economies "work better" when governments keep out of the way and allow voluntary market exchanges to operate within a legal framework that protects property rights and enforces contracts. And to "work better" means to produce a higher valued bundle of goods and services. But governments do not restrict their activities to protective functions; governments, everywhere, in greater or lesser degree, interfere with the workings of markets. Economic reform, then, becomes the inclusive term that refers to institutional changes in the direction of liberating free exchange from politicized intervention.

What is the starting point? Why is economic reform needed at all? Why is it so difficult to achieve? What are the prospects for economic reform in the 1990s? These questions dictate the organization of my efforts in this [selection].

1. HERE AND NOW

As many of you know, I have always insisted that would-be reformers of economic and political institutions acknowledge the simple existential fact that reform, improvement, or change is tethered to the "here and now" as a starting point. I continue to be surprised by those romanticists among us who advance policy nostrums in blissful ignorance of this fact. But "here and now" embodies a multiplicity of dimensions and this cautionary warning gets us nowhere in itself. We need to go further and to specify what we are talking about. That which exists in the "here and now" which is relevant for my discussion is described in a set of individuals who are organized variously in an interlinked set of institutional arrangements, including a polity, normally a nation-state. These individuals have, in turn, a set of rights, claims, duties, and obligations to or against the other participants-members through the institutions in which they cooperate, and these rights, claims, duties, and obligations are themselves defined in the same set of rules or procedures that specify both constraints on individual and institutional behavior and procedures for changing the rules. In summary, we can say that a "constitution" offers a comprehensive description of the rules within which the socio-economic-political game is played. The constitution that exists defines the "here and now" that becomes relevant for my purpose, and effective improvement or reform must involve changes in this defined structure of rules.

2. BUT HOW DO WE KNOW THAT IMPROVEMENT IS POSSIBLE?

Let it be acknowledged that change commences with the status quo.... Why does not the very existence of the rules for social order imply their functional rationality? Absent some rational role, why would the rules that we observe have ever evolved into everyday usage or have been explicitly chosen and maintained through time? And, indeed, is not the primary task for social scientists, and especially political economists, one of locating explanations for observed institutions of order? And does not any diagnosis of structural defects reflect the presumptive arrogance of "rationalist constructivism," against which [Friedrich A.] Hayek has warned us?

I place myself on record here in opposition to this element in Hayek's thought, and, more specifically, in opposition to other modern political economists (many of whom have Chicago moorings), who invoke "transactions costs" barriers to explain the absence of the complex trades or agreements on rules changes that might seem to be mutually beneficial by the criteria of theoretical welfare economics. But I also, and at the same time, place myself on record alongside William H. Hutt, who never ceased from diagnosing putative structural failures when he observed the existence of politicized barriers to voluntary exchanges.

In a 1959 paper, I suggested that the analysis derived from theoretical welfare economics did offer the political economist the bases for advancing hypotheses for changes in rules, hypotheses that could find confirmation only in the attainment of consensus, hypotheses that would be effectively falsified in the absence of such attainment. This stance allows the political economist to infer, by hypothesis, a shortfall in potential well-being when he or she observes politicized barriers to voluntary exchanges among persons, but it does not allow the derivative normative inference that such barriers should necessarily be removed by a presumed benevolent government. The stance here forces upon the economist the secondary chore of working out schemes of compensations between potential net gainers and potential net losers that any changes in rules must involve. The distributional elements of any proposal for reform are necessarily combined with allocational elements in any search for prospective consensus.

3. THE SIMPLE LOGIC OF AGREEMENT ON PARETO-RELEVANT REFORM

In this section, I shall first present the basic logical principles of the Pareto optimality construction in abstract terms, but applied to the stance of the political economist outlined above. I shall then proceed to illustrate these principles through a simple and familiar example, that of politicized control over the price of rental housing.

The political economist observes some politicized interference with the freedom of persons to engage in voluntary exchange transactions. The existing situation is adjudged to be nonoptimal or inefficient in the Pareto sense. There must then exist some alternative situation in which all persons could be made better off, by their own evaluation, or some persons made better off and no other worse off than in the existing setting. From this definitional or classificatory starting point, there follows the conclusion that there must also exist some means of moving from the initial, nonoptimal position to an alternative, optimal position in a way that will damage no one in the economic nexus. This allows the further inference that there must then exist some means of securing agreement on the part of all parties to make the shift in question.

Let us now apply this analysis to rent control. The economist diagnoses rent control to be inefficient. The rental price on old housing is below equilibrium levels, there is a shortage of such housing, and waiting lists and various "key price" arrangements have become substitute rationing devices. The price of new housing, which is exempt from control, is above the price of old housing by more than any meaningful equilibrium price differential.

If presented as a simple proposal to abolish rent control, there would be immediate opposition by those persons who claim rights to existing old housing units. This opposition would prevent the emergence of consensus on the proposal for change. The task for the political economist is to work out the minimal set of compensations that would be required to "buy out" the claims held by those who live in the old housing subject to control and, at the same time, work out some scheme whereby these compensations may be voluntarily financed by others in the community. Owners of old housing could be a major source for such "taxes," and prospective tenants who have previously been denied easy access to such housing would also be willing to meet some share of these financing requirements.

The logic is straightforward. If the rent control rule is Pareto inefficient or nonoptimal, there must exist some scheme of potential compensations and payments that will prove possible and upon which consensus may be attained. If there is no such scheme possible, the observing political economist must acknowledge that his initial classification of the rule as inefficient is in error.

4. WHY AND HOW, THEN, CAN INEFFICIENT ARRANGEMENTS CONTINUE TO EXIST?

The reasoning is impeccable, and there is little or no disagreement among economists in the classification of politicized interferences into value-reducing and value-enhancing sets. Why, then, do we observe pervasive and continuing politicized restrictions on voluntary exchanges among persons, restrictions that almost all economists would label value reducing, like rent controls? And why do such restrictions persist once they are in place? And, further, why do new intrusions into the liberty of persons to make voluntary exchanges continue to emerge from political process? If such intrusions are genuinely value reducing, as economists agree, what prevents the working out of agreed upon schemes that will both eliminate existing interferences and prevent new ones from arising?

I shall discuss these two questions separately. First, I shall address the issues that arise in attempts to secure economic reform by removing existing interferences with voluntary exchanges. Second, I shall extend the analysis to efforts to forestall or prevent the politicization of markets that are operating without specific controls. I shall, in both cases, use the rent control example where applicable.

Suppose that an observing political economist adjudges an existing regime (for example, rent control) to be value reducing. Accepting the stance outlined above, this economist advances a reform package that includes removal of the controls along with compensation payments to those who claim rights or entitlements in the status quo, and, also, tax payments or contributions from those members of the community who could expect to secure net gains from the removal of the restrictions. (With rent control, the package would involve removal of controls over rental housing prices, along with compensations to those who claim "tenant rights," financed by tax payments from those who are expected gainers, owners of controlled units and others who are denied access to the stock.) The elementary logic suggests that there should exist many such schemes that could command generalized assent.

The economist, whom we presume has done his or her work well, is likely to be shocked by the negative reactions to this proposal, when it is advanced as a hypothesis for general approval. And this economist is likely to face continuing frustration when, as, and if differing schemes for effecting the reform are put forward. Persons and groups whose well-being would be predicted to increase, and perhaps substantially, may nonetheless reject, out of hand, any and all schemes that involve their payment of compensation to other persons who would be predicted to lose, and perhaps substantially, from the proposed change in market restrictions.

To understand the central problem in achieving economic reform it is necessary to examine the bases for the apparent refusal of potential gainers to participate in the "complex exchange" that promises to yield net benefits to all members of the community. Why do such persons, (such as the owners of controlled housing units), act in ways that seem contrary to their own economic interests?

Two separate but somewhat related explanations may be suggested. The potential gainers from suggested reform may refuse to acknowledge the *entitlements* or *rights* of those who would be damaged by removal of the restrictions on market exchanges. To offer compensations to those who seem to be unfairly advantaged by existing arrangements, even if it is recognized that such compensations would be required to secure the agreement needed to make the reforms, would violate canons of rough justice. And these canons or principles may dominate the straightforward calculus of economic self-interest.

A separate, but somewhat related, reason why potential gainers from proposed economic reform may refuse to participate in any overall scheme that requires any contribution toward the financing of compensations to potential losers emerges when we examine the political calculus of the former. Full treatment here would require an intellectual excursion through much of elementary public choice theory; a summary description must suffice. Most politicized restrictions or controls over the liberties of persons to enter into voluntary exchanges emerge from the workings of ordinary democratic politics, within which decisions are reached by *majority* coalitions in legislative assemblies or parliaments, decisions which are then imposed on the full membership of the polity. Those who are losers, in some opportunity cost sense, from prior enactments of market restrictions, may consider themselves to have been coerced by the will of an opposing majority coalition. And these losers, who would be the potential gainers from the removal of the restrictions, may hold out positive prospects for the organization of a different and politically successful majority coalition that will, in its turn, impose its own will on members of the majority that enacted the restrictive legislation in the first place. In this imagined scenario, those who stand to gain by economic reform may anticipate securing the desired reform without compensation paid to those who stand to lose. And a rational calculus may dictate that investment in efforts to build new majority coalitions may be more productive than investment in the direct payment of compensation designed to secure the agreement or acquiescence of the potential losers from the proposed change.

The effects of this political choice calculus in preventing agreement on economic reform measures that promise to yield benefits to all parties, given appropriate compensations, are related to differentials in expectations among the separate groups of participants. If prospective gainers from removal of market restrictions anticipate the effective formation of a new majority coalition which will act to repeal the restrictions, why should they pay compensations to the losers? But if these expectations are in error, and those who are in place and protected by existing controls (for example, tenants in old housing) anticipate continuing political dominance, the status quo can surely be predicted to prevail. In contrast, to the extent that prospective gainers become less hopeful of being able to form successful new majority coalitions they become more willing to finance compensations. And, conversely, to the extent that prospective losers become less secure in their maintenance of majority support, they become more willing to accept compensations that are within the relevant choice-set of those who must finance them.

We now shift attention to the different, but related, set of questions involving possible ways and means of preventing the interferences that seem to be characteristic of the working of democratic politics. If, in some way, political behavior could be constrained to insure that value-reducing restrictions on exchanges would never be imposed, there would never arise the need for economic "reform" of the sort under discussion here.

Again, we can locate a source of difficulty in a failure of majoritarian politics to allow a separation to be made between allocational and distributional objectives. A majority coalition may impose economic control measures that clearly reduce value in order to attain desired distributional results. (For example, if tenants in old housing units form a majority coalition, they may impose rent controls simply to keep their own housing costs down, with no regard to the overall waste in economic resources that the control generates.) If, before any such measure could be enacted, prospective beneficiaries should be required to get the agreement of prospective losers, no value-reducing restrictions could be put in place. But, or so the argument might go, why should members of an effective majority coalition, or their legislative representatives, feel obliged to attain the consent, through appropriate compensations or otherwise, of those who are members of the opposing minority? Does not "democracy" mean "rule by majority"?

So long as such an attitude describes both public and intellectual-academic understanding of what "democracy" is all about, we can only predict continued, politically motivated interferences with the liberties of persons to enter freely into exchanges one with another. Until and unless *constitutional* constraints are placed upon the authority of legislative majorities to intervene in the workings of the economy, there will be no means of forestalling the continuing need for economic "reform," defined as the dismantling of prior interventions.

To suggest that political actions aimed at intervening in economic exchanges must pass a constitutional test need not rule out, in any way, all such interventions. Constitutions contain within their rules further rules that define how changes in rules are to be made. But constitutional politics is necessarily more inclusive than within- or postconstitutional politics. A simple majority is not (or should not be) sufficient to implement genuine constitutional change. Hence, proponents and advocates of economic intervention would be required to secure the assent of something more than a bare majority. And in an idealized, and admittedly limiting, case, constitutionally authorized political interventions into markets could take place *only* if such interventions are value enhancing rather than value reducing.

Merely to suggest that intervention into the economic process should be placed out of bounds for majoritarian legislative politics may be labeled subversive, especially in view of a century of socialist inspired and romanticized misunderstandings about the relative efficacies of markets and politicized alternatives. But this century of confusion has surely come close to running its course. It is time to restore an understanding of the relationship between effective democracy and constitutional order.

5. ECONOMIC REFORM AND DISTRIBUTIONAL CONFLICT

The discussion to this point suggests that the central problem of achieving economic reform, or of preventing institutional changes that would make future reform desirable, is not, in itself, *economic*. The problem is, instead, that *the economy* (by which term I refer to the interaction of persons and groups in an interlinked nexus of market transactions), becomes the institutional setting within which *distributional* conflicts are resolved through *political* means. The logic of the Paretian welfare economics sketched out in section 3 is based on the implicit presumption that such conflicts have been resolved or, alternatively, have been relegated for resolution to some arena that is independent of economic process. This logical exercise is helpful in suggesting that a separation between the basic conflicts over claims to value among persons and groups and the voluntary contractual exchanges of values among persons and groups is conceptually, and also institutionally, within the possible.

The political economist, as such, can contribute nothing directly to the dialogue concerning conflicting claims and rights to shares in value. The political economist can, however, provide a measure of the social waste of value that is involved when conflicts over claims are settled through politicized intervention into markets. (Return to the rent control example. The political economist cannot offer a scientific judgment concerning whether or not the tenants of old housing units should be subsidized at the expense of other groups in the community. The political economist can, however, demonstrate that the subsidization in the form of rent ceilings destroys potential value.)

The possible achievement of economic reform through some institutional conversion of indirect subsidization of particular groups through market intervention into direct subsidization through fiscal transfers faces much the same difficulty discussed earlier with reference to the payment of compensations. Groups that benefit through indirect subsidization or protection by market distortions recognize that direct fiscal subsidization intended to generate equivalent distributional patterns will secure relatively less political support. Arbitrary and discriminatory programs of direct fiscal transfers designed to match the distributional effects of piecemeal interferences with market exchanges would not stand scrutiny when evaluated against generalized criteria of fairness or justice, no matter what ultimate form these criteria may take. And the political economist can, indeed, offer some assistance here in pointing out the discrepancy between the attainment of idealized distributive norms and the arbitrary patterns that emerge from politicized markets, quite apart from the demonstrable resource waste. Through such an exercise, the advocates of continued market distortion can be forced into blatant expressions of particularized distributional objectives and away from arguments cloaked in terms of advancing generalized forms.

6. ECONOMICS, POLITICS, AND PROSPECTS

The logic of Paretian welfare economics tells us that the removal of politicized intervention in voluntary market exchange can be orchestrated in such a way that everyone in an economy can be made better off, and by his or her own reckoning. This theorem provides the economist with both a scientific raison d'être and a basis for hope. The economist need not take sides among gainers and losers since, by the Paretian logic, all persons can become gainers from economic reform. And because persons can be presumed to pursue their own interests, there must always remain the hope that, ultimately, rationality will prevail in the choice among institutions.

At the same time, however, the logic of democratic politics, and especially majoritarian politics, tells us that the separation between the operation of the market economy and persisting distributional conflict is unlikely to be secured, thereby insuring that the economist's hopes will remain unfulfilled. It does remain possible however, to say something further about the prospects for reform, at least in terms of an attempted identification of those situations and settings in which economic reform seems most likely to occur.

First, consider a setting where major shocks have essentially destroyed and disrupted the legal-economic-political order; specifically, consider the upheavals generated in the aftermath of major war or revolution. In this setting, there exist no effective rights and claims to values in a status quo; hence, there can be little overt opposition to the emergence of relatively nonpoliticized exchange arrangements that may not have been present prior to the disruption.

And, if there are economists in the wings who have prepared a reform agenda, we might predict that a market order substantially free of political encumbrances might emerge, with the predictable consequences of economic prosperity and growth. Mancur Olson has used this argument persuasively to explain the economic rise of Germany and Japan in the years following World War II, a war that destroyed the institutional base in both countries. William H. Hutt also relied on the disruptions of the institutional arrangements in Great Britain during World War II to make possible his proposed plan for reconstruction which did involve compensatory adjustments for groups that might make claims against some return to the prewar status quo ante. As we know, Hutt's proposal did not succeed.

It is important to emphasize that, even when possibly favorable conditions for economic reform exist, there must be an available agenda for action ready for implementation, an agenda that has been prepared by political economists. The Freiberg or Ordnungspolitik school served this function admirably in postwar Germany, as did the so-called Chicago boys in post-Allende Chile.

Prospects would remain bleak indeed if economic reform could only take place in the upheavals of major wars or revolutions. We can identify a different, and nonwar, setting that offers the opportunity for effective removal of politicized controls over the workings of markets. If a national economy undergoes a historical experience during which, due both to falsified theoretical principles and to the workings of interest-group majoritarian politics, many separate markets have come to be politicized, either by direct interferences with freely established prices or, alternatively, by direct governmental enterprise operation, a "constitutionlike" shift toward the opening of markets may come to be feasible. The economy that has come to be overburdened with a whole set of restrictions will be inefficient in a readily demonstrable sense, and especially so in comparison with other national economies. Participants even in politically protected markets will be able to reckon the general costs of continued widespread politicization. Resistance to depoliticization (privatization) will be less acute on the part of members even of protected industry and consumer groups if the proposed reform is presented as a "package" that embodies similar treatment over a whole set of industries. That is to say, generalized economic reform that incorporates changes in the organization, operation, and control over many sectors may offer more prospects for political success than piecemeal reforms that pick off one or a few industries at a time. If stated as a hypothesis, we could say that the more socialized is the economy, the higher the prospects for economic reform.

I noted only in passing the relevance of the openness of an economy to international comparisons. Almost regardless of internal distributional pressures, a nation cannot long retain inefficient politicized controls over those sectors of its economy that produce for foreign markets. And, further, to the extent that inefficiencies in nonexport sectors exert spillover effects on economies generally, we should predict that small national economies with important export sectors should experience fewer difficulties with securing effective depoliticization than large national economies. This sketch of an analysis yields a hypothesis. If, as, and when the small national economies of Eastern Europe (Hungary, Poland) come to be increasingly opened, we can expect more by way of growth-producing economic reform than elsewhere over the ensuing decades. By comparison, in large internal economies where conflicts among domestic distributional interests dominate international considerations, and where socialization-politicization has not been extended to absurd limits (for example, United States), we must, I think, remain relatively pessimistic about the implementation of economic reform.

To this point, I have not mentioned ideology or conversion to organizational principles as a source or motivation for economic reform. But the influence of ideology should not be totally left out of the account. The depoliticization of the British economy that occurred during the late eighteenth and early nineteenth centuries was surely due, in part, to the conversion of political leaders to the normative principles advanced by the classical political economists. Sober assessment of the modern mind-set in the academies of the 1990s suggests that there is scant prospect for any intellectually led rediscovery of laissez-faire as an explicit normative ideal for social organization. This negative assessment must, however, be accompanied by an acknowledgement of near total uncertainty about the direction to be taken by the intellectuals of the world in the post-Marxist, postsocialist epoch that has so suddenly emerged upon us. Confronted with the discredited socialist alternatives, where are the intellectual critics of free markets to turn?

It seems at least to be within the possible that the leading centers of effective economic reform will be the postsocialist economies, which may well outdistance those mixed economies where extensive politicization did not describe the middle century but where, at the same time, the politicization that did occur is held in place by the exigencies of domestic distributional conflict.

10.4 THOMAS SOWELL

Economic Trade-Offs

Thomas Sowell was born in 1936 in Gastonia, North Carolina. His numerous teaching and research appointments have occurred at institutions such as the U.S. Department of Labor, Douglass College, Howard University, AT&T, Cornell University, Brandeis University, the University of California at Los Angeles, and currently, the Hoover Institution at Stanford University.

A conservative economist, Sowell's early work was in the area of economic theory being directed toward a clarification of the relationships between current and past economic issues. Later, his interest shifted to racial and ethnic issues, for which he issued a warning on the strong feelings caused by a politicization of race. Sowell recommended the integration of multiple groups into a competitive society that dissolves cultural barriers. In *The Economics and Politics of Race: An International Perspective* (W. Morrow, 1983), *Migrations and Cultures: A World View* (Basic Books, 1996), and *Race and Culture: A World View* (Basic Books, 1994), he advanced the notion that because of history and geography, different ethnic groups have different values and skills. As evidence, Sowell cited examples of occupations that are passed on in families and minorities who had succeeded in alien lands first by achieving economic freedom followed by political representation. In the following excerpt, taken from *Knowledge and Decisions* (Basic Books, 1980), he applies the economic approach to social theory in general, stating that the development of knowledge is the most important feature of modern markets. Sowell describes the process by which knowledge, often fragmented and incomplete, is used in making decisions that have important consequences for political and economic processes. He also defines economic trade-offs, with the scarcity of resources leading to certain alternatives being pursued at the expense of others. From a macroeconomic perspective, says Sowell, any economy focuses on maximizing the output from a few key inputs, resulting in substitution in both production and consumption. However, as substitution is not perfect, there is no need to choose any one product to the exclusion of others; resources just need to be directed to producing relatively more of one product and less of another.

Key Concept: economic trade-offs

An economic system is a system for the production and distribution of goods and services. But what is crucial for understanding the way it functions is that it is a system for *rationing* goods and services that are *inadequate* to supply all that people want. This is true of any economic system, whether it is called capitalism, socialism, feudalism, or by any other name. The Garden of Eden was not an economic system, even though it produced and distributed goods and services, because it produced them in such abundance that rationing was unnecessary. A utopia would not be an economic system, for the same reason. In short, while economic systems of various sorts boast of their achievements in bringing goods and services to people, what makes them all economic systems is that they have systematic procedures for *preventing* people from getting goods and services, denying them access to natural resources, tools or equipment for production, and limiting their ability to work at the tasks they would prefer. Capitalist systems use capitalist methods of denial, socialist systems use socialist methods of denial, but all economic systems must use some method of denial.

Looked at another way, there are *inherent* constraints, given the limitations of nature and the unlimited desires of man, and economic systems are simply artificial schemes for administering the inherent scarcities. The scarcities themselves exist independently of the particular economic systems, and would exist if there were no economic system at all and people simply fought over everything they wanted. Economic institutions exist to introduce elements of rationality or efficiency into the use of inputs and outputs.

The classic definition of economics is that it is the study of the allocation of scarce resources which have alternative uses. If resources—the ingredients of production—were not scarce, there would be no economics. We would be in an Eden or a utopia. Similarly, if each resource had only one possible use, we would simply use as much of each resource as was available to produce as much of its unique output as we could, and the only economic problem would be deciding which particular individual should produce it or consume it. But economics is much more complicated than that because, in the real world, the same resource can be used to produce a wide variety of products. Coal, for example, can produce dyes, electric power, heat, nylon, or liquid automotive fuel, and milk can produce ice cream, yogurt, and innumerable kinds of cheeses, as well as providing an ingredient in a virtually limitless variety of cooked foods. An economic system must determine how much of each resource shall go to each of its various uses, under the inherent constraint that all of the desires for all of the users cannot possibly be satisfied simultaneously.

While economic systems may become very complex, the economic situation or predicament is quite simple: there just is not enough to go around. Like so many simple and important realities, it often gets lost sight of, or is completely ignored, in the midst of complicated reasoning or emotionally powerful rhetoric. For example, some social commentators point to the existence of "unmet needs" in society as evidence of the "failure" of the economic system. But, in fact, because economic systems are essentially systems of rationing, any successfully functioning economic system would have "unmet needs" *everywhere.* The alternative would be to completely satisfy all of some category of needs—the most urgent, the moderately important, and the trivially marginal —thereby leaving still more unsatisfied (and more urgent) needs unmet elsewhere in the economy. We could, for example, completely solve the downtown parking problem in every city in the country, so that anyone could easily find a convenient parking space at any hour of the day or night—but the resources needed to do this would mean severe cutbacks in municipal hospitals, schools, and water supply. The mundane fact of insufficiency must be insisted upon and reiterated because so many discussions of "unmet needs" proceed as if "better" policies, practices, or attitudes would "solve" the problem at hand without creating deficiencies elsewhere. Typical of this attitude is the comment that, "If we can send a man to the moon, why can't we—" followed by whatever project the speaker favors. The fact that we sent a man to the moon is part of the reason why many other things could not be done.

KNOWLEDGE IN THE ECONOMY

When economics is mentioned, many people think of money, and in fact the word "resources" is often used simply as a genteel synonym for money. But in reality, a nation's economic success is far more likely to depend upon its real resources—land, machinery, work skills, etc.—rather than on the number or denomination of the pieces of green paper printed by the government. For an individual, the amount of money at his disposal determines his wealth, but for a nation as a whole, its wealth is its food, housing, transportation, medical care, etc.—not the green paper used to transfer this wealth around within its population. A nation is wealthier, its standard of living is higher, when it has more of these real things, not when bigger numbers are printed on its currency.

Since an economy functions with scarce resources which have alternative uses, there must be some method of coordinating the rationing process and getting the most output from the available input. There are as many different ways of doing this as there are different economic systems. All of these involve the use of knowledge, and how effectively that knowledge is used is crucial. After all, the cavemen had the same natural resources at their disposal as we have today, and the difference between their standard of living and ours is a difference between the knowledge they could bring to bear on those resources and the knowledge used today. Although we speak loosely of "production," man neither creates nor destroys matter, but only transforms it—and the knowledge of how to make these transformations is a key economic factor. Even among contemporary nations, differences in their economic conditions are often far more related to differences in their technological and organizational knowledge than to their respective endowments in natural resources. Japan, for example, has achieved a relatively high level of prosperity while importing many of its inputs and exporting much of its output. What they are essentially doing is selling their knowledge and skills to the rest of the world. Although it is physical material that consumers are buying, this material could have been shipped directly from the supplying country to the consuming country, without passing through Japan—except that the Japanese can transform it from inputs to outputs more efficiently than the consuming nation could.

More pervasively than is generally appreciated, economic transactions are purchases and sales of knowledge. Even the hiring of an "unskilled" worker to pump gas involves the purchase of a knowledge of the importance of dependability, punctuality, and an ability to get along with customers and co-workers, quite aside from the modest technological knowledge required to operate the gasoline pump. This is sometimes dramatically brought home when American corporations attempt to set up businesses in less developed countries, and find that they cannot adequately fill their "unskilled" jobs, even though the country may be full of people who are both poor and unemployed.

Even within an economically advanced nation, where certain skills are so taken for granted that those with them are labeled "unskilled," there are still such differences in the degree of mastery of these forms of knowledge that some employees are preferred to others, and some have to be fired for failure to apply the necessary knowledge. For example, a gas station attendant who does not show up promptly and dependably to help with rush hour business can cause some drivers to take their cars to another gas station, where they can get filled up without waiting in such a long line. By the same token, another gas station attendant who is especially efficient, attentive or pleasant to the customers can add to the volume of business. The gas station owner is therefore in a position to make significant distinctions among employees who are lumped together as "unskilled" workers by distant "experts."

Of course, everyone "knows" the importance of punctuality, dependability, etc., in the abstract or intellectual sense of knowing—just as we "know" in a general sense how to milk a cow, though most of us could not actually go out to the barn with an empty pail and come back with milk. But in an economy, it is not the superficial possession of knowledge in the abstract that counts, but the *effective* application of it. As in the case of Pearl Harbor, the abstract existence of knowledge means nothing unless it is applied at the point of decision and action.

More complex operations obviously involve more complex knowledge —often far more complex than any given individual can master. The person who can successfully man a gas pump or even manage a filling station probably knows little or nothing about the molecular chemistry of petroleum, and a molecular chemist is probably equally uninformed or misinformed as to the problems of finance, product mix, location, and other factors which determine the success or failure of a filling station, and both the manager and the chemist probably know virtually nothing about the geological principles which determine the best way and best places to explore for oil—or about the financial complexities of the speculative investments which pay for this costly and uncertain process. It has been said that no one knows how to make even a simple lead pencil. That is, there is no single person who knows how to mine the graphite, grow the wood, produce the rubber, process the metal, and handle all the financial complications of running a successful business. In short, we are all in the business of selling and buying knowledge from one another, because we are each so profoundly ignorant of what it takes to complete the whole process of which we are a part.

COSTS AND INCREMENTAL SUBSTITUTION

Given the inherent factor of scarcity, any kind of economy tries to maximize the output from its given inputs—or, in other words, to get the most value for its costs. Because resources have alternative uses, and because alternative products produce consumer satisfaction, *substitution* is a crucial factor of economic life, both in production and in consumption. We have already noted how the same ingredient can go into many different products. It should also be recognized that many different products can be ingredients in a consumer's sense of well-being. We normally think of physically similar things as substitutes: Plymouths and Chevrolets, rye bread and whole wheat, vodka and gin, etc. But in fact people may choose between spending their disposable cash on adding another room to the house or on taking a vacation abroad, between stocking their wine cellar and buying a season's pass to the baseball games, or between retiring early and sending a child to college. The particular nature of the satisfactions need not be the same.

Substitution does not imply perfect substitutions. There are all degrees of substitutability: most people would consider two pints of milk as a perfect substitute for a quart of milk, but would consider a cold shower a very poor substitute for sex. How well one thing substitutes for another cannot be determined by how similar they are in physical characteristics, or indeed, by any purely objective criteria. Economists define substitutability in terms of people's subjective preferences as revealed by their overt behavior. If a rise in the price of coffee causes people to buy more tea, then economically speaking, we can say that they are substitutes without having to investigate the chemical or physical characteristics of either. Similarly, if an increase in the price of stereo equipment causes people to buy more clothes instead, then economically these two goods are substitutes, without regard to their material disparities or even the implausibility of the connection.

Substitution takes place in production as well as consumption. Electric wires can be made of copper, steel, or aluminum, and the proportions of the three vary according to the relationship of their respective costs. Again, substitutes need not be *perfect* substitutes; the weight advantage of aluminum is more important for some purposes, while for other purposes any price differential will cause the immediate substitution of steel or copper. Through substitution, an economy can—in effect—transform one product into another by shifting some of their common inputs. For example, the economy can easily accomplish the old alchemists' dream of transforming lead into gold by simply shifting the labor, machinery, and managerial skills used to make lead into the production of gold instead. From an economic point of view, it does not matter that this is not "really" transforming one metal physically into another. What matters is that a reduction in the output of one leads to an increase in the output of the other. In World War II, we transformed our automobiles and refrigerators into tanks and airplanes by this very process of redirecting resource inputs into other product outputs.

Neither in production nor consumption does substitution imply total substitution. More likely, it means an incremental substitution, accepting somewhat less of one thing in order to get somewhat more of another. We almost never have to attempt anything as difficult as deciding categorical priorities—whether vegetables are more important than shoes, or vacations more important than music. Moreover, because we usually decide to have some of each option, even the relative importance of each possible choice changes as the respective quantities that we already have change. For example, if we had a dozen oranges and a bushel of apples, we would probably be less interested in another bag of apples than in another bag of oranges, and we might give up either for one pineapple or a pound of grapes, even though we might have the opposite preferences if we started from a position in which we had no fruit at all, or in which we had a bushel of oranges and ten pounds of grapes. In other words, substitution ratios are incrementally variable rather than categorically fixed.

Simple as all this is, it goes completely counter to rhetoric that is often heard, and sometimes heeded, about the urgent need to "establish priorities" either nationally or in a business or other organization. At the instant that such rhetoric is uttered, there may indeed be an urgent need for more of one thing at the expense of something else, but it is only a matter of time before the changing proportions of the two things change the relative urgency of adding more of each. Categorical priorities ignore this fact, unless they are very flexible and reversible—in which case they are not really "priorities." But because sober analysis seldom has the appeal of ringing rhetoric, priorities often do get established, and outlive the necessities that gave rise to them. One of the major problems of public policy is to determine what kinds of social institutions lead to flexible and reversible transformations, which permit continuous adjustment to changing circumstances, and which kinds of institutions lead to enduring categorical priorities, which can become as counterproductive under new circumstances as they may have been necessary under the old.

Costs and Values

Once it is clear that an economy—any kind of economy—is basically a system of rationing inadequate supplies, and a system of incremental substitutions, the concept of "cost" assumes a new significance. The cost of any good is the cost of its ingredients, and their cost, in turn, is *whatever alternative good had to be foregone* in order to use them where they are used. For example, the real cost of a piece of cheese is the ice cream or powdered milk that could have been produced with the same original resource. Indeed, if more cows had been slaughtered instead of being kept alive for their milk, there would have been more steaks, baseball gloves, and other cowhide products, so that the real cost of yogurt includes catchers' mitts.

This is not merely a philosophical way of looking at things. It is the way economies operate in the real world. If the demand for yogurt increased many times, yogurt production would absorb milk that would otherwise have gone into ice cream, cheese, and other dairy products. This would cause more cows to be used to increase total milk production and fewer to be slaughtered—and this in turn would mean less cowhide and higher prices for catchers' mitts. In an economy not coordinated by prices but by government directives, the same end result could occur through an issuing of orders by a central economic planning board, and the more stringent rationing of catchers' mitts would be accomplished by waiting lines or waiting lists instead of by higher prices. The physical dissimilarities between dairy products and cowhide products has nothing to do with their substitutability in the production process. How much, and in which direction, the incremental substitution takes place depends upon their respective values. These values are wholly subjective. To say that people want more yogurt is to say that yogurt has become more valuable to them. Either statement conveys exactly the same information. There is no "objective" value of yogurt which could be determined in a chemical laboratory or under a microscope, nor would any political or philosophical process determine what it is "really" worth.

Value being ultimately subjective, it varies not only from person to person but from time to time with the same person, and varies also according to how much of the given good he already has. Obviously a man in the desert dying of thirst would sacrifice much more for a glass of water than he would in his home, with water available from his faucet. In short, even for the same individual, the value of water can vary from virtually everything he has down to zero—or even below zero, since he would pay to have water taken away if his basement were flooded.

The cost of a given good can be determined in purely physical terms. If so many gallons of milk are required to produce ten pounds of yogurt, and if we know how much ice cream could have been produced with that same amount of milk, then we know the physical rate at which ice cream can be "transformed" into yogurt through incremental substitutions in the production process. However, this statement of physical possibilities says nothing about how much yogurt will in fact be produced relative to ice cream. That depends also on the relative values of these goods to their respective consumers. The knowledge of these changing values may be transmitted by price fluctuations in a market economy, or by voting changes in a politically-controlled ("planned") economy, or by direct orders in a nondemocratic, politically-controlled economy (communism, fascism, etc.).

In other words, while an individual or an economy may appear at first to be weighing the subjective value of a good against its objective cost, ultimately what is being weighed is the subjective value of one good against the subjective value of another good. Faced with identical technology and resources setting the limits of what is possible at a given time, different combinations of goods may be produced, according to the subjective preferences of the decision makers, whether those decision makers are consumers, central planners, or royalty. None of these differing assortments of goods—and therefore different resource uses—need be more "efficient" than any other. Efficiency in turning inputs into outputs can be measured only after specifying the subjective values involved. Even in the apparently objective physical sciences this is also the case. The objective "efficiency" of an automobile engine can be determined only after specifying the subjectively determined goal as the forward movement of the automobile. Otherwise, every engine is 100 percent efficient in the sense that all the energy input is used, either in the forward motion of the car, overcoming the internal friction of engine parts, or in random shaking of the automobile.

Although neither value nor efficiency is wholly objective, the idea that they are dies hard. Denunciations of "inefficiency" and "waste" are often nothing more than statements of a different set of preferences. Schemes to turn particular decisions or processes over to "experts" who will promote scientifically neutral "efficiency" are often simply ways of allowing one group of people to impose their subjective preferences on others. For example, proposals for a city-manager form of government to take municipal decisions "out of politics" are in reality proposals to make local decision making responsive to a different set of interests other than the general electorate. The merits of such a change can be debated from various viewpoints in particular cases, but the point here is the inaccuracy of the usual description of what is going on, and the misconceptions (or dishonesty) behind such descriptions. As a mechanism for the utilization of knowledge in society the city manager arrangement screens out some of the knowledge (from the electorate), allowing more weight to the knowledge of others who have greater access to, or implicit control over, the administration.

Average Versus Incremental Costs

When people casually speak of "the" cost of producing something, they usually mean the average cost—that is, the total cost of running the enterprise divided by the number of units of output it produces. But for actual decision-making purposes at any given time, the *incremental* cost is more crucial. The total cost of running an airline obviously includes the cost of airplanes, but in deciding whether or not to make a particular flight, what matters at that point is whether the incremental cost of that flight will be covered by its incremental value to the passengers, as revealed by what they are willing to pay for it. This question has to be faced whether the airline is a private company in an unregulated economy, a government-owned enterprise in a socialist state, or any other combination of economic and political institutions. The mechanisms by which the decision is made will be different, and of course the actual decision may be influenced or even determined by the nature of the institutional mechanism, but the point here is that the problem itself is independent of institutions, and institutions can be assessed in terms of how well they resolve the problem.

An airplane which would otherwise remain idle on the ground during a particular time has a very low cost in the economic sense of cost as a *foregone alternative.* If a plane that would otherwise remain in a hangar overnight is instead brought out at midnight to fly a party of vacationers to a nearby resort, the cost of this short flight that does not interfere with its other schedule of flights is much less than the "average" cost of an airplane flight. In this case, the incremental cost of the flight is little more than the cost of fuel and a flight crew, since the plane itself is there for another purpose anyway. In a price-coordinated economy, the amount of payment by the passengers required to induce the airline to fly under these conditions will tend to be much lower than the amount required to induce the same airline to set aside planes to fly the same distance on a regular schedule. For the latter decision, the passengers would have to pay an amount sufficient to cover not only the fuel and flight crew but to cover also the cost of the plane itself and the airline's various "overhead" expenses. In an economy coordinated by government decisions, the same economic resolution would be efficient, though it would have to be reached institutionally through a political or administrative process. Whether the same resolution would be reached in fact would depend upon the extent to which the particular institutional arrangements convey the same knowledge of consumer preferences (incremental trade-offs) and production costs (incremental trade-offs), and whether that knowledge was conveyed in a form that was "effective" in the sense of constituting a personal incentive to the decision maker.

It often costs much more to make a commitment in advance to produce a given good or service than it does to produce the same good or service with equipment already provided for other purposes. In some substitutions incremental costs are less than average costs—sometimes only a tiny fraction of average costs. By the same token, if the existing equipment is already being used at its normal capacity, the additional use may cost even more than the normal use, as in the case of additional demand for electricity at a time when the generators are already straining. The difference between average cost and incremental cost is crucial not only in economic institutions in various economic systems but it is also crucial in political, legal, and other systems as well. The incremental cost of a telephone's ringing may be quite low to a resting and slightly bored housewife, but may be maddeningly high to a housewife who is already simultaneously coping with a crying baby, a pot boiling over on the stove, and a fight among her other children. The incremental cost of making certain precedent-setting judicial decisions is not simply the cost in that individual case but the cost of committing legal institutions to settling similar future cases on a similar basis. This cost may be hundreds or thousands of times as large as the individual decision in itself. Looked at another way, where certain decisions may be made in any of a number of different institutions within a given social system, the institutional location of that decision-making process may raise or lower the costs entailed by large multiples of what is involved in the individual decision as such.

CHAPTER 11 Trade Economics in the 1950s

11.1 JAMES E. MEADE

The Theory of Customs Unions

James E. Meade (1907–1995) was born in Bath, England. He was educated at Malvern College, and entered the University of Cambridge in 1925. Meade later studied at Oxford University where he obtained his second bachelor's degree in 1930. His professional career included various faculty appointments at Oxford and service in the economics section of the League of Nations. In 1977, he shared the Nobel Prize in economics with Bertil Ohlin for his analysis of the consequences of international trade and labor policy in open economies.

Meade's first book, *An Introduction to Economic Analysis and Policy* (1936), was one of the first texts to explain Keynesian theory. His major contribution to international trade theory was his ability to forsee the effects of trade on employment, wages, prices, and foreign exchange, with a view toward developing effective policy. In *Balance of Payments* (1951), Meade set forth a policy model that achieved the dual objectives of full employment in the domestic economy through fiscal policy, with equilibrium in external balance of payments through monetary policy. In the following excerpt from *The Theory of Customs Unions* (North-Holland Publishing, 1955), Meade discusses whether the removal of trade barriers between two countries leads to more or less effective employment of existing economic resources. He shows that exchange rate variation eases the achievement of balance of payments equilibrium between partners in a customs union. Meade concludes that if the exchange rate is kept constant between the partners and varied with outside currencies, then the partners can ease adjustment by jointly appreciating or depreciating their currencies instead of severely deflating their domestic economies or significantly removing joint restrictions on payments to outside countries.

Key Concept: the impact of the removal of trade barriers

[For purposes of this discussion,] I shall simply assume that certain countries (which for convenience I will henceforth call the Netherlands and Belgium) have finally succeeded in forming a full customs union (which I will call Benelux) in which there is complete freedom for the movement of goods and services between the partner countries, though obstacles to trade remain between the outside world and the partner countries.

The problem which I want to discuss [here] is whether this removal of barriers to trade between the two partner countries is likely to lead to a more or to a less economic use of the world's economic resources. It is not my intention to inquire into the possible effects of the formation of the union upon the level of economic activity within the various parts of the world. I shall assume that policies are adopted in all the relevant countries which result in the maintenance both of "full employment" for all economic resources and also of equilibrium in all balances of payments. The question which I intend to raise is whether, within such a balanced world economy, the removal of the barriers on their mutual trade by the Netherlands and by Belgium—all other protective barriers to trade remaining unchanged—is likely to lead to the employment of existing economic resources in more or in less economic ways.

But before we proceed to the examination of this issue it is necessary to spend more time considering the various types of policy which the partner countries may adopt for the maintenance of full employment and balance-of-payments equilibrium in their economies. For . . . the type of policy adopted for this purpose may affect in an important way the answer to our central question.

Now when the Netherlands and Belgium form their economic union, they cannot, of course, any longer make use of the control of imports from each other, or the control of payments to each other, as a means of keeping their balances of payments in equilibrium. It is of the essence of the economic union that trade and payments between the partners should be free. But they can, of course, still impose import restrictions or exchange controls on balance-of-payments grounds, in so far as their transactions with outside countries are concerned. But if they do so, they must have a joint and common Benelux programme for such controls. The reasons for this are familiar. If Belgium does not restrict imports from third countries, then any restrictions imposed by the Netherlands will merely be circumvented by the import of outside goods into the Netherlands via Belgium over the uncontrolled Belgian–Dutch frontier. Of if Belgium does not control payments to the outside world and payments from the Netherlands to Belgium are uncontrolled, then Dutchmen can always make payments to the outside world via Belgium.

Let us suppose that the Netherlands and Belgium wish to remove the barriers to trade and payments between them with the minimum amount of unification of their domestic financial institutions and policies. Each country maintains its own separate currency, banking system, gold reserve, and budgetary policy. Our immediate task is to consider what combinations of policy are compatible with the maintenance of full employment and balance-of-payments equilibrium for the customs union. We will consider this problem first on the assumption that all rates of exchange are fixed, and we will then consider the modifications in our analysis which it would be necessary to make if foreign exchange rates could be varied.

We will first deal very briefly with the problem which would arise if the Netherlands and Belgium made up a world of their own and had no contacts with any outside countries. Suppose that the Netherlands was in deficit with Belgium. In our present case this deficit must be removed; for this is now a measure of the total balance-of-payments disequilibrium in our very restricted world. Now this can be done either by a policy of financial expansion in Belgium or by a policy of financial contraction in the Netherlands. In other words, either the surplus country by means of a monetary or budgetary policy of expansion must raise its domestic prices, costs, and incomes or else the deficit country by a monetary or budgetary policy of contraction must reduce its domestic prices, costs, and incomes. But which country should take the necessary action or in what way should the necessary domestic readjustment be shared between them?

It is not really sensible to argue that in all circumstances the action should be equally shared between them. The answer depends upon the domestic economic situation in the Benelux union as a whole. If throughout Benelux there is an existing tendency towards inflation, then the action necessary to correct the bilateral balance should take the form of deflation in the deficit country rather than of inflation in the surplus country; and conversely, if there is an existing tendency towards deflation and unemployment in Benelux.

But while the adjustment of the balance of payments can in this way be made with some regard to the domestic financial situation within the union as a whole, it is, of course, impossible to take into account the domestic financial requirements of the two partners separately. If Belgium is already suffering from some inflationary tendencies from the point of view of its domestic requirements and if the Netherlands is already suffering from some deflation and unemployment domestically, that is just too bad; the removal of the deficit on the Dutch balance of payments requires some further inflation in Belgium or deflation in the Netherlands. Thus this system will enable balance-of-payments equilibrium to be combined with stable full employment only if wage rates and other costs within both partner countries are sufficiently flexible to fit in with the necessary degrees of domestic inflation or deflation.

We can now approach much nearer to reality by considering the position when there is an outside world with which both Belgium and the Netherlands have commercial dealings. But at first we will limit the problem by assuming that the outside world consists of a single outside currency area. This case might take any one of three different forms. First, if there were only one outside country there would, of course, be only that country's currency beside the Dutch and Belgium currencies. Secondly, if all the currencies of all the outside countries were fully and freely convertible into each other, the result would be the same so far as the Netherlands and Belgium are concerned; any earnings of any one currency could be freely used to finance a payment in any other external currency. Thirdly, suppose that the outside currencies were not fully and freely convertible into each other, but suppose that the Netherlands and Belgium felt strong enough financially to behave as hard-currency countries and to insist in all their payments and trade agreements with third countries that all their bilateral balances should be settled 100 per cent in gold or convertible currency; this might hamper their trade with some soft-currency countries; but it would mean that for our present problem they could behave as if there were only one external currency to be considered.

In such cases the Netherlands and Belgium can regard all foreign currencies as being convertible into each other. In these conditions any bilateral deficit of the Netherlands with Belgium can be cleared in a way which leaves all balances of payments in equilibrium if, and only if, the Netherlands has a surplus with the outside world equal to her deficit with Belgium and if Belgium has a deficit with the outside world equal to her surplus with the Netherlands. In this case the Netherlands will have earned a surplus of outside currency to use to pay to Belgium to discharge her debt to Belgium, and this receipt of outside currency by Belgium will be just sufficient to finance Belgium's deficit with the outside world. This situation will be automatically brought about if the Dutch overall balance of payments is in equilibrium and if the Belgian overall balance of payments is also in equilibrium; for in that case the Dutch deficit with Belgium must be matched by an equal surplus with the outside world, and the Belgian surplus with the Netherlands must be automatically matched by an equal deficit with the outside world.

How is this result to be achieved? There are at least two distinct ways of looking at the solution of this problem. I shall call these two methods of solution the National Method and the Economic Union Method respectively. I give them these two names because the former puts the first emphasis on the separate obligations of the two governments in their national economic policies, whereas the latter puts the main emphasis on the common programmes and policies of the Union as a whole. But as I hope to make clear in what follows, both methods lead to exactly the same result if each is carried out in all its stages with 100 per cent efficiency. But as in the real world one can never hope for 100 per cent efficiency in economic policies—especially when their implementation depends upon necessarily imprecise estimates of the quantitative effects of particular acts of policy and upon co-operative action by two sovereign independent governments—there may in fact be a very real issue in the choice of method.

(1) *The National Method* would require that each country should adopt a domestic financial policy which would keep its own overall balance of payments in equilibrium. Thus the Netherlands must adopt a policy for the internal deflation (or inflation) of her own domestic prices, costs, and incomes according as her own overall balance of payments is in deficit (or surplus); and Belgium must adopt a similar policy. If these policies are successfully carried out, then the Netherlands will automatically have a surplus with the outside world to fi-

nance her deficit with Belgium; and Belgium will have a deficit with the outside world which can just be financed out of her surplus with the Netherlands. For this system to work successfully it is, of course, as necessary that each of the two partner countries should inflate effectively when it is in overall surplus as that it should deflate when it is in overall deficit. For example, if the Netherlands were in overall deficit and Belgium in overall surplus, part of the adjustment must be brought about by an inflation in Belgium which will help to reduce the Netherlands' bilateral deficit with Belgium.

But we have so far solved the balance of payments problem without using one of the instruments of control which lies ready to hand, namely the joint Benelux programme of direct controls over payments to the outside world. In any situation it is possible to improve the joint balance with the outside world by a tightening of the joint restrictions on imports from or on payments to the outside world. Suppose that in any situation these controls over payments to the outside world are tightened. Then this will tend to improve the overall balance of payments for both the partner countries. Each country will, therefore, need to inflate more or to deflate less internally in order to preserve equilibrium in its overall balance of payments. In other words, Belgium and the Netherlands must inflate or deflate relatively to each other in order to keep their balances of payments in equilibrium; but whether this shall be done mainly by an inflation in the country which is in a relatively favourable overall balance-of-payments situation or by a deflation in the country which is in a relatively unfavourable overall balance-of-payments situation is still a question which can be determined in the light of the internal financial requirements of the union as a whole. If throughout the union there is a general threat of inflation, then restrictions on imports from the outside world can be relaxed so that more strict domestic financial policies are required on balance-of-payments grounds: if within the union unemployment and deflation is threatened, then a stricter joint policy of import control can be adopted so that a more expansive domestic policy in each country is compatible with that country's balance-of-payments equilibrium.

It is easy to see how conflicts of interest may arise in the use of this joint instrument of control over payments to the outside world. If one of the two partner countries is threatened with a domestic inflation and the other with a domestic deflation and unemployment, then the former will tend to lay the emphasis on a liberal joint import policy combined with stricter domestic financial policies, while the latter is likely to want a less liberal joint import policy combined with more expansionary domestic financial policies. Moreover, imports from the outside world may be more essential for the economy of one of the partner countries than they are for the other partner, so that the former will give relatively more weight to a liberal joint import policy while the latter may put more stress on maintaining an expansionary financial policy within the union. Finally, a joint policy for the control of payments to outside countries is comprised of many elements,—control over capital movements, control over tourist expenditures and other current invisible items, control over imports of foodstuffs, raw materials, machinery, textiles etc., and, possibly, special measures for the encouragement or discouragement of various lines of export to the outside world. It is not difficult to imagine cases in which, even when agreement has been reached upon the need to relax or to tighten controls over outside payments by a certain amount, there may be far-reaching conflicts of interest over the choice of the particular measures of liberalisation or of control which will be selected for this purpose.

(2) *The Economic Union Method* would put the primary emphasis on joint action by the union authorities. In this case the two governments would agree: first, to co-ordinate their two independent domestic financial policies in the interests of preserving domestic equilibrium inside the union, i.e. to avoid overall inflationary or deflationary pressures within the union as a whole which threaten to lead to undesirable price rises or to stagnation and unemployment; and second, to use their joint programme of control over payments to the outside world in order to keep the balance of payments of the union as a whole in equilibrium with the rest of the world. In other words, they would jointly inflate or deflate domestically to fit in with the requirements of the internal economic and financial position within the union as a whole, and they would relax or tighten up their joint controls over external payment according as the combined balance of payments of Belgium and the Netherlands with the outside world was in surplus or deficit.

If this last objective were successfully attained, any deficit of Belgium with the outside world would be offset by an equal surplus of the Netherlands with the outside world, so that the Netherlands would be earning the outside currencies needed to finance Belgium's deficit with the outside world. But there would not necessarily be a full equilibrium in all balances of payments. Suppose that Belgium's surplus with the Netherlands were less than her deficit with the outside world (and therefore also less than the Dutch surplus with the outside world since Benelux as a whole is now in equilibrium with the outside world); then Belgium will be in overall balance-of-payments deficit and the Netherlands in an equal overall balance-of-payments surplus. Since, *ex hypothesi,* direct controls may not be imposed between the partner countries, this can be corrected only by a deflation of incomes, prices, and costs in Belgium or an inflation in the Netherlands. In other words, in order that full equilibrium should be maintained it is not only necessary that Belgium and the Netherlands should co-ordinate their domestic financial policies so as to achieve the desired level of total monetary demand in Benelux as a whole; it is also necessary that this position should be achieved by means of the proper relative inflation or deflation of incomes in the two countries. Thus suppose that there is need for some total expansion of monetary demand inside Benelux to offset some growth of unemployment in Benelux, but that at the same time Belgium is in overall balance-of-payments deficit and the Netherlands in overall balance-of-payments surplus. Then the reflation within Benelux as a whole must rely primarily upon reflation within the Netherlands without any similar financial expansion within Belgium.

Suppose next that Belgium and the Netherlands are trading with two distinct outside currency areas which we will call the Dollar area and the Sterling area. Suppose further that there is not full and free convertibility in both directions between the holdings by Belgium and the Netherlands of these two currencies. For example, while Dollars may be freely convertible into Sterling, Sterling holdings may not be freely convertible into Dollars. In order now that all balances of payments can be readily cleared it is no longer sufficient that the joint Benelux balance of payments should be in balance with the outside world as a whole. It is now also necessary that the joint Benelux balance of payments with the Dollar area should not be in deficit since this cannot be financed by a surplus with the Sterling area. If this additional condition is fulfilled, and if at the same time all the other conditions discussed above are also satisfied, then balances of payments can once more be readily cleared. If one partner is in deficit with the Dollar area, then the other partner will be in at least an equal surplus with the Dollar area which it can transfer to the former for the settlement of its debts to the Dollar area.

In principle the modifications required for this purpose to the two systems of adjustment previously outlined are easy to understand, though in fact their detailed application may give rise to serious conflicts of interest. What is now needed is to introduce an element of discrimination into the joint external commercial and financial controls of Benelux which ensures that the union as a whole shall not be in deficit with the Dollar area or in surplus with the Sterling area. In the particular example which we have taken it is not necessary to ensure that the union as a whole shall not be in surplus with the Dollar area and deficit with the Sterling area, since ex hypothesi earnings of Dollars can be freely used for expenditure in Sterling.

So far I have merely enumerated the conditions, the fulfillment of which would effectively ensure that the Netherlands always possessed foreign currencies which were in total just sufficient to settle her bilateral balance with Belgium and were in kind of a sort which Belgium required to settle her net balances with outside countries. Indeed, it is only if these conditions are fulfilled that a settlement can be found which is fully satisfactory to both partners and which is compatible with the maintenance of full freedom of trade and payments with the economic union. In this case it would obviously be immaterial which of the two following rules of settlement were adopted.

(1) The Netherlands might be put under an obligation to pay to Belgium in settlement of her bilateral balance with Belgium whatever currencies Belgium needed to settle her balances with the outside world.

(2) Belgium might be put under an obligation to take from the Netherlands in settlement of her bilateral surplus with the Netherlands whatever currencies the Netherlands had available from her balances with the outside world.

But, of course, in the cruel and wicked world of reality even with the best will on both sides to operate either the National Method or the Economic Union Method an exact adjustment will never be reached from year to year. Some compromise between the two techniques of settlement would in fact have to be sought. Perhaps a working system could be devised whereby at the close of each accounting period the Netherlands were to declare what currencies she had available from her balances with the outside world and Belgium were to declare what currencies she needed to settle her balances with the outside world and in some way the difference between the two were divided between the two countries. The Netherlands would have to pay rather more than she would like in the currencies which Belgium needed, and Belgium would have to take rather more than she would like in the currencies which the Netherlands had available. Such a system, if it were practicable, would at least give both countries the maximum incentive to rearrange effectively for the next period their

FIGURE 1

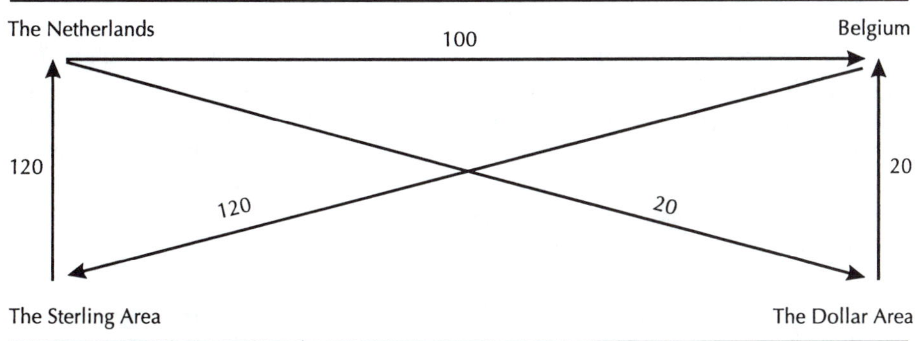

coordinated policies for domestic inflation and deflation and their joint policies for control of their payments to outside countries.

But let us suppose that the National Method or the Economic Union Method has worked fully effectively. It is important to realise that this does not mean that the Netherlands should or could settle the whole of her bilateral balance with Belgium in gold or convertible currency. The . . . very extreme and most improbable example [shown in Figure 1] is devised merely to give a vivid illustration of the point of principle.

The Netherlands has a bilateral deficit of 100 with Belgium and of 20 with the Dollar area, offset by a surplus of 120 with the Sterling area. Belgium, in addition to her surplus of 100 with the Netherlands, has a surplus of 20 with the Dollar area, these two surpluses being offset by her deficit of 120 with the Sterling area. The Dutch deficit of 100 with Belgium must in this case be settled by a payment of 120 in Sterling from the Netherlands to Belgium offset by a payment of 20 in dollars from Belgium to the Netherlands. In this case hard currency must actually pass from the partner, Belgium, which is in bilateral surplus within Benelux to the partner, the Netherlands, which is in bilateral deficit.

This example will also serve to illustrate another point. Suppose that the Netherlands, Belgium, and the Sterling area are all members of some common clearing system (the European Payments Union), while the Dollar area is not a member of it. Then in our example the Netherlands will have a surplus of 20 with the European Payments Union (100 deficit with Belgium offset by a 120 surplus with the Sterling area); and Belgium will have a deficit of 20 with the European Payments Union (100 surplus with the Netherlands offset by a 120 deficit with the Sterling area). At the same time Belgium will be earning 20 in gold or dollars from the Dollar area, while the Netherlands must pay 20 to the Dollar area. The accounts can now be cleared by a payment of 20 in gold from Belgium to the Netherlands offset by a payment of 20 through the European Payments Union from the Netherlands to Belgium. This is, of course, only one more particular example of the general principle that the Netherlands settles her bilateral balance with Belgium with the outside currencies which the Netherlands has available, which in turn coincide with those which Belgium requires,—provided that the principles of the balance-of-payments policies which we have already discussed are effectively carried out.

So far we have assumed that rates of exchange between national currencies are all fixed and constant. It is my personal opinion that this is an undesirable assumption which unnecessarily sacrifices one of the most potent and least obnoxious forms of adjustment. The use of the weapon of exchange rate variations would, in my opinion, usually ease the achievement of balance-of-payments equilibrium and the maintenance of real freedom of trade and payments within an economic union.

We can discuss this issue under separate headings. First we can assume that the rate of exchange between the Dutch and Belgian currencies is fixed, but that the rate of exchange of these currencies with outside currencies can be altered. Second, we can assume that the exchange value of the Dutch and Belgian currency can be separately altered.

In the first case, the two partners can consider a joint change in the exchange value of their currencies as an alternative to a change in their common policy of restriction over imports and other payments to outside countries. In some cases this might considerably ease the process of adjustment. Thus a case might arise (e.g. through a serious recession of business activity in the outside countries) in which the adoption of either the National Method or the Economic Union Method of adjustment discussed above might involve a very severe restriction of imports if the partner countries are to preserve equilibrium in their balances of payments without too severe policies of domestic deflation. This dilemma might be partially removed if they were to allow the exchange value of their currencies to fall somewhat. In other cases (e.g. a serious inflationary tendency in the rest of the world) the National Method or the Economic Union Method might involve a very great unilateral removal of their joint restrictions on payments to outside countries which would be difficult for one or both of them to accept. In this case they could consider the alternative of a joint appreciation of the exchange value of their currencies.

But a still more radical change would be brought about if the rate of exchange between the partners' currencies was also capable of variation. Not only would it be possible to consider the choice just mentioned between import control and exchange rate variation for the reconciliation of internal and external balance for the union as a whole. It would now be possible to adjust the balance of payments of one partner relatively to the balance of payments of the other by means of an exchange rate variation as well as by means of domestic inflation and deflation within the two countries.

Now it is of the essential nature of Benelux that the balance of payments of Belgium cannot be adjusted relatively to the balance of payments of the Netherlands by direct controls, since this would involve the imposition of restrictions or payments between the Netherlands and Belgium. In the absence of exchange rate variations this can be done only by inflation or deflation in the Netherlands relatively to Belgium. For this reason in all the systems which we have so far examined the Netherlands and Belgium have each had to surrender the power to determine its domestic financial policy with a view to its own domestic requirements.

But if the exchange rate can be varied between their currencies, then this freedom is restored. Each can devise a domestic financial policy which suits its domestic requirements, and its balance of payments relatively to the other partner can be adjusted by means of an exchange rate variation. This makes possible a true National Method of adjustment in which a true economic union with full freedom for all trade and payments between the partners is compatible with a real independence of national monetary systems.

11.2 ELI F. HECKSCHER AND BERTIL OHLIN

Interregional Trade Under Simplifying Assumptions About Factor Mobility

Eli F. Heckscher (1879–1952), the Swedish economist and historian, became the first professor of economics and statistics at the Stockholm School of Economics in 1909. Twenty years later a chair was specially opened for him at the Stockholm Institute of Economic History. Heckscher is chiefly remembered for his 1919 article entitled "The Effect of Foreign Trade on the Distribution of Income," in which he supported free trade over protection by demonstrating the ability of factor endowments to confer comparative advantage upon nations. His involvement in public policy led to *The Continental System* (1918), in which he set forth an interpretation of Napoleonic policy, and *An Economic History of Sweden* (1941), in which he addressed the "backwardness" problems of the Swedish economy in the Middle Ages and the lateness of its industrialization. His most significant historical work was his indictment of mercantilism in *Mercantilism* (1935), in which he objected to its protectionism and conceptualization of the role of money.

Bertil Ohlin (1899–1979) was born in Klippan, a village in southern Sweden. After obtaining his Ph.D. in economics in 1924, he was appointed as a professor of economics at the University of Copenhagen. In 1930 Ohlin succeeded Heckscher at the Stockholm School of Economics. He launched a political career in 1944 by heading the Swedish Liberal Party and serving as minister of trade in a coalition government. In 1977, Ohlin shared the Nobel Prize in economics with James E. Meade for laying the foundation of theories in international trade and capital movements.

In 1933, Ohlin published his dissertation, *Interregional and International Trade,* based on Heckscher's 1919 article. It presented the Heckscher-Ohlin model, in which international trade occurs between countries with different factor endowments of land, labor, capital, and technology. According to the model, different factor endowments produce different relative prices, which leads to exports of products produced from abundant factor endowments and imports of products produced from scarce factor endowments. For example, if Country A has abundant land and scarce labor, it will export land-intensive goods and import labor-intensive goods from Country

B, which has abundant labor and limited land. If this trade theory is linked to general equilibrium theory, it results in the factor-price equalization theorem, which holds that trade equalizes factor prices among trading partners. Over time, the price of land in Country A and labor in Country B will rise until they equalize. Ohlin's other work has focused on savings and investment relationships. In *The Problem of Employment Stabilization* (1949), he theorized that national income results from a sequential process in which one period's investment and consumption plans affect employment in the next, and so on. Furthermore, excess demand from social spending programs can cause chronic inflation in successive periods. In this selection from Henry Flam and M. June Flanders, trans. and eds., *Heckscher-Ohlin Trade Theory* (MIT Press, 1991), Heckscher and Ohlin describe the causes and effects of interregional trade under the assumption of factor mobility.

Key Concept: causes and effects of interregional trade

THE CAUSES OF INTERREGIONAL TRADE

Our task now is to study *interregional* (i.e., interlocal) trade.... [T]he point of departure is the general theory of price determination in a *single* market. Thus we need not explore here the tendency of trade both to direct each factor to that activity in which it is most effective and also to diminish the obstacles posed by indivisibilities. Rather, we are investigating precisely and exclusively those issues raised by the spatial dimensions of exchange. To simplify as much as possible, we initially assume that factors of production are perfectly divisible; that is, large- and small-scale production are equally profitable. General price theory deals with the problems of indivisibility. We need consider here only the second cause of interregional trade, differences in the endowment of productive factors. The relationship will be clearer than if we considered both of these causes simultaneously. We can readily modify the analysis later to present a complete picture of the price mechanism. Furthermore, for simplicity, we shall not introduce transport costs for commodities [here].

We start with two regions that have been isolated from each other and explore the circumstances under which trade will develop when relations between them are opened up.

The proximate reason for interregional trade is that some goods can be bought more cheaply from outside than they can be produced "domestically." In other words, the reason is a difference in prices between the several regions because of differences in costs of production. However, one cannot speak of a difference in *absolute* prices, since we are dealing with regions emerging from isolation. Such regions cannot have a common monetary system or an exchange rate linking their currencies. The condition for exchange to develop, then, must be a difference between *relative* commodity prices. This difference is both a sufficient and a necessary condition for trade to arise. It can readily be seen that with the lifting of isolation, this inequality results in the establishment of an exchange rate between the two currencies such that some commodities rise in price in one region, others in the other region; commodity trade must then take place. Let us call the two regions *A* and *B*. Assume that before exchange becomes possible, the relative commodity prices in the two regions are different. Then it is manifestly unthinkable that an exchange rate could arise at which all commodity prices in *A* were higher than the corresponding prices in *B* (or conversely), measured in terms of the monetary unit of either region. If that were the case, commodities would tend to flow from the cheaper to the more expensive region. But since *A* would be unable to export in order to pay for its imports, the rate of exchange would have to rise. Measured in *A*'s monetary units at the going exchange rate, *B*'s prices would not be higher, and some commodities would become more expensive in *B* than in *A* and could be exported from the latter. Only then would equilibrium occur. Third, it is impossible that all prices should be equal across regions in the absence of trade because this contradicts the assumption about differences in relative commodity prices. Consequently this assumption necessarily implies that when the possibility of trade is established, some goods become absolutely cheaper in region *A*, others in region *B*. As a result trade will occur, and each region can apply itself to the output of those goods that it can produce most cheaply.

What then are the causes of differences in production costs between regions, differences that lead to interregional commodity exchange?

The costs of production of a commodity depend on the quantities of the various factors of production used in its production and on their prices. If certain conditions on these quantities and prices are fulfilled, it is conceivable that the costs of production of all commodities in one region will match those of the other region and that there will therefore be no trade between them. But if these conditions are not fulfilled, production costs must differ. It is then profitable to produce some goods exclusively in one region, others exclusively in the other region, and to exchange them for one another.

Rather than asking under what circumstances production costs will differ and trade arise, it is preferable to inquire under what conditions these costs will coincide and therefore trade will *not* occur. When we have answered this question we can conclude that in all other cases costs will differ and trade will take place. We shall therefore explore the conditions necessary for equality both of the prices of the factors of production and of the quantities necessary for production of the several commodities so that production costs of all commodities correspond, in which case interregional trade is both unnecessary and impossible.

Suppose the relative prices of the productive factors are equal in the two regions. This means that different qualities of land, labor, and capital have the same relative prices in *A* and *B*. Thus, for example, if mechanics of a given level of skill receive double the wage of a common laborer in the first region, then the relationship must be the same in the other region. In this instance the productive factors will be used in the same proportions in the production of a given good in *A* as in *B*. The proportions can differ as between goods, but they must, under all circumstances, coincide in *A* and *B*. It is unthinkable that substitution of one factor for another could be worthwhile in one region and not in the other. Consequently for each good the factors of production must be used in the same proportions in both region. The relative commodity prices will then correspond.

Consider an abstract example, for clarification. Assume that there are three factors of production and that their prices are a, b, and c in A and a_1, b_1, and c_1, in B. Since A and B are assumed initially to be isolated from one another, there can be no rate of exchange between them for the time being; a, b, and c must therefore be expressed in A's monetary unit and a_1, b_1, and c_1 in B's monetary unit. If now the relative prices of these productive factors coincide, one can substitute ka for a_1, kb for b_1, and kc for c_1 (k is an arbitrary positive constant). Assume further that the costs of production of the three goods in A and B are, respectively, as follows:

	A	B
I	$3a + 2b + c$	$3a_1 + 2b_1 + c_1 = (3a + 2b + c)k$
II	$2a + 3b + c$	$2a_1 + 3b_1 + c_1 = (2a + 3b + c)k$
III	$a + b + 3c$	$a_1 + b_1 + 3c_1 = (a + b + 3c)k$

Comparison between the two columns shows that as soon as the relative prices of the productive factors are the same in both regions, the relative prices of the goods coincide; in such a case therefore no interregional trade can arise. *Differences in the relative scarcity of the factors of production thus constitute a necessary condition for the establishment of interregional trade.* It is probably also a sufficient condition, because as long as the relative prices of the factors of production do not match, it is practically inconceivable that the relative commodity prices and costs of production should be the same in different regions, thus precluding the occurrence of trade. The conclusion therefore is that under the assumptions stated above the cause of interregional trade lies in differences in the relative scarcity of factors of production.

Thus far we have assumed that the two regions have independent monetary systems. This assumption, however, is not important. One can just as well study two regions that trade with many other regions and that might therefore have a common monetary system or in any case a given exchange rate, regardless of whether or not they trade with each other. Under what circumstances is it conceivable that trade could not occur[1] between two regions with a common monetary system, for example, England and Scotland? Only if the *absolute* commodity prices correspond, that is, if the production costs for all commodities are the same in both regions. This presupposes that the absolute prices of the factors of production are also the same. The existence of trade, on the other hand, shows that some commodities can be produced more cheaply in England and others in Scotland. This dissimilarity in absolute commodity prices implies a disparity between the absolute prices of the factors of production. Obviously some factors must be cheaper in England than in Scotland, while the converse is true for other factors. The distinction between this case and the previous one is only that the difference between the absolute prices results directly from the difference in relative prices in conjunction with a common monetary system. In the previous case the absolute difference could not appear until a rate of exchange between the currencies of the two regions had been established.

The conclusion therefore is that the cause of interregional trade lies in a difference in the relative scarcity of productive factors, which in each region manifests itself in lower absolute prices of some factors and goods and higher prices of other factors and goods relative to those "abroad."[2] It is this difference in the absolute costs of production and prices that is the immediate cause of trade and that leads to each region's specializing in the output of those goods that it can produce more cheaply than others.

A few illustrations will help elucidate this point. Assume that region *A* is abundantly endowed with some factors of production, the prices of which are therefore relatively low and has a correspondingly smaller endowment of other factors, the prices of which are therefore relatively high. *A* will under such circumstances be able to produce cheaply those goods the production of which requires large quantities of the cheaper factors, while other goods will be relatively expensive. In *B*, where there is a relatively abundant endowment of factors that are particularly scarce in *A*, those commodities the production of which is intensive in those factors are relatively cheap, while other goods command relatively higher prices. Expressed in absolute terms, the conclusion is thus that *A* can produce at lower costs those goods the production of which requires relatively large quantities of those factors that are cheaper in *A* than in *B* and relatively small quantities of the factors that are more expensive in *A* than in *B*. Other goods, the production of which demands large quantities of the latter factors, could be produced more cheaply in *B*. Each region has an advantage in the production of those goods intensive in the factors of production that are particularly cheap in that region.

Australia has a small population and an abundant supply of land, much of it not very fertile. Land is consequently cheap and wages high, in relation to most other countries. It would therefore seem profitable to produce goods requiring large areas of less fertile land but relatively little labor. Such is the case, for example, in wool production. Sheep farming requires large quantities of such land but low inputs of labor. Wool can therefore be produced more cheaply than in countries where land rents are high, even if wages are somewhat lower than in Australia.

Similarly, regions well endowed with technically trained labor and capital will specialize in industrial production. These factors are cheaper than in regions such as Australia, where some of them are willing to work only for high rewards, if at all.

Thus, if in a particular region those goods can be produced cheaply that are relatively intensive in the low-priced factors of production and if, further, cheap goods are exported, then the conclusion must be the following: Exports from one region to another will on the whole consist of goods that are intensive in those factors with which this region is abundantly endowed and the prices of which are therefore low. If, on the other hand, those goods that would be expensive to produce in *A* are imported from other regions, then it follows that imports generally consist of goods that embody relatively large quantities of factors that are relatively scarce and expensive in the importing region. In short, commodities that embody large quantities of particularly scarce factors are imported, and commodities intensive in relatively abundant factors are exported. In other words, factors of production in abundant supply are exchanged for those the supply of which is scarce. Australia exchanges wool and wheat for industrial products since the former embody much land and little labor while the opposite is true of industrial products. Australian land is thus exchanged for European labor.

Consider another example. One reason for the superiority of the German chemical industry is that scientifically educated chemists are cheap in Germany and that this kind of labor is used in great quantities in the production of dyes, for example.

The essence of this [discussion] is thus the following: If interregional trade did not take place, the relative scarcity of factors of production and of commodities would be different in different regions. Trade comes about because the exchange rate converts the relative difference into an absolute difference. In this way each region comes to be engaged in the production of those goods that it can produce at lower cost than others, that is, those goods intensive in its low-priced factors of production. Again, those commodities requiring large amounts of the relatively scarce factors will be imported from regions where those factors are less scarce. Indirectly therefore abundant factors of production are exported and scarce factors imported.

THE EFFECTS OF INTERREGIONAL TRADE

The immediate result of interregional trade is equalization of commodity prices between the several regions. But it is evident... that equalization of the prices of factors of production is also involved. This is because imports on the whole consist of those commodities that require large quantities of particularly scarce factors of production, while exports, on the other hand, are goods embodying large quantities of factors that are relatively less scarce. Interregional trade and the division of labor thus lead to increased demand for the latter and decreased demand for the former. There is thus a tendency toward interregional equalization of factors prices. A sparsely populated area with abundant land devotes itself primarily to the production of products requiring much land and little labor. If labor-intensive goods were produced, then obviously total demand for labor would be greater and demand for land less than under a system of division of labor and exchange. If, for example, Australia produced its own industrial products rather than importing them from Europe and America in exchange for agricultural products, then, on the one hand, the demand for labor would be greater and wages consequently higher, and on the other the demand for land, and therefore rent, lower than at present. At the same time, in Europe the scarcity of land would be greater and that of labor less than at present if the countries of Europe were constrained to produce for themselves all their agricultural products instead of importing some of them from abroad. Thus trade increases the price of land in Australia and lowers it in Europe, while tending to keep wages down in Australia and up in Europe. The tendency, in other words, is to approach an equalization of the prices of productive factors.

It has been assumed above that factors of production are immobile. Equalization of their relative scarcity in different regions can therefore not be achieved by transfer from one region to another. Obviously trade will achieve such equalization to some extent, thereby serving as a substitute for interregional mobility of factors of production.

It is evident from the preceding discussion that the necessary condition for interregional trade is a difference in the prices of productive factors and that trade tends to equalize these prices and to create a uniform price structure. Trade thus evokes forces that counteract its own cause. This is consistent with the general criterion for equilibrium and does not imply that trade would cease even with complete equalization of the prices of factors of production between regions. On the contrary, it would continue, since otherwise the earlier differences in scarcity of factors would reappear. There could, however, be no further expansion of trade.

This is an appropriate point at which to introduce the question of the limited divisibility of factors of production.... [T]his is *one* cause of exchange and because of the geographical distribution of productive factors it is also an indirect cause of interregional exchange. This in turn implies a tendency to offset the disadvantages of limited divisibility and to achieve as efficient a utilization of factors as would have been possible with complete divisibility. We have now found that interregional trade, to the extent that it is caused by different endowments of productive factors, that is, by their limited mobility, tends to result in a uniform price structure and thereby in as full an exploitation of factors as would have been possible had they been perfectly mobile. Here we clearly have a complete parallel. The effect of interregional trade can be described, in summary, as *a tendency to eliminate the drawbacks of limited divisibility and mobility of the factors of production.*

This tendency, however, cannot be realized completely. Limited divisibility prevents the most effective combination of productive factors, even at large-scale production. For various reasons which we cannot go into here, it is not profitable to increase the scale of production above a certain optimum. Even at optimum firm size, limited divisibility may be a barrier to the fully effective use of productive factors, some of which, but not all, could be used more efficiently at a larger scale of output.

The same conclusion applies to the tendency of interregional trade to eliminate the detrimental effects of limited mobility of factors by establishing a uniform price structure in the several regions. Even in the absence of transport costs trade is probably, in general, incapable of achieving complete equalization of the prices of productive factors, that is of leading to identical price structures. This requires closer investigation. Here it is convenient, as before, to proceed indirectly, first to investigate under what circumstances equalization would be complete and then to inquire to what extent these conditions do hold.

However production is distributed across different regions, all scarce productive factors must be utilized: in other words, the sum of demands for the scarce factors of production from all the industries in any given region must precisely equal their supply. This condition can be fulfilled at some prices of the productive factors in a given region, but not at others. If at a particular price some factors were not used, they would be competing with the rest of the factors of the same kind, forcing their prices down. Through this change in relative prices it becomes profitable to substitute the unemployed factors for others:

equilibrium is achieved only when all factors commanding any price at all are employed.

Now in order for the relative prices of the productive factors to be the same in different regions, it is necessary that *at these prices* the demand for factors in each region precisely correspond to the supply. In other words, production must be allocated in such a way that the total demand of every firm in a region for factors of production just corresponds to the supply. It is evident that this condition cannot be fulfilled easily. The possibility of finding a combination of commodities that at these prices require productive factors in such proportion that the total demand corresponds to supply within each region depends on the relation between supply of each factor and the requirement of different factors in the production of each good. The supply might be so uneven that no combination of goods could use factors of production in this proportion. A sparsely populated agrarian country may have so little labor that at the same ratio of workers' wages to land rent as abroad only a small fraction of the land would be used. There may be no commodities that require so little labor and so much land. The result will be that land rent will be lower relative to wages than in other countries and that a more extensive agriculture will be carried out. This is only one example of the effects of a disproportionate relationship between the factors. There are numerous other possibilities. Even if there were a combination of industries that required productive factors in the same proportion as the supply in a given region, it might happen that the demand for such commodities in all regions combined would be so limited that the given region could not devote itself exclusively to their production. The necessity of producing other commodities as well then implies a divergence of the relative scarcity of factors from that which would imply conformity with other regions.

It is important to note that the range of possible combinations of industries within each region is tightly constrained by the fact that small-scale production is not profitable. Suppose, for example, that the production of certain commodities in certain quantities would require precisely that supply of productive factors that actually exists in a region. These quantities, however, may be relatively small for certain commodities, and production on such a small, unprofitable scale cannot take place. The tendency to take advantage of economies of scale will thus prevent an allocation of production that equalizes factor prices. Particularly when one considers small regions, the limited divisibility of productive factors must greatly limit the possibility of achieving uniformity in the prices of factors across regions. The number of goods produced in each region will be strictly limited, reducing the probability that the demand for productive factors at prices common to all regions will correspond to their supply.

It is difficult to give precise meaning to the conditions for complete equalization of the prices of factors of production. The closest one could come, it seems, would be that there must be a specific relationship between (1) the technical characteristics of the goods and the factors of production, including the limited divisibility of the latter, (2) the supply of the factors of production, (3) the nature of demand. This relation must be such that at certain prices of the factors, common to all regions, there is a particular combination of industries in region that uses the factors in precisely the same proportions as they are supplied.... [T]his condition can be satisfied only if there is an appropriate relationship between the three elements stated above, which must be considered to be given in the price determination problem. Unfortunately it is impossible to assess the likelihood of this occurring, and there is therefore no justification for assuming that it will. A purely mathematical analysis shows that it is far more probable that particular constants will not fulfill the required conditions than that they will do so. Under such conditions the conclusion is that the tendency of interregional trade to effect a uniform price structure will not be fully realized.

NOTES

1. Remember that transport costs and other costs of moving commodities are not considered here.
2. In order that the exposition is not weighed down by too many peculiar expressions and terms the word "abroad" will be used occasionally, even though we are discussing regions, to denote: in the other region. Similarly the expression "foreign" will be used in the sense of extraregional.

CHAPTER 12 Economics of Growth and Development

12.1 JOSEPH A. SCHUMPETER

Stability and Progress

Joseph A. Schumpeter (1883–1950) obtained his doctorate in Vienna, Austria, and worked as a lawyer until his appointment to an academic position in Czernowitz in modern Ukraine. In 1919 Schumpeter became Austrian Minister of Finance, a position from which he was dismissed within a year. In 1932 he joined Harvard University, flourishing in the company of such luminaries as Alvin Hansen, Wassily Leontief, and Paul Sweezy as peers and Paul A. Samuelson, James Tobin, and Robert Heilbroner as students.

Schumpeter asserted that industrial expansion is the basic fact of economic growth accompanied by increasing specialization. Economic growth is putting together existing factors of production, embodied in new plants and new firms, which produce new commodities or employ a new method or process, etc. This process of innovation results in producing at a smaller cost per unit, breaking off the old "supply schedule" and starting a new one. It is also the key to all credit and capital, says Schumpeter.

In *Theory of Economic Development* (1912), Schumpeter positioned entrepreneurial innovation as the driver of growth. In *Business Cycles* (1939) and *Capitalism, Socialism, and Democracy* (1942), he defined three types of business cycles that fueled growth. The shortest cycles rise from inventory changes generating slow growth, minor innovations such as calculators and electromechanical machines producing moderate growth, with long cycles such as the discovery of electricity or airplane ravel signifying cataclysmic change.

In the following excerpt from Richard V. Clemence, ed., *Essays on Entrepreneurs, Innovations, Business Cycles, and the Evolution of Capitalism* (Addison-Wesley Press, 1951), Schumpeter argues that economic progress in a capitalist system is accompanied by disturbances and dislocations that give rise to a new equilibrium. A new equilibrium always emerges or tends to emerge, which absorbs the results of innovation carried out in the preceding periods of prosperity. Therefore, the instabilities that arise from the process of innovation tend to right themselves. Schumpeter's conclusion is that although there is instability in the capitalist system, there is no instability of order.

Key Concept: causes of instability in the capitalist system

This might very well be all: Economic life, or the economic element in, or aspect of, social life might well be essentially passive and adaptive and *therefore, in itself, essentially stable.* The fact that Reality is full of discontinuous change would be no disproof of this. For such change could without absurdity be explained by influences from without, upsetting equilibria that would, in the absence of such influences, obtain or only shift by small and determined steps along with what we have called continuous growth. We could, of course, even then fit trend lines through the facts succeeding one another historically; but they would merely be expressions of whatever has happened, not of distinct forces or mechanisms; they would be statistical, not theoretical; they would have to be interpreted in terms of particular historic events, such as the opening up of new countries in the nineteenth century, acting on a given rate of growth —and not in terms of the working of an economic mechanism *sui generis.* And if analysis could not detect any purely economic forces within the system making for qualitative and discontinuous change, we should evidently be driven to this conclusion, which can never lack verification, as there are always outside influences to point to, and as a great part of the facts of non-equilibrium must in any case be explained largely on such lines, whether there be a definite piece of non-static mechanism in them or not.

Now it is always unsafe, and it may often be unfair, to attribute to any given author or group of authors clear-cut views of comprehensive social processes, the diagnosis of which must always rest largely on social vision as distinguished from provable argument. For no author or group of authors can help recognising many heterogeneous elements, and it is always easy to quote passages in proof of this. The treatment of the history of the analysis of value, cost and interest affords examples in point, and it must be left to the reader to form his own opinion about the correctness or otherwise of our thus formulating what seems to us to be received doctrine: Industrial expansion, automatically incident to, and moulded by, general social growth—of which the most important purely economic forces are growth of population and of savings—is the basic fact about economic change or evolution or "progress"; wants and possibilities develop, industry expands in response, and this expansion, carrying automatically in its wake increasing specialisation and environmental facilities, accounts for the rest, changing continuously and organically its own *data.*

Grounds for dissent from this view present themselves on several points, but I am anxious to waive objections in order to make stand out *the* objection. Without being untrue, when taken as a proposition summing up economic history over, say, a thousand years, it is inadequate, or even misleading, when meant to be a description of that mechanism of economic life which it is the task of economic theory to explain, and it is no help towards, but a bar to, the understanding of the problems and phenomena incident to that mechanism. For expansion is *no* basic fact, capable of serving in the rôle of a cause, but is itself the result of a more fundamental "economic force," which accounts both for expansion and the string of consequences emanating from it. This is best seen by splitting up the comprehensive phenomenon of general industrial growth into the expansion of the single industries it consists of. If we do this for the period of predominantly competitive capitalism, we meet indeed at any given time with a class of cases in which both entire industries and single firms are drawn on by demand coming to them from outside and so expanding them automatically; but this additional demand practically always proceeds, as a secondary phenomenon, from a primary change in some other industry—from textiles first, from iron and steam later, from electricity and chemical industry still later—which does not *follow,* but *creates* expansion. It *first*—and by its initiative—expands its own production, thereby creates an expansion of demand for its own and, contingent thereon, other products, and the general expansion of the environment we observe—increase of population included—is the *result* of it, as may be visualised by taking any one of the outstanding instances of the process, such as the rise of railway transportation. The way by which every one of these changes is brought about lends itself easily to general statement: it is by means of new combinations of existing factors of production, embodied in new plants and, typically, new firms producing either new commodities, or by a new, *i.e.* as yet untried, method, or for a new market, or by buying means of production in a new market. What we, unscientifically, call economic progress means essentially putting productive resources to uses *hitherto untried in practice,* and withdrawing them from the uses they have served so far. This is what we call "innovation."

What matters for the subject of this study is merely the essentially discontinuous character of this process, which does not lend itself to description in terms of a theory of equilibrium. But we may conveniently lead up to this by insisting for the moment on the importance of the difference between this view and what I have called the received one. Innovation, unless it consists in producing, and forcing upon the public, a new commodity, means producing at smaller cost per unit, breaking off the old "supply schedule" and starting on a new one. It is quite immaterial whether this is done by making use of a new invention or not; for, on the one hand, there never has been any time when the store of scientific knowledge had yielded all it could in the way of industrial improvement, and, on the other hand, it is not the knowledge that matters, but the successful solution of the task *sui generis* of putting an untried method into practice—there may be, and often is, no scientific novelty involved at all, and even if it be involved, this does not make any difference to the nature of the process. And we should not only, by insisting on invention, emphasise an irrelevant point—irrelevant to our set of problems, although otherwise, of course, just as relevant as, say, climate—and be thereby led away from the relevant one, but we should also be forced to consider inventions as a case of external economies. Now this hides part of the very essence of the capitalist process. This kind of external economies—and, in fact, nearly every kind, even the trade journal must, unless the product of collective action, be somebody's business—characteristically comes about by first being taken up by one firm or a few—by acting, that is, as an internal economy. This firm begins to undersell the others, part of which are thereby definitely pushed into the background to linger there on accumulated reserves and quasi-rents, whilst another part copies the methods of the disturber of the peace. *That* this is so, we can see every day by looking at industrial life; it is precisely what goes on, what is missing in the static apparatus and what accounts both for dissatisfaction with it and for the attempts to force such phenomena into its cracking frame—instead of, as we think it natural to do, recognising and explaining this as a distinct process going on along with the one handled by the static theory. *Why* this is so, is a question which it would lead very far to answer satisfactorily. Successful innovation is, as said before, a task *sui generis*. It is a feat not of intellect, but of will. It is a special case of the social phenomenon of leadership. Its difficulty consisting in the resistances and uncertainties incident to doing what has not been done before, it is accessible for, and appeals to, only a distinct type which is rare. Whilst differences in aptitude for the routine work of "static" management only result in differences of success in doing what every one does, differences in this particular aptitude result in only some being able to do this particular thing at all. To overcome these difficulties incident to change of practice is the function characteristic of the entrepreneur.

Now if this process meant no more than one of many classes of "friction," it certainly would not be worth our while to dissent from the usual exposition on that account, however many facts might come under this heading. But it means more than this: Its analysis yields the explanation of phenomena which cannot be accounted for without it. There is, first, the "entrepreneurial" function as distinct from the mere "managerial" function—although they may, and mostly must, meet one another in the same individual—the nature of which only shows up within the process of innovation. There is, secondly, the explanation of entrepreneurs' gain, which emerges in this process and otherwise gets lost in the compound of "earnings of management," the treating of which as a homogeneous whole is unsatisfactory for precisely the same reason which, by universal consent, makes it unsatisfactory so to treat, say, the income of a peasant tilling his own soil, instead of treating it as a sum of wages, rent, quasi-rent and, possibly, interest. Furthermore, it is *this* entrepreneurs' profit which is the primary source of industrial fortunes, the history of every one of which consists of, or leads back to, successful acts of innovation. And as the rise and decay of industrial fortunes is *the* essential fact about the social structure of capitalist society, both the emergence of what is, in any single instance, an essentially temporary gain, and the elimination of it by the working of the competitive mechanism, obviously are more than "frictional" phenomena, as is that process of underselling by which industrial progress comes about in capitalist society and by which its achievements result in higher real incomes all round.

Nor is this all. This process of innovation in industry by the agency of entrepreneurs supplies the key to all the phenomena of capital and credit. The rôle of credit would be a technical and a subordinate one in the sense that everything fundamental about the economic process could be explained in terms of goods, if industry grew by small steps along coherent curves. For in that case financing could and would be done substantially by means of the current gross revenue, and only small discrepancies would need to be smoothed. If we simplify by assuming that the whole circular process of production and consumption takes exactly one period of account, no instruments or consumers' goods surviving into the next, capital—defined as a monetary concept—and income would be exactly equal, and only different phases of one and the same monetary stream. As, however, innovation, being discontinuous and involving considerable change and being, in competitive capitalism, typically embodied in new firms, requires large expenditure previous to the emergence of any revenue, credit becomes an essential element of the process. And we cannot turn to savings in order to account for the existence of a fund from which these credits are to flow. For this would imply the existence of previous profits, without which there would not be anything like the required amount—even as it is, savings usually lag behind requirements—and assuming previous profits would mean, in an explanation of principles, circular reasoning. "Credit-creation," therefore, becomes an essential part both of the mechanism of the process and of the theory explaining it. Hence, saving, properly so called, turns out to be of less importance than the received doctrine implies, for which the continuous growth of saving—accummulation—is a mainstay of explanation. Credit-creation is the method by which the putting to new uses of existing means of production is brought about through a rise in price enforcing the "saving" of the necessary amount of them out of the uses they hitherto served ("enforced savings"—cp. Mr. Robertson's "imposed lacking").

Finally, it cannot be said that whilst all this applies to individual firms, the development of whole industries might still be looked at as a continuous process, a comprehensive view "ironing out" the discontinuities which occur in every single case. Even then individual discontinuities would be the carriers of essential phenomena. But, besides, for a definite reason that is not so. As shown both by the typical rise of general prices and the equally typical activity of the constructional trades in the prosperity phase of the business cycle, innovations cluster densely together. So densely, in fact, that the resultant disturbance produces a distinct period of adjustment—which precisely is what the depression phase of the business cycle consists in. *Why* this should be so, the present writer has attempted to show elsewhere. *That* it is so, is the best single verification and justification of the view submitted, whether we apply the criterion of its being "true to life" or the criterion of its yielding explanation of a phenomena *not itself implied in its fundamental principle.*

If, then, the putting to new uses of existing resources is what "progress" fundamentally consists in; if it is the nature of the entrepreneur's function to act as the propelling force of the process; if entrepreneur's profits, credit, and the cycle prove to be essential parts of its mechanism—the writer even believes this to be true of interest—then industrial expansion *per se* is better described as a consequence than as a cause; and we should be inclined to turn the other way round what we have termed the received chain of causation. In this case, and as those phenomena link up so as to form a coherent and self-contained logical whole, it is obviously conducive to clearness to bring them out boldly; to relegate to one distinct body of doctrine the concept of equilibrium, the continuous curves and small marginal variations, all of which, in their turn, link up with the circuit flow of economic routine under constant data; and to build, alongside of this, and *before* taking account of the full complexity of the "real" phenomenon—secondary waves, chance occurrences, "growth" and so on—a theory of capitalist change, assuming, in so doing, that noneconomic conditions or data are constant and automatic and gradual change in economic conditions is absent. But there is no difficulty in inserting all this. And it would seem to follow that the organic analogy is less adapted to express faithfully the nature of the process than many of us think; although, of course, being a mere analogy, it may be so interpreted as not to imply anything positively wrong and as to avoid the idea of an equilibrium growth *ad instar* of the growth of a tree, which it may, but need not necessarily, suggest.

Summing up the argument and applying it to the subject in hand, we see that there is, indeed, one element in the capitalist process, embodied in the type and function of the entrepreneur, which will, *by its mere working and from within*—in the absence of all outside impulses or disturbances and even of "growth"—destroy any equilibrium that may have established itself or been in process of being established; that the action of that element is not amenable to description by means of infinitesimal steps; and that it produces the cyclical "waves" which are essentially the form "progress" takes in competitive capitalism and could be discovered by the theory of it, if we did not know of them by experience. But by a mechanism at work in, and explaining the features of, periods of depression, a new equilibrium always emerges, or tends to emerge, which absorbs the results of innovation carried out in the preceding periods of prosperity. The new elements find their equilibrium proportions; the old ones adapt themselves or drop out; incomes are rearranged; prosperity inflation is corrected by automatic self-deflation through the repayment of credits out of profits, through the new consumers' goods entering the markets and through saving stepping into the place of "created" credits. So the instabilities, which arise from the process of innovation, tend to right themselves, and do not go on accumulating. And we may phrase the result we reach in our terminology by saying that there is, though instability of the *System*, no economic instability of the *Order*.

The instability due to what we conceive to be the basic factor of purely economic change is, however, of very different importance in the two historic types of capitalism, which we have distinguished.

Innovation in competitive capitalism is typically embodied in the foundation of new firms—the main lever, in fact, of the rise of industrial families; improvement is forced on the whole branch by the processes of underselling and of withdrawing from them their means of production, workmen and so on shifting to the new firms; all of which not only means a large amount of disturbance as an incident, but is also effective in bringing about the result, and to change "internal" economies into "external" ones, only *as far* as it means disturbance. The new processes do not, and generally cannot, evolve out of the old firms, but place themselves side by side with them and attack them. Furthermore, for a firm of comparatively small size, which is no power on the money market and cannot afford scientific departments or experimental production and so on, innovation in commercial or technical practice is an extremely risky and difficult thing, requiring supernormal energy and courage to embark upon. But as soon as the success is before everyone's eyes, everything is made very much easier by this very fact. It can now, with much-diminished difficulty, be copied, even improved upon, and a whole crowd invariably does copy it—which accounts for the leaps and bounds of progress as well as for setbacks, carrying in their wake not only the primary disturbance, inherent to the process, but a whole string of secondary ones and *possibilities,* although no more than possibilities, of recurrent catastrophes or crises.

All this is different in "trustified" capitalism. Innovation is, in this case, not any more embodied *typically* in new firms, but goes on, within the big units now existing, largely independently of individual persons. It meets with much less friction, as failure in any particular case loses its dangers, and tends to be carried out as a matter of course on the advice of specialists. Conscious policy towards demand and taking a long-time view towards investment becomes possible. Although credit creation still plays a rôle, both the power to accumulate reserves and the direct access to the money market tend to reduce the importance of this element in the life of a trust—which, incidentally, accounts for the phenomenon of prosperity coexisting with stable, or nearly stable, prices which we have had the opportunity of witnessing in the United States 1923–1926. It is easy to see that the three causes alluded to, whilst they accentuated the waves in competitive, must tend to soften them down in trustified, capitalism. Progress becomes "automatised," increasingly impersonal and decreasingly a matter of leadership and individual initiative. This amounts to a fundamental change in many respects, some of which reach far out of the sphere of things economic. It means the passing out of existence of a system of selection of leaders which had the unique characteristic that success in *rising* to a position and success in *filling* it were essentially the same thing—as were success of the firm and success of the man in charge—and its being replaced by another more akin to the principles of appointment or election, which characteristically divorce success of the concern from success of the man, and call, just as political elections do, for aptitudes in a candidate for, say, the presidency of a combine, which have little to do with the aptitudes of a good president. There is an Italian saying, "Who enters the conclave as prospective pope, will leave it as a cardinal," which well expresses what we mean. The types which rise, and the types which are kept under, in a trustified society are different from what they are in a competitive society, and the change is spreading rapidly to motives, stimuli and styles of life. For our purpose, however, it is sufficient to recognise that the only fundamental cause of instability inherent to the capitalist system is losing in importance as time goes on, and may even be expected to disappear.

Instead of summing up a very fragmentary argument, I wish to emphasise once more, in concluding, that no account whatsoever has been taken of any but purely economic facts and problems. Our diagnosis is, therefore, no more sufficient as a basis for prediction than a doctor's diagnosis to the effect that a man has no cancer is a sufficient basis for the prediction that he will go on living indefinitely. Capitalism is, on the contrary, in so obvious a process of transformation into something else, that it is not the fact, but only the interpretation of this fact, about which it is possible to disagree. Towards this interpretation I have wished to contribute a negative result. But it may be well, in order to avoid misunderstanding, to state expressly what I believe would be the positive result of a more ambitious diagnostic venture, if I may presume to do so in one short and imperfect sentence: Capitalism, whilst economically stable, and even gaining in stability, creates, by rationalising the human mind, a mentality and a style of life incompatible with its own fundamental conditions, motives and social institutions, and will be changed, although not by economic necessity and probably even at some sacrifice of economic welfare, into an order of things which it will be merely matter of taste and terminology to call Socialism or not.

12.2 ROBERT WILLIAM FOGEL

The Development of the Southern Economy

Robert William Fogel was born in New York City in 1926. He received his B.A. from Cornell University (1948), M.A. from Columbia University (1960), and Ph.D. from Johns Hopkins University (1963). He taught at several universities before joining the University of Chicago in 1981 to become director of the Walgreen Foundation as well as director of the Center of Population Economics. In 1993, he was awarded the Nobel Prize along with Douglass C. North for pioneering the discipline of cliometrics, the study of economic history through quantitative analysis.

Fogel's contribution to economic history involves the reinterpretation of the past, such as the economic effects of American railroads in the nineteenth century in *Railroads and American Economic Growth* (John Hopkins Press, 1964). He argued that the role of the railroads in shaping economic development had been overestimated. Using cost-benefit analysis and counterfactual arguments that examined the consequences of an absence of railroads, he demonstrated that railroads contributed only about 3 percent to the growth in gross domestic product (GDP). In his provocative book *Time on the Cross: The Economics of American Negro Slavery* (Little, Brown, 1974), Fogel set forth that slavery was profitable. In a subsequent book, *Without Consent or Contract: The Rise and Fall of American Slavery* (W. W. Norton, 1989), from which the following selection has been taken, he claims that moral rather than economic reasons ended slavery. In this selection Fogel discovers that the demand for slaves was inelastic in the South, creating an advantage for agricultural production while simultaneously imposing a barrier to industrialization. He also discusses the criticism leveled at the application of cliometric approaches to southern economic development.

Key Concept: inelasticity of demand for slaves

EXPLAINING THE LAG IN SOUTHERN INDUSTRIALIZATION AND URBANIZATION

Recent research by both cliometricians and traditional historians has clarified some of the issues surrounding the debate over the lag in southern industrialization. Robert S. Starobin and Charles B. Dew made the first big breakthroughs on this problem. Their independent studies of small samples of manufacturing firms that used slave labor led both scholars to reject the abolitionist charge that slaves could not perform "the difficult and delicate operations which most manufacturing and mechanical processes involve." They found that slaves not only performed well in the routine aspects of factory production but equaled, and sometimes exceeded, the effectiveness of free men in engineering and supervisory posts. Many southern manufacturers preferred slaves because they were more reliable than free workers, and some firms mixed slaves and free men at all levels of production. These scholars also found that firms using slaves both as ordinary hands and in technical and supervisory posts were as profitable as those that relied exclusively on free labor (some firms were even more profitable). The sample on which the first of these two studies was based was not only small but confined primarily to firms engaged in the processing of such agricultural products as tobacco, cotton, and turpentine. The second study, which was based on a sample of firms in the iron industry, came to similar conclusions regarding the effectiveness of slaves in heavy industry, including their mastery of the "difficult and delicate" arts of the furnace masters, and of the profitability of firms that employed slaves in such occupations.

These findings have been buttressed by cliometric techniques. The factors most frequently cited to support the proposition that slavery was incompatible with urbanization—the increasing cost of control, the hostility of white workers, the fear of rebellion on the part of slaveowners—should all have worked to reduce the level of demand for slaves in the cities. Yet the measurement of the course of demand indicates no such downward trend, either for the urban South as a whole or for any of its leading cities. Not only did the total urban demand for slaves rise in every decade between 1820 and 1860, but the demand for slaves actually increased more rapidly in the cities than in the countryside. Declines in the urban demand for slaves occurred only in isolated instances.

Cliometricians have shown that the factors impinging on the urban demand for slaves were quite diverse. Some conditions, such as the increasing competition from white immigrant labor, served to reduce the urban demand for slaves as antislavery critics had stressed. But other forces worked in the opposite direction. Both the rapid rise in the free population of southern cities and the rise in income per capita swelled the urban demand for slaves in the crafts, in trade, and in domestic service. On balance, the factors that increased the demand for slaves in the cities proved to be substantially stronger than those that served to depress it.

Why then did the slave population of the cities decline between 1850 and 1860? Because the cities had to compete with the countryside for a supply of slaves whose growth was limited to the rate of natural increase. During decades in which the combined rural and urban demand was growing more rapidly than the supply of slaves, such as the decade of the 1850s, prices of slaves were forced up. Both the city and the countryside reacted to the rise in price, but in substantially different ways. In the rural areas there were no close substitutes for slave labor. In the cities, however, free labor, particularly immigrant labor, proved to be an effective substitute. Consequently, as the competition between the cities and the countryside forced the price of slaves up relative to the price of free labor, the cities shifted toward the relatively cheaper form of labor. In other words, slaves were shifted from the cities to the countryside not because the cities did not want slaves, but because as slave prices rose it was easier for the cities than for the countryside to find acceptable lower cost alternatives to slave labor.

That the demand for slaves was much more inelastic in the countryside than in the cities is a discovery of major importance. This highly inelastic demand means that slavery provided masters with a special advantage in the countryside that could not be obtained with free labor. Moreover, the advantage was confined to large plantations based on the gang system, for, as we have seen, slaves working on small farms were neither more nor less efficient than free laborers. The gang system was so obnoxious to free men that they could not be lured to work in gangs even when offered wage premiums to do so.

The discovery of the inelastic rural demand for slaves has raised the possibility that the very advantage that slavery created for agricultural production simultaneously created a barrier to the industrialization of the South. This ironic possibility represents a significant departure from the traditional view of the question. Whereas abolitionists argued that the southern lag in industrialization was the consequence of the weakness of the southern economy, some cliometric theorists now argue that it was a consequence of the strength of its agricultural sector. Their approach implies that, at least for the short run, the policy of specializing in agriculture may indeed have maximized southern per capita income. But the new approach also suggests that slavery thwarted the long-run development of the South by restricting the rise of an entrepreneurial class and of a labor force that could capitalize on the many opportunities for economic growth thrown up by the succession of technological innovations that emanated from the nonagricultural sectors of the economy, particularly from manufacturing, during the century following 1860.

The critical aspect of the new approach is the emphasis placed on the scale of the units engaged in gang-system agriculture. Some cliometricians believe that the existence of these large-scale units kept the return to capital and to entrepreneurial ability much higher in southern than in northern agriculture. The northern devotion to family-sized farms, they argue, made it impossible to expand the size of northern farms, while maintaining the optimal ratio of capital to labor. The desire of farmers to restrict their hands to members of their families (or the unwillingness of hands to work for long on farms other than those managed by themselves or another family member) created an "obstacle to farm expansion and hence to the accumulation of a large absolute fortune within agriculture." Northern farms thus tended to expand not by adding many workers to each unit, as happened in the South, but by adding capital to a farm with a limited number of workers. This practice led to a relatively high level of capital per worker, and so tended to lower the rate of return to capital within agriculture. Consequently, Northerners tended to search for more profitable outlets for their savings in manufacturing and in commerce.

The northern limitation on the size of farms might also have had a beneficial effect on the northern pool of entrepreneurial talent. Two aspects of this question have been stressed. Some believe that northern agriculture was unable to satisfy the ambition of the most talented entrepreneurs that it spawned. Although especially talented entrepreneurs in the South "could achieve and expand and use productively a large personal fortune within the agricultural sector," Northerners had to turn to manufacturing or commerce to satisfy their ambitions. It is also argued that the large number of small farms in the North permitted a larger proportion of individuals to acquire entrepreneurial skills than did the huge agribusinesses of southern agriculture. The point here is that gang-system plantations were vertically integrated and so brought a variety of enterprises under a single management. In the North the typical farm was too small to support by itself a flour mill, a blacksmith shop, a textile shop, a carpentry shop, and a barrel-making shop. Consequently, the North gave rise to a large number of small firms in each of these crafts, the heads of which had to become adept not only in the techniques of their crafts but also in the arts of winning markets, acquiring raw materials, and managing capital.

The plantations of the South, however, were often so large that they could, by themselves, fully support a rice-cleaning mill or a cotton gin (and sometimes both), a cloth house, a tailoring and dress shop, and a variety of handicraft shops. In such instances the craftsmen were not petty capitalists, forced to cope with the daily challenges of the market, but merely laborers trained in particular techniques, who worked at the direction of the planter (or his overseer) for an assured market and with an assured supply of raw materials. Indeed, these craftsmen could not usually even search for better-paying employers or quit the employment of the planter in order to establish their own businesses since, in most cases, they were slaves. Moreover, because of the central role of these agribusinesses, the typical manufacturing unit of the South remained small, and these small manufacturing and handicraft shops were widely dispersed in rural areas, rather than concentrated in towns. Consequently, towns and cities, which many argue were the source of structural change and modernization, were far less numerous in the South than in the West and the North.

Initial tests of the South's performance in allocating resources between agricultural and nonagricultural activities suggest a higher degree of flexibility than many suspected, but the results are far from conclusive. An analysis of the scale of operation reveals that the optimum size of manufacturing firms at the end of the antebellum era was not very large. The South was as well represented in this optimum range of firm sizes (at which production costs are minimized) as were the North Central states.

The most novel, and perhaps the most important, of the cliometric discoveries about the factors influencing the course of industrialization concerns the role of women. Analyses of the data in the manufacturing censuses indicate that the large-scale factories that characterized the Northeast were designed to make use of its relatively large, low-cost labor pool of women and children. The Northeast was unique not only because the top 5 percent of its manufacturing firms were far larger than the top 5 percent of any other region, but also because women comprised a much larger proportion of its manufacturing labor force. Women and young boys were particularly important during the 1820s and 1830s, when the Northeast pulled away from the South in the race for industrialization. The 1832 survey of manufacturing reveals that the majority of workers in northeastern factories with 16 or more employees were adult women or children. For cotton textile firms, the figure was in excess of 80 percent. Moreover, the proportion of the manufacturing labor force that was female was strongly influenced by the relative cheapness of female labor. In the Northeast, females could be hired from farm households at about 40 percent of the male wage. But in the South, where women represented just 10 percent of the manufacturing labor force, the hire rates for farm women were between 60 and 70 percent of those for men. In other words, southern factory owners had to pay much higher wages to women to lure them from the farms than did their northern counterparts, because the nature of the crops in the respective regions made the labor of females much more valuable on southern farms than on northern ones.

It thus appears that the rise of southern manufacturing was retarded because women were much more effective in the production of cotton and tobacco than in the production of wheat and other northern staples. Cotton and tobacco were not only more labor-intensive crops than wheat, but much of the labor required nimbleness rather than strength. In other words, the labor characteristics of southern staples appear to have deprived the region of the pool of cheap female and child labor that was so important in the early rise of the factory.

Still another source of cheap labor promoted the rise of factories in the Northeast. The large influx of Irish and German immigrants during the late 1840s and early 1850s not only led to labor gluts, but caused the wages of common laborers to fall more rapidly than those of skilled artisans. This development increased the competitive advantage of factories in the marketplace over artisan shops, permitting a further penetration of factory-produced goods into markets once served by artisanal products. Beginning in the late 1840s, large factories began substituting the relatively cheap labor of foreign-born workers for that of native-born workers, which led to substantial reductions in unit labor costs and to increases in profits—developments that fueled the rapid expansion of manufacturing during 1844–1854. In the long run, the rise of manufacturing was a great boon to northern labor, but during the last two decades of the antebellum era the rise of manufacturing was associated with the immiseration of substantial sections of the nonagricultural labor force.

RECENT CRITICISMS OF CLIOMETRIC APPROACHES TO THE QUESTION OF SOUTHERN ECONOMIC DEVELOPMENT

One strand of recent research is critical of the cliometric preoccupation with mechanization and large-scale manufacturing in the antebellum economy. Scholars engaged in this research place far greater emphasis on the dynamic role of artisan shops and of the trade and service sectors, arguing that large-scale manufacturing did not gain ascendancy until the end of the nineteenth century. They attribute the preoccupation with large-scale manufacturing partly to research undertaken during the first half of the twentieth century when the influence of the "smokestack" industries was at its zenith. To some extent this tendency reflected the abundance of data on manufacturing and the sparseness of data on services. Not only is the output of the service sector intangible, but with the exception of transportation, the firms in the service sector were typically small, so that their records have been difficult to recover. Some progress has been made in solving the problem of the recovery of data, and the new work suggests that the trade and service sectors were far more dynamic throughout the nineteenth century than has been appreciated. "Dynamic" does not mean that all of the changes in the economy associated with these sectors were desirable. . . .

Historians of southern politics have triggered another, but complementary, set of criticisms of the cliometric approach to southern economic development. Their studies have revealed that white society was more deeply divided over changes in southern life wrought by the rapid penetration of the market economy than cliometricians have realized. These political historians depict "a southern version of a modernization crisis" that until now has been "identified too exclusively with the antebellum North." Because the rapid development of southern commerce threatened the traditional or "precapitalist" structure of southern life, "banks, railroads, corporations, the expanding influence of distant merchants, and the rapid growth of state power" became "crucial issues" in antebellum southern politics.

It was not the yeoman farmers (whom cliometricians, whatever their views of planters, have made bearers of modernity) but the wealthy slaveowners who led the drive for state-sponsored economic development. Because they were not merely landed aristocrats but railroad speculators, merchants, bankers, and corporate stockholders, when the wealthy slaveholders gained control over a state's legislature and judiciary, as they did in Alabama during the 1850s, for example, they used their power to expand greatly the role of the state in the promotion of economic development. It was this policy of statism that provoked the widespread political backlash of Alabama's yeomen, "especially those outside of the cotton belt." Similar patterns have been described for North Carolina, Virginia, and Georgia. Taken as a group, these studies invert the traditional view not only of southern politics, but of the economic issues that defined much of the politics. This inversion does not undermine the principal technical results of the cliometricians, but it does place their economic findings in a different context than the cliometricians have generally presumed. It suggests that cliometricians may have exaggerated the role of manufacturing and romanticized the economic dynamism of the yeomen.

12.3 DOUGLASS C. NORTH

Institutions, Economic Theory, and Economic Performance

Douglass C. North was born in Cambridge, Massachusetts, in 1920. His postsecondary education was completed at the University of California (B.A., 1942; Ph.D., 1952). Much of North's career has been confined to a single institution, the University of Washington, where he served from 1950 to 1983. Since then he has served as the Stephen Olin Professor of Economics at Washington University in St. Louis, Missouri. In 1993, North was granted the Nobel Prize along with Robert William Fogel for pioneering the discipline of cliometrics.

In *Structure and Change in Economic History* (Norton, 1981), *Economic Growth of the United States,* and most notably, *Institutions, Institutional Change and Economic Performance* (Cambridge University Press, 1990), from which the following selection has been taken, North developed a framework for studying the impact of institutions on economic growth. Using the analogy of competitive sport, he challenged neoclassical economics, which assumes that players always obey the rules and that no cheating ever takes place. As cheating is inevitable, in North's view, three types of social and political teams are needed to maintain fair competition. The first type would detect violations and resolve conflict formally through the judicial system and informally by parents at home and managers in commercial enterprises. The second type would teach the individual the rules of the game. The third type would seek institutional change through the services of lobbyists or the introduction of technology.

In the following selection, North underscores the importance of institutions in determining the long-run performance of the economy. He chronicles the parallel development of institutions in England and Spain over several centuries to demonstrate that England's economy, as early as the thirteenth century, had developed institutional incentives geared toward growth, including the accumulation of capital and decentralization in decision making. In contrast, Spain's centralized bureaucracy controlled economic and political resources, which led to stagnation. North's theory is equally applicable to modern inequities in development. For example, China's acceptance of property rights and incentives for entrepreneurs has resulted in a fourfold increase in incomes over a fifteen-year period. The presence of institutions that permit wealth-creation in conjunction with a legal system that protects property rights and promotes competition is the key to economic growth, concludes North.

Key Concept: institutions as determinants of economic performance

We cannot see, feel, touch, or even measure institutions; they are constructs of the human mind. But even the most convinced neoclassical economists admit their existence and typically make them parameters (implicitly or explicitly) in their models. Do institutions matter? Do tariffs, regulations, and rules matter? Does government make a difference? Can we explain the radical change in economic well-being when we step across the boundary between the United States and Mexico? What makes markets work or not work? Does honesty in exchange make a difference; does it pay?... I wish to assert a much more fundamental role for institutions in societies; they are the underlying determinant of the long-run performance of economies. If we are ever to construct a dynamic theory of change—something missing in mainstream economics and only very imperfectly dealt with in Marxian theory—it must be built on a model of institutional change. Although some of the pieces of the puzzle are still missing, the outline of the direction to be taken is, I believe, clear.

In the sections that follow I (1) specify what changes must be made in neoclassical theory to incorporate institutional analysis into that theory, (2) outline the implications for the *static* analysis of economic performance, and (3) explore the implications of institutional analysis for the construction of a dynamic theory of long-run economic change.

I

Information processing by the actors as a result of the costliness of transacting underlies the formation of institutions. At issue are both the meaning of rationality and the characteristics of transacting that prevent the actors from achieving the joint maximization result of the zero transaction cost model.

The instrumental rationality postulate of neoclassical theory assumes that the actors possess information necessary to evaluate correctly the alternatives and in consequence make choices that will achieve the desired ends. In fact, such a postulate has implicitly assumed the existence of a particular set of institutions and information. If institutions play a purely passive role so that they do not constrain the choices of the actors and the actors are in possession of the information necessary to make correct choices, then the instrumental rationality postulate is the correct building block. If, on the other hand, the actors are incompletely informed, devise subjective models as guides to choices, and can only very imperfectly correct their models with information feedback, then a procedural rationality postulate... is the essential building block to theorizing.

The former postulate evolved in the context of the highly developed, efficient markets of the Western world and has served as a useful tool of analysis in such a context. But those markets are characterized by the exceptional condition of low or negligible transaction costs. I know of no way to analyze most markets in the contemporary world and throughout history with such a behavioral postulate. A procedural rationality postulate, on the other hand, not only can account for the incomplete and imperfect markets that characterize much of the present and the past world, but also leads the researcher to the key issues of just what it is that makes markets imperfect. That leads us to the costs of transacting.

The costs of transacting arise because information is costly and asymmetrically held by the parties to exchange and also because any way that the actors develop institutions to structure human interaction results in some degree of imperfection of the markets. In effect, the incentive consequences of institutions provide mixed signals to the participants, so that even in those cases where the institutional framework is conducive to capturing more of the gains from trade as compared to an earlier institutional framework, there will still be incentives to cheat, free ride, and so forth that will contribute to market imperfections. Given the behavioral characteristics of human beings, there is simply no way to devise institutions that solve the complex exchange problems and at the same time are free of some incompatible incentives. As a result, much of the recent literature of industrial organization and political economy has attempted to come to grips with incentive incompatibility in economic and political organization (see Miller, *Managerial Dilemmas: The Political Economy of Hierarchies*, forthcoming). The success stories of economic history describe the institutional innovations that have lowered the costs of transacting and permitted capturing more of the gains from trade and hence permitted the expansion of markets. But such innovations, for the most part, have not created the conditions necessary for the efficient markets of the neoclassical model. The polity specifies and enforces the property rights of the economic marketplace, and the characteristics of the political market are the essential key to understanding the imperfections of markets.

What would make the political market approximate the zero transaction cost model for efficient economic exchange? The condition is easily stated. Legislation would be enacted which increased aggregate income and in which the gainers compensated losers at a transaction cost that is low enough to make it jointly worthwhile. The informational and institutional conditions necessary to realize such exchange are:

1. The affected parties must have the information and correct model to know that the bill affects them and to know the amount of gains or losses they would incur.
2. The results can be communicated to their agent (the legislator) who will faithfully vote accordingly.

3. Votes will be weighted by the aggregate net gains or losses so that the net result can be ascertained and the losers appropriately compensated.
4. This exchange can be accomplished at a low enough cost of transacting to make it worthwhile.

The institutional structure most favorable to approximating such conditions is a modern democratic society with universal suffrage. Vote trading, log rolling, and the incentive of an incumbent's opponents to bring his or her *deficiencies* before constituents and hence reduce agency problems all contribute to *better* outcomes.

But look at the disincentives built into the system. Rational voter ignorance is not just a buzzword of the public choice literature. Not only could the voter never acquire the information to be even vaguely informed about the myriad bills that affect his or her welfare, but there is no way that the constituent (or even the legislator) could ever possess accurate models to weigh the consequences. Agency theory has provided abundant, if controversial, evidence of the degree to which the legislator acts independently of constituent interests. Whereas the legislator is going to trade votes on the basis of perceived number of votes he or she stands to gain or lose, that is frequently a long way from reflecting net gains or losses to all the constituents. And how often is there an incentive to compensate losers? There is a vast gap between *better* and *efficient* (in the neoclassical meaning of that term) outcomes, as a vast literature in modern political economy will attest. For my purpose, it is necessary to emphasize two essential conditions that loom large. They are that the affected parties have both the information and the correct model to accurately appraise the consequences and that all the affected parties have equal access to the decision-making process. These conditions are not even approximately met in the most favorable institutional framework in all of history for efficient political decision making.

Because polities make and enforce economic rules, it is not surprising that property rights are seldom efficient (North, 1981). But even when efficient property rights are devised, they will still typically have features that will be very costly to monitor or enforce, reflecting built-in disincentives or at the very least aspects of the exchange that provide temptation to renege, shirk, steal, or cheat. In many cases informal constraints will evolve to mitigate these disincentive consequences. And the modern Western world provides abundant evidence of markets that work and even approximate the neoclassical ideal. But they are exceptional and difficult to come by, and the institutional requirements are stringent.

II

The consequences of institutions for contemporary economic analysis can be summarized as follows:

1. Economic (and political) models are specific to particular constellations of institutional constraints that vary radically both through time and cross sectionally in different economies. The models are institution specific and in

many cases highly sensitive to altered institutional constraints. A self-conscious awareness of these constraints is essential both for improved theory construction and for issues of public policy. It is not just how well would the model play in Bangladesh or in the United States during the nineteenth century, but much more immediately, how would it play in another developed country like Japan or even in the United States next year?

Even more important is that the specific institutional constraints dictate the margins at which organizations operate and hence make intelligible the interplay between the rules of the game and the behavior of the actors. If organizations—firms, trade unions, farm groups, political parties, and congressional committees to name a few—devote their efforts to *unproductive activity,* the institutional constraints have provided the incentive structure for such activity. Third World countries are poor because the institutional constraints define a set of payoffs to political/economic activity that do not encourage productive activity. Socialist economies are just beginning to appreciate that the underlying institutional framework is the source of their current poor performance and are attempting to grapple with ways to restructure the institutional framework to redirect incentives that in turn will direct organizations along productivity-increasing paths. And as for the first world, we not only need to appreciate the importance of an overall institutional framework that has been responsible for the growth of the economy, but to be self-conscious about the consequences of the ongoing marginal changes that are continually occurring—not only on overall performance but also on specific sectors of the economy. We have long been aware that the tax structure, regulations, judicial decisions, and statute laws, to name but a few formal constraints, shape the policies of firms, trade unions, and other organizations and hence determine specific aspects of economic performance; but such awareness has not led to a focusing of economic theory on modeling the political/economic process that produces these results.

2. A self-conscious incorporation of institutions will force social scientists in general, and economists in particular, to question the behavioral models that underlie their disciplines and, in consequence, to explore much more systematically than we have done so far the implications of the costly and imperfect processing of information for the consequent behavior of the actors. Social scientists have incorporated the costliness of information in their models, but have not come to grips with the subjective mental constructs by which individuals process information and arrive at conclusions that shape their choices. There is in economics a (largely) implicit assumption that the actors can correctly identify the reason for their predicaments (i.e., have *true* theories), know the costs and benefits of alternative choices, and know how to act upon them (see, for example, Becker, 1983). Our preoccupation with rational choice and efficient market hypotheses has blinded us to the implications of incomplete information and the complexity of environments and subjective perceptions of the external world that individuals hold. There is nothing the matter with the rational actor paradigm that could not be cured by a healthy awareness of the complexity of human motivation and the problems that arise from information processing. Social scientists would then understand not only why institutions exist, but also how they influence outcomes.

3. Ideas and ideologies matter, and institutions play a major role in determining just how much they matter. Ideas and ideologies shape the subjective mental constructs that individuals use to interpret the world around them and make choices. Moreover, by structuring the interaction of human beings in certain ways, formal institutions affect the price we pay for our actions, and to the degree the formal institutions are deliberately or accidentally structured to lower the price of acting on one's ideas, they provide the freedom to individuals to incorporate their ideas and ideologies into the choices they make. A key consequence of formal institutions is mechanisms, like voting systems in democracies or organizational structures in hierarchies, that enable individuals who are agents to express their own views and to have a very different impact upon outcomes than those implied by the simple interest-group modeling that has characterized so much of economic and public choice theory.

4. The polity and the economy are inextricably interlinked in any understanding of the performance of an economy and therefore we must develop a true political economy discipline. A set of institutional constraints defines the exchange relationships between the two and therefore determines the way a political/economic system works. Not only do polities specify and enforce property rights that shape the basic incentive structure of an economy, in the modern world the share of gross national product going through government and the ubiquitous and ever-changing regulations imposed by it are the most important keys to economic performance. A useful model of the macroaspect or even microaspects of an economy must build the institutional constraints into the model. Modern macroeconomic theory, for example, will never resolve the problems that it confronts unless its practitioners recognize that the decisions made by the political process critically affect the functioning of economies. Although at an ad hoc level we have begun to recognize this, much more integration of politics and economics than has been accomplished so far is needed. This can only be done by a modeling of the political-economic process that incorporates the specific institutions involved and the consequent structure of political and economic exchange.

III

Integrating institutional analysis into *static* neoclassical theory entails modifying the existing body of theory. But devising a model of economic change requires the construction of an entire theoretical framework, because no such model exists. Path dependence is the key to an analytical understanding of long-run economic change. The promise of this approach is that it extends the most constructive building blocks of neoclassical theory—both the scarcity/competition postulate and incentives as the driving force—but modifies that theory by incorporating incomplete information and subjective models of *reality* and the increasing returns characteristic of institutions. The result is an approach that offers the promise of connecting microlevel economic activity with the macrolevel incentives provided by the institutional framework. The source of incremental change is the gains to be obtained by organizations and their entrepreneurs from acquiring skills, knowledge, and information that will enhance their objectives. Path dependence comes from the increasing returns mechanisms that reinforce the direction once on a given path. Alterations in the path come from unanticipated consequences of choices, external effects, and sometimes forces exogenous to the analytical framework. Reversal of paths (from stagnation to growth or vice versa) may come from the above described sources of path alteration, but will typically occur through changes in the polity.

I can expand on the sequential characteristics of path dependence by [exploring] the contrast between the British-North American path and the Spanish-Latin American path. . . .

The Background

At the beginning of the sixteenth century, England and Spain had evolved very differently. England had developed a relatively centralized feudalism, as a result of the Norman conquest, and had recently established the Tudors with the Battle of Bosworth (1485). Spain, in contrast, had just emerged from seven centuries of Moorish domination of the Iberian Peninsula. It was not a unified country. Although the marriage of Ferdinand and Isabella brought Castile and Aragon together, they continued to maintain separate rules, Cortes, and policies.

However, both England and Spain faced, in common with the rest of the emerging European nation-states, a critical problem: the need to acquire additional revenue to survive in the face of the rising costs of warfare. The king traditionally lived on his own, that is, off the revenue from his estates together with the traditional feudal dues; but these resources were insufficient in the face of the new military technology associated with the effective use of the crossbow, longbow, pike, and gunpowder. This fiscal crisis of the state, first described by Joseph Schumpeter (1954), forced rulers to make bargains with constituents. In both countries, the consequence was the development of some form of representation on the part of constituents (Parliament in England and the Cortes in Spain) in return for revenue. In both countries, the wool trade became a major source of crown revenue. But the consequences of the common relative price change arising from the new military technology were radically different in the two countries. In one, it led to the evolution of a polity and economy that solved the fiscal crisis and went on to dominate the Western world. In the other, in spite of initially more favorable conditions, it led to unresolved fiscal crises, bankruptcies, confiscation of assets, and insecure property rights and to three centuries of relative stagnation.

In England, the tension between ruler and constituent (although the barons at Runnymede might have caviled at that term) surfaced with the Magna Carta in 1215. The fiscal crisis came later with the Hundred Years War. Stubbs describes the consequence as follows: "The admission of the right of parliament to legislate, to enquire into abuses, and to share in the guidance of national policy, was practically purchased by the money granted to Edward I and Edward III" (Stubbs, 1896, p. 599). The subsequent history to 1689 and the final triumph of Parliament is well known.

In Spain, the union of Aragon (comprising approximately Valencia, Aragon, and Catalonia) and Castile joined two very different regions. Aragon had been reconquered from the Arabs in the last half of the thirteenth century and had become a major commercial empire extending into Sardinia, Sicily, and parts of Greece. The Cortes reflected the interests of merchants and played a significant role in public affairs. In contrast, Castile was continually engaged in warfare, either against the Moors or in internal strife, and although the Cortes existed it was seldom summoned. In the fifteen years after their union, Isabella succeeded in gaining control not only over the unruly warlike barons, but over church policy in Castile as well. Although the role of the Castilian Cortes has, in recent scholarly work, been somewhat upgraded, nevertheless there was a centralized monarchy and bureaucracy in Castile, and it was Castile that defined the institutional evolution of both Spain and Latin America.

The Institutional Framework

It was not simply centralization or decentralization in the polity that differentiated the two societies. Nevertheless, this feature made a critical difference and was symptomatic of the broad differences in both the polity and the economy. Not only did the Parliament in England provide the beginning of representative government and a reduction in the *rent-seeking* behavior that had characterized the financially hard-pressed Stuart monarchs, but also Parliament's triumph betokened increased security of property rights and a more effective, impartial judicial system.

Spain's polity consisted of a large centralized bureaucracy that "administered the ever-growing body of decrees and juridical directives, which both legitimized the administrative machinery and laid down its course of action" (Glade, 1969, p. 58). Every detail of the economy as well as the polity was structured with the objective of furthering the interests of the crown in the creation of the most powerful empire since Rome. But with the revolt of the Netherlands and the decline in the inflow of New World treasure, the fiscal demands far outstripped revenue, and the result was bankruptcy, increased internal taxation, confiscations, and insecure property rights.

The Organizational Implications

In England, Parliament created the Bank of England and a fiscal system in which expenditures were tied to tax revenues. The consequent financial revolution not only finally put the government on a sound financial basis, but laid the ground for the development of the private capital market. More secure property rights, the decline of mercantilist restrictions, and the escape of textile firms from urban guild restrictions combined to provide expanding opportunities for firms in domestic and international markets. Both the growing markets and the patent law encouraged the growth of innovative activity. But all this and much more is a familiar story.

In Spain, repeated bankruptcies between 1557 and 1647 were coupled with desperate measures to stave off disaster. War, the church, and administering the complex bureaucratic system provided the major organizational opportunities in Spain and in consequence the military, priesthood, and the judiciary were rewarding occupations. The expulsion of the Moors and Jews, rent ceilings on land and price ceilings on wheat, confiscations of silver remittances to merchants in Seville (who were compensated with relatively worthless bonds called *juros*) were symptomatic of the disincentives to productive activity.

Path Dependence

To make the contrasting brief stories convincing illustrations of path dependence would entail an account of the political, economic, and judicial systems of each society as a web of interconnected formal rules and informal constraints that together made up the institutional matrix and led the economies down different paths. It would be necessary to demonstrate the network externalities that limited the actors' choices and prevented them from radically altering the institutional framework. Such an undertaking is far beyond the kinds of existing empirical evidence with which I am familiar. I can only indirectly infer such implications from the evidence.

In a controversial study, *The Origins of English Individualism* (1978), Alan Macfarlane maintains that at least from the thirteenth century the English were different than the traditional picture we possess of peasant societies. The traditional characteristics—patriarchal domination, extended family, low status of women, tight knit and closed peasant villages, self-sufficiency, and the family as the work unit—all were conspicuously absent by the thirteenth century. Instead, Macfarlane paints a picture of a fluid, individualistically oriented set of attitudes involving the structure of the family, the organization of work, and the social relationships of the village community complemented by an array of formal rules dealing with property, inheritance, and the legal status of women. Macfarlane wants to make the point that England was different and that the difference went way back in time, but in doing so he amasses evidence to make clear the complex interdependent network of formal and informal constraints that made for the increasing returns characteristic of path dependence.

The most telling evidence of the increasing returns feature of the Spanish institutional fabric was the inability of the crown and its bureaucracy to alter the direction of the Spanish path in spite of their awareness of the decay and decline overcoming the country. In a century—the seventeenth—Spain declined from the most powerful nation in the Western world since the Roman empire to a second-rate power. The depopulation of the countryside, the stagnation of industry, and the collapse of Seville's trading system with the New World were paralleled in the political realm by the revolt of Catalonia and Portugal. The proximate cause was recurrent war and a fiscal crisis that led Olivares (1621 to 1640) to pursue the desperate measures that only exacerbated the fundamental problems. Indeed, the policies that were considered feasible in the context of the institutional constraints and perceptions of the actors were price controls, tax increases, and repeated confiscations. As for the perceptions of the actors,

Jan De Vries in his study (1976) of Europe in the age of crisis describes the effort to reverse the decline as follows:

> But this was not a society unaware of what was happening. A whole school of economic reformers... wrote mountains of tracts pleading for new measures.... Indeed, in 1623 a *Junta de Reformacion* recommended to the new King, Philip IV, a series of measures including taxes to encourage earlier marriage (and, hence, population growth), limitations on the number of servants, the establishment of a bank, prohibitions on the import of luxuries, the closing of brothels, and the prohibition of the teaching of Latin in small towns (to reduce the flight from agriculture of peasants who had acquired a smattering of education). But no willpower could be found to follow through on these recommendations.... It is said that the only accomplishment of the reform movement was the abolition of the ruff collar, a fashion which had imposed ruinous laundry bills on the aristocracy. (De Vries, 1976, p. 28)

It appears doubtful that instrumental rationality could be applied to the reasoning of the Junta.

Both England and Spain faced fiscal crises in the seventeenth century, but the contrasting paths that they took appear to have reflected deep underlying institutional characteristics of the societies.

The Downstream Consequences

U.S. economic history has been characterized by a federal political system, checks and balances, and a basic structure of property rights that have encouraged the long-term contracting essential to the creation of capital markets and economic growth. Even one of the most costly civil wars in all of history failed to alter the basic institutional matrix.

Latin American economic history, in contrast, has perpetuated the centralized, bureaucratic traditions carried over from its Spanish/Portuguese heritage. Here is John Coatsworth's characterization of the institutional environment of nineteenth-century Mexico:

> The interventionist and pervasively arbitrary nature of the institutional environment forced every enterprise, urban or rural, to operate in a highly politicized manner, using kinship networks, political influence, and family prestige to gain privileged access to subsidized credit, to aid various strategems for recruiting labor, to collect debts or enforce contracts, to evade taxes or circumvent the courts, and to defend or assert titles to lands. Success or failure in the economic arena always depended on the relationship of the producer with political authorities—local officials for arranging matters close at hand and the central government of the colony for sympathetic interpretations of the law and intervention at the local level when conditions required it. Small enterprise, excluded from the system of corporate privilege and political favors, was forced to operate in a permanent state of semiclandestiny, always at the margin of the law, at the mercy of petty officials, never secure from arbitrary acts and never protected against the rights of those more powerful. (Coatsworth, 1978, p. 94)

The divergent paths established by England and Spain in the New World have not converged despite the mediating factors of common ideological influences. In the former, an institutional framework has evolved that permits the complex impersonal exchange necessary to political stability and to capture the potential economic gains of modern technology. In the latter, personalistic relationships are still the key to much of the political and economic exchange. They are a consequence of an evolving institutional framework that produces neither political stability nor consistent realization of the potential of modern technology.

12.4 JOHN R. COMMONS

Property, Liberty and Value

John R. Commons (1862–1945) was born in Hollandsburg, Ohio. He was an architect of New Deal legislation and was considered the leading authority on labor during the early twentieth century. Commons studied at Oberlin College and Johns Hopkins University and held faculty positions at Wesleyan University, Oberlin College, Syracuse University, and the University of Wisconsin. He successfully divided his time between teaching and service on numerous government commissions responsible for drafting reform legislation to regulate public utilities and resolve labor disputes. A prolific author, Commons is best known for *History of Labor in the United States, Institutional Economics: Its Place in Political Economy* (Macmillan, 1934), and *Legal Foundations of Capitalism* (University of Wisconsin Press, 1957), from which the following selection has been taken.

Commons viewed the individual as the basic unit of society. He believed that other groups, including social institutions, the government, and industry, act as vehicles for the advancement of individual freedom and the fulfillment of individual expectations. Given that there is a fundamental imbalance of power in such relationships, with external forces dominating the individual, power must be effectively channelled through the adoption of public procedures and the establishment of rules that limit the exercise of power. In the following selection, Commons distinguishes between use-value and exchange-value, citing historical court cases to justify the transition from use-value to exchange-value.

Key Concept: the transition in the meaning of property from use-value to exchange-value

USE-VALUE AND EXCHANGE-VALUE

In the year 1872 the Supreme Court of the United States was called upon, in the Slaughter House Cases, to interpret the meanings of the words Property and Liberty as used in the Constitution of the United States. The Thirteenth Amendment to the Federal Constitution, adopted in 1865, prohibited slavery and involuntary servitude except as punishment for crime, and the Fourteenth Amendment, adopted three years later, prohibited a state from depriving any person of "life, liberty, or property" without "due process of law," and gave to the federal courts jurisdiction. The legislature of Louisiana had granted to a corporation a monopoly to maintain slaughtering places for stock in the city of New Orleans, and had regulated the charges to be made to other butchers who used these facilities. The latter, through their attorneys, contended that the statute deprived them of both their property and their liberty without due process of law. The Supreme Court divided. If the court should hold that property meant exchange-value, then the federal court would take jurisdiction under the Amendments. But if property meant only the use-value of physical things, then the court would not interfere with the legislature of Louisiana. Justice Miller, for the majority, declared that the act was not a deprivation of property or liberty as the terms were used in the Thirteenth and Fourteenth Amendments. The term "liberty," he said, should be construed with reference to the well-known purpose of those Amendments, namely, to establish freedom from slavery or personal servitude. Even conceding that the term "liberty," as popularly used, might mean "civil liberty" or the right to buy and sell, yet that aspect of liberty was not included in the meaning of the term as used in the Amendments. Prior to the adoption of these amendments the liberty of citizens, whether personal, civil or economic, was, for the most part, in the keeping of the states. The Thirteenth and Fourteenth Amendments only transferred from the states to the federal government the protection of such fraction of the total concept of liberty as was comprehended in freedom from personal slavery. All other aspects of liberty were left, as they had been, to the keeping of the states. And as to the meaning of the term "property," as used in the Fourteenth Amendment, he held that the term retained its common-law meaning of physical things held exclusively for one's own use. Property, according to the Fourteenth Amendment meant use-value, not exchange-value. "Under no construction of that provision that we have ever seen," he said, "can the restraint imposed by the state of Louisiana upon the exercise of their trade by the butchers of New Orleans be held to be a deprivation of property within the meaning of that provision." The state of Louisiana had not deprived the butchers of the use-value of their property—it had deprived them of its exchange-value.

The minority of the court, however, contended that the police power (which they admitted, of course, might justly deprive a person of liberty or property for public purposes without compensation), could have been exercised in this case without resorting to a monopoly, by merely regulating all of the butchers alike in the interest of public health, but that the monopoly feature of the law deprived the other butchers of their liberty and property and turned it over to the monopolist. They then went on to define the property and liberty which was thus unjustly taken away, not by a proper exercise of the police power, but by a special privilege granted to the slaughter-house monopolist. A man's "calling," his "occupation," his "trade," his "labor," was property, as well as the physical things, which he might own; and "liberty" included his "right of choice," his right to choose a calling, to choose an occupation or trade, to choose the direction in which he would exercise his labor. Justice Bradley, of the minority, for example, declared that the "right to choose one's calling is an essential part of that liberty which it is the object of government to protect; and a calling, when chosen, is a man's property and right.... Their right of choice is a portion of their liberty; their occupation is their property." (116, 122.) Justice Field, also of the minority, desired to change the meaning of "slavery" from physical coercion to economic coercion. He said, "A person allowed to pursue only one trade or calling, and only in one locality of the country, would not be, in the strict sense of the term, in a condition of slavery, but probably none would deny that he would be in a condition of servitude.... The compulsion which would force him to labor even for his own benefit only in one direction, or in one place, would be almost as oppressive and nearly as great an invasion of his liberty as the compulsion which would force him to labor for the benefit or pleasure of another, and would equally constitute an element of servitude." (90.) Thus Justice Field described slavery as physical coercion and servitude as economic coercion. And Justice Swayne declared, "Property is everything which has exchangeable value, and the right of property includes the power to dispose of it according to the will of the owner. Labor is property, and as such merits protection. The right to make it available is next in importance to the rights of life and liberty." (127.) Thus Justice Swayne defined property as the exchange-value of one's ability to work, and liberty as the right to realize that exchange-value on the labor market.

These minority definitions of liberty and property as exchange-value were unavailing in the Slaughter House Cases. The majority held to the older meaning of use-value. Twelve years later the municipal authorities of New Orleans, acting under a new constitution for the state, granted to another company privileges in conflict with those of the original monopolist, thus infringing upon their exclusive right. This time, therefore, the Slaughter House company was plaintiff against the municipality. The majority of the court now retained its original definition of property and liberty, but now held that not only the original act, as they had contended before, but also this annulling act were a proper exercise of the police power. But Justices Bradley and Field, while concurring in the court's decision, placed it on the grounds of their dissenting opinions in the original Slaughter House Cases, and repeated their earlier views that the original act was itself an unlawful deprivation of liberty and property. In their earlier dissent the minority had not cited any cases where the term property had been used in the sense of a trade, occupation, calling, or one's labor, whose value to the owner is in its exchange-value, though they asserted that it *ought* to have that meaning. Thus, in the constitutional sense of the term, they had not been able to controvert Justice Miller's denial that that meaning had ever been given to it. In the later case, however, they suggested the origin of their new definition. Justice Field now stated that this meaning of property was derived from Adam Smith who had said: "The property which every man has in his own labor, as it is the original foundation of all other property, so it is the most sacred and inviolable." And Justice Bradley contented himself with saying, "If a man's right to his calling is property, *as many maintain,* then those who had already adopted the prohibited pursuits in New Orleans, were deprived, by the law in question, of their property, as well as their liberty, without due process of law." Thus the new meanings of property and liberty were found in Adam Smith and the customs of business, and not in the Constitution of the United States.

After the Slaughter House Cases the minority definitions of property and liberty began to creep into the constitutional definitions given by state and federal courts, as indeed was inevitable and proper if the thing itself was thus changing. Finally, in the first Minnesota Rate Case, in 1890 the Supreme Court itself made the transition and changed the definition of property from physical things having only use-value to the exchange-value of anything.

This decision was a partial reversal of the decision of the court in the case of Munn *v.* Illinois in 1876. In the Munn Case the Supreme Court had held, agreeably to its holding in the Slaughter House Cases, that when a state legislature reduced the prices which a warehouse company charged for the use of its services the resulting reduction in exchange-value of the business was not a deprivation of property in the sense in which the word was used in the Fourteenth Amendment and therefore was not an act which the federal courts might restrain. It was only a regulation of the "use and enjoyment" of property under the police power of the state. The court went so far as to declare that, if the legislature abused its power, "the people must resort to the polls, not to the courts."

That the state legislatures might possibly abuse their power had been clearly suggested in the decision of the Supreme Court of Illinois in sustaining the act of the Illinois legislature, when the Munn Case was before that court. The Illinois court had held that the authority was not abused in that case by the Illinois legislature, since the property of the owner was not "taken" from him, in that he was not deprived of the "title and possession" of the property. In this respect the Illinois court adhered to the primitive definition of property as the mere holding of physical objects for one's own use and enjoyment. The legislature, under the police power of the state, might reduce the charges which a warehouse company had established for its services, but that was not "taking" their property. The owners continued to hold their physical property even though deprived of the power to fix the prices for its use. To this Justice Field had rightly answered, "There is indeed no protection of any value under the constitutional provision which does not extend to the use and income of the property, as well as to its title and possession." For, of course, the title of ownership or the possession of physical property is empty as a business asset if the owner is deprived of his liberty to fix a price on the sale of the product of that property.

But Justice Field in the Munn Case had gone too far. He denied the authority of *both* the legislature *and* the courts to fix the compensation. The majority had only denied the authority of the court to fix it. Fourteen years after Munn *v.* Illinois this further issue came up in the Minnesota Rate Case, and the petitioners for the railroads asked the court to review the decision in the Munn and similar cases and to restrain the state legislature from fixing finally the prices charged for the use of property. (445.) The court now acceded, and Justice Blatchford, for the majority, wrote, "This power to regulate [police power] is not a power to destroy, and limitation is not the equivalent of confiscation." (456.) And confiscation, or the reasonableness of a rate, "is eminently a question for judicial investigation, requiring due process of law for its determination." (458.) Thus Justice Field's definition of property as the exchange-value of property was approved and, therefore, the protection of that property was brought under the jurisdiction of the federal courts conformably to the Fourteenth Amendment.

But Justice Bradley, who in the Slaughter House Cases had agreed with Justice Field, now again dissented (supported by two other justices) and held that the majority opinion asserted an "assumption of authority on the part of the judiciary which... it has no right to make." (418, 463.) "If not in terms, yet in effect," he said, "the present cases are treated as if the constitutional prohibition was, that no state shall take private property for public use without just compensation—and as if it was our duty to judge of the compensation. But there is no such clause in the Constitution of the United States." (465.) "There was," he said, "in truth, no deprivation of property in these cases at all. There was merely a regulation as to the enjoyment of property, made by a strictly competent authority, in a matter entirely within its jurisdiction." (466.) In this respect he, like the Illinois court in the Munn Case, continued to adhere to the primitive definition of property as the mere exclusive holding of objects for one's own use, a kind of property that is not taken from the owner unless he is deprived of its title and possession, for which he is entitled to just compensation.

The majority, however, now held, as they had not held in the Munn Case, that not merely physical things are objects of property, but the *expected earning power* of those things is property; and property is taken from the owner, not merely under the power of *eminent domain* which takes *title* and *possession*, but also under the police power which takes its *exchange-value.* To deprive the owners of the *exchange-value* of their property is equivalent to depriving them of their property. Hence, differently from the Munn Case decision, they now held that, under the Fourteenth Amendment, it is the province of the court and not the legislature, to determine the extent to which that "taking" of the value of property might go and yet not pass beyond the point of confiscation. They thus extended to the exercise of the police power the judicial authority to ascertain just compensation which the judiciary had exercised over the power of eminent domain.

Thus the transition in the definition of property from physical objects to exchange-value was completed. "Title and possession" of physical property could be taken from its owner for public purposes under the power of eminent domain, but only on condition that equivalent value should be paid, such that the owners' assets should not be reduced; and this equivalent value, or just compensation, is a judicial question. Now it is enlarged to read: The exchange-value of property may be taken from its owners under the police power, but only to the extent that they retain sufficient bargaining power to maintain the same exchange-value that they had, and this also is a judicial question. The definition of property is changed from physical things to the exchange-value of anything, and the federal courts now take jurisdiction.

Evidently, however, the exchange-value of property has no existence if either the owner or expected purchasers are forbidden access to markets where they can sell and buy the property. Hence liberty of access to markets is essential to the definition of exchange-value. This attribute was finally added seven years after the Minnesota Rate Case, in the Allgeyer Case, and the minority definition of liberty in 1872 became the unanimous definition of liberty in 1897. The court now said: "The liberty mentioned in that Amendment [Fourteenth] means not only the right of the citizen to be free from physical restraint of his person, but the term is deemed to embrace the right of the citizen to be free in the enjoyment of all his faculties; to be free to use them in all lawful ways; to live and work where he will; to earn his livelihood by any lawful calling; to pursue any livelihood or avocation, and for that purpose to enter into all contracts which may be proper, necessary, and essential to his carrying out to a successful conclusion the purposes above mentioned.... His enjoyment upon terms of equality with all others in similar circumstances of the privilege of pursuing an ordinary calling or trade, and of acquiring, holding, and selling property is an essential part of liberty and property as guaranteed by the Fourteenth Amendment."

Furthermore, while liberty of access to markets on the part of an owner is essential to the exchange-value of property, too much liberty of access on the part of would-be competitors is destructive of that exchange-value. During the past three hundred years this excessive liberty has been restrained by the courts in the long line of cases going under the name of "goodwill" or "unfair competition." Evidently, these decisions of the courts had been designed to protect the exchange-value of property, and now that the definition of property itself had been changed from physical things to the exchange-value of anything, it was an easy step to change the definition of goodwill from "fair competition" to "property." The long-recognized goodwill of a business which had always possessed exchange-value, but which was merely the expected beneficial behavior of other people, now became simply a special case of property. Other courts followed, and the transition from the meaning of property as physical things to that of the most ethereal invisibility was reached in 1902 in a case involving the right to exclusive telephonic communication of news to the daily press by mere word of mouth. The lower court then said, "Property... is not, in its modern sense, confined to that which may be touched by the hand, or seen by the eye. What is called tangible property has come to be, in most great enterprises, but the embodiment, physically, of an underlying life—a life that, in its contribution to success, is immeasurably more effective than the mere physical embodiment." And, in 1911, by another lower court, Justice Swayne's definition in 1872 of labor as property became "the right to labor in any calling or profession in the future."

The foregoing cases, it will be noted, have turned on a double meaning of property, and the transition is from one of the meanings to both of the meanings. Property, in the popular ordinary usage, the usage of the old common law and the one adhered to in the Slaughter House Cases and the Munn Case, meant any tangible thing owned. Property, in the later decisions, means any of the expected activities implied with regard to the thing owned, comprehended in the activities of acquiring, using and disposing of the thing. One is Property, the other is Business. The one is property in the sense of Things owned, the other is property in the sense of exchange-value of things. One is physical objects, the other is marketable assets.

Thus it is that "corporeal property," in the original meaning of the term, has disappeared, or, rather, has been relegated to what may be described as the internal "economy" of a going concern or a household in the various processes of producing and consuming physical objects, according to what the economists call their "use-value." And, instead of the use-value of corporeal property, the courts are concerned with its exchange-value. This exchange-value is not corporeal—it is behavioristic. It is the market-value expected to be obtained in exchange for the thing in any of the markets where the thing can or might be sold. In the course of time this exchange-value has come to be known as "intangible property," that is, the kind of property whose value depends upon right of access to a commodity market, a labor market, a money market, and so on. Consequently, in conformity with the customs and usages of business, there are only two kinds of property, both of them invisible and behavioristic, since their value depends on expected activities on the commodity and money markets. One of these may technically be distinguished as "incorporeal property," consisting of debts, credits, bonds, mortgages, in short, of promises to pay; the other may be distinguished as "intangible property" consisting of the exchange-value of anything whether corporeal property or incorporeal property or even intangible property. The short name for intangible property is *assets.* Assets is the expected exchange-value of anything, whether it be one's reputation, one's horse, house or land, one's ability to work, one's goodwill, patent right, good credit, stocks, bonds or bank deposit, in short, intangible property is anything that enables one to obtain from others an income in the process of buying and selling, borrowing and lending, hiring and hiring out, renting and leasing, in any of the transactions of modern business. We shall identify these two classes of property as "encumbrances" and "opportunities." Encumbrances are incorporeal property, that is, promises to pay, enforced by government; opportunities are intangible property, that is, accessibility to markets, also enforced by government.

Going back, therefore, to the common-law meaning of property as physical things held for the owner's use, we find that what property really signified, even in that original sense, was not the physical thing itself but the expected "uses" of the thing, that is, various activities regarding the thing. These uses, or activities, arose from the producing and consuming power of a person in control of, or working with, the thing. The legal terms carry this futuristic, behavioristic meaning. The legal term "use," is said to have been derived from the Latin *opus,* meaning work or working, through the Anglo-French *oeps* and the Old French *oes.* It means the work a person can do with a thing, his behavior respecting the thing. Thus it differs from the economic term, "utility," which is derived from the latin *usus,* through the French *utilité,* and means the satisfaction a person gets in using a thing. Use is behavior. Utility is feeling. The early feudal grants of land to tenants were granted *ad opus*—that is, "to the use" of the tenant in production and consumption. Then when property began to yield exchange-value as well as use-value, the term "uses" was simply enlarged by the courts to include it. It now means both the expected use-values of production and consumption and the expected exchange-values of selling and buying.

The difference is unimportant in the law of private property. In fact, the term "uses" has a social meaning and a business meaning. Socially it means what we understand by producing and consuming things; that is, increasing the supply and enjoyment of things. But in the business sense it means also acquiring and disposing of the thing in transactions with other people. This explains the easy transition from the common-law meaning of property as physical things, valuable to owners on account of the expected physical uses of production and consumption, to the business-law meaning of property as *assets,* valuable to owners on account of their expected bargaining uses as purchasing power in buying and selling.

The common-law and popular notion of property as physical things is, therefore, but an elliptical statement of what common-sense can take for granted without the pedantry of explaining every time that what is meant by property is the *uses* and not the thing. The trouble is that, by using this common-sense notion of uses, not only the courts and business men, but also theoretical economists, pass over from the significance of "uses" in the sense of producing an increase in the supply of goods, to its exact opposite meaning in the business sense of an increase in the power of owners to command goods from other persons in exchange. The one is *producing power* which *increases* the supply of goods in order to increase the quantity of use-values; the other is *bargaining power* which *restricts* the supply of goods in proportion to demand, in order to increase or maintain their exchange-value. Bargaining power is the willful *restriction* of supply in proportion to demand in order to maintain or enlarge the value of business assets; but producing power is the willing *increase* of supply in order to enlarge the wealth of nations.

Hence the transition in the meaning of property from the use-value to the exchange-value of things, and therefore from the producing power that increases use-values to the bargaining power that increases exchange-values, is more than a transition—it is a reversal. The reversal was not at first important when business was small and weak—it becomes important when Capitalism rules the world.

The transition in meanings of property and liberty applies to agriculture as well as manufacturers, commerce and transportation, and to individuals, partnerships and associations as well as corporations. Farming has become a going-business, or a bankrupt business, like other businesses. The isolated, colonial, or frontier farmer might produce and consume things, attentive only to their use-value, but the modern farmer lives by producing "social-use-values" and buying other social-use-values produced and sold by other business men. In this way he also "produces" exchange-value, that is, assets. He farms for sale, not for use, and while he has the doubtful alternative of falling back on his own natural resources if he cannot sell his products, yet his farm and crops are valuable because they are business assets, that is, exchange-values, while his liabilities are his debts and his taxes, all of them measured by his expectations and realizations on the commodity markets and money markets, in terms of exchange-value or price.

This, we take it, is the substance of Capitalism distinguished from the Feudalism or Colonialism which it displaced—production for the use of others and acquisition for the use of self, such that the meaning of property and liberty spreads out from the expected uses of production and consumption to expected transactions on the markets where one's assets and liabilities are determined by the ups and downs of prices. And this is, in substance, the change in the meanings of Property and Liberty, from the Slaughter House Cases in 1872 to the Allgeyer Case in 1897, a change from the use-value of physical things to the exchange-values of anything.

12.5 SIMON KUZNETS

Driving Forces of Economic Growth

Simon Kuznets (1901–1985) was a native of Kharkov, Russia. He emigrated to the United States in 1922 and entered Columbia University, obtaining his bachelor's degree in 1923, his master's degree in 1924, and his doctorate in 1926. A faculty member of the University of Pennsylvania for 24 years, Kuznets also held academic positions at Johns Hopkins University for 6 years and Harvard University for 11 years. In 1971, he was awarded the Nobel Prize in economics for his pioneering work on national income measurements.

In *National Income and Its Composition, 1919–1938* (National Bureau of Economic Research, 1941), Kuznets developed a method by which countries could measure their gross national product (GNP). He devised techniques to sum expenditures by different classes of purchases over different classes of goods, thereby providing the foundation for statistical studies of the relationships between income, consumption, and investment. Decades of work on national income accounts made Kuznets aware of the limitations of gross domestic product (GDP) as a measure of national economic performance and growth. He rejected it as the sole indicator of performance as it ignores working conditions and nonmarket activities. Kuznets discovered long growth cycles, with a life of 20 years, and demonstrated that they were influenced by variations in the rate of population growth. The aggregate propensity to save had remained stable in most industrial economies in the long run. He found that in the short run, however, the propensity to save depended upon cyclical fluctuations. The quantity of real capital continued to decline in proportion to the growth of production. In *Economic Development, the Family, and Income Distribution: Selected Essays* (Cambridge University Press, 1989), from which the following is excerpted, Kuznets explores the driving forces of economic growth from a historical perspective. He makes the startling discovery that the rate of rise in per capita incomes in the developed countries was higher in the period preceding their entry into modern economic growth.

Key Concept: driving forces of economic growth

I. INTRODUCTION

In defining the scope of this paper, we had to answer several questions. First, if one necessarily deals with a limited period in the long history of mankind from the hunting-gathering tribes to the industrial societies of 1980, what should the reference period be? Second, in reflecting on economic growth, what classes and groups of societies, in the wide range of units among which mankind is divided, should we emphasize? Third, while we cannot pursue quantitative analysis here, we should be clear as to the quantitative and related criteria of economic growth. Different criteria will result in focusing our attention on different aspects of economic growth, and on different groups of driving forces. Finally, how do we deal with "driving forces," a concept for which it is difficult to establish *ex ante* empirically observable counterparts?

However carefully considered, the answers to these questions were bound to leave us with a theme so wide as to warrant only selected reflections, rather than tested and documented conclusions. We reflect on the historical record of the last two centuries, viewing it as a distinct epoch of economic growth. Yet the period is too short, in excluding important antecedents in the earlier history, particularly of what are now economically developed countries; and too long, in encompassing changes in growth trends that cannot be adequately noted here. We emphasize the record of the currently developed countries, especially of the earlier entrants, all of which were market economies; and hence neglect the totalitarian developed countries, with their distinctive mechanism and drives. We gauge economic growth by the long-term rise in the volume and diversity of final goods, per capita, with some attention to sectoral structure and shifts; but exclude cases where such rise was due largely to natural resources made valuable by advanced technology elsewhere, or was attained in good part by intensified efforts of workers mobilized to involve a rising proportion of the population. Finally, we comment on selected aspects of the ways by which economic growth had been attained for the range of developed market economies just indicated, in the hope that they will at least suggest the identity and characteristics of the driving forces. The relevance of the latter to economic growth, or lack of it, in countries excluded from direct discussion here, may then be considered; but this cannot be done within the limits of this paper.

The records of growth of the currently developed market economies indicate that, despite a substantial rise in the growth rate of their population, the rate of rise in per capita income was substantially higher than in the centuries preceding their entry into modern economic growth—the entry occurring over the historical span from the last quarter of the 18th century to the recent decades. This acceleration of economic growth was associated with a number of other economic and social processes; and we select a few that seem illuminating of the driving forces involved. The impression which suggests the first topic is that modern economic growth, as exemplified by the group of countries defined above, was accompanied by, and based upon, a high rate of accumulation of useful knowledge and of technological innovations derived from it. The second important associated process was that of shifts in the production structure of the economy, in the shares of different production sectors in output, labor, and capital, with a close relation between the high rate of growth of per capita product and a high rate of shift among the various production sectors. The third major strand in the unfolding of modern economic growth was the complex of functions and influences associated with the national sovereign state.

II. TECHNOLOGICAL INNOVATIONS AND CAPITAL FORMATION

By a technological innovation we mean a new way of producing old goods, or a necessarily original way of producing new goods. Since we deal here with technological innovations that have materialized, the results of unsuccessful attempts having long vanished, we assume that the new ways, the new methods of production, were better than the old, and thus should have contributed to growing productivity, and hence to economic growth. Note that technology here is confined to control over nature (including man only in his physiological, not social aspects) for human purposes, economic purposes among them; hence the association between technological innovation and rising productivity. In the present connection, the high rate of technological innovations and their large cumulative impact on economic growth is reflected in the known succession of major innovations in a variety of fields; in the pervasiveness of new technology in extending to even the oldest production sectors (like agriculture); and in the large proportion of new goods, and of old goods produced by new methods, in the total product of developed countries.

We emphasize major technological innovations, major in that they affect large components of final consumption and of intermediate demand for reproducible capital, and thus contribute substantially to growth of product and productivity. A familiar illustration is provided by the innovations in the production of light and washable fabrics like cotton cloth, of a new industrial material like iron and eventually steel, and of a new source of industrial power like steam, the three major innovations of the "first" industrial revolution; and more illustrations could be easily provided. This emphasis focuses our attention on the long periods over which the unfolding of such innovations takes place, from the pioneering demonstrations of their technical feasibility and of their great potential as a framework for a host of subsidiary innovations and improvements; to the complementary changes that are called for in the institutional structure of the economic enterprises and in conditions of work and life of the actively engaged workers, to channel the innovation into efficient uses; to the retardation phase that follows maturity of the given innovation in the pioneer country, once its lesser potential for further cost reduction, lower price elasticity of demand, and the competitive pressures of either emerging foreign followers or of more recent innovations, make for slower growth and lessened impact on the country's advance in product per worker. These long sequences of interplay between the growth-promoting effects of the extending application of a major technological innovation, with increasingly effective institutional and human response, and the eventual exhaustion of these effects because of both internal and external pressures, represent slices of a long and complex growth process. They should be illuminating and suggestive of both the driving forces of economic growth and of those that limit the latter, when confined to one sector of a country's economy, or even to one country, as compared with others.

The key feature of an innovation is that it is *new*—and thus a peculiar combination of new *knowledge* sufficiently useful and promising to warrant the attempt to apply it; and of *ignorance* of the full range of possibilities and improvements that can be learned only in extended application. A major invention is a crude framework, major in the sense that it is a new base to which a wide variety of subinventions and improvements can be applied—but that are yet unknown, and rarely foreseen. Clearly, one of the requirements of a high rate of technological innovation is a society (or a related group of them) that encourages the continuous production of a variety of new knowledge relevant, directly or indirectly, to problems of economic production; that contains an entrepreneurial group perceptive of such new knowledge, and capable of venturing attempts to apply it on a scale sufficient to reveal its potentials; and a capacity to generate, without costly breakdowns, institutional changes and group adjustments that may be needed to channel efficiently the new technology—with its distinctive constraints. The driving forces or permissive factors are those involved in man's search for new knowledge of nature and of the universe within which we live, including the inventive links between it and production; and the capacity of societies both to encourage technological innovations, and to accommodate them, despite the disruptive unevenness of their impact on different social groups.

The major role of rapidly advancing observational and experimental science, i.e., systematic study of the universe, in creating increasing opportunities for invention and technological innovation, is a distinctive characteristic of modern economic growth, and is directly relevant here. Whatever science discovers about the properties of the physical world is of possible application in technology, which deals with rearrangement of the physical world for human ends. Hence, the advance in the stock of useful knowledge contributes to an explanation of the continuous *succession* of major innovations and of the rising power of technology. The aspect of most interest here is the reinforcing relation between technological innovation and additions to useful knowledge, observational and experimental science among it. Once technological innovations embody new, yet incomplete knowledge, they imply an important learning process, dispelling ignorance of hitherto unknown, yet relevant, aspects of nature. This adds to the data and puzzles of science and thus stimulates further observation and search. In addition, mass application of major inventions may generate new observational tools hitherto not available for scientific use. And, of course, the addition to economic resources made by a successful innovation may provide the wherewithal and stimulus for the search for further useful knowledge. One should stress that the contribution of a technological innovation to *learning* is most directly a function of the "ignorance" component: were the innovation based on complete knowledge of the process or material in question, no learning would have occurred and the contribution to new knowledge would have been limited to effects of cost reduction and of greater potential availability of economic resources.

A notable aspect of technological innovations associated with modern economic growth was the large volume of fixed, reproducible capital required. The demand for the latter, revealed by the capital intensity of the production of new types of industrial power and of the use of this power in the mechanization of a wide variety of formerly labor-intensive processes, was due to distinctive features of the new technology. To illustrate, if steam expansion could deliver large charges of concentrated power, with a reliability, economy, and flexibility of location hitherto unknown, the very large magnitude of physical power made available required a durable and costly envelope for controlling and channeling this power into beneficial rather than destructive uses. Also, the application of stationary steam engines to say manufacturing operations required tools of a material that could withstand continuity and high velocity of turn, again a new industrial material with a high capital intensity of output. What was true of stationary steam power was even more applicable to its use in land transport—with large fixed capital embodied not only in rolling stock but also in the roadbeds and associated facilities. But large amounts of fixed capital meant a large scale of plant and economic enterprise, with increasing economies of scale continuously pushing upwards the optimum scale involved. There was thus a direct line of connection between the greater productivity available in the new technology, the greater volume of physical nonhuman power that the latter employed in the mechanization of a variety of productive processes, the increasing demand for fixed capital that embodied and controlled the new power, and the rising scale of plant and of the economic firm unit. Somewhat different, yet essentially similar connections between the technological features of the new and changing technology, and economic implications in the way of demand for fixed reproducible capital and scale of plant and enterprise, can be suggested for more recent clusters of technological innovations, e.g., those associated with electric power or with the internal combustion engine.

The large demand for fixed capital exercised a restraining influence on the rate of application of new technology, alongside with the limited supply of technological talent capable of exploiting the potential of major inventions through the generation of subinventions and improvements, and with scarcity of entrepreneurial talent capable of innovative organizational tasks in the mobilization of capital, labor skills, and administrative capacity. These several constraints serve to explain why over given intervals of economic growth, long enough to reveal the extent of the latter but short enough to permit observing secular changes, major technological innovations were limited to a few sectors in the economy—the identity of which changed from one period to the next. This concentration on foci of growth did not mean absence of technological advance elsewhere in the economy: it only meant a higher growth rate in the favored industries and sectors and a lower growth rate, but still increasing productivity, in the preponderant majority of others.

One should note here the changes in economic and social institutions that were required to respond to the capital demands and other corollaries of the distinctive features of the new technology. If large volumes of durable, reproducible capital and large-scale plants and hence firms were involved, new devices for mobilizing savings and of channeling them into the new uses, and legal innovations for the proper organization of investors, entrepreneurs, and workers in effective economic enterprise were called for. There was, consequently, a connection between say the emergence of steam railroads, on the one hand, and major changes in financial institutions engaged in mobilization and channeling of savings and the emergence of the modern corporation as the increasingly dominant form of organization of private economic enterprise, on the other hand. Furthermore, if the fixed capital structure of private enterprise in some sectors resulted in a kind of competition that ended up in monopoly and in spreading of the latter to other sectors, new forms of government intervention had to be devised to mitigate the undesirable effects of such a development. Thus, the unfolding of major technological innovations or of clusters of them, with their large demand for fixed capital and associated changes in size, structure, and behavior of plants and enterprises, involved a sequence of technological and institutional changes. The latter responded to the former, as an effective way of channeling the innovations; but also generated trends of their own, some of which may have facilitated and others may have impeded further growth in product per capita or per worker.

This brings us to another related aspect of major technological innovations, the unpredictability of their long-term consequences. It applies particularly to *clusters* of related innovations, many of the latter major—such clusters representing innovations in the several steps of a given industry's production process from the raw material to the finished product, or the several innovations that emerge from the widening application of a new industrial material or of a new source of industrial power. It is these clusters that are important, because a technical breakthrough in one step of a production process or in one use of a new source of power is bound to stimulate related innovations in the sequence or in the range. But when we consider the long-term cumulative consequences of the unfolding of such a cluster, we find a long, interrelated chain of changes in technology and changes in institutional and social adjustments, spread over decades and occurring in a complex and changing national and international environment. It is difficult to assume that anyone at the end of the 18th century could have predicted the magnitude and character of the contributions of steam power to economic growth and structure of the advanced economies in the 19th century; or that anyone at the end of the 19th century could have foreseen the contribution, the widespread positive, and some problematical, effects of the internal combustion engine. This is not to deny the descriptive prescience of some early advocates of the great merits of science, and of science-fiction writers of the 19th and 20th centuries. It is only to emphasize that predictability of the more sober type, one that would yield acceptably firm expectations of direction and magnitude, was not possible, because the chain of connections began with a technological innovation that contained a substantial component of unknown and hence of ignorance, to be overcome only with extended application; and continued to generate a long chain of interweaving links of technological and social change in a sequence of uncertain speed and mixture of successes and temporary failures.

Given such unpredictability, the opportunity for taking steps in good time to maximize the positive contributions of a major innovation and to forestall or minimize the negative, was narrowly limited. This meant that there was little automatic about growth based on the cumulative contributions of technological innovations: the latter could generate pressures and bottlenecks, which could be resolved, but which could also mean delays and breaks in the resulting growth. A record of a high rate of sustained economic growth, powered largely by technological innovation, implies that the society has sufficient capacity to overcome either technological or institutional bottlenecks without incurring such heavy costs as to reduce the advance of net product per worker.

In the discussion so far I chose to emphasize the sustaining elements in technological innovation in their feedback relation with the advance of systematic observational and experimental knowledge; the interplay of technological change with social changes and innovations; the elements of unpredictability and hence of occurrence of bottlenecks and delays; and the pattern of exhaustion of growth opportunities within a sector or a country that once benefited from a cluster of major technological innovations. This is a selective view, and the discussion fails to touch upon a variety of important related aspects. Some of these can be listed as illustrations of unanswered questions.

The discussion above failed to deal with the possibility of a trend—from empirically derived innovations, with inventive response to pressing bottlenecks suggesting necessity as the mother of invention, to invention and innovation that were applications of new knowledge to the production of new goods where invention was the mother of what eventually became a deeply integrated necessity. The discussion also neglected the difference between the mixture of new knowledge and ignorance associated with a major innovation in a *pioneer* country, from that faced in a *follower* country, which can profit from greater knowledge attained by the pioneer but must make up for its greater backwardness in attempting to exploit the already known but still new technology. Above all, the discussion failed to deal directly with the old, and still persisting, issue of the limits imposed by scarcity of natural resources relative to the growth of world population and its needs. The issue could be posed at least in the sense that, advanced economic growth having so far been limited to not more than a quarter of world population, modern technology could afford to be generous in its use of natural resources. Such use might not be feasible with the widening spread of economic growth to rising proportions of mankind, with resulting challenges that perhaps could not be met easily. The omission of the first two topics was due largely to difficulties of summarizing diverse and incomplete evidence; while the last topic involved long-term projections, requiring venturesome assumptions concerning feasible advance of science and technology.

III. STRUCTURAL SHIFTS

The high rate of increase of product per worker or per capita, characteristic of modern economic growth, was inevitably associated with a high rate of structural shifts. These were changes in the shares of production sectors in the country's output, capital, and labor force, with implicit changes in shares of various labor-status groups among the gainfully engaged and in the conditions of their work and life; of different types of capital and forms of economic enterprise; and in the structure of the country's trade and other economic interchanges with the rest of the world. The implications of such structural shifts for the changing position of the several socioeconomic groups were particularly important, because the responses of these groups to the impacts of advancing technology shaped modern society.

The shifts in the proportions of population actively engaged in the several production sectors, the latter distinguished by different types of product, of production process, and, particularly important here, of conditions of work and hence life of the actively engaged, were due to several complexes of factors. One was the differential impact of technological innovations, which, over any limited secular period, tended to be concentrated in a few industries, old or new. Another was the differing income elasticity of domestic demand, in response to the cost-reducing effects of advancing technology in the old goods and to the availability of new goods. A third was provided by the shifts in comparative advantage in international trade in tradable goods. In the long run, technological advance was all-pervasive, affecting old as well as new sectors; so that, e.g., the decline of the share of labor force in agriculture was due to a combination of low income elasticity of domestic demand for its product, the advance of labor productivity within the sector, and the adverse shifts in comparative advantage in trade with less developed countries.

The consequences of rapid shifts in the distribution of the economically active population (and their dependents) among the several production sectors were numerous, and crucial in the transformation and modernization of developed countries. One major consequence was the discontinuity, the disjunction between the sectoral attachment of successive generations—of a magnitude that could not be accommodated by differences in rates of natural increase or by differing changes in labor force participation proportions. If, to illustrate, the share of total labor force attached to agriculture declined, over a two decade period, from 50 to 43 percent, a not unusual drop, and total labor force grew over the period by 30 percent, the result was that the agricultural labor force grew from 50 to 55.9 or less than 12 percent, while the nonagricultural labor force grew from 50 to 74.1, or over 48 percent. Such differences in growth rates of what we take to be employment opportunities in the two sectors could not be accommodated by lower rates of natural increase or by a more rapid drop in labor force participation proportions in the agricultural sector. In fact, as the rates of natural increase and labor force participation proportions declined (with the spread of lower birth rates and lower labor force participation proportions among the young and the old), they declined less among the agricultural, rural population than among the nonagricultural, urban population. Even if we assume the same growth rate of 30 percent over the two decades for the initial agricultural and nonagricultural labor force, the indicated migration of labor force between the two sectors would amount to 65.0 minus 55.9, or 9 percent of total labor force at the start of the period. But this is only part of the process: change of attachment and intergenerational migration would be amplified by the higher rate of natural increase and slower decline in labor force participation proportions among the slowly growing, more traditional sectors and occupations; a more detailed sectoring would increase the calculated migration streams; and the latter would have occurred *within* sectors, between the smaller scale, more traditional units and the larger scale, more modern firms.

Associated with this large volume of internal migration and mobility, both spatial and inter- and intrasectoral, was the rise in requirements in education and skill for the succeeding generations of workers. This trend was largely powered by the demand of advancing technology for a greater capacity on the part of the economically active population to deal with the application of new knowledge to production problems. But it was also partly a response to the increase of the migratory component within the additions to labor force supply: migrants had to be evaluated in terms of their potential capacities in the performance of their production tasks, and such evaluation had to be based on objective criteria, if only for lack of information concerning their personal "roots." Yet the shift to overt criteria of capacity to perform, away from criteria of social status and origin, was essentially due to the doubt that the status and social affiliation of the parental generation conveyed adequate assurance as to the performance capacity of the younger generation.

The decline in the importance of status and the rise in the weight of objectively tested criteria of capacity and skill of the person was, like many other modern trends, qualified by exceptions and discrimination that represented survival of earlier and more traditional views. Yet the significance of this trend, and its connection with the increasing contribution of new knowledge and technological innovation to economic growth, and with the disjunction between the sectoral attachments of the older and the younger generations, cannot be denied. It was manifested in, and strengthened by, the demographic transition, the shift from the more traditional to modern patterns of population growth. In this transition, reduction in mortality, due either to higher income levels or to scientific advance in medical arts or to both, was a crucial step, particularly in that it most affected mortality in the infant and the younger ages. It was combined, after some lag, with reduced birth rates, the latter reflecting the growing need for greater human capital investment in the younger generation. This involved the parental generation in greater input for the benefit of children, reversing the earlier traditional views of the children being for the benefit of family and older generation. This also meant that it was the younger generation that was the carrier of the new knowledge, acquired by formal education and by learning on the job—neither of which was secured from the blood-related parental generation.

One could argue that there was, partly in consequence of the trends mentioned, a deauthorization of the traditions carried by the older generation. If so, structural shifts under discussion were an important strand in the whole process of modernization, in the movement away from the premodern and hence to us traditional views—as was the case with the effects of science on traditional religion, or with the emphasis on man as the master of his destiny on traditional views concerning sources of political and social authority.

The suggested connection between new-knowledge originated technological innovations and rapid structural shifts, on the one hand, and changing views on the role of man within society, on the other, is particularly relevant because the shifts among the socioeconomic groups were not without breakdowns and conflicts. If a technological innovation rendered a major group of older handicraft firms obsolete, or if a combination of advancing labor productivity and low income elasticity of demand for products of agriculture displaced large groups of agricultural workers, the rate of impact could easily have resulted in prolonged and costly technological unemployment. If established groups, attached to large economic sectors, suffered, or foresaw, contraction in the share and role of their base in economic society, with the possibility of shift problematic and costly, they were likely to resist by using political pressure to slow down the process. If the classes that were in power in premodern society observed reduction in the economic base of their power because of the emergence of new foci of growth, the natural reaction was to resist the change, unless promised assurance of retention of some part of former power by enforceable action of accepted social authority. Historical illustrations abound of such conflicts, engendered by the unequal impact of modern economic growth on the several socioeconomic groups, and of resulting resistance by some of these groups to modernization and growth. If these conflicts were to be resolved so as to preserve a sufficient consensus for growth and change, and yet not at a cost that would retard it unduly, some resolution mechanism was needed—acceptable to, and consistent with, the modern view on man and society.

This mechanism was the national sovereign state, a form of social organization that relies on a sense of community, of belonging together, of common interest, among its individual and group members, in order to serve as overriding arbiter of intranational group conflicts; as authoritative referee among new institutional devices needed to channel advancing technology into efficient use, or to mitigate the negative effects of economic change in order to reduce resistance to growth. The secularization and strengthening of the national sovereign state played a strategic part in modern economic growth. It proved to be so far, with some qualifications, the one form of organization of society that, while discarding the status-bound discriminations of traditional authority of religious and religiously anointed royalty (and aristocracy, or castes, etc.), preserved a unity and centralization of decisions compatible with the modern view on man as the basic source of social authority. Considering that the modern state was meant to formulate and advance the short- and long-term interests of the society over which it was sovereign, its major role in setting the rules and monitoring the conditions for economic growth is hardly surprising....

There is another series of implications of the changes in conditions of work and life of the various socioeconomic groups in modern economic growth—bearing partly on comparative valuation of different types of final goods that comprise net product, partly on the distinction between intermediate and final goods in defining net product under changing conditions. These implications reveal some aspects of the driving force in economic growth, and some difficulties in measuring its full costs and benefits for guidance in generating an adequate social response.

If we think of final product as the sum of consumer outlays by individual and group consumers and of capital formation, and of the weights of physical units of these components as prices reflective of social valuation, the common finding is that weighting the final goods by initial-year prices yields greater aggregate growth than the weighting of the physical units by end-year prices. The reason for this difference, between the Paasche and Laspeyres indexes, is the negative correlation between temporal change in quantity and temporal change in price: those goods that decline in unit price relative to other prices tend to reflect greater cost-reducing effects of technological innovation—and the expected response of demand (domestic or foreign) warrants greater growth. This difference may also be expressed by saying that the earlier generation, looking *forward* to growth, values it more highly than the later generation, looking *back* at growth that has occurred. This contrast suggests one aspect of the driving force in economic growth—the tendency to value the new more highly than the old, and to treat the already established as a low cost necessity. Of course, if anything happens to affect the latter adversely, without adequate substitution, the driving pressure of the resulting bottleneck is all the greater.

The implication of changed conditions of work and life for the distinction between intermediate goods, i.e., those used to produce the final goods, and final product, results in more intricate problems. If the changed requirement for active participation in economic production is more education, should it be viewed as a capital asset—as has been argued in much of the recent literature; and if so, how does one distinguish the consumption from the capital component of educational outlay? If the requirement for modern jobs is living in urban communities, or serving as an employee rather than as a self-employed worker, should one try to estimate comparative costs of living in the countryside and in the cities, taking into account some of the positive and negative externalities in both? And how does one evaluate the net human cost (or benefit) of shifting from self-employed to employee status?

One should note that the economic accounts of even the advanced countries, from which we derive the parameters of modern economic growth, neglect every one of the questions just raised. All we have so far are experimental analyses by individual scholars. But the important point is not statistical lacunae: it is the inevitable presence, in a society within which social groups shift from one set of conditions of work and life to another, of a mixture of gains and losses for which the market does not provide an agreed-upon social valuation. The scope of these unreflected gains and losses would only widen, were we to add other noneconomic concomitants and conditions of economic growth that are of obvious bearing upon its quality.

12.6 GUNNAR MYRDAL

Investment in Man

Gunnar Myrdal (1898–1987) was born in Solvarbo, Sweden. In 1923, he graduated from the law school of Stockholm University and began practicing law while continuing his studies at the university. He briefly joined the Institute of International Studies in Geneva, Switzerland, before he was appointed to the Lars Hierta Chair of Political Economy and Public Finance at the University of Stockholm in 1933. In 1974, Myrdal was awarded the Nobel Prize jointly with Friedrich A. Hayek for his analysis of the interdependence of social, economic, and institutional phenomena.

Myrdal's early work was devoted to pure economic theory. In *Monetary Equilibrium* (1939), he introduced the concepts of ex ante, or the predicted value of a variable, and ex post, or the realized value of that variable. According to Myrdal, consumers base purchasing decisions on ex ante or anticipated prices, which in turn affect ex post or actual prices. At the behest of the Carnegie Corporation, Myrdal directed a study of American blacks, which was later published as *An American Dilemma: The Negro Problem and Modern Democracy* (Harper & Brothers, 1944). This study is widely regarded as one of the most significant analyses of American race relations. Its general optimism contrasts with his grim view of Asian poverty in the following selection taken from *Asian Drama: An Inquiry into the Poverty of Nations* (Twentieth Century Fund, 1968). In it he posits that extensive reforms in population control, agriculture, health care, and education rather than foreign aid are necessary to propel these countries into development.

Key Concept: a framework for analyzing poverty in Asia

RISING INTEREST IN IMPROVING HEALTH AND EDUCATION: OBSTACLES AND INHIBITIONS

In recent times a number of developments have conspired to stimulate interest in health and education in South Asia. The South Asian states formulated their planning goals in terms of the ideals of the modern Western welfare states and in so doing were impressed by the importance these states attach to health andeducational improvements. The Communist countries have placed even greater emphasis on improving conditions of education and health for the masses of people, so ideological influences from this source have only strengthened the esteem in which these objectives are held. The planning ideology itself has to some degree directed attention to the instrumental value of advances in these fields.

The formation in 1948 of the World Health Organization and the activities of that organization, which have been directed very largely toward ameliorating conditions in the underdeveloped countries, have strengthened the zeal for an improved level of health in South Asia. Of particular importance in this connection has been the availability since the Second World War of cheap but effective means of fighting many of the area's most disastrous diseases. The work of UNESCO [United Nations Educational, Scientific and Cultural Organization] has been important in the field of education. If this organization has occasionally exerted a less positive influence than the World Health Organization, it must be remembered that the task of raising educational standards is more complex and difficult and that UNESCO has had nothing to offer comparable to the new wonder drugs.

These influences have had their impact on the educated and articulate strata in the South Asian countries—except insofar as their thinking has been distorted by conventional economic theory (see below). But the broad masses of people in these countries have been touched only slightly as yet by the heightened interest in improving health conditions. An indication of this is the fact that the authorities encounter difficulties when they attempt to induce people to behave more rationally in regard to sanitation and hygiene. The masses are perhaps more interested in better schooling, even though they often resist the changes in attitudes that are intended to be among its effects. Governments have shown an increased readiness to take action in both fields, but on a limited scale. Except for a few measures, like anti-malaria campaigns, which have been, predictably, inexpensive but highly productive of results, health policies have not been given a high priority. Measures to raise educational standards have been more prominent in the plans. That they have not bad a greater effect on development is due partly to the explosive rise in the school-age population and partly, as we shall find, to faults and weaknesses in the direction of the educational effort.

The relatively low priority given to genuine and radical reforms in the fields of health and education is traceable to the prevailing philosophy of development, which stresses the over-riding importance of physical investment. As we have noted throughout this study, the economic literature and the plans have been dominated by theories based on an uncritical application of Western concepts and analytical models to the South Asian situation. Models centered on the concept of a capital/output ratio have dictated the direction of economic planning in underdeveloped countries. One implication of this "modern approach" is the assumption that "noneconomic" factors—not only institutions and attitudes but also levels of living, including health and educational facilities—can be disregarded. The primary and often exclusive importance given to investment in physical capital for economic development requires this assumption.

THE RECENT ECONOMIC THEORY OF "INVESTMENT IN MAN"

The capital/output approach was in line with neo-classical economic theory, where an "unchanged state of the arts" in a very inclusive sense was often assumed. In the post-war years this approach gained in popularity among economists because of several studies that purported to show a close relationship between capital formation and economic growth in the United States and certain highly developed West European countries. In fact, the capital/output ratio came to be regarded as akin to the constants that have made it possible to advance knowledge of the physical universe by purely abstract mathematical reasoning. In very recent years, however, more intensive studies of economic growth in the same advanced countries revealed that only a part of it could be explained by the amount of investment in physical capital (and the increase in the labor force). While estimates of the unexplained residual vary within a wide range, they generally support the view that it is considerably bigger than that part of economic growth which is explained by capital investment.

This important negative finding demolished the foundations of the planning model cast in terms of physical investment alone, and threw the door wide open to speculation about other operative factors in development. A wide variety of factors presented themselves: education, health, research, technology, organization, management, government, administration, and so on. Significantly, economists were not prepared to abandon the capital/output model; instead, they widened the concept of capital investment to include, besides physical investment, "investment in man," sometimes labelled "investment in human capability" or "investment in human resources." To accomplish this, it was necessary to reduce the wide variety of specific factors exemplified above to one or a few categories for which definite amounts of expenditure could be calculated. From the beginning, interest has focussed on education, though health has occasionally shared the spotlight; the more elaborate models all reduce investment in man to the one factor, education. Improvements in the other factors must then be thought of as effects of education—part of its "return." Another consequence of treating education as investment—and the same would hold true of health or any other factor if it was similarly treated—is that it must then be described in the separate and aggregate form of financial expenditure.

Once economists identified the residual factor in economic growth with investment in man and the latter with education, this approach derived support from various research undertakings that were themselves inspired by it. A positive correlation was found to exist between the level of development and literacy or some other easily available measure of educational "level" in different countries and during different periods. Although it was, of course, recognized that statistical correlation does not establish what is cause and what is effect, these calculations served to confirm in a general and vague way the theory that education is a form of investment and a vital one.

Events themselves gave support to the view that education is an important developmental factor, lending further spurious support to the new theory. When W. Leontief found that, as far as international trade was concerned, the

United States specialized in selling labor-intensive rather than capital-intensive products, this invited the explanation that the United States had a greater comparative advantage in the skills possessed by its labor force (including organizational abilities, assumed to be imparted by education) than in its abundance of capital. The Marshall Plan in Western Europe turned out to be a greater and more rapid success than most economists had foreseen, while economic aid to underdeveloped countries generally proved to be less effective than had been expected. It seemed reasonable to suppose that the accumulated "educational capital" of the West European countries was a factor in this result. Another influence was the delayed realization that the Soviet Union had made strenuous efforts to increase educational facilities on all levels, and the inference that her rapid emergence from a state of relative underdevelopment was partly attributable to these efforts.

Not only the initial finding of a "residual" in development, impossible to explain by physical investment, but also all of the various calculations inspired by and vaguely supporting the theory that education can be treated as investment in the conventional capital/output model of development were based on statistics relating to some of the highly advanced Western countries: no underdeveloped country compiles statistical series of the kind needed for such studies. Nevertheless, economists have not hesitated to apply this theory to the underdeveloped countries. Some economists point to the fact that since the underdeveloped countries must use modern techniques as worked out in the advanced countries, if they are to progress, investment in education is even more important to them than it was to the Western countries when they were in the early stages of development. Except for such general considerations, there has been little interest in determining the effect of education under the very different conditions that prevail in the underdeveloped countries. The new theory has simply been applied by analogy.

As far as underdeveloped countries are concerned, the newest approach—as we shall call it in order to distinguish it from the "modern approach" in the post-war period that has treated development as a function of physical capital investment—has thus remained merely a new approach and has hardly been used in any real research. The situation is somewhat paradoxical. While most of the planning in South Asia and the other underdeveloped regions, and most of the economic literature on development, continues to be based on the notion that physical investment is the engine of development, there are today an increasing number of economists who denounce that view and who regard development, particularly in underdeveloped countries, as primarily an educational process. The members of this newest school of thought are aware of the fact that they are thereby repudiating the dominant trend of economic thinking about development in underdeveloped countries as it evolved since the end of the Second World War; before that time there had been little interest in the development issue, particularly in regard to underdeveloped countries. Of fresh research, guided by the newest theory and going deeply into their educational problems, very little has been seen.

The vision is there, however. To quote one exegesis of the newest school:

> Much of the past discussion of economic growth—in developed as well as in underdeveloped countries—appears to be as obsolete as the abandoned and useless furniture in the attic of an old family homestead.... Clearly... a new concept of "capital"—and a new *political* economy—is in the process of formulation since the old concepts, which were limited to tangible property, are now manifestly inadequate. The main shift in the present development is characterized by the tendency to think of the cause of economic growth as the *capacity* to create wealth rather than the creation of wealth itself. The direction of the change in thought is suggested by the question: Can we formulate a theory of human capital which accounts for economic growth in terms of changes in the quality of human beings?

The same spokesman contrasts this view to the still dominant one:

> ... orthodox economic and fiscal opinion continues to ignore the drift of current development and the significance to public policy of the new insight which is emerging. We continue to build models of economic growth on strictly materialist assumptions which overlook the role of capital investment in human beings in our own experience.... We disregard the role of the development of human skills and trained imagination in our own achievements... by presenting a picture of exclusive preoccupation with physical and material achievement.

Against the background of the common approach to development problems in the post-war period the idea that education can be treated as investment in the conventional model takes on the character of a discovery. The newest school can, however, point out that the orthodoxy they fight against was not always the ruling one. Alfred Marshall regarded education as a "national investment"—although, unlike members of the newest school, he used the word "investment" only in a figurative sense as he repudiated calculations of returns—and he was only following in the tradition established by many of the classical economists, among them John Stuart Mill, Malthus, and Adam Smith. The basic practical and political valuation inherent in this view is illustrated by the following quotation from Theodore W. Schultz:

> When poor countries... enter upon the process of developing a modern agriculture and industry, with some notable exceptions they invest too little in human capital relative to what they invest in nonhuman capital; skills and knowledge useful in their economic endeavor are neglected as they concentrate on new plants and equipment. Thus, an imbalance arises and as a consequence they fail, often by a wide margin, to attain their optimum rate of economic growth.

Leaving aside for the moment the question whether it is possible and correct to treat education in financial terms as simply an investment (see next section), educationists in South Asia and elsewhere certainly agree with the newest school of economists that education is important for development. And they formed this opinion long before a group of economists in very recent years hit on the idea, though they have never been able to effectively challenge the modern materialist orthodoxy. It is a remarkable fact, testifying to the damaging compartmentalization of the social sciences and, in particular, the insularity of traditional economics, that economists after the Second World War could build up a theory of development based solely on physical investment—a theory so incapable of explaining the process of economic growth that a group of them later "discovered" investment in man—while all the time they were apparently unaware of the thinking and writings of students and practitioners who specialized in this field (and also of the theorizing by earlier members of their own profession). As one commentator has observed, "the economists have not properly taken account of a long history of pedagogical research and practice."

This history is long indeed. When the Scandinavian countries began to legislate universal and compulsory elementary education in the beginning of the nineteenth century, this great reform movement was spurred by the argument that education was a prerequisite for improving agriculture, promoting industrialization, and for a general speed-up of what we now call "development." Another motivating factor was the belief that only a broadening of the educational base could make popular participation in government more effective. Somewhat later, similar reasoning led several states of the United States to include in their constitutions the right of all children to free elementary education. The French were inclined to trace their defeat in the war of 1870–71 to the superiority of German training programs, especially in the vocational and technical fields, and this belief helped to bring about a reform of the French educational system. Closer to South Asia, Japan has long acted on the belief that educational improvement would help it to emulate the industrial progress of the West. In fact, with the major exception of the post-war economic theorizing and planning for development in underdeveloped countries, nowhere in the world in modern history has there been any discussion of economic development that did not give educational improvement a predominant role. Indeed, for well over a century education for development has been a central theme of pedagogical literature. Economic historians have regularly paid a great deal of attention to education and educational reform when seeking to explain why the rate of economic development has varied in different epochs and in different countries. As one writer observes: "It might seem somewhat surprising that such a common-sense hypothesis [that education can raise productivity of workers] should not have been accepted by economists until quite recently." But none in this tradition has tried to put educational reform into the conceptual strait jacket of a quantity of financial investment, accounted for in a capital/output ratio. This is the only innovation in the newest economic approach.

CRITICAL COMMENTS ON THE NEWEST WESTERN APPROACH

The present writer, who for more fundamental reasons has felt it necessary to apply an out-and-out institutional approach to the development problems in the underdeveloped countries of South Asia, can only welcome the newest school's repudiation of the orthodoxy of the modern and still prevalent theory, which awards to physical investment the role of engendering development. Nevertheless, he has reservations concerning this school. In his opinion its members do not go far enough, either in their criticisms or in their innovations.

Economists of the newest school restrict themselves to widening the concept of investment in the capital/output model, so as to include investment in man, usually simplified to mean only education. But . . . the model itself is based on a number of unwarranted assumptions. In this instance it requires the assumption that education is a homogeneous magnitude, measurable in terms of financial expenditures. The model also implies that prevailing attitudes and institutions, items in the levels of living other than educational facilities, are of no consequence for the problem, and that the effect of all other policy measures applied at the same time can be completely disregarded. As these assumptions are logically inconsistent and inadequate to reality, use of the capital/output model can only block the way to realistic and relevant research.

In the present context this criticism will be spelled out solely in regard to the invalid and unrealistic assumption made about institutions—specifically, those in agriculture. Our study of this sector . . . clearly indicates that the low productivity of labor and land is related to the social structure and the attitudes supported by that structure, the widespread existence of absentee land ownership and tenancy being of particular importance. Because of these institutions the peasants have little possibility or incentive to avail themselves of new techniques or otherwise try to increase their output. If productivity in agriculture is to increase, there must be institutional reform. Unless land reform of one type or another is introduced, improved farming methods have little chance of being applied. More precisely, the productivity-raising effects of education, and even people's interest in acquiring education, will depend on the extent to which institutional reforms take place. Such reforms can come about only through legislative and administrative means, and they require many additional policy measures to make them effective.

The tendency to exclude this institutional policy factor when planning is done in terms of even an extended capital/output model is plainly evident in the writings of members of the newest school. Thus James C. Maddox defines his "prescription for increasing agricultural productivity" as "the mixture of education, research, fertilizer, insecticides, high yielding seeds, and a few tractors." Lee R. Martin explains that "the full productive potential of a country is a joint function of its natural resources (defined by worldwide technology, not technology in local use), the number of workers, and the most advanced state of the production arts." Theodore W. Schultz has recently published a book, *Transforming Traditional Agriculture,* which, while interesting, entirely bypasses the problems of the institutional setting and the need for institutional reform.

Much more generally, the treatment of education in terms of investment implies a bypassing of the inequality issue. . . . [We believe that] social and economic inequality determines the effects of attempts to improve education, and [that] educational advance often serves to stratify inequality. This newest theory of investment in man is, consequently, heavily biased, and in a way that conflicts with our value premises.

The critique in the last three paragraphs is not, of course, meant to deprecate efforts in the educational field, or, for that matter, to deny the importance of physical investment. The point is that an analysis which does not fully take into account the institutional framework within which the economic variables operate, and which aggregates disparate activities, while isolating them from other, complementary activities, is bound to be not only superficial but misleading.... [A]bstraction from the institutional framework—and from the attitudes that are molded in that framework and, in turn, support it—is opportunistic both in South Asia and in the West; it is a biased approach. In a brilliant paper, Thomas Balogh suggests that calculations made about the profitability of education are "not merely fallacious in a technical economic sense but... immoral politically"; what he says about a particular species of model can be generalized to the whole genus of development models we are now discussing.

> I admit the attractiveness of this mathematical approach. Land reform, the creation of agricultural extention services and of an adequate agricultural credit system, the reorganisation of the civil service, the establishment of state industrial corporations—all these are complex matters. They involve a change of attitudes, a reform of institutions. They hurt vested interests. They cause political difficulties. How much simpler to lift out of a residual, representing complex conditions of progress, a particular factor—in this case 'the vast heavy investment which all countries undertake at all times in the development of their human resources'—and assign to it a definite causal force, having obtained the residual after accounting for the equally complex influence on economic progress of the growth of 'land, labour and capital' in a most cavalier and illegitimate way.

ADDED DIFFICULTIES WHEN HEALTH IS INCLUDED IN THE MODEL

The tendency has been to restrict the category investment in man to financial expenditures on education. The question must at last be raised: why have economists focussed their attention on education and almost entirely ignored the other dimension of population quality, health?

The answer cannot be the difficulty of defining health or health objectives, as it is at least equally difficult to define educational levels. Measuring efforts put forth and their effectiveness in financial terms is no more feasible in the case of education than in the case of health. Factual information is about equally lacking in both instances. In any event, neither definitional difficulties nor a lack of empirical data have ever deterred economists, and least of all the model-builders among them, from tackling problems and presenting solutions that pretend knowledge. The fact that improved health is regularly accompanied by demographic changes (a fall in the death rate and perhaps a rise in the fertility rate) which exert a downward pressure on income per head and living levels, does not justify leaving the health factor out of development theories, especially since allowance could be made for these secondary changes by slightly complicating the models.

Some clue may be found in the fact that the concept of investment in man had its origin largely in the analysis of the recent growth history of certain highly developed countries. It can be assumed that health conditions in these countries have been so relatively favorable in recent decades that an improvement in health facilities—with the application at any point of time of the then known medical techniques—has not at the margin made any very great contribution to the utilization and productivity of the labor force. However, the same is true of education, particularly elementary schooling. Further speculation along these lines would seem profitless. There can be no warrant for leaving health out of the development picture. Ill health is a very serious deterrent to a rise in labor input and efficiency in the underdeveloped countries in South Asia.

But if we do add investment in health to investment in education and define human resources in terms of the two dimensions of population quality—as occasional references invite—we must include all costs involved in improving conditions of health, not just expenditures on health facilities. In all South Asian countries and particularly in the biggest and poorest of them, India and Pakistan, a major cause of ill health—specifically, of incipient disease, apathy, and bodily and mental weakness—is serious undernutrition and malnutrition among the masses of the people. The majority of South Asians spend much more than half their income on food, and still they are undernourished. Nor do they have access to the clothing, housing, and sanitary facilities they need to keep them reasonably fit. On the margin, then, increases in the consumption of essentials, food especially, or the expenditures that make such increases possible, are bound to be productive of better health, which is not the case in the highly developed countries. The implication is that the new term "investment in man" should include not only the consumption of educational and health facilities, but *practically all essential consumption,* if the underlying reasoning is to be logically consistent. *The productivity effect on the margin of the various items of consumption differs, however*—some consumption is relatively unproductive, and some has a negative value for health. The *real planning problem* is how to squeeze and twist consumption in such a way as to speed up development. This problem would not be clarified to any degree by the statement that much of the consumption in these poor countries constitutes investment in man. What the planners need to know is the effect on productivity of increases in the consumption of various items, and here the model offers no guidance at all.

CONCLUDING REMARKS

To sum up, the most recent opposition of some economists to the modern approach is certainly wholesome, insofar as it challenges the exclusive role given in the post-war period to physical investment in the models that still form the basis for planning in South Asian countries. The general policy judgment of the rebel school—though it is usually not indicated, or is indicated only by a few illustrations of what educators have been hammering at for many decades—

that greater efforts to improve education, if wisely planned and directed, can be more conducive to development than some physical investment, is probably correct, though it does not follow as a conclusion from use of the conventional model with only a broadened definition of capital investment. The same probably holds true of greater efforts to improve health, though these efforts would have to have as a major objective the increasing of essential consumption and, in particular, food intake. Again, this would not follow from the use of a capital/output model, even if the model took health measures into account. The investment approach entirely ignores the fact that institutional and attitudinal reforms, which depend on political decisions rather than budgetary considerations, are needed to make investments in education "pay off," and the broader consideration that the success of educational programs depends on the policies pursued in all other fields as well as the direction of the educational programs themselves. It is possible that some members of the school of economists whose views have been discussed in the preceding two sections would agree generally with our evaluation. But *if the concept "investment in man" is revised to take account of these criticisms, it becomes virtually empty of theoretical content; it becomes merely a vague propaganda term for a more rational and circumspect development planning that takes into account not only physical investment but all other induced changes.* That concept does not by itself contain even the beginning of a valid theory, and should not invite the type of abstract and carelessly constructed models referred to above....

To avoid any misunderstanding it should again be stressed that we are not averse to the use of models. Still less are we opposed to efforts to make quantitative judgments. We are not in sympathy with the view that some factors are "qualitative"; in principle, social scientists must strive constantly to translate all of their knowledge into measurable quantities. However, *both models and quantitative pronouncements must be logically consistent and thoroughly grounded in facts.* We need much more specific and precise information about actual health and educational conditions in South Asia and their relationship to a vast number of other socio-economic conditions. In particular, we need research to shed light on the effect of various programs on physiological and mental vigor, skills, knowledge and attitudes, labor input and efficiency. We need to know more about how different development efforts affect one another and how they are affected by institutional settings. When more data become available there will be plenty of room for models that are clear, specific, logically consistent, and adequate to reality.

The judgment that the South Asian countries would be well advised to devote more resources to improving health and education is probably correct as far as it goes, but it is vague and it does not clarify the really important issues, namely: where should health and educational programs be directed, how far should they be pushed, what means should they employ, and what other policy measures are needed? The criticism of the modern, conventional approach to planning, which relates development to physical investment alone, is valid—but for reasons more fundamental than those advanced by the newest school of economists. These two assertions are not in the slightest degree strengthened or rendered more precise by a general "theory" of investment in man as the engine of economic growth. The quantitative inferences frequently arrived at by the use of the new, extended models are as fictitious as, for instance, the calculations of the percentage of the labor force that is "underemployed"; by presenting an elegant appearance of knowledge, where none exists, they make it easy to avoid the laborious task of studying reality in all its complexity. The abstract criticism [here] is intended to help clear the deck of useless theories, based on preconceptions, that obstruct and misdirect scientific advance.

12.7 W. ARTHUR LEWIS

Savings

Developmental economist W. Arthur Lewis (1915–1991) was born on the island of St. Lucia in the British West Indies. He served on the faculty of the University of London until 1948, when he was appointed professor at the University of Manchester. In 1963 he joined Princeton University as professor of economics and international affairs. In 1979 he was awarded the Nobel Prize for his insightful analysis of the problems of economic development.

Lewis's theory of economic development may be traced to the United Nations report *Economic Development in Low-Income Countries* (1951) and his influential book *The Theory of Economic Growth* (Richard D. Irwin, 1955), from which the following selection has been taken. He disagreed with Western economists who, flushed with the success of the Marshall Plan, viewed trade and foreign capital as twin engines of economic growth in that exports of manufactured products would generate rising profits, which should be reinvested in plant and equipment to achieve further growth. Lewis failed to see any developmental benefits from increasing trade or external investment. Focusing on human capital, he posited that large investments in education would yield trained employees engaged in increasingly productive employment in the manufacturing sector. Rising profits would provide the capital to stimulate growth. Likewise, productivity in agriculture would yield similar savings, which could be invested profitably in the growing industrial sector. In the following selection, Lewis describes the mechanism of development. Its central proposition is the need to raise the national savings rate from 4–5 percent to 12 percent. Comparing the behavior of various social classes in developing countries, he concludes that development will be led by entrepreneurs who are the only group with the motivation to save at the preferred rate.

Key Concept: national savings as a stimulus of growth

The central problem in the theory of economic growth is to understand the process by which a community is converted from being a 5 per cent to a 12 per cent saver—with all the changes in attitudes, in institutions and in techniques which accompany this conversion.

It is customary to account for this conversion in terms of increasing thrift, and of better use of savings. That thrift increases is true, but it is also very misleading if it suggests that the essential change is that all classes of society become more thrifty or less wasteful. For the essential change is rather the emergence of a new class in society—the profit making entrepreneurs—which is more thrifty than all the other classes (the landlords, the wage-earners, the peasants, the salaried middle-classes), and whose share of the national income increases relatively to that of all others. In private capitalism these entrepreneurs have made private profits, and have reinvested on private account; whereas in the U.S.S.R. the great increase in profits has been concealed as a 'turnover tax', which the planners have reinvested on public account. But, in either case, the essential feature of the conversion from 5 to 12 per cent saving is an enormous increase in the share of profits in the national income.

A relative increase in profits is not necessarily the same as an increase in the inequality of income distribution, since this increase may be associated with a corresponding decline in the relative importance of income from rent. In fact, the communities in which income is most unevenly divided are not those wealthy economies where profits are large, but rather those impoverished, overpopulated economies where rents are large. In Ceylon or Puerto Rico the top 10 per cent of income receivers get about 40 per cent of the total of personal incomes, whereas in the United Kingdom or the United States of America the top 10 per cent receives, before taxation, nearer 30 per cent. These figures are somewhat misleading, since the undistributed profits of companies are not included in the assessment of personal incomes; when account is taken of undistributed profits there may not be much difference either way. In any case, it is not possible to make a general comparison between more and less developed economies, in the matter of inequality. The less developed differ amongst themselves, according to whether land is scarce or plentiful, and widely distributed or concentrated in ownership; and also according to whether there has been considerable development of capitalist enterprises within them, such as mines or plantations. The more developed also differ amongst themselves, and their distribution of personal income is also less unequal (before taxation) today than it was twenty years ago (though this is mainly because of the increase of undistributed relatively to distributed profits). The fact that there is no unique difference between more and less developed economies in this respect serves, however, only to reinforce our conclusion. The ratio of savings to national income is a function not just of inequality, but more precisely, of the ratio of profits to national income.

Large rent incomes do not result in saving because a landed aristocracy does not think in terms of using its income for productive investment—at any rate did not think in these terms until there was a capitalist example to imitate. Traditionally rent incomes are used to buy more land, to carry a large number of retainers (including a private army if the central government is weak), to build churches, temples, tombs and monuments, to extend charity, and to entertain lavishly. With the passage of time these habits change under capitalist pressure; the combination of taxation of rents and the example of profitable capitalist investment tends to make landlords more thrifty, and in advanced capitalist societies rent may even be a source (a minor source) of saving for productive investment. This, however, happens after the event; so an increase in the thriftiness of landlords cannot be used to explain why the community changes from a 5 to a 12 per cent saver.

The same goes for the peasant class. The peasants are a class who paradoxically combine a thrifty temperament with a high propensity to be burdened by debt. Peasants learn to be thrifty because they know how near they live to the brink of disaster. In some communities hardly a year passes without flood, or drought, or locusts, or cattle plague or some other Act of God which reduces to destitution all the peasants except those who have some savings to fall back on. These recurrent disasters are part of the explanation of the propensity to incur debt. At the same time, those peasants who save tend to invest either in lending to less fortunate peasants, or else in buying land, and in neither case is the result an increase in capital formation. Buying land raises the price and alters the distribution of land, but it does not make land more productive. If the peasants own the land, they may invest in improving it, but most of the techniques of improving land involve a temporary reduction in its yield (fallows, rotations, afforestation, grass strips, erosion control), and are not popular in areas where the pressure on the land is considerable. Peasants also like to invest in cattle, but the attitude of many peasants in Asia and in Africa to cattle is not commercial, so that in many cases this investment is a burden rather than a source of profit. Considering the precarious life of the peasant, and his non-commercial attitude towards his land and his cattle, it is not surprising that net capital formation by peasants is only a very small part of the national income.

The wage and salary earning classes have a more regular income than the peasants, and usually also even the unskilled urban worker earns more than the average peasant. Yet these classes save very little because their mentality is directed towards spending rather than towards saving. Workers' savings are very small. The salaried middle classes save a little, but in practically every community the savings of the middle classes out of their salaries are of little consequence for productive investment. This is especially so in countries where the ruling class differs in race from the middle and lower classes, since the middle classes then seem to distinguish themselves in conspicuous consumption, in their zeal to demonstrate that they are as good as their foreign rulers. Low savings out of salaries are in any case almost universal. Most members of the middle class are engaged in the perpetual struggle to keep up with the Jones's; if they manage to save enough to buy the house in which they live, they are doing well. They may save to educate their children, or to subsist in their old age, but this saving is virtually offset by the savings being used up for the same purposes. The offset is not complete if income or population is growing, since the amount set aside by each generation is then larger than the amount set aside by the previous generation and now being consumed. These savings are of course very important to the individual saver. It is important to have something put by for a rainy day, even in a welfare state, and social reformers have always been right to urge people to save. However, the very fact that these savings are merely a postponement of future consumption, and are thus largely offset by other postponed consumption, means that they are not important in the context of productive investment.

The low level of savings of the salaried middle classes also bears out the point that saving and inequality of income are not directly related. Middle class earnings are much higher in relation to average earnings, or to the earnings of small farmers or unskilled workers, in the less developed than they are in the industrial countries. This is partly due to the greater shortage of middle class skills, but it is also due to the greater mobility of the middle classes, as between richer and poorer countries, which enables them to demand in poorer countries as high a standard of living as they could get in richer countries; in fact, because the poor countries have to attract middle class skills from the rich, the middle classes tend even to have a higher standard of living in the poor than they do in the rich countries. Thus the greater inequality of income is associated with a larger proportion of national income going into middle class consumption.

There is very little evidence on savings out of wages, salaries and peasant incomes. Such evidence as there is suggests that even in the richest countries these savings seldom exceed 4 per cent of the national income. Japan is a notable exception; figures as high as 8 or 10 per cent have been quoted in her case. In the less developed countries small savings seem to be much nearer 1 per cent of national income, according to the best calculations so far made. Needless to say, even 1 or 2 or 3 per cent of the national income is not to be despised: it is well worth while pursuing measures designed to push small savings up from 1 to 2 or 3 per cent. These measures lie in the directions of institutions, of propaganda, and of financial incentives. There is a whole range of savings institutions that can be developed—post office savings, friendly societies, co-operative credit societies, co-operative retail societies, insurance policies, building societies and the like. Experience shows that the amount of saving depends partly on how widespread these facilities are; if they are pushed right under the individual's nose, to the extent of having street savings groups, or factory groups, or even deductions from earnings at source, people save more than if the nearest savings institution is some distance away. Saving is also a habit, which can to some extent be created by propaganda. People save more if they are given some acceptable reason for saving. They save more in wartime partly because they are persuaded that this is the patriotic thing to do; they might also save more in countries launching upon development programmes if these programmes caught their imagination, and if they were persuaded that this is a way of making their contribution. In addition people can be persuaded to save in their own individual or family interest, for education, for old age, for house purchase, for weddings or funerals, or as a safeguard against sickness or disaster. Even if these savings are largely offset by consumption, the habit of self-reliance and the avoidance of destitution are compelling reasons for doing all that we can to stimulate them. The principle of insurance appeals easily, and a cheap well advertised system of personal insurance stimulates saving. In addition, the financial incentives for saving should be adequate, in the sense that the rate of interest should be attractive. It is customary to pay only rates of 2 to 3 per cent on small savings, partly because the cost of collecting and using small savings tend to be high; but there may well be a case for subsidising the rate of interest offered on small savings, so that more attractive rates can be offered. If the community is also using inflation for the purpose of capital formation, with the result that the value of money is falling, there is something to be said for guaranteeing the real value of small savings; otherwise small savers are discriminated against (since the value of other assets rises as prices rise), and small savings are discouraged.

It is particularly important to stimulate saving among the peasants, because of the role which agriculture has to play in economic development. Economic growth results in the expansion of all other activities relatively to agriculture—because the income elasticity of demand for food is less than one. Relatively speaking, therefore, other occupations are growing all the time, and the people in these occupations have to be fed out of the produce of the farmers remaining in agriculture. Hence economic growth requires that the produce of farmers per head must increase, to provide a growing surplus per head from which to feed the non-farmers. At the lowest levels of productivity each farm family is producing food for itself and half a non-farm family; whereas at the highest contemporary levels each farm family feeds itself and seven other families.

Savings enter into this process at two points. In the first place, the required growth of productivity in agriculture usually means that more capital must be invested in agriculture. Sums of money can be set aside for this purpose by the government, and lent to the farmers through rural banks or credit societies. This involves, however, an absorption of capital into agriculture from other sectors of the economy (unless the money comes from taxes on landlords), and since all other sectors are simultaneously clamouring for capital, the more the farmers can finance themselves the better. This gives special point to savings campaigns and savings institutions in rural areas.

Saving may also be involved in the process in another way. If agricultural productivity is rising, and providing a larger surplus which can be used to feed the towns, governments are frequently tempted to tax this surplus away from the peasants, and to use it to finance expansion in other sectors, including capital formation in public utilities or in manufacturing. There is a double temptation, since taxing the farmers opens up one opportunity of finding resources sorely needed, and since also, if the farmers are not taxed, the rise in their real incomes may make it necessary to raise real wages and salaries in the cities and in other occupations, so as to continue to attract labour from agriculture, and this increase in real wages and salaries in the cities and in other occupations, so as to continue to attract labour from agriculture, and this increase in real wages and salaries reduces the share of profits and therefore of saving in the national income. Hence in a number of cases an increase in the productivity of farming has been accompanied by heavy taxation of farmers, which has been used to finance capital formation in other sectors, and it has been true to say in these cases that, far from agriculture absorbing capital from other sectors, it has been the farmers who have been forced to finance the industrial revolution. Japan is a case in point. In that country productivity per person engaged in agriculture doubled between 1885 and 1915, but much of the increase was taken from the farmers in higher rents or taxes, and used to finance the rest of the economy.... The U.S.S.R. is another case where farm incomes per head were kept down, between the world wars, in spite of farm mechanization and the considerable release of labour to the towns. This was done jointly by raising the prices of manufacturers relatively to farm products, and by levying heavy taxes upon the collective farms. Current examples are provided also by the Gold Coast,

Burma, and Uganda, three countries whose governments have withheld from their farmers a very large part of the increase in the price of farm produce since 1945, and who are using part of the proceeds to finance economic development in other sectors of the economy.

Economic development can take place without levying upon the peasants to finance capital formation if the necessary savings are forthcoming from some other group. In practice the only other major source of savings in the past has been the profits of business enterprise, which, as we shall see in a moment, tend to grow relatively to national income in less developed countries if circumstances are favourable. If it is desired to accelerate capital formation at a time when profits are still a small proportion of national income there is in practice no other way of doing this than to levy substantially upon agriculture, both because agriculture constitutes 50 to 60 per cent or more of the national income, and also because levying upon other sectors is handicapped by the fact that it is desirable to have these other sectors expand as part of the process of economic growth. Levying on agriculture is in turn politically very difficult to do, as the U.S.S.R. discovered, unless the productivity of agriculture is rising rapidly so that the levy can be effected without reducing the standard of living of the peasants. The model of how it can be done is provided not by the U.S.S.R. but by Japan, and the moral is that any programme for industrialization and heavy capital formation should have as its counterpart measures for increasing agricultural productivity rapidly—not mainly with tractors or with new economic structures, but mainly with new seeds, fertilizers, pesticides and water. Behind this again lies a political problem of whether countries in which the peasants have political power are capable of launching upon programmes of this sort. . . .

Apart from the cases where the farmers are squeezed to provide for capital formation, the main source of savings in any economy is profits, distributed or undistributed. If one enquires why the profit making class is more prone to thrift and to productive investment than all other classes, the answer is probably to be found in its place in the social hierarchy. Unlike the salaried middle classes, capitalists do not have to engage in conspicuous consumption in order to impress upon other people their social importance, since the mere fact of their independent status as profit makers and as employers of other people, combined with their known wealth, assures them some social prestige; the middle and lower classes can never save much, no matter how high their real incomes may rise, since they are always imitating the consumption standards of those richer than themselves, whereas the rich can save because their incomes are more than adequate for their accepted standards of consumption. The profit makers have lower social status than the landed aristocracy, but they know that they cannot attain the prestige of the aristocracy simply by spending conspicuously, and so only a few of them try to do this. Like the aristocracy, they are ambitious for power, but their road to power lies in a different direction. The aristocracy achieve power by increasing the size of their estates, and (in feudal and early capitalist stages) by monopolizing the highest political, military and religious offices. The profit maker, on the other hand, knows that his power lies in his money; he therefore saves, and invests his money as profitably as he can. Some of his money is invested, as the peasant invests money, simply in financing other people's consumption, or in buying land, two forms of 'investment' which do not increase capital formation. But the profit maker knows that the most profitable investments are those which exploit new techniques, or open up new resources, and these also pander to his ambition for power because the greater his productive investments, the larger the number of people he has working under him. The capitalist is therefore the only person whose ambition drives in the direction of using his income to create an empire of bricks and steel; all other classes fulfill their ambitions in other ways—the salaried middle classes by conspicuous consumption, and the agricultural classes by buying land, or by holding office. In the later stages of capitalism these distinctions are blurred; capitalists buy or marry their way into the landed aristocracy and make a bid for political office; landowners go into the City, and invest their rents productively; and even peasants get the idea that it is just as good to use money to improve the land one has already, as to use it to buy still more land. In the later stages thrift and productive investment spread to all classes of the community, but in origin productive investment is essentially the mark of the capitalist class.

12.8 THEODORE W. SCHULTZ

From Propositions to Implications

Theodore W. Schultz, pioneer of human capital theory, was born in 1902 in Arlington, South Dakota. His postsecondary education in agricultural economics was completed at South Dakota State College (B.A.), and the University of Wisconsin (M.A. and Ph.D.). Schultz's academic appointments have occurred at Iowa State College and the University of Chicago, where his academic reponsibilities have been supplemented by investigations of agriculture in developing countries. In 1979, he was awarded the Nobel Prize for the dual research streams of developmental economics based on agriculture and human capital investments.

In *Transforming Traditional Agriculture* (Yale University Press, 1964), Schultz laid the framework for a balanced approach to agriculture, which was validated in the field with the Green Revolution in India, Pakistan, and the Philippines. Integrating the introduction of new seed varieties, pest control, and modern farm machinery with traditional values and practices, the Green Revolution transformed the agricultural landscape in these countries. Schultz pioneered the idea that the developed world's investment in education and research, termed human capital, was higher than its return on physical capital (plant and equipment) and was one of the sources of disparity between developed and developing countries. In 1960 he formalized this thesis with numerical estimates of the value of human capital, including such hitherto overlooked variables as earnings foregone by students. In the selection that follows, which is from *Investment in Human Capital: The Role of Education and of Research* (The Free Press, 1971), Schultz presents seven propositions to guide educators in planning and financing education. He justifies higher education as a form of human capital; explores its functions of discovering talent, instruction, and research; analyzes difficulties in measuring the productivity of labor entering higher education; and discusses the uncertainties that plague estimates of long-term demand for higher education.

Key Concept: education as a form of human capital

While altruism is not at the heart of the relationship between education and economics, both gain from an exchange of products. To broaden the exchange, economists are offering some new propositions that should prove useful in planning and in financing education. I shall present seven. Let me indicate what they are about. Organized education produces an array of different forms of human capital of varying durability. Higher education is engaged in three major types of production activities, which entail discovering talent, instruction, and research. But it is not renowned for its gains in the productivity of teachers and students. Educational planning overlooks most of the real costs of higher education because of its omission of the earnings foregone by students. Long-term projections of the demand for higher education are conjectures that undervalue flexibility and overvalue formulas. The advantages of thinking in terms of the rates of return to investment in education and the requirement of efficiency prices in allocating investment resources in accordance with the standard set by the relative rates of return to alternative investment opportunities are strong and clear. There is, however, much confusion with regard to the welfare consequences of higher education, including the consequences of the way in which it is financed and the resulting personal distribution of costs and benefits. I now turn to the meaning of these propositions.

1 *Education is a form of human capital.* It is *human* because it becomes a part of man, and it is *capital* because it is a source of future satisfactions, or of future earnings, or both. Thus far, however, the concept of human capital has contributed more to economic thinking than it has to the solution of problems in education. In economics, it has become a seminal concept entering into many parts of economic analysis. In international trade, it points to the solution of the Leontief paradox, showing why capital-rich countries nevertheless export labor-intensive goods—we discover that labor entering into these goods requires much human capital. The differences among countries in their capital endowments, when both physical and human capital are taken into account and under the assumption of factor-price equalization, go a long way toward explaining the differences in income per worker among them. When considering the international movement of human capital and the growing international markets for particular high skills, the so-called brain drain is straightaway a form of maximizing economic behavior. In internal migration, also, human capital is a critical explanatory factor. In solving the long-standing puzzle of the *residual*, where the rate of increase in output exceeds the rate of increase in inputs, it has contributed much. As a part of an all-inclusive concept of capital, advances in specification and measurement of the services of capital would appear to explain most of the observable economic growth. Furthermore, it sets the stage for a generalized theory of capital accumulation in which investment resources are allocated in accordance with the priorities set by the relative rates of return to all material and human investment opportunities.

There are the following particular implications of this proposition for planning and financing higher education: 1) The human capital that is formed by higher education is far from homogeneous. Parts of it are for consumption and parts are for production. Moreover, both the consumer and producer components are of many different types. To lump them in allocating resources to higher education is bad economics. 2) The value of each type of human capital depends on the value of the services it renders and not on its original costs;

mistakes in the composition and size of the stock of each type, once made, are sunk investments. 3) The formation of most of these types of capital requires a long horizon because the capabilities that the student acquires are part of him during the rest of his life. 4) The value of the benefits of higher education accruing to students privately consists of future earnings and of future nonpecuniary satisfactions. It is difficult to measure the latter, but they are nevertheless real and important. 5) Although human capital, as such, cannot be bought and sold, it is comparatively easy to estimate the value of the producer services of this capital because they are priced in terms of wages and salaries in the labor market. 6) Human capital, like reproducible material capital, is subject to obsolescence. The traditional tax treatment of depreciation is outmoded inasmuch as it excludes human capital. Although earnings foregone do not enter into taxable income, none of the direct private costs is treated as capital formation. The upper limit of the life of this capital is the remaining life span of individuals after they have completed their formal education. An increase in longevity may decrease the rate of depreciation; earlier retirements may work in the opposite direction. More important is the obsolescence from changes in demand for high skills, changes that are a consequence of the characteristics of our type of economic growth. It should be possible to provide instruction that would be less subject to this type of obsolescence than it is presently. Educational planning should search for ways and means of improving higher education in this respect by substituting long-life for short-life instructional components so that it can serve better the changing demands for high skills. Continuing education after graduation is a form of maintenance. 7) Capital formation by education sets the stage for thinking of education as an investment.

2 *The Three major functions of higher education are discovering talent, instruction, and research.* Each of these activities requires analysis to determine how efficiently it is organized and whether too few or too many resources are allocated to it. But it must be admitted in all honesty that hard facts and valid inferences pertaining to these issues are about as scarce as they are in the pork barrel realm of rivers and harbors. What is an efficient organization of each of these three activities in higher education in terms of scale of organization, specialization, location of colleges and universities, and importantly, the *complementarity between the discovery of talent, instruction, and research*?

Taking the system of higher education as it is, with regard to instruction, economists have made substantial progress in specifying and identifying the economic value of higher education as it increases the value productivity of human agents as workers. Less, although some, progress has been made in getting at the economic value of university research. The much-neglected activity is that of discovering talent. It, too, can be approached by treating it as a process that provides students with opportunities to discover whether they have the particular capabilities required for the type and level of education at which they are working.

The value of the research function has received a lot of puffing but little analysis. It has prestige, but what about performance? With regard to organized agricultural research, where it is a part of land-grant universities, there are some studies with some hard facts. The payoff on this type of research has been very high. But there are no economic studies to my knowledge of other types of organized university research. Is it organized efficiently in terms of combinations of scientific talent, scale of organization, complementarity with Ph.D. research and with other research centers, and division of labor between basic and applied research? Is it for profit or on public account? Despite the importance of these questions and the wide array of experience from which we can learn, scientists are woefully unscientific in the impressionistic answers they give to this question.

There are many signs that indicate that one of the strongest features of higher education in the United States is in discovering talent. Although we are far ahead of western Europe in this activity, the payoff to additional resources used for this purpose is still in all probability very high. If so, three implications are worthy of note: 1) relatively more resources should be committed to this activity; 2) resources should be allocated specifically to support it; and 3) the organization and budgets of higher education should be planned to perform this activity efficiently.

3 *There appear to be few or no gains in the measured productivity of labor entering into higher education.* It follows that if the price of this labor rises and if its productivity remains constant (other things unchanged), the price of the services it renders must rise; that is, the cost of higher education per student must rise. The crude facts, as we observe them, are consistent with this proposition. But these facts do not measure changes in the quality of the educational product, which has been rising markedly in many fields. The advance in knowledge is probably the main reason, and here we have a strong clue to the complementarity between instruction and research.

Nor do we know the possibilities of economizing on the labor entering into education by substituting other educational inputs for this labor or by reorganizing the educational process and thereby obtaining gains in the productivity of teachers and students in terms of the time they spend teaching and learning. These possibilities are undoubtedly of substantial importance, but it is doubtful that they will be found predominantly in new learning machines, in television instruction, or in the computerization of educational activities; instead, they are mainly to be achieved through many small innovative reorganizations of the instructional interplay between teachers and students that will reduce the time spent by each in attaining a given educational product.

The reasons why it is so difficult to make these gains are fairly obvious. The product of teaching and learning is highly labor-intensive like that of barbers. At best, it would appear that there is little room for nonlabor inputs. Nor are cheaper labor inputs the solution; that is, substituting low quality, less costly teachers and students for high quality persons. Although the difficulties here may seem insurmountable, it should be remembered that in classical economics, manufacturing carried the promise of decreasing cost whereas the outlook for agriculture was increasing cost per unit of product. But economic development in western countries has more than offset the drag of diminishing returns to land in farming, and the gains in labor productivity in agriculture have been exceeding those in manufacturing. Not so long ago the conventional view was that the retail sector could not gain appreciably from labor-saving developments, but it has in fact made much progress on this score. The present conventional view that the educational sector is destined to continue as it is regarding the amount of time required of students and teachers also may prove wrong.

The major real problems awaiting solution in higher education in economizing on the time of students and teachers are, in large part, a consequence of the traditional decision-making process in colleges and universities, the ambiguity that conceals the added value of the product, and the lack of strong incentives to innovate. On theoretical grounds there is room for more progress. Decision-making theory is not empty as a guide in improving the traditional process. A theory of the allocation of time is now at hand for determining how efficiently the time of students is allocated. Requiring college students to spend 20 hours a week in class, as is required of many students, may be anything but efficient. The implication is that we might find 15 or 10 or even fewer hours more efficient. But we really will not know what could be achieved by such innovations until we have undertaken carefully planned experiments to discover what the results would be. The specifications of the value added to the capabilities of students by the educational process are being clarified, for example, in the search for a better mix of instructional components that would have a longer life than the present mix.

4 *Earnings foregone by students are well over half of the real costs of the human capital formation by higher education.* Earnings foregone by college and university students in the United States exceeded in 1959–1960 the "direct" expenditures in the same period for higher education (minus auxiliary enterprises and capital outlay plus implicit interest and depreciation of physical property), which came to about $4,350 million. Yet we omit these earnings foregone in our planning and financing approach to higher education. We keep them concealed by not entering them in our college and university plans nor in our national income and capital formation accounts. The omission of these earnings foregone by students seriously distorts our view of the economics of higher education. Let me turn to the major implications of this omission of earnings foregone: 1) higher education (leaving university research aside) is more than twice as costly as is revealed in our budgets; 2) it is simply impossible to plan efficiently when over half of the real costs are treated as "free" resources; 3) there is no incentive to economize on the time of students in educational planning under existing circumstances; 4) educational planners receive no signals that the value of the time of students is rising relative to material inputs; 5) the rate of return to investment in higher education is grossly overestimated when earnings foregone are omitted; 6) so-called "free" education is far from free to students and their parents, which, in turn, implies that many families with low incomes cannot afford to forego the earnings of their children; and 7) savings, investment, and capital formation are all substantially understated in terms of national accounting.

5 *Long-term projections of the demand for higher education are beset with all manner of uncertainty.* They are conjectures that can be very misleading. As a consequence, flexibility is undervalued and formulas are overvalued in educational

planning. Economic logic tells us that in coping with uncertainty, it is necessary to remain sufficiently flexible so that one can act efficiently when new and better information becomes available. But such flexibility is not costless; thus the prospective additional gains from flexibility must be reckoned against the additional costs. Furthermore, to the extent that these projections can be made more reliable, the need for and cost of acquiring flexibility can be reduced.

The available projections of the demands for higher education can be substantially improved. What we have are numbers, which are not a reliable source of information. The concept of demand for education requires clarification; as it is presently used, it is beset with ambiguity. So-called need is not demand because the concept of demand implies prices and quantities. But the relevant prices, whether they are shadow prices or actual prices, are not specified in the numbers being projected. The demand behavior of students for places in colleges and universities is a useful approach. Another approach is to determine the demands for the particular capabilities that come from the teaching and learning in higher education—demands that are derived from the production activity of the economy. But it is unfortunately true that there is as yet no satisfactory theory connecting *ex post* rates of increase in the demands for the satisfactions and earnings that accrue to college and university students with future rates of increase in these demands. Projections abound, but they are in principle as naive as exponential population projections. You can take your choice, and if you happen to be correct, it will not be because of reason but because of luck. Manpower studies do not provide the answer, nor are the sophisticated programming models as yet providing an answer.

The rise in per family income undoubtedly increases the demand for the consumer satisfactions from higher education; the income elasticity of the demand for this consumer component is probably such that it is a superior good with a fairly high elasticity. But the demand for the producer component is very hard to determine because it is derived from the production activity of the economy and because the sources of changes in these derived demands over time are still far from clear. Furthermore, the observable responses of students to the array of different prices that students pay for higher education are confounded by all manner of pricing policies and changes in these policies over time.

The lessons to be drawn from all of this are as follows: 1) The game of numbers as it is now played produces unreliable projections of the demand for higher education. 2) Some improvements can be achieved by clarifying and analyzing the economic demands in terms of the factors that determine changes in these demands. 3) But this approach is also severely limited because as yet there is no economic theory for determining the changes in the demands for higher education that are derived from our type of economic growth. 4) At best, any long-term projections of the demands for higher education are subject to many unknowns and to much uncertainty. 5) To be prepared to cope with these, it is the better part of wisdom to pay the price of developing flexibility in the institutional structure of higher education and also within colleges and universities so that they will be capable of adapting their activities to new information with regard to demands as it becomes available. 6) Fixed formulas, like the parity formula in agriculture, lead to inflexibility and, over time, to serious distortions, and they should therefore be avoided in planning and financing higher education.

6 *Seeing that education is an investment in human capital, the central economic concept in planning and financing it should be the rate of return to investment.* The advantages of this concept are that it has a firm foundation in economic theory, that it is applicable to both private and public allocative decisions, that in practical economic affairs it is widely used and understood, and that it leads to efficient allocations when all investments are made in accordance with the priorities set by the relative rates of return to alternative investment opportunities. Although it is difficult to use this concept as an allocative guide in view of the way in which education is organized, it is the economist's key in solving the problem of allocating resources; the solution is in equalizing the rates by always allocating investment resources in favor of the highest rate of return.

The practical difficulties in using this concept in education are predominantly consequences of a type of organization that is not designed to provide most of the necessary information and that lacks strong incentives to use the available information. Consider the cost of college and university instruction: earnings foregone by students, which are well over half of the real cost, are concealed; the depreciation and the rate of interest on the investment in buildings used for classrooms, laboratories, offices, and library are as a rule also concealed; the cost of university research and of discovering talent is rarely identified and separated from the cost of instruction. It is also true that the price that the student pays for educational services is only remotely related to the real cost of producing them, and therefore private choices by students, however efficient they are privately, are not necessarily efficient socially. Nor can the allocation of public funds to higher education be made socially efficient under circumstances where information on cost is so inadequate. Consider also the returns that accrue to students and society from these educational services: the organization of higher education provides little or no economic information on returns, pecuniary and nonpecuniary, to guide students in making their career choices, not even with regard to the starting salaries of college graduates; foundation and public subsidies are accepted and awarded to students to get them to enter particular fields without regard to the depressing effects of the increase in supply that is thereby induced upon the lifetime earnings of those who are and will be in these fields; there is inadequate information on the effects upon returns of differences in innate ability of students, in their motivations, and of the differences in the effectiveness of college teaching; although these returns are subject to uncertainty, it is not a unique, distinguishing mark because other investments are also subject to uncertainty. In general, colleges and universities and public bodies that provide funds are poorly organized to provide the necessary information on cost and returns or to use whatever information is available.

Meanwhile, economists who have taken a hand in estimating the returns to education have made substantial progress. These estimates and those pertaining to cost have reached the stage where they are becoming useful allocative guides. But so far the returns from the nonpecuniary satisfactions that accrue to

TABLE 1

Estimates of Private Rates of Return, United States

	High School Graduates: White Males after Personal Taxes (percent)	*College Graduates: White Males after Personal Taxes* (percent)	*Corporate Manufacturing Firms: after Profit but before Personal Taxes* (percent)	*U.S.Private Domestic Economy: Implicit Rate of Return after Profit Taxes but before Personal Taxes* (percent)
1939	16	14.5		
1949	20	13.+	7.0 (for period 1947–57)	12.6
1956	25	12.4		14.4 (1955–56)
1958	28	14.8		12.3 (1957–58)
1959	Slightly higher than in 1958			9.7
1961	Slightly higher than in 1958			11.2 (1960–61)
1963–65				13.3

students have not been reckoned. Nor are the estimates of social returns in good repair.

Turning back to the rate of return as the central concept, the alternative investment opportunities are of course numerous, not only between human and material capital but within each of these two sets. Is there evidence that private educational choices are privately efficient; that is, do private rates of return to education tend 1) to be equal among educational options and 2) to be comparable to private rates of return to other private investments? The evidence implies inefficiencies. To illustrate, consider the available estimates on alternatives within education. In terms of equalizing the rates of return, elementary and secondary schooling appear to have priority. All of the estimates known to me show the highest private rates of return to elementary schooling, and we need to remind ourselves that there are still some children who are not completing the elementary grades. What is more important is the underinvestment in the quality of elementary schooling, especially in many rural areas. While the private rate of return to investment resources entering into high school education is not as high as that for elementary schooling, it nevertheless appears to be about twice as high as that indicated for private investment in completing college. In Table 1, the private rates of return to white males after personal taxes, in 1958, are 28 percent for high school graduates and 14.8 percent for college graduates. Thus, in allocating resources within education with a view to equalizing the rates of return, the implication is that elementary and secondary schooling appears to be subject to underinvestment relative to higher education. Nevertheless, comparing columns (2) and (4) in Table 1, the private rates of return to white male college graduates after personal taxes, without any allowance for the private satisfactions that accrue to students, are on a par with the private implicit rates of return to material capital *before personal taxes* on the income from this capital.

7 *Education changes the personal distribution of income.* The general extension of education and the additional earnings from these forms of human capital have probably been a major factor during recent decades in changing the distribution of personal income. Not only has the supply of educational opportunities increased markedly over time, but the inequality in the differences in the supply of these opportunities has, without doubt, been reduced in elementary and secondary schooling. The differences in the innate capacity of individuals to benefit from investment in education probably remains unchanged for the population as a whole, but the distribution of this capacity of those attending college changes over time as the proportion of individuals of particular age classes attending college increases. Human capital is in fact treated as the key to a theory of the personal distribution of personal income in a pioneering study by Gary S. Becker.

Higher education is certainly *not neutral* in its personal income distribution effects; some individuals and families undoubtedly gain future income streams partly at the expense of others. Whether it is in general regressive or progressive depends on the distribution of the personal costs and personal benefits of higher education. There are all too few hard facts on this issue.

In clarifying public policy choices, it is necessary to distinguish between the objective of economic efficiency and that of reducing the inequality in the personal distribution of income. There are circumstances when a particular policy will advance the economy toward both objectives; for example, when there is excessive unemployment, a fiscal-monetary policy that reduces such unemployment would normally contribute to both objectives. Similarly, when there is an underinvestment in elementary schooling—that is, a high rate of return to additional investment in such schooling—a policy to invest more in universal elementary schooling of high quality contributes both to economic efficiency and to reducing the inequality in personal income. But under other circumstances, the attainment of one of these objectives is in part at the expense of the other. At this point, the rating of social values underlying such policy choices enters.

I assume that it is not necessary to belabor the fact that economic efficiency rates high among the social values of our society. This assumption is implicit in my formulation of the six propositions already considered; the principal implications derived from them all pertain to economic efficiency. But how high a social value does our society place on reducing the inequality in personal income? The rating of this social value is not so clear as that which is socially assigned to economic efficiency. Nevertheless, there are strong indications that it also is an important social value. I shall proceed on the assumption that there is a social preference for less inequality in the personal distribution of income than that which prevails presently. Moreover, I shall assume that this social preference is such that society is prepared, should it be necessary, to forego some economic efficiency to bring about somewhat less inequality in the distribution of personal income. Proceeding on this assumption, it becomes relevant and important to determine what the income distribution effects of higher education are and how they can be altered for the better at the least cost in terms of allocative efficiency.

Although higher education is in all probability far from neutral in its effects on the distribution of personal income, it is surprising how little is actually known about these effects. It could be that the financing of higher education is in general quite regressive. It is plausible that it is regressive because it adds to the value of the human capital of those who attend college relative to those who do not go to college, because it increases the lifetime earnings of college graduates in part at the expense of others, and, closely related, because higher education provides educational services predominantly for students from middle and upper income families, a part of the cost of these educational services being paid for by taxes on poor families, as [W. Lee] Hansen and [Burton A.] Weisbrod show in their study of California. It appears to be true that a much smaller proportion of the undergraduate students in publicly financed institutions receive financial aid for reasons of their having inadequate income than do undergraduate students in private colleges and universities. In either case, the financing is such that substantial amounts of valuable assets are being transferred by society to a particular intellectually elite set of individuals.

In retrospect, given the type of growth that has characterized our economy and the remarkable increase in the stock of education per worker in the labor force, the gains in elementary and secondary schooling and in higher education taken as a whole have been instrumental, it seems to me, in reducing the inequality in the distribution of personal income. The hypothesis I proposed... with regard to this issue continues to be consistent with the evidence thus far available. In terms of the income effects of additional education per worker, this hypothesis is: The rise in the investment in education relative to that invested in nonhuman capital increases total earnings relative to total property income, and property income is distributed much less equally than the earnings of persons from labor. Therefore, investment in schooling reduces the inequality in the distribution of personal income. The hypothesis proposed here is that these patterns of investment are an important part of the explanation of the observed reductions in the distribution of personal income.

Becker and Barry R. Chiswick have been analyzing the effects of schooling on the distribution of personal income. For adult white males and for the states within the United States, they report that "about one-third of the differences in inequality between states is directly explained by schooling, one-third directly by the residual and the remaining one-third by both together through the positive correlation between them."

In a more recent report, Chiswick gives the following results from his analysis of North-South differences: "The education component... can 'explain' half of the North-South differences in income inequality. The proportion is slightly lower for white males and slightly higher for all males." But neither the hypothesis I have advanced nor the evidence on the income effects of schooling from Becker and Chiswick implies that the income effects of higher education per se are progressive rather than regressive.

In developing an analytical approach bringing economic theory to bear on the effects of human capital on the personal distribution of income, Becker's

1967 work is full of promise. His distinction between the "egalitarian" and "elite" views is helpful in clarifying the problem. He identifies the egalitarian view with supply conditions; the objective is to reduce the inequality in the differences in the supply of educational opportunities. The elite view, on the other hand, turns on the demand conditions: the actual investment and earning differences are primarily a consequence of differences in the capacity of individuals to benefit from investment in education and from other forms of human capital. What Becker's analytical approach will show when it is applied to higher education is still in the realm of unfinished business. Hansen and Weisbrod, using a cost-benefits approach, show that public higher education in California is highly regressive.

ACKNOWLEDGMENTS

1.1 From Thomas Mun, *England's Treasure by Forraign Trade* (1664).

1.2 From William Petty, *A Treatise of Taxes and Contributions* (1662).

2.1 From François Quesnay, *Quesnay's Tableau Économique,* ed. and trans. Marguerite Kuczynski and Ronald L. Meek (Macmillan, 1972). Copyright © 1972 by The Royal Economic Society. Reprinted by permission of Macmillan Press Ltd. Notes omitted.

2.2 From Anne-Robert-Jacques Turgot, *Reflections on the Formation and Distribution of Wealth* (1774).

3.1 From David Hume, *Essays: Moral, Political, and Literary,* rev. ed., ed. Eugene F. Miller (Liberty Classics, 1987). Copyright © 1985, 1987 by Eugene F. Miller. Reprinted by permission of The Liberty Fund, Inc. Notes omitted.

3.2 From Adam Smith, *An Inquiry into the Nature and Causes of the Wealth of Nations,* ed. Edwin Cannan (1937). Notes omitted.

3.3 From Thomas Robert Malthus, *An Essay on the Principle of Population,* ed. Philip Appleman (W. W. Norton, 1976). Copyright © 1976 by W. W. Norton & Company, Inc. Reprinted by permission. Notes omitted.

3.4 From David Ricardo, *The Principles of Political Economy and Taxation* (Everyman's Library, 1911). Reprinted by permission of Everyman's Library, David Campbell Publishers. Notes omitted.

3.5 From Jean-Baptiste Say, *A Treatise on Political Economy, or the Production, Distribution, and Consumption of Wealth* (Augustus M. Kelley, 1971). Reprinted by permission of Augustus M. Kelley Publishers. Notes omitted.

3.6 From John Stuart Mill, *Principles of Political Economy,* ed. William Ashley (Augustus M. Kelley, 1987). Reprinted by permission of Augustus M. Kelley Publishers. Notes omitted.

4.1 From Karl Marx, *Capital: A Critique of Political Economy, vol. 1,* trans. Ben Fowkes (Vintage Books, 1977). Copyright © 1976 by New Left Review. Reprinted by permission of New Left Review. Notes omitted.

4.2 From Friedrich Engels, *The Origin of the Family, Private Property and the State* (Penguin Books, 1985). Copyright © 1946 by Lawrence & Wishart. Reprinted by permission of Lawrence & Wishart. Notes omitted.

5.1 From Alfred Marshall, *Principles of Economics,* 9th ed. (Macmillan, 1961). Copyright © 1961 by Macmillan and Co., Ltd. Reprinted by permission of Macmillan Press Ltd. Notes omitted.

5.2 From Irving Fisher, *The Theory of Interest as Determined by Impatience to Spend Income and Opportunity to Invest It* (Macmillan, 1930). Notes omitted.

5.3 From Joan Robinson, *The Rate of Interest and Other Essays* (Macmillan, 1954). Copyright © 1954 by Macmillan and Co., Ltd. Reprinted by permission of Macmillan Press Ltd. Notes omitted.

6.1 From Carl Menger, *Principles of Economics,* trans. and ed. James Dingwall and Bert F. Hoselitz (Free Press, 1950). Copyright © 1950 by The Free Press. Reprinted by permission of Libertarian Press, Inc., P.O. Box 309, Grove City, PA 16127. Notes omitted.

6.2 From William Stanley Jevons, "Brief Account of a General Mathematical Theory of Political Economy," *Journal of the Royal Statistical Society* (June 1866). References omitted.

6.3 From Friedrich A. Hayek, *Prices and Production* (Routledge & Kegan Paul, 1960). Reprinted by permission of Routledge, Ltd. Notes omitted.

7.1 From Frank H. Knight, *Risk, Uncertainty and Profit* (Augustus M. Kelley, 1964). Reprinted by permission of Augustus M. Kelley Publishers. Notes omitted.

7.2 From Milton Friedman and Anna Jacobson Schwartz, *A Monetary History of the United States, 1867–1960* (Princeton University Press, 1963). Copyright © 1963 by The National Bureau of Economic Research. Reprinted by permission of Princeton University Press. Notes omitted.

7.3 From Gary S. Becker, *Human Capital: A Theoretical and Empirical Analysis, With Special Reference to Education*, 2d ed. (Columbia University Press, 1975). Copyright © 1975 by The National Bureau of Economic Research, Inc. Reprinted by permission of University of Chicago Press. Notes omitted.

7.4 From George J. Stigler, *The Citizen and the State: Essays on Regulation* (University of Chicago Press, 1975). Copyright © 1975 by The University of Chicago. Reprinted by permission. Notes and references omitted.

8.1 From John Maynard Keynes, *The General Theory of Employment, Interest, and Money* (Harcourt Brace Jovanovich, 1964). Copyright © 1964 by Harcourt Brace & Company. Reprinted by permission. Notes omitted.

8.2 From Alvin H. Hansen, *A Guide to Keynes* (McGraw-Hill, 1953). Copyright © 1953 by Marian Hansen Merrifield and Mildred Furiya. Reprinted by permission of the author. Notes omitted.

8.3 From James Tobin, *Essays in Economics: National and International* (MIT Press, 1996). Originally published in *Journal of Money, Credit, and Banking*, vol. 15, no. 4 (November 1983). Copyright © 1983 by Ohio State University Press. Reprinted by permission.

9.1 From Thorstein Veblen, *The Theory of Business Enterprise* (Augustus M. Kelley, 1975). Reprinted by permission of Augustus M. Kelley Publishers. Notes omitted.

9.2 From John Kenneth Galbraith, *The Affluent Society* (Houghton Mifflin, 1958). Copyright © 1958, 1969, 1976, 1984 by John Kenneth Galbraith. Reprinted by permission of Houghton Mifflin Company. Notes omitted.

10.1 From Vilfredo Pareto, *Vilfredo Pareto: Selections from His Treatise* (Thomas Y. Crowell, 1965). Copyright © 1965 by Thomas Y. Crowell Company. Reprinted by permission of HarperCollins Publishers, Inc.

10.2 From A. C. Pigou, *Socialism Versus Capitalism* (Macmillan, 1937). Copyright © 1937 by Macmillan and Co., Limited. Reprinted by permission of Macmillan Press Ltd. Notes omitted.

10.3 From James M. Buchanan, *The Economics and the Ethics of Constitutional Order* (University of Michigan Press, 1991). Copyright © 1991 by The University of Michigan. Reprinted by permission.

10.4 From Thomas Sowell, *Knowledge and Decisions* (Basic Books, 1980). Copyright © 1980 by Basic Books, Inc. Reprinted by permission of Basic Books, a member of Perseus Books, L.L.C. Notes omitted.

11.1 From James E. Meade, *The Theory of Customs Unions* (North-Holland, 1955). Notes omitted.

11.2 From Eli F. Heckscher and Bertil Ohlin, *Heckscher-Ohlin Trade Theory,* trans. and ed. Harry Flam and M. June Flanders (MIT Press, 1991). Copyright © 1991 by The Massachusetts Institute of Technology. Reprinted by permission of MIT Press. Notes omitted.

12.1 From Joseph A. Schumpeter, *Essays on Entrepreneurs, Innovations, Business Cycles, and the Evolution of Capitalism,* ed. Richard V. Clemence (Transaction, 1989). Copyright © 1989 by Transaction Publishers. Reprinted by permission. Notes omitted.

12.2 From Robert William Fogel, *Without Consent or Contract: The Rise and Fall of American Slavery* (W. W. Norton, 1989). Copyright © 1989 by Robert W. Fogel. Reprinted by permission of W. W. Norton & Company, Inc. Notes omitted.

12.3 From Douglass C. North, *Institutions, Institutional Change and Economic Performance* (Cambridge University Press, 1990). Copyright © 1990 by Cambridge University Press. Reprinted by permission. References omitted.

12.4 From John R. Commons, *Legal Foundations of Capitalism* (University of Wisconsin Press, 1957). Notes omitted.

12.5 From Simon Kuznets, *Economic Development, the Family, and Income Distribution: Selected Essays* (Cambridge University Press, 1989). Copyright © 1989 by Cambridge University Press. Reprinted by permission. Notes omitted.

12.6 From Gunnar Myrdal, *Asian Drama: An Inquiry into the Poverty of Nations* (Twentieth Century Fund, 1968). Copyright © 1968 by the City of Stockholm. Reprinted by permission of the City of Stockholm, Board of Culture. Notes omitted.

12.7 From W. Arthur Lewis, *The Theory of Economic Growth* (Richard D. Irwin, 1955). Copyright © 1955 by Richard D. Irwin, Inc. Reprinted by permission of Routledge Ltd.

12.8 From Theodore W. Schultz, *Investment in Human Capital: The Role of Education and of Research* (Free Press, 1971). Copyright © 1971 by The Free Press. Reprinted by permission of The Free Press, a division of Simon & Schuster, Inc. Notes omitted.

Index